PENGUIN BOO

THE MASKS OF GOD: PRIMI

Joseph Campbell has been interested in mythology since his childhood in New York, when he read books about American Indians, frequently visited the American Museum of Natural History, and was fascinated by the museum's collection of totem poles. He earned his B.A. and M.A. degrees at Columbia in 1925 and 1927 and went on to study medieval French and Sanskrit at the universities of Paris and Munich. After a period in California, where he encountered John Steinbeck and the biologist Ed Ricketts, he taught at the Canterbury School, then, in 1934, joined the literature department at Sarah Lawrence College, a post he retained for many years. During the 1940s and '50s, he helped Swami Nikhilananda to translate the Upanishads and *The Gospel of Sri Ramakrishna.* The many books by Professor Campbell include *The Hero with a Thousand Faces, Myths to Live By, The Flight of the Wild Gander,* and *The Mythic Image*. He has edited *The Portable Arabian Nights*, *The Portable Jung*, and other works.

ALSO BY JOSEPH CAMPBELL

A Skeleton Key to Finnegans Wake

(WITH HENRY MORTON ROBINSON)

The Hero with a Thousand Faces

The Masks of God: Primitive Mythology

The Masks of God: Oriental Mythology

The Masks of God: Occidental Mythology

The Flight of the Wild Gander

Myths to Live By

EDITED BY JOSEPH CAMPBELL

The Portable Arabian Nights

The Portable Jung

JOSEPH CAMPBELL

THE MASKS OF GOD: PRIMITIVE MYTHOLOGY

PENGUIN BOOKS

Penguin Books Ltd, Harmondsworth, Middlesex, England
Penguin Books, 625 Madison Avenue, New York, New York 10022, U.S.A.
Penguin Books Australia Ltd, Ringwood, Victoria, Australia
Penguin Books Canada Ltd, 2801 John Street, Markham, Ontario, Canada L3R 1B4
Penguin Books (N.Z.) Ltd, 182–190 Wairau Road, Auckland 10, New Zealand

First published by The Viking Press 1959
Revised edition published 1969
Viking Compass Edition published 1970
Reprinted 1971 (twice), 1972, 1973, 1974, 1975, 1976
Published in Penguin Books 1976
Reprinted 1977

LIBRARY OF CONGRESS CATALOGING IN PUBLICATION DATA

Campbell, Joseph, 1904—
Primitive mythology.

(His The Masks of God; v. 1)
Includes bibliographical references and index.
1. Religion, Primitive. 2. Mythology. I. Title. II. Series.
[GN470.C33 1976] 291.1'3 76-25192
ISBN 0 14 00.4304 7

Printed in the United States of America by
Offset Paperback Mfrs., Inc., Dallas, Pennsylvania
Set in Linotype Times Roman

Portions of the Prologue appeared in *Daedalus*

The author wishes to acknowledge with gratitude the generous support of his researches by the Bollingen Foundation.

Foreword

ON COMPLETION OF *The Masks of God*

Looking back today over the twelve delightful years that I spent on this richly rewarding enterprise, I find that its main result for me has been its confirmation of a thought I have long and faithfully entertained: of the unity of the race of man, not only in its biology but also in its spiritual history, which has everywhere unfolded in the manner of a single symphony, with its themes announced, developed, amplified and turned about, distorted, reasserted, and, today, in a grand *fortissimo* of all sections sounding together, irresistibly advancing to some kind of mighty climax, out of which the next great movement will emerge. And I can see no reason why anyone should suppose that in the future the same motifs already heard will not be sounding still—in new relationships indeed, but ever the same motifs. They are all given here, in these volumes, with many clues, besides, suggesting ways in which they might be put to use by reasonable men to reasonable ends—or by poets to poetic ends—or by madmen to nonsense and disaster. For, as in the words of James Joyce in *Finnegans Wake:* "utterly impossible as are all these events they are probably as like those which may have taken place as any others which never took person at all are ever likely to be."

A Note on the 1969 Edition of *Primitive Mythology*

Hardly two years after the publication, 1959, of this first volume of *The Masks of God,* a series of sensational revelations from the

Olduvai Gorge in Tanganyika, East Africa, set back the date by more than a million years for the earliest known appearances of manlike species on this earth. Whereas the previous specimens, from half a dozen South African sites (see below, pp. 357–60), had been dated circa 600,000 B.C., the Tanganyika finds were in 1961 determined by the newly developed Argon-40 method to be approximately 1,750,000 years old.[1] * Moreover, at least two distinctly different types of hominid were found to have existed at that time. The one called Zinjanthropus—the "Ethiopian anthropoid" (from the Arabic *Balad al-Zinj,* "Land of the Ethiopians") —was a heavy-jawed eater of largely vegetable food, while the other, smaller, was an eater of meat, apparently a competent hunter, and a user of flaked stone tools. Dr. L. S. B. Leakey, the excavator of Olduvai, regards the latter as the more likely prototype of our own fully human species and has named him, accordingly, Homo, "man"—Homo habilis, "able or competent man." [2] All the rest, both of earliest Tanganyika and of the later South African sites, are now generally regarded as off the main evolutionary line toward Homo sapiens and classified under one rubric, Australopithecus, "southern ape." The more flattering title that I have used on page 357, Plesianthropus, "near man," is restricted to but one assortment of skulls, teeth, and bones—that from Sterkfontein, South Africa: which, according to the leading expert on these matters, Dr. Carleton S. Coon, seems to represent a rather special case, pointing, as do none of the other South African Australopithecines, forward along the evolutionary line, to ourselves.[3]

A second highly significant—though very different—field of research in which discoveries relevant to the argument of this volume were announced almost immediately after its publication was that of the archaeology of the nuclear Near East, where a series of disclosures from the Anatolian plain of Southern Turkey revealed an unsuspected period of beginnings, antecedent to the earliest evidences of the known neolithic cultures. As a consequence: I. *The proto-neolithic* (see below, pp. 135–38 and 401–402) has been carried back two thousand years, to circa 9500

* Reference notes to the Foreword are on page 488.

B.C., and II. *The basal neolithic* (pp. 138–40 and 402) now appears to have first arisen neither in Iraq, Iran, Palestine, nor Syria, but in Asia Minor, circa 7500 B.C., and to have developed there in three stages:

1. A formerly unsuspected stage, known now as the pre-pottery or aceramic neolithic, which has been identified in Palestine (at Jericho) as well as at Hacilar, Çatal Hüyük, and certain other Anatolian sites.[4] The apparent luxury of the settlements, with their tidy little brick houses and the sense throughout of a manner of life already well established, suggests that the arts of agriculture and stock breeding must already have been mastered, though still supplemented by the hunt. And of the greatest interest, furthermore, both at Hacilar and at Jericho, is the evidence of a domestic skull cult of some kind (compare below, p. 127).

2. Then at Çatal Hüyük, circa 6500 B.C., ceramic wares suddenly appear, and, as the excavator, Dr. James Mellaart, observes: "we can actually study the transition from an aceramic Neolithic with baskets and wooden vessels to a ceramic Neolithic with the first pottery."[5] Along with this pottery, furthermore, which is the earliest yet discovered anywhere, there have also come to light the earliest known neolithic figurines, in association with some forty or more symbolically ornamented chapels—revealing, in superb display, practically all the basic motifs of the great mother-goddess mythologies of later ages. And these earliest known neolithic figurines are of an easy, natural, lifelike grace, not the least "archaic," primitive, or stilted.

3. It is only in the next and final stage of the early Anatolian development, and then gradually also in neighboring areas—circa 5500–4500 B.C.—that those well-known, unlifelike, conventionalized naked-goddess figurines appear that have been generally associated with the earliest village arts. A trend from naturalism to abstraction, from visual to conceptual thought, would seem thus to be indicated. And in the Anatolian sphere, meanwhile, which is still in advance of all, signs have begun appearing of the dawn of the earliest age of metals, the early chalcolithic: beads and little tubes of copper and lead, various trinkets, and even a few metal tools. A truly superb painted pottery is also being manu-

factured, pointing toward the great ceramic styles of the following millennium (Halaf wares, Samarra wares, Obeid wares, etc., as discussed in the body of my text, pp. 140–43). The expansion southward and eastward of the arts and manners of settled village life now has begun to cover the whole of the Near East, new centers of creative transformation are developing, and—as reviewed below, pp. 143 ff.—the stage has been set for the rise in Mesopotamia, circa 4000 B.C., of the first of the great historic civilizations.

A third area of archaeological research—and the last that I shall mention here—where a startling discovery transformed the situation almost immediately after the publication of this book, was the coast of Ecuador, where, in December 1960, a piece of Japanese pottery was picked up on a beach. Subsequent excavations yielded many fragments more, all of the early Jomon ("cord-marked") style of circa 3000 B.C.—which is the earliest date for pottery yet registered for the New World. A number of ceramic female figurines turned up, also, in these digs, and these are the earliest figurines—indeed the earliest works of art—yet unearthed in the Americas.[6] I take note of this with considerable glee, as supporting most dramatically the argument of my chapter on the possibility of an early trans-Pacific diffusion of culture traits to the New World (pp. 202–215). And meanwhile, as for researches into the beginnings of the planting and agricultural traditions of pre-Columbian America: an extremely well-conducted program of excavations in Mexico, in the once-inhabited caves of southwest Tamaulipas and the Valley of Tehuacán, has lately shown that by about 3500 B.C. (plus or minus a few centuries) some sort of plant domestication was being practiced by cave-dwelling hunting and fishing folk. Maize, it seems, was then first cultivated; and during the next two thousand years the signs increase of a developing horticulture, until, by circa 1500 B.C., the beginning of something like a genuine neolithic stage of village farming seems to have been attained.[7]

Now all three of the fields of research into man's past of which I have here taken note are today in such rapid and promising transformation that there will, no doubt, be as many astonishing disclosures during the seventies and eighties as there were in the decade of the sixties. In the main (I suspect) they will support, as have these, the arguments of my pages: but if not, the reader (I dare to hope) will know how to add and subtract.

—JOSEPH CAMPBELL

New York City
Christmas Day, 1968

CONTENTS

CONTENTS

ILLUSTRATIONS

Sketches for illustrations on pages 288, 300, 301, 302, 303, 309, 326, 382 are by John L. Mackey.

THE MASKS OF GOD: PRIMITIVE MYTHOLOGY

TOWARD A NATURAL HISTORY OF THE GODS AND HEROES

1. The Lineaments of a New Science

The comparative study of the mythologies of the world compels us to view the cultural history of mankind as a unit; for we find that such themes as the fire-theft, deluge, land of the dead, virgin birth, and resurrected hero have a worldwide distribution—appearing everywhere in new combinations while remaining, like the elements of a kaleidoscope, only a few and always the same. Furthermore, whereas in tales told for entertainment such mythical themes are taken lightly—in a spirit, obviously, of play—they appear also in religious contexts, where they are accepted not only as factually true but even as revelations of the verities to which the whole culture is a living witness and from which it derives both its spiritual authority and its temporal power. No human society has yet been found in which such mythological motifs have not been rehearsed in liturgies; interpreted by seers, poets, theologians, or philosophers; presented in art; magnified in song; and ecstatically experienced in life-empowering visions. Indeed, the chronicle of our species, from its earliest page, has been not simply an account of the progress of man the tool-maker, but—more tragically—a history of the pouring of blazing visions into the minds of seers and the efforts of earthly communities to incarnate unearthly covenants. Every people has received its own seal and sign of supernatural designation, communicated to its heroes and daily proved in the lives and experience of its folk. And though many who bow with closed eyes in the sanctuaries of their own tradition rationally scrutinize and disqualify the sacraments of others, an honest comparison immediately reveals that all have been built from one fund of mythological motifs—variously selected, organized, interpreted, and ritualized, according to local need, but revered by every people on earth.

A fascinating psychological, as well as historical, problem is thus presented. Man, apparently, cannot maintain himself in the universe without belief in some arrangement of the general inheritance of myth. In fact, the fullness of his life would even seem to stand in a direct ratio to the depth and range not of his rational thought but of his local mythology. Whence the force of these unsubstantial themes, by which they are empowered to galvanize populations, creating of them civilizations, each with a beauty and self-compelling destiny of its own? And why should it be that whenever men have looked for something solid on which to found their lives, they have chosen not the facts in which the world abounds, but the myths of an immemorial imagination—preferring even to make life a hell for themselves and their neighbors, in the name of some violent god, to accepting gracefully the bounty the world affords?

Are the modern civilizations to remain spiritually locked from each other in their local notions of the sense of the general tradition; or can we not now break through to some more profoundly based point and counterpoint of human understanding? For it is a fact that the myths of our several cultures work upon us, whether consciously or unconsciously, as energy-releasing, life-motivating and -directing agents; so that even though our rational minds may be in agreement, the myths by which we are living—or by which our fathers lived—can be driving us, at that very moment, diametrically apart.

No one, as far as I know, has yet tried to compose into a single picture the new perspectives that have been opened in the fields of comparative symbolism, religion, mythology, and philosophy by the scholarship of recent years. The richly rewarded archaeological researches of the past few decades; astonishing clarifications, simplifications, and coordinations achieved by intensive studies in the spheres of philology, ethnology, philosophy, art history, folklore, and religion; fresh insights in psychological research; and the many priceless contributions to our science by the scholars, monks, and literary men of Asia, have combined to suggest a new image of the fundamental unity of the spiritual history of mankind. Without straining beyond the treasuries of evidence already on hand in these widely scattered departments of our subject, therefore, but simply gathering from them the *membra disjuncta* of a unitary mythological science, I attempt in the following pages the first sketch of a natural history of the gods and heroes, such as in its final form should include in its purview all divine beings—as zoology includes all animals and botany all plants—not regarding any as sacrosanct or beyond its scientific domain. For, as in the visible world of the vegetable and animal kingdoms, so also in the visionary world of the gods: there has been a history, an evolution, a series of mutations, governed by laws; and to show forth such laws is the proper aim of science.

II. The Well of the Past

"Very deep," wrote Thomas Mann at the opening of his mythologically conceived tetralogy, *Joseph and His Brothers,* "is the well of the past. Should we not call it bottomless?" And he then observed: "The deeper we sound, the further down into the lower world of the past we probe and press, the more do we find that the earliest foundations of humanity, its history and culture, reveal themselves unfathomable." [1] *

Our initial task must be to ask if this be true. And to this end we shall explore first the psychological aspect of the question, to learn whether in the human psychosomatic system there have been found any structures or dynamic tendencies to which the origins of myth and ritual might be referred; and turn only then to the archaeological and ethnological evidences, to learn what the earliest discoverable patterns of mythological ideation may have been.

However, as Mann has already warned, concerning the foundations for which we are seeking, "No matter to what hazardous

* Numbered reference notes begin on page 473.

lengths we let out our line they still withdraw, again and further into the depths." For beneath the first depth, namely that of the earliest civilizations—which are but the foreground of the long backward reach of the prehistory of our race—there rest the centuries, millenniums, indeed the centuries of millenniums of primitive man, the mighty hunter, the more primitive root-and-bug collector, back for more than half a million years. And there is a third depth, even deeper and darker, below that—below the ultimate horizon of humanity. For we shall find the ritual dance among the birds, the fish, the apes, and the bees. And it therefore has to be asked whether man, like those other members of the kingdom, does not possess any innate tendencies to respond, in strictly patterned racial ways, to certain signals flashed by his environment and his own kind.

The concept of a natural science of the gods, matching the compass of the materials already classified in the pertinent scientific files, must therefore include in its ken the primitive and prehistoric as well as recent strata of human experience; and not merely summarily and sketchily, as a kind of protasis to the main subject. For the roots of civilization are deep. Our cities do not rest, like stones, upon the surface. The first, rich, great, and terrible chapter in the textbook of this subject will have to be developed no less fully than the second, third, and fourth. And its range will be immensely greater than theirs; for it will extend into "the dark backward and abysm of time" that is the racial counterpart of that psychological unconscious which has been recently exposed—sensationally—within the individual. Fathoming the grottoes of the Crô-Magnon artist-wizards of the Great Hunt; deeper still, the dens of the crouching cannibals of the glacial ages, lapping the brains of their neighbors, raw, from cracked skulls; and still beyond, examining the enigmatic chalky, skeletal remains of what now would seem to have been chimpanzee-like hunter-pygmies on the open plains of the early Transvaal, we shall be finding clues to the deepest secrets not only of the high cultures of both the Orient and the Occident, but also of our own most inward expectations, spontaneous responses, and obsessive fears.

The present volume, therefore, explores with what light is available the deep, very deep well of the past. And, like the aim of Bacon's *Advancement of Learning,* its intent is "to point out what part of knowledge has been already labored and perfected, and what portions left unfinished or entirely neglected." Moreover, where the view is broad and certain distinctive, suggestive landmarks can be descried, occasional guesses are ventured as to indicated implications. But the whole review—rich and colorful though its materials—together with its ventured hypotheses, is necessarily in the way rather of a prospectus than of a definition; for these materials have never before been gathered to a single summation, pointing to a science of the roots of revelation.

Furthermore, after this study of the spiritual resources of prehistoric man, I shall in three subsequent volumes review the forms, successively, of Oriental mythology, Occidental mythology, and what I propose to call creative mythology, as representing the remaining natural divisions of this subject. For under the rubric "Oriental" can be readily comprised all the traditions of that broad and various, yet essentially unified, major province represented by the philosophical myths and mythological philosophies of India, Southeast Asia, China, and Japan—to which can be joined the earlier yet closely related mythological cosmologies of archaic Mesopotamia and Egypt, as well as the later, remoter, yet essentially comparable systems of pre-Columbian Middle America and Peru. And under the rubric "Occidental" the progressively, ethically oriented mythologies of Zoroastrianism, Judaism, Christianity, and Islam naturally fall, in relationship and counterplay to the Greco-Roman pantheons and the Celto-Germanic. And finally, as "creative mythology," will be considered that most important mythological tradition of the modern world, which can be said to have had its origin with the Greeks, to have come of age in the Renaissance, and to be flourishing today in continuous, healthy growth, in the works of those artists, poets, and philosophers of the West for whom the wonder of the world itself—as it is now being analyzed by science—is the ultimate revelation.

Moreover, since it is true, as Mann has said, that while in the life of the human race the mythical is an early and primitive way of thought, in the life of the individual it is a late and mature one,[2] an impressive accord will be heard resounding through all the modulations of this subject, from the primitive to the most mature.

III. The Dialogue of Scholarship and Romance

The quest for a scientific approach to mythology was hampered until the end of the last century by the magnitude of the field and scattered character of the evidence. The conflict of authorities, theories, and opinions that raged in the course, particularly, of the nineteenth century, when the ranges of knowledge were expanding in every field of research (classical and Oriental scholarship, comparative philology, folklore, Egyptology, Bible criticism, anthropology, etc.) resembled the mad tumult of the old Buddhist parable of "The Blind Men and the Elephant." The blind men feeling the animal's head declared, "An elephant is like a water pot"; but those at his ears, "He is like a winnowing basket"; those at his tusks, "No, indeed, he is like a plowshare"; and those at his trunk, "He is like a plow pole." There were a number feeling his belly. "Why," they cried, "he is like a storage bin!" Those feeling his legs argued that he was like pillars; those at his rectum, that he was like a mortar; those at his member, that he was like a pestle; while the remainder, at his tail, were shouting, "An elephant is like a fan." And they fought furiously among themselves with their fists, shouting and crying, "This is what an elephant is like; that is not what an elephant is like"; "This is not what an elephant is like; that is what an elephant is like."

"And precisely so," then runs the moral of the Buddha, "the company of heretics, monks, Brahmans, and wandering ascetics, patient of heresy, delighting in heresy, relying upon the reliance of heretical views, are blind, without eyes: knowing not good, knowing not evil, knowing not right, knowing not wrong, they quarrel and brawl and wrangle and strike one another with the daggers of their tongues, saying, 'This is right, that is not right'; 'This is not right, that is right.' "[3]

The two learned disciplines from which the lineaments of a

sound comparative science might first have emerged were those of the classics and the Bible. However, a fundamental tenet of the Christian tradition made it appear to be an act of blasphemy to compare the two on the same plane of thought; for, while the myths of the Greeks were recognized to be of the natural order, those of the Bible were supposed to be supernatural. Hence, while the prodigies of the classical heroes (Herakles, Theseus, Perseus, etc.) were studied as literature, those of the Hebrews (Noah, Moses, Joshua, Jesus, Peter, etc.), had to be argued as objective history; whereas, actually, the fabulous elements common to the two precisely contemporary, Eastern Mediterranean traditions were derived equally from the preceding, bronze-age civilization of Mesopotamia—as no one before the development of the modern science of archaeology could have guessed.

A third, and ultimately the most disturbing, discipline contributing to the tumult of the scene was the rapidly developing science of Aryan, Indo-Germanic, or Indo-European Philology. As early as 1767 a French Jesuit in India, Father Cœurdoux, had observed that Sanskrit and Latin were remarkably alike.[4] Sir William Jones (1746–1794)—the West's first considerable Sanskritist, judge of the supreme court of judicature at Calcutta, and founder of the Bengal Asiatic Society—was the next to observe the relationship, and from a comparative study of the grammatical structures of Latin, Greek, and Sanskrit concluded that all three had "sprung," as he phrased it, "from some common source, which perhaps no longer exists."[5] Franz Bopp (1791–1867), published in 1816 a comparative study of the Sanskrit, Greek, Latin, Persian, and Germanic systems of conjugation.[6] And finally, by the middle of the century it was perfectly clear that a prodigious distribution of closely related tongues could be identified over the greater part of the civilized world: a single, broadly scattered family of languages that must have sprung from a single source, and which includes, besides Sanskrit and Pali (the language of the Buddhist scriptures), most of the tongues of northern India as well as Singhalese (the language of Ceylon), Persian, Armenian, Albanian, and Bulgarian; Polish, Russian, and the other Slavic tongues; Greek, Latin and all the languages of Europe except Esthonian, Finnish, Lapp, Magyar, and Basque. Thus a continuum from Ireland to India had been revealed. And not only the languages, but also the civilizations and religions, mythologies, literary forms, and modes of thought of the peoples involved could be readily compared: for example, the Vedic pantheon of ancient India, the Eddic of medieval Iceland, and the Olympian of the Greeks. No wonder the leading scholars and philosophers of the century were impressed!

The discovery appeared to indicate that the most productive, as well as philosophically mature, constellation of peoples in the history of civilization had been associated with this prodigious ethnic diffusion; for it seemed that even in the Orient, the homeland of many darker races, it had been the lighter-skinned Indo-Aryans who had given the chief impulse to the paramount cultural trend—namely that represented in its earliest recorded phase by the Sanskrit Vedas and the Vedic pantheon (so close in form and spirit to the Homeric hymns and Olympic pantheon of the Greeks that the Alexandrians had had no difficulty in recognizing analogies), and in its later, more highly developed phase, by the gospel of Gautama Buddha, whose princely mind, inspired by what many scholars throughout Europe took to be a characteristically Aryan type of spirituality, had touched with magic the whole of the Orient, lifting temples and pagodas not to any God but to Buddhahood: that is to say, the purified, perfected, fully flowered, and fully illuminated consciousness of man himself.

It was a fateful, potentially very dangerous discovery; for, even though announced in the terminology of tranquil scholarship, it coincided with a certain emotional tendency of the time. In the light of the numerous discoveries then being made in every quarter of the broadly opening fields of the physical, biological, and geographical sciences, the mythological Creation story in the Old Testament could no longer be accepted as literally true. Already in the early seventeenth century the heliocentric universe had been condemned as contrary to Holy Scripture, both by Luther and by the Roman Catholic Inquisition: in the nineteenth century the tendency of the learned world was rather to reject Holy Scripture as contrary to fact. And with the Hebrew Scripture went the Hebrew God, and the Christian claim to divine authority as well.

The Renaissance had opposed to the Judeo-Christian ideal of obedience to a supposed revelation of God's law, the humanism of the Greeks. And with the discovery, now, of this impressive ethnic continuity, uniting that humanism, on the one hand, with the profound, non-theological religiosity of the Indian Upanishads and Buddhist Sutras, and on the other hand, with the primitive vitality of the pagan Germans, who had shattered Christianized Rome only to be subdued and Christianized themselves in turn, the cause of the pagan against the Judeo-Christian portion of the European cultural inheritance seemed to be greatly enhanced. Moreover, since the evidence appeared to point to Europe itself as the homeland from which this profoundly inspired and vigorously creative spiritual tradition sprang—and, specifically, the area of the Germanies *—a shock of romantic European elation quivered through the scientific world. The Grimm brothers, Jacob and Wilhelm (1785–1863 and 1786–1859), gathered the fairy tales of their collection with the belief that there might be discovered in them the broken remains of a nuclear Indo-European mythology. Schopenhauer greeted the Sanskrit Upanishads as "the most rewarding and elevating reading possible in the world."[7] And Wagner found in the old Germanic mythologies of Wotan, Loki, Siegfried, and the Rhine-maidens the proper vehicle of his German genius.

Thus it was that when a couple of dilettantes with creative imagination brought this sensational product of philological research out of the studies of the scholars, where thought leads to further thought, into the field of political life, where thought leads to action and one thought is enough, a potentially very dangerous situation was created. The first step in this direction was taken in

* For a modern review of this evidence, see Paul Thieme, "The Indo-European Language," *Scientific American,* Vol. 199, No. 4 (October 1958), pp. 63–74, and Peter Giles' article, "Indo-Europeans," *Encyclopædia Britannica,* 14th edition (1929), Vol. 12, pp. 262–63. The homeland of the nuclear folk is placed by Thieme in an area between the Vistula and the Elbe, in the late fourth millennium B.C., and by Giles roughly in the area of the old Austro-Hungarian Empire. A. Meillet and Marcel Cohen, on the other hand, in their great work on *Les Langues du monde* (Paris: H. Champion, 1952), p. 6, place the area "in the plains of southern Russia and perhaps earlier in Central Asia."

1839, when a French aristocrat, Courtet de l'Isle, proposed a theory of politics on the basis of what he conceived to be the new science, in a work entitled *La Science politique fondée sur la science de l'homme; ou, Etude des races humaines* (Paris: 1839). The tendency was developed in Count Arthur de Gobineau's four-volume *Essai sur l'inégalité des races humaines* (1853–1855), and Count Vacher de Lapouge's *L'Aryen et son rôle social* (1899), and required, finally, only the celebrated work of Wagner's English son-in-law, Houston Stewart Chamberlain, *The Foundations of the Nineteenth Century* (1890–1891), to supply the background for Alfred Rosenberg's *Der Mythus des 20. Jahrhunderts* (1930) and break the planet into flames.

Clearly, mythology is no toy for children. Nor is it a matter of archaic, merely scholarly concern, of no moment to modern men of action. For its symbols (whether in the tangible form of images or in the abstract form of ideas) touch and release the deepest centers of motivation, moving literate and illiterate alike, moving mobs, moving civilizations. There is a real danger, therefore, in the incongruity of focus that has brought the latest findings of technological research into the foreground of modern life, joining the world in a single community, while leaving the anthropological and psychological discoveries from which a commensurable moral system might have been developed in the learned publications where they first appeared. For surely it is folly to preach to children who will be riding rockets to the moon a morality and cosmology based on concepts of the Good Society and of man's place in nature that were coined before the harnessing of the horse! And the world is now far too small, and men's stake in sanity too great, for any more of those old games of Chosen Folk (whether of Jehovah, Allah, Wotan, Manu, or the Devil) by which tribesmen were sustained against their enemies in the days when the serpent still could talk.

The ghostly, anachronistic sounds of Aryan battle cries faded rapidly from the nineteenth-century theaters of learning as a broader realization of the community of man developed—due primarily to a mass of completely unforeseen information from the pioneers of archaeology and anthropology. For example, it soon appeared not only that the earliest Indo-European tribes must already have been mixed of a number of races, but also that the greater part of what had been taken to be of their invention actually had been derived from the earlier, very much more highly developed cultures of ancient Egypt, Crete, and Mesopotamia. Moreover, the worldwide diffusion of the major themes of classical as well as biblical mythology and religious lore—far beyond any possible influence either of Aryan or of Semite—so greatly magnified the frame of the prehistory of civilization that the old problems, prides, and prejudices were rendered out of date.

A sense of the import of these new discoveries for the nineteenth-century image of man can be gained from a summary schedule of a number of representative moments; for example:

1821	Jean François Champollion derived from the Rosetta Stone the key to Egyptian hieroglyphics, thus unveiling a civilized religious literature earlier than the Greek and Hebrew by about two thousand years.
1833	William Ellis, *Polynesian Researches* (4 vols.), opened to view the myths and customs of the South Sea Islands.
1839	Henry Rowe Schoolcraft, *Algic Researches* (2 vols.), offered the first considerable collection of North American Indian myths.
1845–50	Sir Austen Henry Layard excavated ancient Nineveh and Babylon, opening the treasuries of the Mesopotamian civilization.
1847–65	Jacques Boucher de Crèvecœur de Perthes, *Antiquités celtiques et antédiluviennes* (3 vols.), established the existence of man in Europe in the Pleistocene Period (that is to say, more than a hundred thousand years ago) and, on the basis of his classification of flint tools, identified three Old Stone Age periods, which he termed: (1) "the Cave Bear Age," (2) "the Mammoth and Woolly Rhinoceros Age," and (3) "the Reindeer Age."
1856	Johann Karl Fuhlrott discovered in a cave in eastern Germany the bones of Neanderthal Man (Homo neanderthalensis), mighty hunter of the Cave Bear and Mammoth Ages.
1859	Charles Darwin's great work, *On the Origin of Species,* appeared.

1860–65 Edouard Lartet, in southern France, unearthed the remains of Crô-Magnon Man, by whom Neanderthal Man had been displaced in Europe during the Reindeer Age, at the end of the Pleistocene.

1861 The *Popol Vuh,* an ancient Central American mythological text, was introduced to the learned world by the Abbé Brasseur de Bourbourg.

From this momentous decade of the sixties onward, the universality of the basic themes and motifs of mythology was generally conceded, the usual assumption being that some sort of psychological explanation would presently be found; and so it was that from two remote quarters of the learned world the following

1868 comparative studies appeared simultaneously: in Philadelphia, Daniel G. Brinton's *The Myths of the New World,* comparing the primitive and high-culture mythologies of the Old World and the New; and in Berlin, Adolf Bastian's *Das Beständige in den Menschenrassen und die Spielweite ihrer Veränderlichkeit,* applying the point of view of comparative psychology and biology to the problems, first, of the "constants" and then of the "variables" in the mythologies of mankind.

1871 Edward B. Tylor, in his *Primitive Culture: Researches into the Development of Mythology, Philosophy, Religion, Language, Art, and Custom,* directed a psychological explanation of the concept of "animism" to a systematic interpretation of the whole range of primitive thought.

1872–85 Heinrich Schliemann, excavating Troy (Hissarlik) and Mycenae, probed the pre-Homeric, pre-classical levels of Greek civilization.

1879 Don Marcelino de Sautuola discovered on his property in northern Spain (Altamira) the magnificent cave-painting art of the Mammoth and Reindeer Ages.

1890 Sir James George Frazer published the culminating work of this whole period of anthropological research, *The Golden Bough.*

1891–92 In Central Java, on the Solo River, near Trinil, Eugène Dubois unearthed the bones and teeth of "the Missing Link," Pithecanthropus erectus ("the Ape-man who walks erect")—with a brain capacity halfway between that of the largest-brained gorilla (about 600 cc.) and that of the average modern man (about 1400 cc.).

1893 Sir Arthur Evans commenced his Cretan excavations.

1898 Leo Frobenius announced a new approach to the study of primitive cultures (the *Kulturkreislehre,* "culture area theory"), wherein he identified a primitive cultural continuum, extending from equatorial West Africa eastward, through India and Indonesia, Melanesia and Polynesia, across the Pacific to equatorial America and the northwest coast.[8] This was a radical challenge to the older "parallel development" or "psychological" schools of interpretation, such as Brinton, Bastian, Tylor, and Frazer had represented, inasmuch as it brought the broad and bold theory of a primitive trans-oceanic "diffusion" to bear upon the question of the distribution of so-called "universal" themes.

And so it was that, during that epochal century of almost unbelievable spiritual and technological transformations, the old horizons were dissolved and the center of gravity of all learning shifted from the little areas of local pride to a broad science of man himself in his new and single world. The older, eighteenth-century disciplines, which formerly had seemed to fill sufficiently the field of humanistic concern, had become but provinces of a much larger subject. And whereas formerly the prime question seemed to have been that of man's supernatural as against merely natural endowment, now, with the recognition of the universality of those mythological themes that formerly had been taken as evidence of the divine source of the higher religions, "surpassing man's natural knowledge," as St. Thomas Aquinas argued, and therefore proving that "God is far above all that man can possibly think of God"; [9] with the realization that these supernatural motifs were not peculiar to any single tradition but common to the religious lore of mankind, the tension between "orthodox" and "gentile," "high" and "primitive," simply dissolved. And the major questions, the problems of man's highest concern, now became, first, whether such mythological themes as death-and-resurrection, the virgin birth, and creation from nothing should be rationally dismissed as mere vestiges of primitive ignorance (superstitions), or, on the contrary, interpreted as rendering values beyond the faculty of reason (transcendent symbols); and, second, whether, as products of the spontaneous operations of the psyche, they can have appeared independently in various quarters of the world (theories of parallel development), or rather, as the inventions of particular times and persons, must have been spread about either by early migrations or by later commerce (theories of diffusion).

Few in the nineteenth century were competent to face either of these questions without prejudice or to control the necessary evidence for their analysis; for the psychology of the time had simply not come into possession either of the information or of the hypotheses necessary for a probing of the psyche in depth. The eminent physiologist, psychologist, and philosopher Wilhelm Wundt (1832–1920), who in 1857 began lecturing at Heidelberg and in 1875 at the University of Leipzig, masterfully reviewed the whole ethnological field from a psychological point of view in his numerous works on ethnological psychology (*Völkerpsychologie*); but he realized and frankly averred that the breadth and depth of this richly promising subject had not yet been adequately measured.[10] A scientific probing of the psyche in depth, however, had already been initiated at the neurological clinic of Salpêtrière, in Paris, where Jean Martin Charcot (1825–1893), professor of pathological anatomy in the medical faculty of the university, was opening new horizons in his studies of hysteria, paralysis, brain disease, senility, and hypnosis.[11] The young Sigmund Freud (1856–1939) and Carl G. Jung (b. 1875) were among his pupils; and something of the force and direction of his researches may be judged from their distinguished careers in exploration of the dark, inaccessible reaches of the psyche. However, the application of the new realizations concerning the phenomenology of the "unconscious" of the neurotic individual to a systematic interpretation of ethnological materials had to wait for the twentieth-century movement initiated by Jung's *Wandlungen und Symbole der Libido* (1912),[12] and Freud's *Totem und Tabu* (1913).[13] The orientations and researches of Wundt and Charcot prepared the way, but the full-scale application of the laws and hypotheses of the science of the unconscious to the fields of religion, prehistory, mythology and folklore, literature and the history of art, which has been one of the outstanding factors in the development of twentieth-century thought, we find only suggested as a richly promising possibility in the science of their day.

And yet, as Thomas Mann observed in his important speech on "Freud and the Future," delivered in Vienna on the occasion of Dr. Sigmund Freud's eightieth birthday, the profound and natural sympathy between the two spheres of literature and the science of the unconscious had for a long time existed unperceived. The romantic-biologic fantasies of Novalis (1772–1801); Schopenhauer's dream psychology and philosophy of instinct (1788–1860); the Christian zeal of Kierkegaard (1813–1855), which had led him to extremes of penetrating psychological insight; Ibsen's view of the lie as indispensable to life (1828–1906); and, above all, Nietzsche's translation of the metaphysical pretensions of theology, mythology, and moral philosophy into the language of an empirical psychology (1844–1900)—these not only anticipated, but in scope and richness sometimes even surpassed, the wonderful insights that were now being coolly systematized in the formidable hypotheses and terminologies of scientific exactitude. In fact, as Mann suggested in his somewhat ironical praise of the eminent scientist whose scientific exactitude had not permitted him to regard philosophy very highly, it might with justice even be claimed that the modern science of the unconscious no more than writes the *quod erat demonstrandum* to the whole great tradition of metaphysical and psychological insights represented by the romantic poets, poet-philosophers, and artists, who, throughout the course of the nineteenth century, had walked step by step alongside the men of analytical knowledge and experience.[14]

One thinks of Goethe, in every line of whose *Faust* there is evident a thoroughly seasoned comprehension of the force of the traditional symbolism of the psyche, in relation not only to individual biography but also to the psychological dynamics of civilization. One thinks of Wagner, whose masterworks were conceived in a realization of the import of symbolic forms so far in advance of the allegorical readings suggested by the Orientalists and ethnologists of his time that even with the dates before one (Wagner, 1813–1883; Max Müller, 1823–1900; Sir James George Frazer, 1854–1941) it is difficult to think of the artist's work as having *preceded* the comparatively fumbling efforts of the men of science to interpret symbols. Or one thinks of Melville (1819–1891), captured by cannibals on the South Sea island of Nukahiva and even scheduled to become an item on the menu, in whose *Moby Dick* (1851) and *Pierre* (1852) the profundity of the author's psychological insight is rendered through an infallible use of the language of symbol.

"The myth," as Thomas Mann has seen, and as many of the depth psychologists would agree, "is the foundation of life, the timeless *schema,* the pious formula into which life flows when it reproduces its traits out of the unconscious." [15] But on the other hand—as any ethnologist, archaeologist, or historian would observe—the myths of the differing civilizations have sensibly varied throughout the centuries and broad reaches of mankind's residence in the world, indeed to such a degree that the "virtue" of one mythology has often been the "vice" of another, and the heaven of one the other's hell. Moreover, with the old horizons now gone that formerly separated and protected the various culture worlds and their pantheons, a veritable *Götterdämmerung* has flung its flames across the universe. Communities that once were comfortable in the consciousness of their own mythologically guaranteed godliness find, abruptly, that they are devils in the eyes of their neighbors. Evidently some mythology of a broader, deeper kind than anything envisioned anywhere in the past is now required: some *arcanum arcanorum* far more fluid, more sophisticated, than the separate visions of the local traditions, wherein those mythologies themselves will be known to be but the masks of a larger—all their shining pantheons but the flickering modes of a "timeless *schema*" that is no *schema*.

But that, precisely, is the great mystery pageant only waiting to be noticed as it lies before us, so to say, in sections, in the halls and museums of the various sciences, yet already living, too, in the works of our greatest men of art. To make it serve the present hour, we have only to assemble—or reassemble—it in its full dimension, scientifically, and then bring it to life as our own, in the way of art: the way of wonder—sympathetic, instructive delight; not judging morally, but participating with our own awakened humanity in the festival of the passing forms.

Part One

THE PSYCHOLOGY OF MYTH

Introduction

THE LESSON OF THE MASK

The artist eye, as Thomas Mann has said,[1] has a mythical slant upon life; therefore, the mythological realm—the world of the gods and demons, the carnival of their masks and the curious game of "as if" in which the festival of the lived myth abrogates all the laws of time, letting the dead swim back to life, and the "once upon a time" become the very present—we must approach and first regard with the artist's eye. For, indeed, in the primitive world, where most of the clues to the origin of mythology must be sought, the gods and demons are not conceived in the way of hard and fast, positive realities. A god can be simultaneously in two or more places—like a melody, or like the form of a traditional mask. And wherever he comes, the impact of his presence is the same: it is not reduced through multiplication. Moreover, the mask in a primitive festival is revered and experienced as a veritable apparition of the mythical being that it represents—even though everyone knows that a man made the mask and that a man is wearing it. The one wearing it, furthermore, is identified with the god during the time of the ritual of which the mask is a part. He does not merely represent the god; he *is* the god. The literal fact that the apparition is composed of A, a mask, B, its reference to a mythical being, and C, a man, is dismissed from the mind, and the presentation is allowed to work without correction upon the sentiments of both the beholder and the actor. In other words, there has been a shift of view from the logic of the normal secular sphere, where things are understood to be distinct from one another, to a theatrical or play sphere, where they are accepted for what they are *experienced* as being and the logic is that of "make believe"—"as if."

We all know the convention, surely! It is a primary, spontaneous device of childhood, a magical device, by which the world can be transformed from banality to magic in a trice. And its inevitability in childhood is one of those universal characteristics of man that unite us in one family. It is a primary datum, consequently, of the science of myth, which is concerned precisely with the phenomenon of self-induced belief.

"A professor," wrote Leo Frobenius in a celebrated paper on the force of the daemonic world of childhood, "is writing at his desk and his four-year-old little daughter is running about the room. She has nothing to do and is disturbing him. So he gives her three burnt matches, saying, 'Here! Play!' and, sitting on the rug, she begins to play with the matches, Hansel, Gretel, and the witch. A considerable time elapses, during which the professor concentrates upon his task, undisturbed. But then, suddenly, the child shrieks in terror. The father jumps. 'What is it? What has happened?' The little girl comes running to him, showing every sign of great fright. 'Daddy, Daddy,' she cries, 'take the witch away! I can't touch the witch any more!' "

"An eruption of emotion," Frobenius observes,

> is characteristic of the spontaneous shift of an idea from the level of the sentiments (*Gemüt*) to that of sensual consciousness (*sinnliches Bewusstsein*). Furthermore, the appearance of such an eruption obviously means that a certain spiritual process has reached a conclusion. The match is not a witch; nor was it a witch for the child at the beginning of the game. The process, therefore, rests on the fact that the match has *become* a witch on the level of the sentiments and the conclusion of the process coincides with the transfer of this idea to the plane of consciousness. The observation of the process escapes the test of conscious thought, since it enters consciousness only after or at the moment of completion. However, inasmuch as the idea *is,* it must have *become*. The process is creative, in the highest sense of the word; for, as we have seen, in a little girl a match can become a witch. Briefly stated,

then: the phase of *becoming* takes place on the level of the sentiments, while that of *being* is on the conscious plane.[2]

This vivid, convincing example of a child's seizure by a witch while in the act of play may be taken to represent an intense degree of the daemonic mythological experience. However, the attitude of mind represented by the game itself, before the seizure supervened, also belongs within the sphere of our subject. For, as J. Huizinga has pointed out in his brilliant study of the play element in culture, the whole point, at the beginning, is the *fun* of play, not the rapture of seizure. "In all the wild imaginings of mythology a fanciful spirit is playing," he writes, "on the border-line between jest and earnest."[3] "As far as I know, ethnologists and anthropologists concur in the opinion that the mental attitude in which the great religious feasts of savages are celebrated and witnessed is not one of complete illusion. There is an underlying consciousness of things 'not being real.' "[4] And he quotes, among others, R. R. Marett, who, in his chapter on "Primitive Credulity" in *The Threshold of Religion,* develops the idea that a certain element of "make-believe" is operative in all primitive religions. "The savage," wrote Marett, "is a good actor who can be quite absorbed in his role, like a child at play; and also, like a child, a good spectator who can be frightened to death by the roaring of something he knows perfectly well to be no 'real' lion."[5]

"By considering the whole sphere of so-called primitive culture as a play-sphere," Huizinga then suggests in conclusion, "we pave the way to a more direct and more general understanding of its peculiarities than any meticulous psychological or sociological analysis would allow."[6] And I would concur wholeheartedly with this judgment, only adding that we should extend the consideration to the entire field of our present subject.

In the Roman Catholic mass, for example, when the priest, quoting the words of Christ at the Last Supper, pronounces the formula of consecration—with utmost solemnity—first over the wafer of the host (*Hoc est enim Corpus meum:* "for this is My Body"), then over the chalice of the wine (*Hic est enim Calix Sanguinis mei, novi et aeterni Testamenti: Mysterium fidei: qui pro vobis et pro multis effundetur in remissionem peccatorum:* "For this is the Chalice of My Blood, of the new and eternal testament: the mystery of faith: which shall be shed for you and for many unto the remission of sins"), it is to be supposed that the bread and wine become the body and blood of Christ, that every fragment of the host and every drop of the wine is the actual living Savior of the world. The sacrament, that is to say, is not conceived to be a *reference,* a mere sign or symbol to arouse in us a train of thought, but is God himself, the Creator, Judge, and Savior of the Universe, here come to work upon us directly, to free our souls (created in His image) from the effects of the Fall of Adam and Eve in the Garden of Eden (which we are to suppose existed as a geographical fact).

Comparably, in India it is believed that, in response to consecrating formulae, deities will descend graciously to infuse their divine substance into the temple images, which are then called their throne or seat (*pīṭha*). It is also possible—and in some Indian sects even expected—that the individual himself should become a seat of deity. In the *Gandharva Tantra* it is written, for example, "No one who is not himself divine can successfully worship a divinity"; and again, "Having become the divinity, one should offer it sacrifice." [7]

Furthermore, it is even possible for a really gifted player to discover that everything—absolutely everything—has become the body of a god, or reveals the omnipresence of God as the ground of all being. There is a passage, for example, among the conversations of the nineteenth-century Bengalese spiritual master Ramakrishna, in which he described such an experience. "One day," he is said to have reported, "it was suddenly revealed to me that everything is Pure Spirit. The utensils of worship, the altar, the door frame—all Pure Spirit. Men, animals, and other living beings—all Pure Spirit. Then like a madman I began to shower flowers in all directions. Whatever I saw I worshiped." [8]

Belief—or at least a game of belief—is the first step toward such a divine seizure. The chronicles of the saints abound in accounts of their long ordeals of difficult practice, which preceded their moments of being carried away; and we have also the more spontaneous religious games and exercises of the folk (the amateurs) to illustrate for us the principle involved. The spirit of the festival, the holiday, the holy day of the religious ceremonial, requires that the normal attitude toward the cares of the world should have been temporarily set aside in favor of a particular mood of dressing up. The world is hung with banners. Or in the permanent religious sanctuaries—the temples and cathedrals, where an atmosphere of holiness hangs permanently in the air—the logic of cold, hard fact must not be allowed to intrude and spoil the spell. The gentile, the "spoil sport," the positivist, who cannot or will not play, must be kept aloof. Hence the guardian figures that stand at either side of the entrances to holy places: lions, bulls, or fearsome warriors with uplifted weapons. They are there to keep out the "spoil sports," the advocates of Aristotelean logic, for whom A can never be B; for whom the actor is never to be lost in the part; for whom the mask, the image, the consecrated host, tree, or animal cannot become God, but only a reference. Such heavy thinkers are to remain without. For the whole purpose of entering a sanctuary or participating in a festival is that one should be overtaken by the state known in India as "the other mind" (Sanskrit, *anya-manas:* absent-mindedness, possession by a spirit), where one is "beside oneself," spellbound, set apart from one's logic of self-possession and overpowered by the force of a logic of "indissociation"—wherein A is B, and C also is B.

"One day," said Ramakrishna, "while worshiping Shiva, I was about to offer a bel-leaf on the head of the image, when it was revealed to me that this universe itself is Shiva. Another day, I had been plucking flowers when it was revealed to me that each plant was a bouquet adorning the universal form of God. That was the end of my plucking flowers. I look on man in just the same way. When I see a man, I see that it is God Himself, who walks on earth, rocking to and fro, as it were, like a pillow floating on the waves." [9]

From such a point of view the universe is the seat (*pīṭha*) of a divinity from whose vision our usual state of consciousness excludes us. But in the playing of the game of the gods we take a step toward that reality—which is ultimately the reality of ourselves. Hence the rapture, the feelings of delight, and the sense of refreshment, harmony, and re-creation! In the case of a saint, the game leads to seizure—as in the case of the little girl, to whom the match revealed itself to be a witch. Contact with the orientation of the world may then be lost, the mind remaining rapt in that other state. For such it is impossible to return to this other game, the game of life in the world. They are possessed of God; that is all they know on earth and all they need to know. And they can even infect whole societies, so that these, inspired by their seizures, may likewise break contact with the world and spurn it as delusory, or as evil. Secular life then may be read as a fall—a fall from Grace, Grace being the rapture of the festival of God.

But there is another attitude, more comprehensive, which has given beauty and love to the *two* worlds: that, namely, of the *līlā,* "the play," as it has been termed in the Orient. The world is not condemned and shunned as a fall, but voluntarily entered as a game or dance, wherein the spirit plays.

Ramakrishna closed his eyes. "Is it only this?" he said. "Does God exist only when the eyes are closed, and disappear when the eyes are opened?" He opened his eyes. "The Play belongs to Him to whom Eternity belongs, and Eternity to Him to whom the Play belongs. . . . Some people climb the seven floors of a building and cannot get down; but some climb up and then, at will, visit the lower floors." [10]

The question then becomes only: How far down or up the ladder can one go without losing the sense of a game? Professor Huizinga, in his work already referred to, points out that in Japanese the verb *asobu,* which refers to play in general—recreation, relaxation, amusement, trip or jaunt, dissipation, gambling, lying idle, or being unemployed—also means to study at a university or under a teacher; likewise, to engage in a sham fight; and finally, to participate in the very strict formalities of the tea ceremony. He continues:

> The extraordinary earnestness and profound gravity of the Japanese ideal of life is masked by the fashionable fiction that everything is only play. Like the *chevalerie* of the Christian Middle Ages, Japanese *bushido* took shape almost entirely in

the play-sphere and was enacted in play-forms. The language still preserves this conception in the *asobase-kotoba* (literally play-language) or polite speech, the mode of address used in conversation with persons of higher rank. The convention is that the higher classes are merely playing at all they do. The polite form for "you arrive in Tokyo" is, literally, "you play arrival in Tokyo"; and for "I hear that your father is dead," "I hear that your father has played dying." In other words, the revered person is imagined as living in an elevated sphere where only pleasure or condescension moves to action.[11]

From this supremely aristocratic point of view, any state of seizure, whether by life or by the gods, must represent a fall or drop of spiritual *niveau,* a vulgarization of the play. Nobility of spirit is the grace—or ability—to play, whether in heaven or on earth. And this, I take it, this *noblesse oblige,* which has always been the quality of aristocracy, was precisely the virtue (ἀρετή) of the Greek poets, artists, and philosophers, for whom the gods were true as poetry is true. We may take it also to be the primitive (and proper) mythological point of view, as contrasted with the heavier positivistic; which latter is represented, on the one hand, by religious experiences of the literal sort, where the impact of a daemon, rising to the plane of consciousness from its place of birth on the level of the sentiments, is taken to be objectively real, and, on the other, by science and political economy, for which only measurable facts are objectively real. For if it is true, as the Greek philosopher Antisthenes (born c. 444 B.C.) has said, that "God is not like anything: hence no one can understand him by means of an image," [12] or, as we read in the Indian Upanishad,

> It is other, indeed, than the known
> And, moreover, above the unknown! [13]

then it must be conceded, as a basic principle of our natural history of the gods and heroes, that whenever a myth has been taken literally its sense has been perverted; but also, reciprocally, that whenever it has been dismissed as a mere priestly fraud or sign of inferior intelligence, truth has slipped out the other door.

And so what, then, is the sense that we are to seek, if it be neither here nor there?

Kant, in his *Prolegomena to Every Future System of Metaphysics,* states very carefully that all our thinking about final things can be only by way of *analogy.* "The proper expression for our fallible mode of conception," he declares, "would be: that we imagine the world *as if* its being and inner character were derived from a supreme mind" (italics mine).[14]

Such a highly played game of "as if" frees our mind and spirit, on the one hand, from the presumption of theology, which pretends to know the laws of God, and, on the other, from the bondage of reason, whose laws do not apply beyond the horizon of human experience.

I am willing to accept the word of Kant, as representing the view of a considerable metaphysician. And applying it to the range of festival games and attitudes just reviewed—from the mask to the consecrated host and temple image, transubstantiated worshiper and transubstantiated world—I can see, or believe I can see, that a principle of release operates throughout the series by way of the alchemy of an "as if"; and that, through this, the impact of all so-called "reality" upon the psyche is transubstantiated. The play state and the rapturous seizures sometimes deriving from it represent, therefore, a step rather *toward* than away from the ineluctable truth; and belief—acquiescence in a belief that is not quite belief—is the first step toward the deepened participation that the festival affords in that general will to life which, in its metaphysical aspect, is antecedent to, and the creator of, all life's laws.

The opaque weight of the world—both of life on earth and of death, heaven, and hell—is dissolved, and the spirit freed, not *from* anything, for there was nothing from which to be freed except a myth too solidly believed, but *for* something, something fresh and new, a spontaneous act.

From the position of secular man (Homo sapiens), that is to say, we are to enter the play sphere of the festival, acquiescing in a game of belief, where fun, joy, and rapture rule in ascending series. The laws of life in time and space—economics, politics, and even morality—will thereupon dissolve. Whereafter, re-created by that return to paradise before the Fall, before the knowledge of good and evil, right and wrong, true and false, belief and disbelief, we are to carry the point of view and spirit of man the player (Homo ludens) back into life; as in the play of children, where, undaunted by the banal actualities of life's meager possibilities, the spontaneous impulse of the spirit to identify itself with something other than itself for the sheer delight of play, transubstantiates the world—in which, actually, after all, things are not quite as real or permanent, terrible, important, or logical as they seem.

Chapter 1

THE ENIGMA OF THE INHERITED IMAGE

I. The Innate Releasing Mechanism

A number of popular moving-picture films have shown the amazing phenomenon of the laying and hatching of the eggs of the sea turtle. The female leaves the water and crawls to a point on the beach safely above the tide line, where she digs a hole, deposits hundreds of eggs, covers the nest, and turns back to the sea. After eighteen days a multitude of tiny turtles come flipping up through the sand and, like a field of sprinters at the crack of the gun, make for the heavily crashing waves as fast as they can, while gulls drop screaming from overhead to pick them off.

No more vivid representation could be desired of spontaneity and the quest for the not-yet-seen. There is no question here of learning, trial-and-error; nor are the tiny things afraid of the great waves. They know that they must hurry, know how to do it, and know precisely where they are going. And finally, when they enter the sea, they know immediately both how to swim and that swim they must.

Students of animal behavior have coined the term "innate releasing mechanism" (IRM) to designate the inherited structure in the nervous system that enables an animal to respond thus to a circumstance never experienced before, and the factor triggering the response they term a "sign stimulus" or "releaser." It is obvious that the living entity responding to such a sign cannot be said to be the individual, since the individual has had no previous knowledge of the object to which it is reacting. The recognizing and responding subject is, rather, some sort of trans- or super-individual, inhabiting and moving the living creature. Let us not speculate here about the metaphysics of this mystery; for, as Schopenhauer sagely remarks in his paper on *The Will in Nature,* "we are sunk in a sea of riddles and inscrutables, knowing and understanding neither what is around us nor ourselves."

Chicks with their eggshells still adhering to their tails dart for cover when a hawk flies overhead, but not when the bird is a gull or duck, heron or pigeon. Furthermore, if the wooden model of a hawk is drawn over their coop on a wire, they react as though it were alive—unless it be drawn backward, when there is no response.

Here we have an extremely precise image—never seen before, yet recognized with reference not merely to its form but to its form in motion, and linked, furthermore, to an immediate, unplanned, unlearned, and even unintended system of appropriate action: flight, to cover. The image of the inherited enemy is already sleeping in the nervous system, and along with it the well-proven reaction. Furthermore, even if all the hawks in the world were to vanish, their image would still sleep in the soul of the chick—never to be roused, however, unless by some accident of art; for example, a repetition of the clever experiment of the wooden hawk on a wire. With that (for a certain number of generations, at any rate) the obsolete reaction of the flight to cover would recur; and, unless we knew about the earlier danger of hawks to chicks, we should find the sudden eruption difficult to explain. "Whence," we might ask, "this abrupt seizure by an image to which there is no counterpart in the chicken's world? Living gulls and ducks, herons and pigeons, leave it cold; but the work of art strikes some very deep chord!"

Have we here a clue to the problem of the image of the witch in the nervous system of the child? Some psychologists would say so. C. G. Jung, for example, identifies two fundamentally different systems of unconsciously motivated response in the human being. One he terms the personal unconscious. It is based on a context of forgotten, neglected, or suppressed memory images derived from personal experience (infantile impressions, shocks, frustrations, satisfactions, etc.), such as Sigmund Freud recognized and analyzed in his therapy. The other he names the collective unconscious. Its contents—which he calls archetypes—are just such images as that of the hawk in the nervous system of the chick. No one has yet been able to tell us how it got there; but there it is!

"A personal image," he writes, "has neither archaic character nor collective significance, but expresses unconscious contents of a personal nature and a personally conditioned conscious inclination.

"The primary image (*urtümliches Bild*), which I have termed 'archetype,' is always collective, i.e. common to at least whole peoples or periods of history. The chief mythological motifs of all times and races are very probably of this order; for example, in the dreams and fantasies of neurotics of pure Negro stock I have been able to identify a series of motifs of Greek mythology.

"The primary image," he then suggests, "is a memory deposit, an engram, derived from a condensation of innumerable similar experiences . . . the psychic expression of an anatomically, physiologically determined natural tendency." [1]

Jung's idea of the "archetypes" is one of the leading theories, today, in the field of our subject. It is a development of the earlier theory of Adolf Bastian (1826–1905), who recognized, in the course of his extensive travels, the uniformity of what he termed the "elementary ideas" (*Elementargedanke*) of mankind. Remarking also, however, that in the various provinces of human culture these ideas are differently articulated and elaborated, he coined the term "ethnic ideas" (*Völkergedanke*) for the actual, local manifestations of the universal forms. Nowhere, he noted, are the "elementary ideas" to be found in a pure state, abstracted from the locally conditioned "ethnic ideas" through which they are substantialized; but rather, like the image of man himself, they are to be known only by way of the rich variety of their extremely interesting, frequently startling, yet always finally recognizable inflections in the panorama of human life.

Two possibilities of emphasis are implicit in this observation of Bastian. The first we may term the psychological and the second the ethnological; and these can be taken to represent, broadly, the two contrasting points of view from which scientists, scholars, and philosophers have approached our subject.

"First," wrote Bastian, "the idea as such must be studied . . . and as second factor, the influence of climatic-geological conditions."[2] Only after that, as a third factor, according to his view, could the influence upon one another of the various ethnic traditions throughout the course of history be profitably surveyed. Bastian, that is to say, stressed the psychological, spontaneous aspect of culture as primary; and this approach has been the usual one of biologists, medical men, and psychologists to the present day. Briefly stated, it assumes that there is in the structure and functioning of the psyche a certain degree of spontaneity and consequent uniformity throughout the history and domain of the human species—an order of psychological laws inhering in the structure of the body, which has not radically altered since the period of the Aurignacian caves and can be as readily identified in the jungles of Brazil as in the cafés of Paris, as readily in the igloos of Baffin Land as in the harems of Marrakech.

But on the other hand, if climate, geography, and massive social forces are to be regarded as of more moment in the shaping of the ideas, ideals, fantasies, and emotions by which men live than the innate structures and capacities of the psyche, then a diametrically contrary philosophical position must be assumed. Psychology in this case becomes a function of ethnology; or, to quote one representative authority, A. R. Radcliffe-Brown, in his work on *The Andaman Islanders:*

> A society depends for its existence on the presence in the minds of its members of a certain system of sentiments by which the conduct of the individual is regulated in conformity with the needs of the society. Every feature of the social system itself and every event or object that in any way affects the well-being or the cohesion of the society becomes an object of this system of sentiments. *In human society the sentiments in question are not innate but are developed in the individual by the action of the society upon him* [italics mine]. The ceremonial customs of a society are a means by which the sentiments in question are given collective expression on appropri-

> ate occasions. The ceremonial (i.e. collective) expression of any sentiment serves both to maintain it at the requisite degree of intensity in the mind of the individual and to transmit it from one generation to another. Without such expression the sentiments involved could not exist.[3]

It will be readily seen that in such a view the ceremonials and mythologies of the differing societies are in no sense manifestations of psychologically grounded "elementary ideas," common to the human race, but of interests locally conditioned; and the fundamental contrast of the two approaches is surely clear.

Was the little girl's reaction to the idea of the witch that she had conjured into her mind comparable to the chick's reaction to the fashioned image of a hawk? Or should we say, rather, that because she had been brought up on the fairy tales collected by the Brothers Grimm, she had learned to associate certain imagined dangers with a German fictional character and these alone were the cause of her fright?

Before being satisfied that we know the answer, we must consider seriously the now well-proven fact that the human nervous system was the governor, guide, and controller of a nomadic hunter, foraging for his food and protecting himself and his family from becoming food in a very dangerous world of animals, for the first 600,000 years of its development; whereas it has been serving comparatively safe and sane farmers, merchants, professors, and their children for scarcely 8000 years (a segment of less than 1½ per cent of the known arc). Who will claim to know what sign stimuli smote our releasing mechanisms when our names were not Homo sapiens but Pithecanthropus and Plesianthropus, or perhaps even—millenniums earlier—Dryopithecus? And who that has knowledge of the numerous vestigial structures of our anatomy, surviving from the days when we were beasts (for example, the muscles of the caudal vertebrae that once wagged our tail), would doubt that in the central nervous system comparable vestiges must remain: images sleeping, whose releasers no longer appear in nature—but might occur in art?

As N. Tinbergen has so well advised in his introductory lectures on *The Study of Instinct,* since generalization based on too narrow a foundation tends to give rise to unnecessary controversy, special emphasis should be placed on the importance of a complete inventory of the behavior patterns of a species before conclusions are announced.[4] For the problem of the relationship of innate to conditioned behavior is far from resolved even for animal species very much less complicated than our own. Nor can general laws be announced for the animal world that will necessarily be valid from one species to the next.

The young of the cuckoo, hatched from an egg laid in the nest of another species and without previous experience of its own kind, when it is fledged flocks only with cuckoos—all of which, likewise, have been raised in the nests of other birds and have never been *taught* to recognize their own kind. But, on the other hand, a duckling will attach itself, as to a parent, to the first creature that greets its eye when it leaves the egg—for example, a mother hen.

The case of the cuckoo, like that of the chicks responding to the hawk, or of the turtles rushing for the sea, illustrates the first point to be emphasized in our brief consideration of this problem of the physiology of the inherited image; namely, the now well-demonstrated fact, already noted, that in the central nervous systems of all animals there exist innate structures that are somehow counterparts of the proper environment of the species. The Gestalt psychologist Wolfgang Köhler has termed these structures in the central nervous system "isomorphs." The animal, directed by innate endowment, comes to terms with its natural environment not as a consequence of any long, slow learning through experience, through trial-and-error, but immediately and with the certainty of recognition. The case of the duckling, on the other hand, illustrates a second point that must be noted if we are to appreciate the relevance of these studies to our own problem of the mythological archetypes; namely, the fact that although in many instances the sign stimuli that release animal responses are immutable and correspond to the inner readiness of the creature as precisely as key to lock (in fact, have been termed "key-tumbler" structures), there also are systems of response that are established by individual experience. In such the structure of the IRM is described as "open." It is susceptible to "impression" or "imprint" (*Prägung*). Moreover—as in the instance of the duckling—where these "open structures" exist the first imprint is definitive, requires sometimes less than a minute for its completion, and is irreversible.

Furthermore, according to Professor Tinbergen, who has given particular attention to the problem of animal learning, not only do differing species have different dispositions to learn, but such innate dispositions come to maturity only in certain critical periods of the animal's growth. "The Eskimo dogs of east Greenland," he writes, for example,

> live in packs of five to ten individuals. The members of a pack defend their group territory against all other dogs. All dogs of an Eskimo settlement have an exact and detailed knowledge of the topography of the territories of other packs; they know where attacks from other packs must be feared. Immature dogs, however, do not defend the territory. Moreover, they often roam through the whole settlement, very often trespassing into other territories, where they are promptly chased. In spite of these frequent attacks, during which they may be severely treated, they do not learn the territories' topography and for the observer their stupidity in this respect is amazing. While the young dogs are growing sexually mature, however, they begin to learn the other territories and within a week their trespassing adventures are over. In two male dogs the first copulation, the first defence of territory, and the first avoidance of strange territory, all occurred within one week.[5]

After the work of Sigmund Freud and his school on the stages of the maturation of the human infant and the force of the imprints acquired in those stages on the responses of the individual throughout life, it will hardly be necessary to argue the relevance of the concepts of "inner readiness" and "imprint" to the sphere of human learning. Much of what the infant has to learn, furthermore, resembles remarkably the sociology of the Eskimo huskies, since it has to do largely with the various aspects of group affiliation. There is, however, in the human sphere a factor that makes all study of instinct and innate structures extremely difficult; for, whereas even the animals most helpless at birth mature very quickly, the human infant is utterly helpless during the first dozen years of its existence and, during this period of the maturation of its character, is completely subject to the pressures and imprints of its local society. In fact, as Adolf Portmann, of Basel, has so well and frequently pointed out, precisely those three endowments of erect posture, speech, and thought, which elevate man above the animal sphere, develop only after birth, and consequently, in the structure of every individual, represent an indissoluble amalgam of innate biological and impressed traditional factors. We cannot think of one without the other.

And so, in the name of science, let us not try to do so!

It is possible, of course, to identify even in man a certain number of innate "key-tumbler" responses: that of the infant to the nipple, for example. It is obvious, also, that in man, just as in the lower animals, there are certain "central excitatory mechanisms" (CEMs), which receive stimulation both from within and from without and move the individual to "appetitive behavior"—sometimes even against his better judgment. A manifest example is the response of the sexual appetite to the stimulus of certain hormones (e.g., testosterone propionate and estrogen) and the reaction, then, even of the innocent individual, to the sign stimuli so well known to the whole species. These phenomena, I should say, require no laboratory tests to warrant our regard. But it must not be forgotten that the entire instinct structure of man is much more open to learning and conditioning than that of animals, so that when evaluating human behavior we have always a very much stronger factor of individual experience to consider than when measuring the central excitatory mechanisms (CEMs) and the innate releasing mechanisms (IRMs) of insect, fish, bird—or even ape.

This important fact may help to clarify the main lines of the problem announced in Bastian's contrast of elementary with ethnic ideas. The elementary, or innate, ideas we must interpret, I believe, as a reference, in nineteenth-century terms, to what now would be called the innate neurological structures (CEMs and IRMs) of the biological species Homo sapiens: those inherited structures in the central nervous system that constitute the elementary foundations of all human experience and reaction. The ethnic ideas, on the other hand, refer to the historically conditioned context of sign stimuli through which the activities of man, in any given society, are released. But since there is no such thing as man *qua* "Man," abstracted from all sociological conditioning, there are very few examples of unimprinted sign stimuli on the level of human ethology—and this is what has made it possible for students of the phenomenology of our species to write, sometimes, as though there were in the human race no inherited structuring system whatsoever. It is now, however, a thoroughly proven fact that the human mind is by no means the mere *tabula rasa* of seventeenth-century epistemology. Indeed, quite the contrary! It is an aggregate of a great many predicating structures, each with its own readiness of response. The mere fact that they are more open than their animal homologues to individual experience must not be allowed to distract us from the more basic fact of their existence—or of their force in establishing and maintaining those basic similarities in human culture the world over which are vastly more massive than the variations. But equally, and on the other hand, we must not be quick to suppose that because an extensive, or even universal, distribution has been established for any given sign stimulus, this then may be regarded as innate and not impressed.

II. The Supernormal Sign Stimulus

It is by now a commonplace of biological thought to observe that man, in his character as animal, is born at least a year too soon, completing in the sphere of society a development that other species accomplish within the womb. It has been observed that our hairlessness is a fetal trait, that our numerous psychological difficulties are functions of the prematurity of our birth, and that—to use Nietzsche's picturesque term—we cannot but expect to remain *das kranke Tier,* "the sick animal," throughout life and to the end of our days. It was the great French naturalist Buffon (1707–1788), I believe, who first remarked that "man is no more than a decadent ape." And it was a Dutch anatomist, Ludwig Bolk, who, in 1926, in a work entitled *The Problem of Human Incarnation,* gave a scientific foundation to this idea by showing that mutations inhibiting maturation actually occur in animals, and suggesting that the evolution of man must have been effected by a series of such modifications. According to Bolk's view, man has been arrested at a stage of growth represented by a late phase in the development of the embryo of a chimpanzee.[6]

A more generous view, however, recognizes in the hairlessness of our species the enhancement of the skin as a sense organ and of the parts of the body as foci of optical interest. For in man the sensory nerves running through the spine are much more numerous than in any of the furry tribes, while the range and subtlety of the sign stimuli afforded not only by our nakedness but also by our various modes of covering and uncovering it evoke responses of considerably more diversity than those of mere animal appetite and consummation. The hairless face has become an organ of exquisite mobility, capable of a range and refinement of social signaling infinitely more versatile than the social "releasers" (the bird cries, flourished antlers, and tail-flashes) of the animal kingdom. The mutation, that is to say, was not negative but positive; and the long gestation, going beyond the capacity of the mother's womb to support it, was the consequence of an advance. For, as Schopenhauer declares, "All great things mature slowly."

And are we to forget, furthermore, the rapid growth, during the first year of extra-uterine life, of this wonderful head and brain? It is perfectly true that, because of the prematurity of our birth, we do not have as many stereotyped, key-tumbler responses as the other vertebrates, and that, having consequently a more open reflex structure than they, we are less rigidly patterned in our instincts, less conservative, dependable, and secure than the animals. But on the other hand, we do have this developed brain, which is three times as great in size as its nearest rival and has given us not only new knowledge (including that of our own inevitable death), but also a capacity to control and even to inhibit our responses.

Best of all, however, is the gift of immaturity itself, which has enabled us to retain in our best, most human, moments the capacity for play. In puppyhood animals show a capacity for play, when they are protected from the dreadful seriousness of the wilderness by the guardianship of parents; and practically all make a charming display of it again in courtship. However, in man—or perhaps we should say, rather, in the best of men, though indeed in the majority of women—the capacity is retained throughout life. It is, in fact, only those who have failed, one way or another, in their manhood or womanhood, who become our penny-dreadfuls, our gorillas and baboons. In a highly suggestive paragraph, the animal psychologist Konrad Lorenz presents an excellent statement of our indebtedness to this capacity of ours for play, reminding us that:

> Every study undertaken by Man was the genuine outcome of curiosity, a kind of game. All the data of natural science, which are responsible for Man's domination of the world, originated in activities that were indulged in exclusively for the sake of amusement. When Benjamin Franklin drew sparks from the tail of his kite he was thinking as little of the lightning conductor as Hertz, when he investigated electrical waves, was thinking of radio transmission. Anyone who has experienced in his own person how easily the inquisitiveness of a child at play can grow into the life work of a naturalist will never doubt the fundamental similarity of games and study. The inquisitive child disappears entirely from the wholly animal nature of the mature chimpanzee. But the child is far from being buried in the man, as Nietzsche thinks. On the contrary, it rules him absolutely.[7]

Animals are without speech—and one reason, surely, is their inability to play with sounds. They are without art—and the reason, again, is their inability to play with forms. Man's capacity for play animates his urge to fashion images and organize forms in such a way as to create new stimuli for himself: sign stimuli, to which his nervous system may then react much in the way of an isomorph to its releaser. We have observed the case of the little girl, seized by her own creation of a witch. Let us consider, now, what can happen to a poet. The following statement, by the British poet and critic A. E. Housman, supplies the most satisfactory definition I know of a certain triggering principle that is effective in the poetic impact:

> Poetry seems to me more physical than intellectual. A year or two ago, in common with others, I received from America

> a request that I would define poetry. I replied that I could no more define poetry than a terrier can define a rat, but that I thought we both recognized the object by the symptoms which it provokes in us. One of these symptoms was described in connection with another object by Eliphaz the Temanite: "A spirit passed before my face: the hair of my flesh stood up." Experience has taught me, when I am shaving of a morning, to keep watch over my thoughts, because if a line of poetry strays into my memory, my skin bristles so that the razor ceases to act. This particular symptom is accompanied by a shiver down the spine; there is another which consists in a constriction of the throat and a precipitation of water to the eyes; and there is a third which I can only describe by borrowing a phrase from one of Keats's last letters, where he says, speaking of Fanny Brawne, "everything that reminds me of her goes through me like a spear." The seat of this sensation is the pit of the stomach.[8]

The reader hardly need be reminded that the images not only of poetry and love but also of religion and patriotism, when effective, are apprehended with actual physical responses: tears, sighs, interior aches, spontaneous groans, cries, bursts of laughter, wrath, and impulsive deeds. Human experience and human art, that is to say, have succeeded in creating for the human species an environment of sign stimuli that release physical responses and direct them to ends no less effectively than do the signs of nature the instincts of the beasts. The biology, psychology, sociology, and history of these sign stimuli may be said to constitute the field of our subject, the science of Comparative Mythology. And although no one has yet devised an effective method for distinguishing between the innate and the acquired, the natural and the culturally conditioned, the "elementary" and the "ethnic" aspects of such human-cultural catalysts and their evoked responses, the radical distinction here made by the poet Housman between images that act upon our nervous structure as energy releasers and those that serve, rather, for the transmission of thought, supplies an excellent criterion for the testing of our themes.

"I cannot satisfy myself," he writes, "that there are any such things as poetical ideas. No truth, it seems to me, is too precious, no observation too profound, and no sentiment too exalted to be expressed in prose. The utmost that I could admit is that some ideas do, while others do not, lend themselves kindly to poetical expression; and that these receive from poetry an enhancement which glorifies and almost transfigures them, and which is not perceived to be a separate thing except by analysis." [9]

When Housman writes that "poetry is not the thing said but a way of saying it," and when he states again "that the intellect is not the fount of poetry, that it may actually hinder its production, and that it cannot even be trusted to recognize poetry when it is produced," [10] he is no more than reaffirming and lucidly formulating the first axiom of all creative art—whether it be in poetry, music, dance, architecture, painting, or sculpture—which is, namely, that art is not, like science, a logic of references but a release from reference and rendition of immediate experience: a presentation of forms, images, or ideas in such a way that they will communicate, not primarily a thought or even a feeling, but an impact.

The axiom is worth recalling here, because mythology was historically the mother of the arts and yet, like so many mythological mothers, the daughter, equally, of her own birth. Mythology is not invented rationally; mythology cannot be rationally understood. Theological interpreters render it ridiculous. Literary criticism reduces it to metaphor. A new and very promising approach is opened, however, when it is viewed in the light of biological psychology as a function of the human nervous system, precisely homologous to the innate and learned sign stimuli that release and direct the energies of nature—of which our brain itself is but the most amazing flower.

One further lesson may be taken from animals. There is a phenomenon known to the students of animal behavior as the "supernormal sign stimulus," which has never been considered, as far as I know, in relation either to art and poetry or to myth; yet which, in the end, may be our surest guide to the seat of their force, and to an appreciation of their function in the quickening of the human dream of life.

"The innate releasing mechanism," Tinbergen declares, "usually seems to correspond more or less with the properties of the environmental object or situation at which the reaction is aimed. . . . However, close study of IRMs reveals the remarkable fact that it is sometimes possible to offer stimulus situations that are even more effective than the natural situation. In other words, the natural situation is not always optimal." [11]

It was found, for instance, that the male of a certain butterfly known as the grayling (*Eumenis semele*), which assumes the initiative in mating by pursuing a passing female in flight, generally prefers females of darker hue to those of lighter—and to such a degree that if a model of even darker hue than anything known in nature is presented, the sexually motivated male will pursue it in preference even to the darkest female of the species.

"Here we find," writes Professor Portmann, in comment, "an 'inclination' that is not satisfied in nature, but which perhaps, one day, if inheritable darker mutations should appear, would play a role in the selection of mating partners. Who knows whether such anticipations of particular sign stimuli may not play their part in the support and furthering of new variants, inasmuch as they may represent one of the factors in the process of selection that determines the direction of evolution?" [12]

Obviously the human female, with her talent for play, recognized many millenniums ago the power of the supernormal sign stimulus: cosmetics for the heightening of the lines of her eyes have been found among the earliest remains of the Neolithic Age. And from there to an appreciation of the force of ritualization, hieratic art, masks, gladiatorial vestments, kingly robes, and every other humanly conceived and realized improvement of nature, is but a step—or a natural series of steps.

Evidence will appear, in the course of our natural history of the gods, of the gods themselves as supernormal sign stimuli; of the ritual forms deriving from their supernatural inspiration acting as catalysts to convert men into gods; and of civilization—this new environment of man that has grown from his own interior and has pressed back the bounds of nature as far as the moon—as a distillate of ritual, and consequently of the gods: that is to say, as an organization of supernormal sign stimuli playing on a set of IRMs never met by nature and yet most properly nature's own, inasmuch as man is her son.

But for the present, it suffices to remark that one cannot assume out of hand that simply because a certain culturally developed sign stimulus appeared late in the course of history, man's response to it must represent a *learned* reaction. The reaction may be, in fact, spontaneous, though never shown before. For the creative imagination may have released precisely here one of those innate "inclinations" of the human organism that have nowhere been fully matched by nature. Hence, not only the ritual arts and the development from them of the archaic civilizations, but also—and even more richly—the later shattering of those arts by the modern arrows of man's flight beyond his own highest dream, would perhaps best be interpreted psychologically, as a history of the supernormal sign stimuli that have released—to our own fright, joy, and amazement—the deepest secrets of our being. Indeed, the depths of the mystery of our subject—which are the depths not only of man but of the living world—have not been plumbed.

In sum, then: Within the field of the study of animal behavior—which is the only area in which controlled experiments have made it possible to arrive at dependable conclusions in the observation of instinct—two orders of innate releasing mechanisms have been identified, namely, the stereotyped, and the open, subject to imprint. In the case of the first, a precise lock-key relationship exists between the inner readiness of the nervous system and the external sign stimulus triggering response; so that, if there exist in the human inheritance many—or even any—IRMs of this order, we may justly speak of "inherited images" in the psyche. The mere fact that no one can yet explain how such lock-key relationships are established does not invalidate the observation of their existence: no one knows how the hawk got into the nervous system of our barnyard fowl, yet numerous tests have shown it to be, *de facto,* there. However, the human psyche has not yet been, to any great extent, satisfactorily tested for such stereotypes, and so, I am afraid, pending further study, we must simply admit that we do not know how far the principle of the inherited image can be carried when interpreting mythological universals. It is no less premature to deny its possibility than to announce it as anything more than a considered opinion.

Nor are we ready, yet, to say whether the obvious, and sometimes very striking, physical differences of the human races represent significant variations of their innate releasing mechanisms. Among the animals such differences do exist—in fact, changes in the IRMs of the major instincts appear to be among the first things affected by mutation.

For example, as Tinbergen observes:

> The herring gull (*Larus argentatus*) and the lesser black-backed gull (*L. fuscus*) in north-western Europe are considered to be extremely diverged geographical races of one species, which, having developed by geographical isolation, have come into contact again by expansion of their ranges. The two forms show many differences in behavior; *L. fuscus* is a definite migrant, traveling to south-western Europe in autumn, whereas *L. argentatus* is of a much more resident habit. *L. fuscus* is much more a bird of the open sea than *L. argentatus*. The breeding-seasons are different. One behavior difference is specially interesting. Both forms have two alarm calls, one expressing alarm of relatively low intensity, the other indicative of extreme alarm. *L. argentatus* gives the high-intensity alarm call much more rarely than *L. fuscus*. The result is that most disturbances are reacted to differently by the two forms. When a human intruder enters a mixed colony, the herring gulls will almost always utter the low-intensity call, while *L. fuscus* utters the high-intensity call. This difference, based upon a shift of degree in the threshold of alarm calls, gives the impression of a qualitative difference in the alarm calls of the two forms, such as might well lead to the total disappearance of one call in one species, of the other in the second species, and thus result in a qualitative difference in the motor-equipment. Apart from this difference in threshold, there is a difference in the pitch of each call.[13]

Between the various human races differences have been noted that suggest psychological as well as merely physiological variation; differences, for example, in their rates of maturing, as Géza Róheim has indicated in his vigorous work on *Psychoanalysis and Anthropology*.[14] However, it is still far from legitimate, on the basis of the mere scraps of controlled observation that have been recorded, to make any such broad generalizations about intellectual ability and moral character as are common in discussions of this subject. Furthermore, within the human species there is such broad variation of innate capacity from individual to individual that generalizations on a racial basis lose much of their point.

In other words, the whole question of the innate stereotypes of the species Homo sapiens is still wide open. Objective and promising studies have been commenced, but they have not yet progressed very far. An interesting series of experiments by E. Kaila,[15] and R. A. Spitz and K. M. Wolf,[16] has shown that between the ages of three and six months the infant reacts with a smile to the appearance of a human face; and by fashioning masks omitting certain of the details of the normal human countenance, the observers were able to establish the fact that in order to evoke response the face had to have two eyes (one-eyed, asymmetrical masks did not work), a smooth forehead (wrinkled foreheads produced no smile), and a nose. Curiously, the mouth could be omitted; the smile, therefore, was not an imitation. The face had to be in some movement and seen from the front. Moreover, nothing else—not even a toy—would evoke this early infant smile. Following the sixth month, a distinction began to be made between familiar and unfamiliar, friendly and unfriendly faces. The richness of the child's experience of its social environment having already increased, the innate releasing mechanism had been altered by impressions from the outer world, and the situation had changed.

It has been remarked that in certain primitive Australian rock paintings of ancestral figures the mouths are omitted, and that a significant number of very early, paleolithic female figurines also lack the mouth. How far one can presume to carry these suggestions toward the conclusion that there is a "parental image" in the central nervous structure of the human infant, however, we cannot say. As Professor Portmann has pointed out: "Since the effect of this form on the infant can be demonstrated with certainty only from the third month, the question remains open as to whether the central nervous structure that makes possible the recognition of the human countenance and the social response of the smile is of the open, i.e. imprinted, type, or entirely innate. All of the indices available to us speak for a largely inherited configuration; and yet, the question remains open." [17]

How much more open, then, the question broached by Professor Lorenz in his paper on "The Innate Forms of Human Experience": [18] the question of the parental response evoked in the adult by the sign stimuli provided by the human baby! The figure tells the story—as far as it goes.

Sign stimuli releasing parental reactions in man (left), compared with counterparts that do not (right). After Lorenz

And finally, it must be noted that there is no consensus among students of the subject even as to what categories of appetite may be regarded as instinctive in the human species. Professor Tinbergen, speaking for the animal world, has named sleep and food-seeking; so also, in many species, flight from danger, fighting in self-defense, and a number of activities functionally related to the reproductive urge, as, for example, sexual fighting and rivalry, courtship, mating, and parental behavior (nest-building, protection of the young, etc.). The list greatly varies, however, from species to species; and how much of it can be carried over into the human sphere is not yet known. Tentatively, it might reasonably be supposed that food-seeking, sleep, self-protection, courtship and mating, and some of the activities of parenthood should be instinctive. But the question—as we have seen—remains open as to what precisely are the sign stimuli that generally trigger these activities in man, or whether any of the stimuli can be said to be as immediately known to the human interior as the hawk to the chick. We do not, therefore, speak of inherited images in the following pages.

The concept of the sign stimulus as an energy-releasing and -directing image clarifies, however, the difference between literary metaphor, which is addressed to the intellect, and mythology, which is aimed primarily at the central excitatory mechanisms (CEMs) and innate releasing mechanisms (IRMs) of the whole person. According to this view, a functioning mythology can be defined as a corpus of culturally maintained sign stimuli fostering the development and activation of a specific type, or constellation of types, of human life. Furthermore, since we now know that no images have been established unquestionably as innate and that our IRMs are not stereotyped but open, whatever "universals" we may find in our comparative study must be assigned rather to common experience than to endowment; while, on the other hand, even where sign stimuli may differ, it need not follow that the responding IRMs differ too. Our science is to be simultaneously biological and historical throughout, with no distinction between "culturally conditioned" and "instinctive" behavior, since all instinctive human behavior is culturally conditioned, and what is culturally conditioned in us all is instinct: specifically, the CEMs and IRMs of this single species.

Therefore, though respecting the possibility—perhaps the probability—of such a psychologically inspired parallel development of mythological imagery as that suggested by Adolf Bastian's theory of elementary ideas and C. G. Jung's of the collective unconscious, we cannot attempt to interpret in such terms any of the remarkable correspondences that will everywhere confront us. On the other hand, however, we must ignore as biologically untenable such sociological theorizing as that represented, for example, by the anthropologist Ralph Linton when he wrote that "a society is a group of biologically distinct and self-contained individuals," [19] since, indeed, we *are* a species and *not* biologically distinct. Our approach is to be, as far as possible, skeptical, historical, and descriptive—and where history fails and something else appears, as in a mirror, darkly, we indicate the considered guesses of the chief authorities in the field and leave the rest to silence, recognizing that in that silence there may be sleeping not only the jungle cry of Dryopithecus, but also a supernormal melody not to be heard for perhaps another million years.

Chapter 2

THE IMPRINTS OF EXPERIENCE

I. Suffering and Rapture

James Joyce, in *A Portrait of the Artist as a Young Man,* supplies an excellent structuring principle for a cross-cultural study of mythology when he defines the material of tragedy as "whatsoever is grave and constant in human sufferings"; [1] for it is from the "grave and constant" that the imprints common to the mythologies of the world must be derived. And of such imprints, suffering itself—the raw material of tragedy—is surely the most general, since it is, in a preliminary sense at least, the sum and effect of all.

Moreover, tragedy—the Greek tragedy—was a poetic inflection of mythology, the tragic catharsis of emotion through pity and terror of which Aristotle wrote being precisely the counterpart, psychologically, of the purgation of spirit (κάθαρσις) effected by a rite. Like the rite, tragedy transmutes suffering into rapture by altering the focus of the mind. The tragic art is a correlate of the discipline termed, in the language of religion, "spiritual cleansing," or "the stripping of the self." Released from attachment to one's mortal part through a contemplation of the grave and constant in human sufferings—"correcting," to use Plato's felicitous phrase, "those circuits of the head that were deranged at birth, by learning to know the harmonies of the world" [2]—one is united, simultaneously, in tragic pity with "the human sufferer" and in tragic terror with "the secret cause," Plato's "likeness of that which intelligence discerns." Whereupon, one day, with a cry of joy, leaving both humanity and intelligence behind, the soul may leap to what it then suddenly recognizes beyond the mask. *Finis tragoediae: incipit comoedia.* The mode of the tragedy dissolves and the myth begins.

"O Lord, how marvelous is Thy face," wrote Nicholas of Cusa,

> Thy face, which a young man, if he strove to imagine it, would conceive as a youth's; a full-grown man, as manly; an aged man as an aged man's! Who could imagine this sole pattern, most true and most adequate, of all faces—of all even as of each—this pattern so very perfectly of each as if it were of none other? He would have need to go beyond all forms of faces that may be formed, and all figures. And how could he imagine a face when he must go beyond all faces, and all likenesses and figures of all faces and all concepts which can be formed of a face, and all color, adornment and beauty of all faces? Wherefore he that goeth forward to behold Thy face, so long as he formeth any concept thereof, is far from Thy face. For all concept of a face falleth short, Lord, of Thy face, and all beauty which can be conceived is less than the beauty of Thy face; every face hath beauty yet none is beauty's self, but Thy face, Lord, hath beauty and this having is being. 'Tis therefore Absolute Beauty itself, which is the form that giveth being to every beautiful form. O face exceedingly comely, whose beauty all things to whom it is granted to behold it, suffice not to admire! In all faces is seen the Face of faces, veiled, and in a riddle; howbeit unveiled it is not seen, until above all faces a man enter into a certain secret and mystic silence where there is no knowledge or concept of a face. This mist, cloud, darkness, or ignorance into which he that seeketh Thy face entereth when he goeth beyond all knowledge or concept is the state below which Thy face cannot be found except veiled; but that very darkness revealeth Thy face to be there, beyond all veils.[3]

Here is the secret cause—known not in terror but in rapture. And its sole beholder is the perfectly purified spirit, gone beyond the normal bounds of human experience, thought, and speech. "There the eye goes not," we read in the Indian *Kena Upanisad,* "speech goes not, nor the mind."[4] And yet the impact has been experienced by a great many on this earth. It has been rendered (though seldom as wonderfully as in this inspired utterance of

Cusanus) in many mythologies and many paeans of the mystics, in many times and many lands. Without question, it is an available experience, and should even, perhaps, be counted paramount among the "grave and constant" in human suffering and joy. Furthermore, the images rendering it must be classified in our science as of one order, no matter how alien they may be to our local forms of religious symbolization.

The Fifth Danish Thule Expedition (1921–1924) across arctic North America, from Greenland to Cape Prince of Wales, Alaska, was conducted by the seasoned scholar and explorer Knud Rasmussen, who, in the course of this extraordinary journey, met and won the confidence of a number of Eskimo shamans: first, a generous-hearted, warmly hospitable, sturdy old man named Aua at Hudson Bay; next, in the harsh Baker Lake area, among the so-called Caribou Eskimo (who are as primitive as any people on earth), a ruthless, highly intelligent, strongly independent savage named Igjugarjuk, who, when as a youth he had wished to take to wife a girl whose family objected, went with his brother to lie in wait not far from the entrance to the young woman's hut and from there shot down her father, mother, brothers, and sisters—seven or eight in all—until only the girl that he wanted remained; and finally, at Nome, an old scalawag named Najagneq, who had just been released from a year in jail for having killed seven or eight members of his community. In his distant village, Najagneq had made a fortress of his house and from there, alone, had waged war with the whole of his tribe—and against the whites too—until he had been taken by stratagem by the captain of a ship and brought to Nome. He was held in jail there until ten witnesses of his killings could be fetched from his settlement; but when these were confronted with him they dropped their charges, much as they would have liked to see him done away with. His small piercing eyes roamed about wildly, and his jaw hung in a bandage that was much too slack, a man who had tried to kill him having injured his face. And when the ten men who would have accused him met his look in the witness box, they lowered their eyes in shame.

It is worth considering for a moment the character of these

rugged shamans, lest we suppose that the highest religious realizations are vouchsafed only to the saintly.

Dr. H. Ostermann, in his report of the Fifth Thule Expedition, wrote:

> Najagneq's powers of imagination had been stimulated in the big town of Nome. Although knowing of nothing except earth huts, sledges and kayaks, he was not at all impressed by the large houses, the steamers and the motor-cars. But he had been fascinated by the sight of a white horse hauling a big lorry. So he now told his astonished fellow villagers that the white men in Nome had killed him ten times that winter, but that he had had ten white horses as helping spirits, and he had sacrificed them one by one and thus saved his life.
>
> This man of "ten-horse-power" had authority in his speech, and he completely swayed those to whom he spoke. He had conceived a curious feeling of mild goodness for Dr. Rasmussen, and when they were alone together he was not afraid to admit that he had pulled the legs of his countrymen somewhat. He was no humbug, but a solitary man accustomed to hold his own against many and therefore had to have his little tricks. But whenever his old visions and his ancestral beliefs were mentioned, his replies, which were brief and to the point, bore the impress of imperturbable gravity. When Dr. Rasmussen asked him if he believed in any of all the powers he spoke of, he answered: "Yes, a power that we call Sila, one that cannot be explained in so many words. A strong spirit, the upholder of the universe, of the weather, in fact all life on earth—so mighty that his speech to man comes not through ordinary words, but through storms, snowfall, rain showers, the tempests of the sea, through all the forces that man fears, or through sunshine, calm seas or small, innocent, playing children who understand nothing. When times are good, Sila has nothing to say to mankind. He has disappeared into his infinite nothingness and remains away as long as people do not abuse life but have respect for their daily food. No one has ever seen Sila. His place of sojourn is so mysterious that he is with us and infinitely far away at the same time."
>
> And Dr. Rasmussen adds [Dr. Ostermann is quoting from the notes found in Rasmussen's posthuma]: "Najagneq's words sound like an echo of the wisdom we admired in the old shamans we encountered everywhere on our travels—in harsh King William Land or in Aua's festive snow hut at Hudson

Bay, or in the primitive Eskimo Igjugarjuk, whose pithy maxim was:

" 'The only true wisdom lives far from mankind, out in the great loneliness, and it can be reached only through suffering. Privation and suffering alone can open the mind of a man to all that is hidden to others.' "[5]

We shall return in a later chapter to Igjugarjuk and his story of the sufferings through which he learned true wisdom. The present point is that from the great Cusanus to the great Igjugarjuk we have a considerable span of human character and experience, as well as of cultural inheritance; yet, unless I am deceived, the ultimate reference of their mutually independent statements is the same. Nor is this the last that we shall learn of the hidden wisdom achieved through suffering, "in the great loneliness," which is "beyond all forms of faces that may be formed, and all figures," or as Najagneq put it, "cannot be explained in so many words."

The "grave and constant" in human suffering, then, leads—or *may* lead—to an experience that is regarded by those who have known it as the apogee of their lives, and which is yet ineffable. And this experience, or at least an approach to it, is the ultimate aim of all religion, the ultimate reference of all myth and rite. Moreover, those by whom the mythological traditions of the world have been developed and maintained have been the shamans, sages, prophets, and priests, many of whom have had an actual experience of this ineffable mystery and all of whom have revered it. One of the ironies of our subject is that much of the research and collecting among primitive tribes has been conducted either by scientists whose minds are sterilized to this experience and for whom the word "mystic" is a term of abuse, or else by missionaries for whom the only valid approach to it is in their own tradition of spiritual metaphor. Yet occasionally a scholar of Rasmussen's stature appears and the truth is out.

The first point to be noticed is that a primitive wizard is perfectly capable not only of uttering as profound a statement concerning the relationship of man to the mystery of his being as any that will be found in the annals of the higher religions, but also of wantonly producing parodies of his own mythology to intimidate and impress his simpler fellows. The fact that valid mythological motifs (for example, death and resurrection) have been used in this way for deception does not mean that in proper context they are still, necessarily, the "opiate of the people." Yet they certainly may become just that; for since the ultimate reference of religion is ineffable, many of those who live most sincerely by its mythology are the most deceived—this deception itself being part of the suffering and darkness through which the mind must pass before the Face-that-is-no-face becomes known.

There is a word in Sanskrit, *upādhi,* which means "deceit, deception, disguise," but also, "limitation, idiosyncrasy, or attribute." The ultimate truth, being without attributes, cannot be contemplated by the mind. As Igjugarjuk says, it "lives far from mankind, out in the great loneliness." Therefore, in rites and meditations designed to ready the mind for an experience of the beauty that is Absolute Beauty, "attributes" (*upādhis*) are assigned to it; for example, in the meditation of Cusanus, the property of being a face—and of being beautiful.

Gerhart Hauptmann has somewhere said that poetry is the art of causing the Word to resound behind words (*Dichten heisst, hinter Worten das Urwort erklingen lassen*).[6] In the same sense, mythology is a rendition of forms through which the formless Form of forms can be known. An inferior object is presented as the representation, or habitation, of a superior. The love or attachment felt for the inferior is a function actually of one's potential establishment in the superior; yet it must be sacrificed (therein the suffering!) if the mind is to pass on to its proper end.

The science of comparative mythology is, then, a comparative study of *upādhis:* the deceptive attributes of being, through which the human mind, in the various eras and areas of its domain, has been united with the secret cause in tragic terror, and with the human sufferer (the self being stripped away) in tragic pity. And these *upādhis* are of two orders: those inevitably deriving from the primary conditions of all human experience whatsoever (*la condition humaine*), and those particular to the various areas and eras of human civilization (*die Völkergedanken*). Of the first we treat in the present chapter; of the others, in the remaining sections of the work.

But all, certainly, will not be of suffering, the tragic *upādhi* (or deception) of suffering; for the paramount theme of mythology is not the agony of quest but the rapture of a revelation, not death but the resurrection: Hallelujah!

"I am she," declared the great goddess of the universe, Queen Isis, when she appeared to Lucius Apuleius, her devotee, at the conclusion of the ordeal described allegorically in his novel, *The Golden Ass:*

> I am she that is the natural mother of all things, mistress and governess of all the elements, the initial progeny of worlds, chief of the powers divine, queen of all that are in hell, the principal of them that dwell in heaven, manifested alone and under one form of all the gods and goddesses. At my will the planets of the sky, the wholesome winds of the seas, and the lamentable silences of hell are disposed; my name, my divinity is adored throughout the world, in divers manners, in variable customs, and by many names.
>
> For the Phrygians that are the first of all men call me the Mother of the gods of Pessinus; the Athenians, which are sprung from their own soil, Cecropian Minerva; the Cyprians, which are girt about by the sea, Paphian Venus; the Cretans, which bear arrows, Dictynian Diana; the Sicilians, which speak three tongues, infernal Proserpine; the Eleusians their ancient goddess Ceres; some Juno, others Bellona, others Hecate, others Ramnusie, and principally both sort of the Ethiopians, which dwell in the Orient and are enlightened by the morning rays of the sun; and the Egyptians, which are excellent in all kind of ancient doctrine, and by their proper ceremonies accustomed to worship me, do call me by my true name, Queen Isis.
>
> Behold I am come to take pity of thy fortune and tribulation; behold I am present to favor and aid thee; leave off thy weeping and lamentation, put away all thy sorrow, for behold the healthful day which is ordained by my providence.[7]

Suffering itself is a deception (*upādhi*); for its core is rapture, which is the attribute (*upādhi*) of illumination.

The imprint of the rapture enclosed in suffering, then, is the foremost "grave and constant" of our science. Compassed in the life wisdom of perhaps but a minority of the human race, it has nevertheless been the matrix and final term of all the mythologies of the world, yielding its radiance to the whole festival of those lesser *upādhis*—or imprints—to which we now must turn.

II. The Structuring Force of Life on Earth

Certainly one force that can never have been absent from human experience, as Adolf Portmann has pointed out in a suggestive paper on "The Earth as the Home of Life," [8] is gravity, which not only works continuously on every aspect of human affairs, but has fundamentally conditioned the form of the body and all its organs. The diurnal alternation of light and dark is another ineluctable factor of experience, to which, indeed, considerable dramatic value accrues as a result of the fact that at night the world sleeps, dangers lurk, and the mind plunges into a realm of dream experience, which differs in its logic from the world of light. In dream, objects shine of themselves, without illumination from without, and, moreover, are of a subtle substance that is capable of magical and rapid transformation, appalling effects, and nonmechanical locomotion. There can be no doubt but that the world of myth has been saturated by dream, or that men were dreaming even when they were little more than apes. And, as Géza Róheim has observed, "there cannot be several 'culturally determined' ways of dreaming, just as there are no two ways of sleeping." [9]

Dawn, and awakening from this world of dream, must always have been associated with the sun and sunrise. The night fears and night charms are dispelled by light, which has always been experienced as coming from above and as furnishing guidance and orientation. Darkness, then, and weight, the pull of gravity and the dark interior of the earth, of the jungle, or of the deep sea, as well as certain extremely poignant fears and delights, must for millenniums have constituted a firm syndrome of human experience, in contrast to the luminous flight of the world-awakening solar sphere into and through immeasurable heights. Hence a polarity of light and dark, above and below, guidance and loss of bearings, confidence and fears (a polarity that we all know from our own tradition of thought and feeling and can find matched in many parts of the world) must be reckoned as inevitable in the way of a structuring principle of human thought. It may or may not be fixed within us as an "isomorph"; * but, in any case, it is certainly a general and very deeply known experience.

The moon, furthermore, and the spectacle of the night sky, the stars and the Milky Way, have constituted, certainly from the beginning, a source of wonder and profound impression. But there is actually a physical influence of the moon upon the earth and its creatures, its tides and our own interior tides, which has long been consciously recognized as well as subliminally experienced. The coincidence of the menstrual cycle with that of the moon is a physical actuality structuring human life and a curiosity that has been observed with wonder. It is in fact likely that the fundamental notion of a life-structuring relationship between the heavenly world and that of man was derived from the realization, both in experience and in thought, of the force of the lunar cycle. The mystery, also, of the death and resurrection of the moon, as well as of its influence on dogs, wolves and foxes, jackals and coyotes, which try to sing to it: this immortal silver dish of wonder, cruising among the beautiful stars and racing through the clouds, turning waking life itself into a sort of dream, has been a force and presence even more powerful in the shaping of mythology than the sun, by which its light and its world of stars, night sounds, erotic moods, and the magic of dream, are daily quenched.

The contrast in physical form and spheres of competence of the male and female surely is another universal of human experience; and we must reckon also, in this context, with the "instinct crossing" between the two, which makes possible—or rather, inevitable, and sometimes even against better judgment—the awakening of the two bodies in synchronization to that curious mutual engagement which the Freudians like to call a "re-enactment of the primal scene," and which many have found to be the one consummation of appetite most difficult to resist. In a number of meticulous studies of animal behavior it has been shown that a trimly meshed sequence of sign stimuli, flashed from the male organism to the

* Cf. supra, p. 35.

female and from the female to the male, can be identified as releasers of the sometimes exceedingly complicated performances that must be undertaken in perfect synchronization before the species can be reproduced; and I do not know anyone outside of the most carefully schooled scientific circles who would suppose for a moment that a comparable criss-cross of isomorphs might not safely be assumed to exist on the human level as well. But since nothing is to be assumed recklessly on the basis of merely personal experience, and no one has yet been able to raise two young human beings in absolute isolation from social conditioning and introduce them to each other when the moon is full, we shall not presume to say how much of what everyone knows about this matter is due to imprint, or how much to inherited image. Let us remark only that the perfumes of flowers, the beautification of the body, night, secret meetings, music, token exchanges, anguish, remorse, rivalry, jealousy, murder, and the whole opera, can be identified in human history as far as our eyes can see.

And we have the voluminous literature of the Freudian school to assure us that the covert as well as obvious analogies, puns, and inflections by which sex, the sex organs, and the sexual act are implicated in our thoughts are known to every tradition in the world, whether oral or literate. In mythology, of course, the image of birth from the womb is an extremely common figure for the origin of the universe, and the sexual intercourse that must have preceded it is represented in ritual action as well as in story. Furthermore, the mysterious (one might even say, magical) functioning of the female body in its menstrual cycle, in the ceasing of the cycle during the period of gestation, and in the agony of birth—and the appearance, then, of the new being; these, certainly, have made profound imprints on the mind. The fear of menstrual blood and isolation of women during their periods, the rites of birth, and all the lore of magic associated with human fecundity make it evident that we are here in the field of one of the major centers of interest of the human imagination. In the earliest ritual art the naked female form is extremely prominent, whereas the male is usually ornamented, or masked, as shaman or hunter in the performance of some act. The fear of woman and the mystery of her motherhood have been for the male no less impressive imprinting forces than the fears and mysteries of the world of nature itself. And there may be found in the mythologies and ritual traditions of our entire species innumerable instances of the unrelenting efforts of the male to relate himself effectively—in the way, so to say, of antagonistic cooperation—to these two alien yet intimately constraining forces: woman and the world.

Still another profoundly important structuring system of experiences that can be said, without question, to constitute a pattern of imprints on our own readiness for life is that of the normal stages of human growth and emotional susceptibility, from the moment of birth to that of death and the stench of decay. A great deal of excellent writing on this subject has been produced recently by the various authorities on child psychology and psychoanalysis, so that to review the whole matter in detail would be only to repeat what is already very well known. However, I am not aware of any work that has yet drawn attention in systematic series to the mythological motifs developed from the imprints of this sociologized biology of human growth.

As we have noted, it requires twenty years for the human organism to mature, and during the greater part of this development it is dependent, utterly, upon parental care. There follows a period of another twenty years or so of maturity, after which the signs of age begin to appear. But the human being is the only animal capable of knowing death as the end inevitable for itself, and the span of old age for this human organism, consciously facing death, is a period of years longer than the whole lifetime of any other primate. So we see three—at least three—distinct periods of growth and susceptibility to imprint as inevitable in a human biography: (1) childhood and youth, with its uncouth charm; (2) maturity, with its competence and authority; and (3) wise old age, nursing its own death and gazing back, either with love or with rancor, at the fading world.

It has been the chief function of much of the mythological lore and ritual practice of our species to carry the mind, feelings, and powers of action of the individual across the critical thresholds from the two decades of infancy to adulthood, and from old age to death; to supply the sign stimuli adequate to release the life energies of the one who is no longer what he was for his new task, the new phase, in a manner appropriate to the well-being of the group. And so we find, on the one hand, as a constant factor in these "rites of passage," the inevitable, and therefore universal, requirements of the human individual at the particular junctures, and on the other hand, as a cultural variable, the historically conditioned requirements and beliefs of the local group. This gives that interesting quality of seeming to be ever the same, though ever changing, to the kaleidoscope of world mythology, which may charm our poets and artists but is a nightmare for the mind that seeks to classify. And yet, with a steady eye, even the phantasmagoria of a nightmare can be catalogued—to a degree.

The remaining sections of the present chapter develop, therefore, in the way of a tentative, preliminary sketch, the main lines and phases of what would appear to have been—up to the present moment, at least—the chief sources of imprint in the course of the archetypal biography of man.

III. The Imprints of Early Infancy

Certain imprints impressed upon the nervous system in the plastic period between birth and maturity are the source of many of the most widely known images of myth. Necessarily the same for all mankind, they have been variously organized in the differing traditions, but everywhere function as potent energy releasers and directors.

The first indelible imprints are those of the moment of birth itself. The congestion of blood and sense of suffocation experienced by the infant before its lungs commence to operate give rise to a brief seizure of terror, the physical effects of which (caught breath, circulatory congestion, dizziness, or even blackout) tend to recur, more or less strongly, whenever there is an abrupt moment of fright. So that the birth trauma, as an archetype of transformation, floods with considerable emotional effect the brief moment of loss of security and threat of death that accompanies any crisis of radical change. In the imagery of mythology and religion this birth (or more often rebirth) theme is extremely prominent; in fact, every threshold passage—not only this from the darkness of the womb to the light of the sun, but also those from childhood to adult life and from the light of the world to whatever mystery of darkness may lie beyond the portal of death—is comparable to a birth and has been ritually represented, practically everywhere, through an imagery of re-entry into the womb. This is one of those mythological universals that surely merit interpretation, rather from a psychological than from an ethnological point of view.

The water image in mythology is intimately associated with this motif, and the goddesses, mermaids, witches, and sirens that often appear as guardians or manifestations of water (wells, water courses, youth-renewing caldrons), Ladies of the Lake and other water nixies, may represent either its life-threatening or its life-furthering aspect.

The Late Classical story of Actaeon, for example, as rendered in Ovid's *Metamorphoses,*[10] tells of a hunter, a vigorous youth in the prime of his young manhood, who, when stalking deer with his dogs, chanced upon a stream that he followed to its source, where he broke upon the goddess Diana bathing, surrounded by a galaxy of naked nymphs. And the youth, not spiritually prepared for such a supernormal image, had only the normal look in his eye; whereupon the goddess, perceiving this, sent forth her power and transformed him into a stag, which his own dogs then immediately scented, pursued, and tore to bits.

On the simple level of a typical Freudian reading, this mythical episode represents the prurient anxiety of a small boy discovering Mother; but according to a more sophisticated, "sublimated" vein of reference, more appropriate to the post-Alexandrian atmosphere of Ovid's elegant art, Diana was a manifestation of that goddess-mother of the world whom we have already met as Queen Isis, and who, as she herself has told us, was known to the cultures of the Mediterranean under many names. The case, surely, is that of an *upādhi:* an inferior object (mother image) serving as symbol of a superior (the mystery of life). Meditating, we may emphasize the superior, in which case we are performing what in India is termed *sampad upāsanā,* "accomplished, or perfected, meditation"; or we may emphasize the inferior, which is termed *adhyāsa upāsanā,* "superimposed, or false, meditation." The first elevates to the supernormal; the second leaves one about as Actaeon: to be psychoanalyzed, finally, to bits and returned to the womb.

At her greatest temple city in Asia Minor, at Ephesus (where, in A.D. 431, the Virgin Mary would be declared to have been truly "the Godbearer"), the great goddess, the mother of all things, was represented as Artemis (Diana) with a multitude of breasts. Innumerable figurines, furthermore, of naked goddesses (or rather, in the spirit of her own perfected teaching, we should say, of the Naked Goddess) have been found throughout the excavated ruins of the ancient world. As Heinrich Zimmer observed in his commentary on a Hindu version of her story:

> If one inquires to know her ultimate origin, the oldest textual remains and images can carry us back only so far, and permit us to say: "Thus she appeared in those early times; so-and-so she may have been named; and in such-and-such a manner she seems to have been revered." But with that we have come to the end of what can be said; with that we have come to the primitive problem of her comprehension and being. She is the *primum mobile,* the first beginning, the material matrix out of which all comes forth. To question beyond her into her antecedents and origin, is not to understand her, is indeed to misunderstand and underestimate, in fact to insult her. And anyone attempting such a thing well might suffer the calamity that befell that smart young adept who undertook to unveil the veiled image of the Goddess in the ancient Egyptian temple of Sais, and whose tongue was paralysed forever by the shock of what he saw. According to the Greek tradition the Goddess has declared of herself: οὐδεὶς ἐμὸν πέπλον ἀνεῖλε, "no one has lifted my veil." It is a question not exactly of the veil, but of the garment that covers her female nakedness—the veil is a later misinterpretation for the sake of decency. The meaning is: I am the Mother without a spouse, the Original Mother; all are my children, and therefore none has ever dared to approach me; the impudent one who should attempt it shames the Mother—and that is the reason for the curse.[11]

In the tale of Actaeon we have this same religious theme rendered in a comparable image. "And though Diana would fain have had her arrow ready," Ovid tells us, "what she had she took up, the water, and flung it into the young man's face. And as she poured the avenging drops upon his hair, she spoke these words, foreboding his coming doom: 'Now you are free to tell that you have seen me unrobed—if you can tell.' "[12]

The water is the vehicle of the power of the goddess; but equally, it is she who personifies the mystery of the waters of birth and dissolution—whether of the individual or of the universe. For in the vein of myth the elemental mode of representation may alternate with that of personification. At the opening of the Book of Genesis is it not written, for example, that "the Spirit [or wind] of God was moving over the face of the waters"? Water and wind, matter and spirit, life and its generator: these pairs of opposites are fused in the experience of life; and their world-creating juncture may be represented elementally, as in this opening of the Bible, or on the other hand, as in the art of the Tantric Buddhism, in the image of a divine male and female in sexual embrace. The mystery of the origin of the "great universe" or macrocosm is read in terms of the procreation of the "little universe," the microcosm; and the amniotic fluid is then precisely comparable to the water that in many mythologies, as well as in the pre-Socratic philosophy of the Greek sage Thales of Miletus (c. 640–546 B.C.), represents the elementary substance of all things.

This manner of homologizing the personal and the universal, which is a basic method of mythological discourse, has made it possible for Freudian psychoanalysts, whose training in the language of symbols has been derived from a study primarily of neurotics, to translate the whole cultural inheritance of mankind back into nursery rhymes. But the problem of the neurotic is, precisely, that instead of accomplishing the passage of the difficult threshold of puberty, dying as infant to be reborn as adult, he has remained with a significant fraction of his personality structure fixed in the condition of dependency. Rejecting emotionally the reorganization of his childhood imprints through the myths and rites of a maturely functioning community, he can read the picture language of his civilization only in terms of the infantile sources of its developed and manipulated figures; whereas in the mythology and rites these have been applied to a cultural and simultaneously metaphysical context of allusions. Freud theoretically devaluated such culturally and philosophically inspired repatternings, terming them mere "secondary elaborations"—which is perhaps appropriate when the case in question is the nightmare of some forty-year-old sub-adolescent, weeping on a couch. But in the reading of myth such a reductive method commits us to the monotony of identifying in every symbolic system only the infantile sources of its elements, neglecting as merely secondary the historical problem of their reorganization: pretty much as though an architect, viewing the structures of Rome, Istanbul, Mohenjo-Daro, and New York, were to content himself with the observation that all are of brick. In the present chapter we are examining bricks. Hereafter we may take bricks for granted and concern ourselves with their employment. For, as a Jungian friend of mine once epitomized the problem: "It is the predicament of the neurotic that he translates everything into the terms of infantile sexuality; but if the doctor does so too, then where do we get?"

The state of the child in the womb is one of bliss, actionless bliss, and this state may be compared to the beatitude visualized for paradise. In the womb, the child is unaware of the alternation of night and day, or of any of the images of temporality. It should not be surprising, therefore, if the metaphors used to represent eternity suggest, to those trained in the symbolism of the infantile unconscious, retreat to the womb.

The fear of the dark, which is so strong in children, has been said to be a function of their fear of returning to the womb: the fear that their recently achieved daylight consciousness and not yet secure individuality should be reabsorbed. In archaic art, the labyrinth—home of the child-consuming Minotaur—was represented in the figure of a spiral. The spiral also appears spontaneously in certain stages of meditation, as well as to people going to sleep under ether. It is a prominent device, furthermore, at the silent entrances and within the dark passages of the ancient Irish kingly burial mound of New Grange. These facts suggest that a constellation of images denoting the plunge and dissolution of consciousness in the darkness of non-being must have been employed intentionally, from an early date, to represent the analogy of threshold rites to the mystery of the entry of the child into the womb for birth. And this suggestion is reinforced by the further fact that the paleolithic caves of southern France and northern Spain, which are now dated by most authorities circa 30,000–10,000 B.C., were certainly sanctuaries not only of hunting magic but also of the male puberty rites. A terrific sense of claustrophobia, and simultaneously of release from every context of the world above, assails the mind impounded in those more than absolutely dark abysses, where darkness no longer is an absence of light but an experienced force. And when a light is flashed to reveal the beautifully painted bulls and mammoths, flocks of reindeer, trotting ponies, woolly rhinos, and dancing shamans of those caves, the images smite the mind as indelible imprints. It is obvious that the idea of death-and-rebirth, rebirth through ritual and with a fresh organization of profoundly impressed sign stimuli, is an extremely ancient one in the history of culture, and that everything was done, even in the period of the paleolithic caves, to inspire in the youngsters being symbolically killed a reactivation of their childhood fear of the dark. The psychological value of such a "shock treatment" for the shattering of a no longer wanted personality structure appears to have been methodically utilized in a time-tested pedagogical crisis of brainwashing and simultaneous reconditioning of the IRMs, for the conversion of babes into men, dependable hunters, and courageous defenders of the tribe.

The concept of the earth as both bearing and nourishing mother has been extremely prominent in the mythologies both of hunting societies and of planters. According to the imagery of the hunters, it is from her womb that the game animals derive, and one discovers their timeless archetypes in the underworld, or dancing ground, of the rites of initiation—those archetypes of which the flocks on earth are but temporal manifestations sent for the nourishment of man. Comparably, according to the planters, it is in the mother's body that the grain is sown: the plowing of the earth is a begetting and the growth of the grain a birth. Furthermore, the idea of the earth as mother and of burial as a re-entry into the womb for rebirth appears to have recommended itself to at least some of the communities of mankind at an extremely early date. The earliest unmistakable evidences of ritual and therewith of mythological thought yet found have been the grave burials of Homo neanderthalensis, a remote predecessor of our own species, whose period is perhaps to be dated as early as 200,000–75,000 B.C.[13] Neanderthal skeletons have been found interred with supplies (suggesting the idea of another life), accompanied by animal sacrifice (wild ox, bison, and wild goat), with attention to an east-west axis (the path of the sun, which is reborn from the same earth in which the dead are placed), in flexed position (as though within the womb), or in a sleeping posture—in one case with a pillow of chips of flint.[14] Sleep and death, awakening and resurrection, the grave as a return to the mother for rebirth; but whether Homo neanderthalensis thought the next awakening would be here again or in some world to come (or even both together) we do not know.

So much, then, for the imagery of birth.

The next constellation of imprints to be noted is that associated with the bliss of the child at the mother's breast; and here again we have a context of enduring force. The relationship of suckling to mother is one of symbiosis: though two, they constitute a unit. In fact, as far as the infant is concerned—who is still far from having conceived even the first notion of a dissociation between subject and object, inside and outside—the affective aspect of its own experience and those external stimuli to which its feeling, needs, and satisfactions correspond are exactly one. Its world, as Jean Piaget has clearly shown in his study of *The Child's Conception of the World,* is a "*continuum* of consciousness,"[15] at once physical and psychic. Whatever impinges upon its unpracticed senses is uncritically identified with the attendant tonalities of its own interior, so that between the external and internal poles of its world there is no distinction. And this undefined, undefining experience of continuity is only emphasized by the readiness of the mother to respond to, or even to anticipate, its requirements.[16] The whole tiny universe of this self-centered mite is "a network of purposive movements, more or less mutually dependent,"[17] and all tending toward the good of—itself.

But the mother cannot anticipate everything. There are moments, consequently, when the universe does not correspond exactly to experienced need. Whereupon the imprints of that first terrifying shock of separation, the birth trauma, which afflicted the whole organism in its initial experience of the assault of life, are more or less forcefully reactivated. The mother is absent; the universe, absent; the bliss of the blessed infant imbibing forever the ambrosia of the madonna's body is gone forever. Melanie Klein, who has devoted particular attention to this very early chapter of our universal biography, has suggested that at such moments an impulse to tear "good body content" from the mother is immediately and simultaneously identified by the child with the danger of its own bodily destruction.[18] Hence, when the mother image begins to assume definition in the gradual dawn of the infantile consciousness, it is already associated not only with a sense of beatitude, but also with fantasies of danger, separation, and terrible destruction.

We all know the fairy tale of the witch who lives in a candy house that would be nice to eat. Indeed, we have seen already what a scare she gave to a child who conjured her up in play. She is kind to children and invites them into her tasty house only because she wants to eat them. She is a cannibal. (And for some six hundred thousand years of human experience cannibals, it should be born in mind—and even cannibal mothers—were grim and gruesome, ever-present realities.) Cannibal ogresses appear in the folklore of peoples, high and low, throughout the world; and on the mythological level the archetype is even magnified into a universal symbol in such cannibal-mother goddesses as the Hindu Kālī, the "Black One," who is a personification of "all-consuming Time"; or in the medieval European figure of the consumer of the wicked dead, the female mouth and belly of Hel.

In a myth of the Melanesian island of Malekula in the New Hebrides, which describes the dangers of the way to the Land of the Dead, it is told that when the soul has been carried on a wind across the waters of death and is approaching the entrance of the underworld, it perceives a female guardian sitting before the entrance, drawing a labyrinth design across the path, of which she erases half as the soul approaches. The voyager must restore the design perfectly if he is to pass through it to the Land of the Dead. Those who fail, the threshold guardian eats. One may understand how very important it must have been, then, to learn the secret of the labyrinth before death; and why the teaching of this secret of immortality is the chief concern of the religious ceremonials of Malekula.

According to a number of authorities cited by W. F. Jackson Knight in a highly interesting and suggestive article on "Maze Symbolism and the Trojan Game," the labyrinth, maze, and spiral were associated in ancient Crete and Babylon with the internal organs of the human anatomy as well as with the underworld, the one being the microcosm of the other. "The object of the tomb-builder would have been to make the tomb as much like the body of the mother as he was able," he writes, since to enter the next world, "the spirit would have to be re-born," [19] "The maze form—which is an elaborated spiral—gives a long and indirect path from the outside of an area to the inside, at a point called the nucleus, generally near the center. Its principle seems to be the provision of a difficult but possible access to some important point. Two ideas are involved: the idea of defence and exclusion, and the idea of the penetration, on correct terms, of this defence." [20] "The maze symbolism," he states further, "seems somehow to be associated with maidenhood. . . . The overcoming of difficulties by a hero frequently precedes union with some hidden princess." [21]

In the celebrated story of Theseus, the labyrinth, and the princess Ariadne, the Cretan labyrinth was difficult to enter and as difficult to leave, but Ariadne's thread supplied the clue. And when the legendary founder of Rome, the hero Aeneas, arrived, in the course of his journey from Troy, at the cavern-entrance of the underworld, he found engraved there, upon the rocky face, a figure of the Cretan labyrinth. And when he and his company had made sacrifice of abundant beeves and lambs to the ultimate deities of that abyss, "Lo! about the first rays of sunrise the ground moaned underfoot, and the woodland ridges began to stir, and dogs seemed to howl through the dusk as the terrible guardian, the Sibyl, arrived. 'Away! Depart, you unsanctified!' she cried. 'Retire from the grove! But thou, Aeneas, come, unsheath thy steel; now is need of courage, now of strong resolve!' Whereupon she plunged in ecstasy into the cavern opening, and he, unflinching, kept pace with his advancing guide." [22]

We have already noted that in the early Irish kingly burial mound of New Grange (which is to be dated somewhere in the second millennium B.C.) labyrinthine spirals are prominent, not only within the narrow passages to the "nucleus" but also, and most conspicuously, on the great threshold-stones at the entrances, where they guard the four gates, one facing in each of the four directions. In ancient Egypt the structure known as the Labyrinth (mentioned by Herodotus and Strabo, and excavated by Flinders Petrie in 1888) was a vast complex of buildings beside an artificial lake, with the tombs of kings and sacred crocodiles in the basement. The relationship (if any) of such megalithic structures and the rituals of their use in Egypt, Crete, and Ireland to the mortuary customs of remote Melanesia, which are also associated both with megaliths and with the symbolism of the spiral and the labyrinth, as well as with animal sacrifice (the sacrificial animal there, however, being the pig), we shall consider when we come to the problem of the origins and diffusion of the mythological motifs of the neolithic and equatorial culture spheres. For the present, it will suffice to remark that in Malekula, when the voyager to the Land of the Dead has proved himself qualified to enter the cave by completing the labyrinth-design of the dangerous guardian, he discovers therein a great water, the Water of Life, on the shore of which grows a tree, which he climbs, and from which he dives into the waters of the subterranean sea.[23]

The Hindu mother-goddess Kālī is represented with her long tongue lolling to lick up the lives and blood of her children. She is the very pattern of the sow that eats her farrow, the cannibal ogress: life itself, the universe, which sends forth beings only to consume them. And yet she is simultaneously the goddess Annapurna (*anna* meaning "food," and *pūrṇā,* "abundance"), India's counterpart of Egyptian Isis with the sun-child Horus at her breast, or of Babylonian Ishtar, nursing the moon-god reborn, the archaic prefigurements in Mediterranean mythology and art of the Madonna of the Middle Ages.

And so, in mythology and rite, as well as in the psychology of the infant, we find the imagery of the mother associated almost equally with beatitude and danger, birth and death, the inexhaustible nourishing breast and the tearing claws of the ogress. The heavenly realm, where the paradisial meal is served forever, and Olympus, the mountain of the gods, where ambrosia flows—these, certainly, are but versions fit for adult saints and heroes of the bliss of the well-nursed child. And the primary imprint of which the fury and fright of the disemboweling maw of hell is the adult amplification is no less certainly the child's own fantasies of its raging body—its whole universe—torn apart.

A third system of imprints that can be assumed to be universal in the development of the mentality of the infant is that deriving from its fascination with its own excrement, which becomes emphatic at the age of about two and a half. In many societies the infant experiences the first impact of severe discipline in the matter of when, where, and how it may permit itself to respond to nature; the worst of it being that for the child, at this period of its life, defecation is experienced as a creative act and its own excrement as a thing of value, suitable for presentation as a gift. In societies in which this pattern of interest and action is regarded as unattractive, a socially determined reorganization of response is imposed sharply and absolutely, the spontaneous interest and evaluations of the earlier period of the child's thought being then strictly repressed. But they cannot be erased. They remain as subordinated, written-over imprints: forbidden images, apt on occasion, or under one disguise or another, to reassert their force.

Throughout the higher mythologies there is abundant evidence of dualistic systems of imagery deriving from this circumstance. They are to be recognized in the prevalence of an association of filth with sin and cleanliness with virtue. Hell is a foul pit and heaven a place of absolute purity, whether in the Buddhist, Zoroastrian, Hindu, Moslem, or Christian organization of the afterworld. Furthermore, there has been a suggestion from Dr. Freud to the effect that the infantile urge to manipulate filth and assign it value survives in our adult interest in the arts—painting, smearing of all kinds, sculpture, and architecture—as well as in the urge to collect precious stones, gold, or money, and in the pleasures derived from the giving and receiving of gifts. The aim of the sixteenth- and seventeenth-century alchemists to sublimate "base matter" (filth and corruption) into gold (which is pure and therefore incorruptible) would represent perfectly, according to this view, an urge to carry the energies locked in the first system of interests into the sphere of the superimposed second, so that, instead of suppression and therewith division, there should be effected a sublimation, or vital fusion, of the two socially opposed systems of the psyche, or, to use the phrase of the poet Blake, a Marriage of Heaven and Hell. And the fact that it was precisely at the time of the collapse (for many) of the authority of the medieval dualism of God and devil that the greatest flowering not only of alchemy but also of the Occidental arts took place may tend to confirm this psychoanalytical reading of the urge that brought them forth. The value of gold, of the marble and clay of the sculptor, and of the materials of the painter may be supposed, furthermore, to have been the greater inasmuch as all were derived from the bowels of the earth—which, according to the system of the saints, had long received an emphatically negative interpretation as the seat of hell.

And it may be noted further, in this connection, that in practically every primitive society ever studied the smearing of paint and clay on the body is thought to give magical protection as well as beauty; that in India, where cowdung is revered as sacred and the ritual distinction between the left hand (used at the toilet) and the right (putting food into the mouth) is an issue of capital moment, a ritual smearing of the forehead and body with colored clays and ash is a prominently developed religious exercise; and, finally, that among many advanced as well as primitive peoples the sacred clowns—who in religious ceremonies are permitted to break taboos and always enact obscene pantomimes—are initiated into their orders by way of a ritual eating of filth.

Among the Jicarilla Apache of New Mexico the members of the clown society are actually called "Striped Excrement."[24] They are smeared with a white clay and have four black horizontal stripes crossing their legs, body, and face.[25] In our own circuses the clown is garishly painted, breaks whatever taboos the police permit, and is a great favorite of the youngsters, who perhaps see reflected in his peculiar charm the paradise of innocence that was theirs before they were taught the knowledge of good and evil, purity and filth.

A fourth constellation of imprints engraved on the maturing psyche of the infant appears (at least in those provinces of our own civilization that have been studied for these effects) at about the age of four, when the physical difference between the sexes becomes a matter of keen concern. The *petite différence* leads the girl to believe (we are told) that she has been castrated, and the boy that he is liable to be. Thereafter, in the masculine imagination all fear of punishment is freighted with an obscurely sensed castration fear, while the female is obsessed with an envy that cannot be quite quenched until she has brought forth from her own body a son. Hence the value, from the female point of view, of the madonna image and the whole system of religious references imputing cosmic significance to her womb and breasts. But in the male the sense of her dangerous envy is ever present. Hence the negative estimate of the woman as a potential spiritual, if not physical, castrator, which in the mind of the child tends to become associated with the image of the ogress and cannibal witch, and in religious traditions where a monastic spirit prevails is an extremely prominent trait.

In this connection it should be noted that there is a motif occurring in certain primitive mythologies, as well as in modern surrealist painting and neurotic dream, which is known to folklore as "the toothed vagina"—the vagina that castrates. And a counterpart, the other way, is the so-called "phallic mother," a motif perfectly illustrated in the long fingers and nose of the witch. According to Freud,[26] the capacity of the sight of a spider to precipitate a crisis of neurotic anxiety—whether in the nursery rhyme of Miss Muffett or in the labyrinths of modern life—derives from an unconscious association of the spider with the image of the phallic mother; to which, perhaps, should be added the observation that the web, the spiral web, may also contribute to the arachnid's force as a fear-releasing sign.

There is a myth of the Andamanese, according to which there were at first no women in the world, only men. Sir Monitor Lizard (whom we shall later meet at leisure) captured one of these, cut off his genitals, and took him to wife. Their progeny became the ancestors of the only race in the world with which the Andamanese and their mythology are concerned—to wit, the Andamanese.[27]

According to another myth—told in New Mexico by the Jicarilla Apache Indians [28]—there once was a murderous monster called Kicking Monster, whose four daughters at that time were the only women in the world possessing vaginas. They were "vagina girls." And they lived in a house that was full of vaginas. "They had the form of women," we are told, "but they were in reality vaginas. Other vaginas were hanging around on the walls, but these four were in the form of girls with legs and all body parts and were walking around." As may be imagined, the rumor of these girls brought many men along the road; but they would be met by Kicking Monster, kicked into the house, and never returned. And so Killer-of-Enemies, a marvelous boy hero, took it upon himself to correct the situation.

Outwitting Kicking Monster, Killer-of-Enemies entered the house, and the four girls approached him, craving intercourse. But he asked, "Where have all the men gone who were kicked into this place?" "We ate them up," they said, "because we like to do that"; and they attempted to embrace him. But he held them off, shouting, "Keep away! That is no way to use the vagina." And then he told them, "First I must give you some medicine, which you have never tasted before, medicine made of sour berries; and then I'll do what you ask." Whereupon he gave them sour berries of four kinds to eat. "The vagina," he said, "is always sweet when you do like this." The berries puckered their mouths, so that finally they could not chew at all, but only swallowed. "They liked it very much, though," declared the teller of the story. "It felt just as if Killer-of-Enemies was having intercourse with them. They were almost unconscious with ecstasy, though really Killer-of-Enemies was doing nothing at all to them. It was the medicine that made them feel that way.

"When Killer-of-Enemies had come to them," the story-teller then concluded, "they had had strong teeth with which they had eaten their victims. But this medicine destroyed their teeth entirely." [29] And so we see how the great boy hero, once upon a time, domesticated the toothed vagina to its proper use.

Now it must have occurred to the reader during the preceding review of a series of imprints that, although a number of the images discussed are no doubt impressed upon our "open" IRMs from without, certain others can be the products only of the nervous structure itself. For where in the world would the cannibal ogress be? Or where the phallic mother and toothed vagina? Judging from the power of such images to release affects in children, as well as in many adults, we should call them sign stimuli of considerable force. Yet they are not in nature, but have been created by the mind. Whence then? Whence the images of nightmare and of dream?

Perhaps a suggestive analogy is to be seen in the case of the grayling moth,* which prefers darker mates to those actually offered by its present species. For if human art can offer to a moth the supernormal sign stimulus to which it responds more eagerly than to the normal offerings of life, it can surely supply supernormal stimuli, also, to the IRMs of man—and not only spontaneously, in dream and nightmare, but even more brilliantly in the contrived folk-tales, fairy tales, mythological landscapes, over- and underworlds, temples and cathedrals, pagodas and gardens, dragons, angels, gods, and guardians of popular and religious art. It is true, of course, that the culturally developed formulations of these wonders have required in many cases centuries, even millenniums, to complete. But it is true also (and this, I believe, is what the present review is showing) that there is a point of support for the reception of such images in the *déjà vu* of the partially self-shaped and self-shaping mind. In other words, whereas in the

* Supra, p. 43.

animal world the "isomorphs," or inherited stereotypes of the central nervous structure, which for the most part match the natural environment, may occasionally contain possibilities of response unmatched by nature, the world of man, which is now largely the product of our own artifice, represents—to a considerable extent, at least—an opposite order of dynamics; namely, that of a living nervous structure and controlled response system fashioning its habitat, and not *vice versa;* but fashioning it not always consciously, by any means; indeed, for the most part, or at least for a very considerable part, fashioning it impetuously, out of its own self-produced images of rage and fear.

A fifth and culminating syndrome of imprints of this kind, mixed of outer and inner impacts, is that of the long and variously argued Oedipus complex, which, according to the orthodox Freudian school, is normally established in the growing child at the age of about five or six, and thereafter constitutes the primary constellating pattern of all impulse, thought and feeling, imaginative art, philosophy, mythology and religion, scientific research, sanity and madness. The claim for the universality of this complex has been vigorously challenged by a number of anthropologists; for example, Bronislaw Malinowski, who, in his work on *Sex and Repression in Savage Society* declares, "The crux of the difficulty lies in the fact that to psychoanalysts the Oedipus complex is something absolute, the primordial source . . . the *fons et origo* of everything. . . . I cannot conceive of the complex as the unique source of culture, of organization and belief," he goes on then to say; "as the metaphysical entity, creative, but not created, prior to all things and not caused by anything else." [30] Géza Róheim, on the other hand, replied in defense of Freud in a strong rebuttal,[31] to which, as far as I know, there has been no response. However, since our problem for the present is not that of the ultimate force or extent in time and space of this imprint, but that simply of the possibility of its derivation from infantile experience, we may say that whether it is quite as universal as strict Freudians believe, or significantly modified in force and character according to the sociology of the tribe or family in question, the fact remains that at about the age of five or six the youngster becomes implicated imaginatively (in our culture world, at least) in a ridiculous tragi-comedy that we may term "the family romance."

In its classical Freudian structuring, this Oedipal romance consists in the more or less unconscious wish of the boy to eliminate his father (Jack-the-Giant-Killer motif) and be alone with his mother; but with a correlative fear, which is also more or less unconscious, of a punishing castration by the father. And so here, at last, the imprint of the Father has entered the psychological picture of the growing child—in the way of a dangerous ogre. As Róheim represents the case in his study of the psychology of primitive warfare, the father is the first enemy, and every enemy is symbolic of the father;[32] indeed, "whatever is killed becomes father."[33] Hence certain aspects of the headhunting rites, to which we shall presently be turning; hence, too, the rites of the paleolithic hunters in connection with the killing and eating of their totem beasts.

For the girl, the corresponding Freudian formula is that of the legend of Electra. She is her mother's rival for the father's love, living in fear that the ogress may kill him and draw herself back into the web of the nightmare of that presexual cannibal feast (formerly paradise!) of the bambino and madonna. For times have changed, and it is now the little girl herself who is to play the madonna—to a brood of dolls.

Since the following chapters furnish abundant instances of this romance of a Lilliputian and two giants, we need not pause to document it here, but observe, simply, that one example has already been supplied in the episode of Killer-of-Enemies (the boy hero), Kicking Monster (the father-ogre), and the Four Vagina Girls (who are dangerous in the father's service but susceptible of domestication). Four is a ritual number in American Indian lore, referring to the four directions of the universe, and appears in this story because the figures have no personal, or historical, but rather a cosmic mythological reference. The girls are personifications of an aspect of the mystery of life.

And so, finally, to conclude this brief sketch of the Freudian notion of the family romance and its variations, the reaction of the very young male who vaguely senses that his mother is a temptress, seducing his imagination to incest and parricide, may be to hide his feelings from his own thoughts by assuming the compensatory, negative attitude of a Hamlet—a mental posture of excessive submission to the jurisdiction of the father (atonement theme), together with a fierce rejection of the female and all the associated charms of the world (the fleshpots of Egypt, whore of Babylon, etc.):

> Yea, from the table of my memory
> I'll wipe away all trivial fond records,
> All saws of books, all forms, all pressures past,
> That youth and observation copied there;
> And thy commandment all alone shall live
> Within the book and volume of my brain,
> Unmixed with baser matter: yes, by heaven!
> O most pernicious woman!
> O villain, villain, smiling, damned villain! [34]

Here we are on the way to the worship of the omnipotent father alone, monkdom, puritanism, Platonism, celibate clergies, homosexuality, and all the rest. And there is much of this, too, to be found in the chapters to come.

For as long as the nuclear unit of human life has been a man, woman, and child, the maturing consciousness has had to come to a knowledge of its world through the medium of this heavily loaded, biologically based triangle of love and aggression, desire and fear, dependency, command, and the urge for release. It is a cooky-mold competent to shape the most recalcitrant dough. So that, even should it finally be shown, somehow, that the human nervous system is without innate form, we should still not be surprised to find in all mythology an order of sign stimuli derived from the engrams of these inevitables.

IV. The Spontaneous Animism of Childhood

It is during the years between six and twelve that youngsters in our culture, and apparently in most others, develop their personal skills and interests, moral judgments, and notions of status. The differentiating factors of the various natural and social environ-

A child's drawing of his dream of the devil. After Piaget

ments now begin to preponderate to such a degree that further talk of common modes of thought and action might seem to be out of place. Yet all the new, structuring impressions, derived from the greatly differing local scenes, whether accidental in their impact or pedagogically systematized in imposed routines of training, are received in terms of the mentality not of adulthood but of growing childhood, which has certain common traits throughout the world.

The enigma of the dream, for example, is at first interpreted as in no sense mental: it is external to the dreamer, even though invisible to others. And the memory of the dream is confused with ordinary memories, so that the two worlds are mixed.[35] A little boy of five years and six months was asked, "Is the dream in your head?" and he answered, "I am in the dream, it is not in my head. When you dream you don't know you are in bed. You know you are walking: you are in the dream. You are in bed, but you don't know you are." [36] Even at the age of seven or eight, when dreams can be recognized as arising in the head instead of coming from outside—from the moon, from the night, from the lights in the room or in the street, or from the sky—they are still regarded as in some way external. "I dreamt that the devil wanted to boil me," said a little fellow of seven, explaining a picture that he had drawn (figure above). On the left (I) was the child himself, in bed. "That's me," he said. "It was specially my eyes that stayed there—to see." In the center was the devil. And on the right of the picture (II) was the little boy again, standing in his nightshirt in front of the devil, who was about to boil him. "I was there twice over," he said in explanation. "When I was in bed I was really there, and then when I was in my dream I was with the devil, and I was really there too."

The reader will not need to be told that we have here a type of logic that is not precisely that of Aristotle, but familiar enough in fairy tale and myth, where the miracle of bi-presence is possible and the same person or object can be in two or more places at the same time. Shamans, we shall presently see, leave their bodies and ride on their drums or mounts beyond the bounds of the visible world, to engage in adventures with devils and gods, or with other shamans, all of whom, likewise, can be in more than one place at a time. Or we may think of the Roman Catholic dogma of the multipresence of Christ in the sacrament of the altar. "There are not as many bodies of Christ as there are tabernacles in the world, or as there are Masses being said at the same time," it is declared in a Catholic catechism of Christian doctrine, "but only one body of Christ, which is everywhere present, whole and entire in the Holy Eucharist, as God is everywhere present, while he is but one God."[37] Or one may think of the multipresence of the Hindu savior, Krishna, when he was dancing with the many milkmaids of Vrindavan; and the charming explanation of the religious experience of multipresence that was given by the maids of Vrindavan to one of their number. "I see Krishna everywhere," the beautiful Radha had said, and they replied, "Darling, you have painted your eyes with the collyrium of love; that is why you see Krishna everywhere."[38]

We have noted that in the world of the infant the solicitude of the parent conduces to a belief that the universe is oriented to the child's own interest and ready to respond to every thought and desire. This flattering circumstance not only reinforces the primary indissociation between inside and out, but even adds to it a further habit of command, linked to an experience of immediate effect. The resultant impression of an omnipotence of thought—the power of thought, desire, a mere nod or shriek, to bring the world to heel—Freud identified as the psychological base of magic, and the researches of Piaget and his school support this view. The child's world is alert and alive, governed by rules of response and command, not by physical laws: a portentous continuum of consciousness, endowed with purpose and intent, either resistant or responsive to the child itself. And as we know, this infantile notion (or something much like it) of a world governed rather by moral than by physical laws, kept under control by a superordinated parental personality instead of impersonal physical forces, and oriented to the weal and woe of man, is an illusion that dominates men's thought in most parts of the world—or even most men's thoughts in all parts of the world—to the very present. We are dealing here with a spontaneous assumption, antecedent to all teaching, which has given rise to, and now supports, certain religious and magical beliefs, and when reinforced in turn by these remains as an absolutely ineradicable conviction, which no amount of rational thought or empirical science can quite erase.

And so now it must be observed that, just as the imprints discussed in Section III of the present chapter are susceptible of either infantile or adult interpretation, so too are these experiences of indissociation. For even from the point of view of a strictly biological observation it can be shown that in a certain sense the indissociation of the child has a deeper validity than the adult experience of individuation. Biologically, the individual organism is in no sense independent of its world. For society is not, as Ralph Linton assumed, "a group of biologically distinct and self-contained individuals." Nor is society, indeed, apart from nature. Between the organism and its environment there exists what Piaget has termed "a continuity of exchanges." [39] An internal and an external pole have to be recognized, "but each term is in a relation of constant equilibrium and natural dependence with respect to the other." And it is only relatively slowly that a notion of individual freedom and sense of independence are developed—which then, however, may conduce not only to a manly sense of self-sufficiency and an order of logic in which subjective and objective are rationally kept apart, but to a deterioration of the unity of the social order as well, and to a sense of separateness, which may end in a general atmosphere of anxiety and neurosis.

It has been one of the chief aims of all religious teaching and ceremonial, therefore, to suppress as much as possible the sense of ego and develop that of participation. Such participation, in primitive cults, is principally in the organism of the community, which itself is conceived as participating in the natural order of the local environment. But to this there may be added the larger notion of a community including the dead as well—as, for example, in the Christian idea of the Church Militant, Suffering, and Triumphant: on earth, in purgatory, and in heaven. And finally, in all mystical effort the great goal is the dissolution of the dewdrop of the self in the ocean of the All: the stripping of self and the beholding of the Face.

"And when Thou didst approach my unworthiness with Thy greatly desired face, which bestows all bliss," wrote Saint Gertrude of Helfta (1256–1302), "I felt that a light, ineffably vivifying, proceeded from Thy divine eyes into mine. Penetrating my entire inner being, it produced in every member a most marvelous effect, inasmuch as it dissolved my flesh and bones to the very marrow; so that I had the feeling that my whole substance was nothing but that divine splendor which, playing upon itself in an indescribably delightful way, was communicating to my soul incomparable serenity and joy." [40]

A like sentiment appears in the well-known verse of the Indian *Bṛhadāraṇyaka Upaniṣad* (c. 800 B.C.): "Just as a man, when in the embrace of a beloved wife, knows nothing within or without, so does this being, when embraced by the Supreme Self, know nothing within or without." [41]

Among the treasures of the Buddhist mystics of Japan we find the following in the journal of the sandal-maker Saichi (c. 1850–1933):

My heart and Thy heart—
The oneness of hearts—
"Homage to Amida Buddha!" [42]

And, once again, in the words of Omar Khayyam (1050–1120):

My being is of Thee, and Thou art mine,
And I am Thine, since I am Lost in Thee! [43]

In childhood the earliest questions asked concerning the origins of things betray the spontaneous assumption that somebody made them. "Who made the sun?" asks the child of two years and a half. "Who puts the stars in the sky at night?" asks another of three and a half.[44] In these early ruminations the first point of focus is the problem of the origin of the child itself, the second, the origin of mankind, and the last, the origin of things; but the compass of the search presents even learned parents with more than they can handle in the way of scientific and metaphysical challenge. One little boy, for example, presented his scholarly father with the following recorded series:

At two years and three months: "Where do eggs come from?" And, when told: "Well, what do mummies lay?"

At two years and six months: "Papa, were there people before us?" Yes. "How did they come there?" They were born, like us. "Was the earth there before there were people on it?" Yes. "How did it get there if there were no people to make it?"

At three years and seven months: "Who made the earth?"

And at four years and five months: "Was there a mummy before the first mummy?"

At four years and nine months: "How did the first man get here without having a mummy?"

And only then, but shortly following: "How was water made?" "What are rocks made of?"[45]

The first notion entertained by the majority of the youngest children seems to be that babies are not born or made, but found. "Mamma, where did you find me?" asked a youngster of three years and six months. "Mamma, where did I come from?" asked another, of three and eight. "Where is the baby now that a lady is going to have next summer?" asked one little genius of four years and ten months; and, when told: "Has she eaten it, then?" Another: "Do people turn back into babies when they get very old?" Or again, at an age of five years and four months: "When you die, do you grow up again?"[46]

As Professor Piaget observes, in this first stage of theorization babies are thought to pre-exist; however, it is realized that parents must have something to do with the mystery. The reader will have noted that the various explanations on this level come very close to certain well-known primitive and archaic ideas; for example, that of conception through eating, which is found in myths and folktales throughout the world; or the idea of rebirth, which is perhaps already suggested even in the burials, circa 100,000 B.C., of Neanderthal Man.*

The second type of infantile question concerning birth involves the problem not only of the whence but also that of the how. By this time the child's interest in his own acts of creation, liquid and solid, has suggested at least two possibilities, which he is not usually willing to formulate, yet may be covertly testing through his questions. The queries just cited concerning the origins of water and rocks are manifest examples. Some sort of mysterious fabrication by the parents is supposed, either outside of their bodies or within, and these vaguely conceived processes then are taken to be possible models for the creation of other things in the world as well. The child begins by assuming that adults were the makers of all things; for they are thought to be omniscient and omnipotent until events make it all too evident that they are neither. Whereupon the cherished image of an all-knowing, all-potent, manually or otherwise creating parent is simply transferred to the vague figure of an anthropomorphic though invisible God, which has already been furnished by parental or other instruction.

The figure of a creative being is practically, if not absolutely, universal in the mythologies of the world, and just as the parental image is associated in childhood not only with the power to make all things but also with the authority to command, so also in religious thought the creator of the universe is commonly the giver and controller of its laws. The two orders—the infantile and the religious—are at least analogous, and it may well be that the latter is simply a translation of the former to a sphere out of range of critical observation. Piaget has pointed out that although the little myths of genesis invented by children to explain the origins of themselves and of things may differ, the basic assumption underlying all is the same: namely, that things have to be made by someone, and that they are alive and responsive to the commands of

* Cf. supra, p. 67.

their creators. The origin myths of the world's mythological systems differ too; but in all except the most rarefied the conviction is held (as in childhood), without proof, that the living universe is the handiwork or emanation—psychical or physical—of some father-mother or mother-father God.

The sense, then, of this world as an undifferentiated continuum of simultaneously subjective and objective experience (participation), which is all alive (animism), and which was produced by some superior being (artificialism), may be said to constitute the axiomatic, spontaneously supposed frame of reference of all childhood experience, no matter what the local details of this experience may happen to be. And these three principles, it is no less apparent, are precisely those most generally represented in the mythologies and religious systems of the whole world.

In fact, the notion of participation—or indissociation between the subjective and objective aspects of experience—goes so far in the usual thinking both of infants and of the archaic philosophical systems that the names of things (which are certainly subjective, simply within the mind, and differ greatly from culture to culture) are thought by all children and by most archaic thinkers to be intrinsic to things, as their audible aspect. In the Hebrew Kabbala, for example, the sounds and forms of the letters of the Hebrew alphabet are regarded as the very elements of reality, so that by correctly pronouncing the names of things, of angels, or even of God, the competent Kabbalist can make use of their force. The pronunciation of the name of God (YHVH), indeed, has always been guarded with great care. In ancient times the sages communicated the pronunciation of the name to their disciples only once in seven years.[47] A scribe inditing biblical scrolls was required to place his mind in a devotional attitude when writing the name of God, and if he made an error in the name, in certain cases the mistake was irremediable and the whole column on which the error occurred had to be withdrawn from use; [48] for the name itself could not be erased. Comparably, in the mystical disciplines of the Indian Tantric tradition, where not Hebrew but Sanskrit is regarded as the primal language of the universe, the pronunciation of the name of any god will cause him to appear and his force to operate, since the name is the audible form of the god himself. The supreme Word, of which the whole universe, visible and invisible, is the manifestation, is in the Indian tradition the syllable AUM. And, of course, then there is that celebrated opening of the Gospel according to John: "In the beginning was the Word, and the Word was with God, and the Word was God. He was in the beginning with God; all things were made through him, and without him was not anything made that was made. In him was life, and the life was the light of men." [49]

"And God said, 'Let there be light'; and there was light." [50]

"If there weren't any words it would be very bad," said a little boy of six years and six months; "you couldn't make anything. How could things have been made?" [51]

The very young child does not remember when or how he first heard the names of things whose names he knows. He commonly believes that he came to know them simply by looking, and that the name comes into being simultaneously with the object. "What are names for?" a child of five years and a half was asked. "They are what you see when you look at things," he replied.[52] The name is a quality of the object, situated within it, and likewise known to the object. "Where is the name of the sun?" "Inside the sun," a child of seven said.[53] "Does a fish know its name?" the same little boy was asked when he was nine, and he answered, "Yes."

What has been termed "creation from nothing," and celebrated by theologians as an extremely elevated notion, is actually—at least in the text in which the notion is supposed to be documented—a creation from the word, through naming the name, which is one of the primary notions of creation entertained by the human infant. Moreover, in the cosmologies of archaic man, as in those of infancy, the main concern of the creator was in the weal and woe of man. Light was made so that we should see; night so that we might sleep; stars to foretell the weather; clouds to warn of rain. The child's view of the world is not only geocentric, but egocentric. And if we add to this simple structure the tendency recognized by Freud, to experience all things in association with the subjective formula of the family romance (Oedipus complex), we have a rather tight and very slight vocabulary of elementary ideas, which we may expect to see variously inflected and applied in the mythologies of the world.

It is already clear from the studies that have been made of children in the West—who are the only ones that have been systematically examined—that the rational logic and scientific views that ultimately replace in their thinking the spontaneous animistic and artificialist theories of infancy only gradually suppress or dissolve the earlier notions. Names are not correctly distinguished from their referents until somewhere about the tenth or eleventh year. Life becomes restricted to animals and plants, and consciousness to animals, hardly before the ages of eleven or twelve. And yet even after the basic laws of physics and chemistry have been learned, which have been so painfully drawn from nature by the long toil of science, when the adult is asked about the mysteries of creation it is seldom that he will answer in other terms than those of the infantile artificialist or animist: the world has been made by some omniscient god for some purpose, and we for some end, which we must learn to know and to serve; or else—in replies somewhat more sophisticated—there is within things themselves some force that makes them, an immanent power out of which they arise and back into which they go.

In the mythologies of the world a great number of origin myths appear, but few more wonderful than the following, spontaneously invented by a nine-year-old when asked concerning the origins of his country.

"How did Switzerland begin?"

"Some people came," he answered.

"Where from?"

"I don't know. There were bubbles on the water and a little worm underneath. Then it got big and came out of the water and fed and grew arms and teeth and feet and a head and it turned into a baby."

"Where did the bubble come from?"

"From the water. The worm came out of the water and the bubble broke and the worm came out."

"What was there at the bottom of the water?"

"The bubble, which came out of the ground."

"And what happened to the baby?"

"He got big and had babies. By the time he died the babies had children. Later on some of them became French, some German, some Savoyards. . . ." [54]

It seems safe to assume, at this point, that no comment on this origin myth is necessary. Most readers can no doubt recall early myths of their own invention that were of somewhat the same order. With this we leave the course of our common childhood behind—the childhood of our species, perhaps, since the hoary days of Neanderthal—and move on to see what the adult shamans, priests, and philosophers have managed to achieve beyond this level, in the reading and representation of the enigma of life.

v. The System of Sentiments of the Local Group

The transformation of the child into the adult, which is achieved in higher societies through years of education, is accomplished on the primitive level more briefly and abruptly by means of the puberty rites that for many tribes are the most important ceremonials of their religious calendar.

When a Central Australian Aranda youngster is between ten and twelve years old, for example, he and the other members of his age group are taken by the men of the village and tossed several times into the air, while the women, dancing around the company, wave their arms and shout. Each boy then is painted on his chest and back with simple designs by a man related to the social group from which his wife must come, and as they paint the patterns the men sing: "May he reach to the stomach of the sky, may he grow up to the stomach of the sky, may he go right into the stomach of the sky." The boy is told that he now has upon him the mark of the particular mythological ancestor of whom he is the living counterpart; for it is thought that the children born to women are the reappearances of beings who lived in the mythological age, in the so-called "dream time," or *altjeringa*. The boys are told that from now on they will not play or camp with the women and girls, but with the men; they will not go with the women to grub for roots and to hunt such small game as rats and lizards, but will join the men and hunt the kangaroo.[55]

In this simple rite it is apparent that the image of birth has been transferred from the mother to the sky and that the concept of the ego has been expanded, simultaneously, beyond the biography of the physical individual. A woman gave birth to the boy's temporal body, but the men will now bring him to spiritual birth. They will continue and consummate his post-uterine gestation, the long process of his growth to a fully human maturity, refashioning his body, and his mind as well, joining him to his eternal portion, beyond time. Furthermore, in the ceremonials that he will presently observe the tasks proper to his manhood will in every detail be linked to mythological fantasies of a time-transcending order, so that not only himself but his whole world and his whole way of life within it will be joined inseparably, through myths and rites, to the field of the spirit.

Henceforth, all life on earth is to be recognized as a projection on the plane of temporal event of forms, objects, and personalities forever present in the permanent no-where, no-when, of the mythological age, the *altjeringa,* "dream time," when all was magical, as it is in dream: the realm that is seen again in dream and shown forth in the rites. The boy is himself a mythological, eternal being who has become incarnate; his fellows, too, are the manifestations of eternal forms; likewise, the kangaroos that he will soon be hunting and the well-known desert reaches where the magical mystery play of the hunt will be enacted in the serious game of life—the mystery play of the death and reappearance of the kangaroo, who is to give his flesh, as a willing victim, to be the food of men. No child—no woman—is aware of the real marvel of this dual mystery, wherein the timeless and the temporal are the same. This secret dimension of the world is the revelation of the men's rites, through which the mind grows to knowledge, and after beholding which one is far above the plane of the mental system of the child. It is a marvel, a source of wonder, well worth the pain and fright of a second birth. And meanwhile, throughout the physical as well as psychological ordeal of transformation, in compensation for the earthly mother lost, the boy's pliant mind and will are to be directed forward to the image of his manhood with an earthly wife.

It is clear what is happening. The imprints irreversibly established in infancy as energy-releasing signs are being reorganized, and through an extremely vivid, increasingly frightening and unforgettable series of controlled experiences are in the end to be so recomposed that the boy's course will be directed forward into manhood: not to any merely open, uncommitted manhood, but specifically to a certain style of thought and feeling, impulse and action, comporting with the requirements of the local group. For it is at this point in his development that the mores, ideology, and motivations of the local system of life are to be assimilated into his psyche, fused with his spiritual substance, and thus made his own, as he is made theirs.

As already remarked, in the words of Radcliffe-Brown: * "A society depends for its existence on the presence in the minds of its members of a certain system of sentiments by which the conduct of the individual is regulated in conformity with the needs of the society"; and further: "the sentiments in question are not innate but are developed in the individual by the action of the society upon him." It is in the rites of initiation that these sentiments of the local system are established through a forced fusion with the primary system of the mentality of childhood, which, as we have seen, is universal—or practically universal—to the human race. The system of sentiments of the local group, however, has been constellated not primarily, or even secondarily, to gratify the crude wishes of the growing adolescent for sensual pleasure and manly power, but rather in the general interest of a group having certain specific local problems and limitations. The crude energies of the young human animal are to be cowed, broken, recoordinated to a larger format, and thus at once domesticated and amplified. Hence, although the rites certainly have a psychological function and must be interpreted in terms of the general psychology of the human species, each local system itself has a long history behind it of a particular sort of social experience and cannot be explained

* Cf. supra, p. 33.

in general psychological terms. It has been closely adjusted to specific, geographically determined conditions of existence, and comprehends, furthermore, certain archaic notions of cosmology that have been derived from millenniums of meditation on the recognized natural order of the living world. From culture to culture, the sign symbols presented in the rites of initiation differ considerably, and they have to be studied, consequently, from a historical as well as from a psychological point of view. It must be recognized that either view alone is an oversimplification.

No functioning mythological system can be explained in terms of the universal images of which it is constituted. These images are developed largely from such infantile imprints as those that we have just reviewed and constitute merely the raw material of myth. They carry the energies of the psyche into the mythological context and weld them to the historical task of the society, where the symbols function, not in the way of a regressive recall of the spirit to the joys and sorrows, desires and terrors of little Oedipus, or of the earlier bambino, but rather as releasers and directors of the energies into the field of adult experience and performance. Mythology, that is to say, is progressive, not regressive. And the rites themselves, through which the new sign symbols are impressed on the minds of the growing young in such a way as to recondition the entire system of their innate releasing mechanisms, constitute one of the most interesting and crucial foci of our subject. For it is precisely here that we confront directly the problem of the meeting of the general and the particular, of the elementary and the ethnic, in the field of myth. The initiation rite is the caldron of their fusion.

And should the fusion not take place?

If it should happen in the case of any particular individual that the impress of the socially enforced reorganization of the infantile imagery should fail of its proper effect, that particular individual's personal system of references, and consequently of sentiments, would remain essentially infantile and therefore aberrant, isolating, shameful, and frightening, so that the sort of disorientation known so well to the psychoanalytic couches of our contemporary, literarily instead of mythologically and ritually educated civilization would inevitably result. In the traumatic experience of his second birth the individual would have suffered an accident precisely comparable to a misbirth or physical accident in the first. In which case, of course, a regressive interpretation of his peculiar mode of experiencing the imagery of local myth would be in order. However, for the psychoanalyst then to make use of the fantasies of that regressive case as a key to the scientific understanding of the progressively functioning mythology and ceremonialism of the social group in question would be about as appropriate as to mistake a pancake for a soufflé.

It is possible that the failure of mythology and ritual to function effectively in our civilization may account for the high incidence among us of the malaise that has led to the characterization of our time as "The Age of Anxiety." Or it may be that it is only among our poets and artists, journalists and Ph.D.s that the impress of our socially framed system of sentiments has failed of effect; so that this notion of the prevalence of anxiety is an invention peculiar to them, based rather on their own sophisticated pathology than on the more naïve state of health of the majority of their fellows. But in either case it would certainly seem that when an essentially cerebral emphasis preponderates in the schooling of the young, as it does in our highly literate society, an alarming incidence of serious failure is to be expected in the difficult passage of the critical threshold from the system of sentiments proper to infancy to that of the responsibilities of the hour—and that, consequently, any attempt to interpret the symbolism of archaic man on the basis of contemporary thought and feeling must be extremely dangerous.

In following the further progress of the puberty rites and ordeals of the Central Australian Aranda, therefore, it will be well to leave the clichés of modern psychology to one side and focus, rather, on the particular character and tasks of the local desert scene, where the temperature at noon is frequently as high as one hundred and forty degrees Fahrenheit; where the normal social unit is a little cluster of intimately known relatives and companions, all of whom, both male and female, are stark naked; where there is no written tradition through which the corpus of tribal knowledge, style of spiritual life, and techniques of subsistence can be communicated; and where the chief object of the hunt is the bounding kangaroo.

The real trials of the growing youngster, and the second stage of his initiation into both the duties and the knowledge of his inevitable estate, commence one evening, suddenly, in the men's camp, when he is pounced upon by three strong young fellows, loudly shouting, who bear him off, frightened and struggling, to a ceremonial ground that has been prepared for his circumcision. The whole community is there to greet him, women as well as men, and when he finds himself among them his struggles cease.

He is placed among the men, and the women at once begin to dance, flourishing shields. They are now the women of the age of dream, the *altjeringa* age, who danced this way when the young men of the age of the ancestors were to be initiated; and the men sing while they perform. When the boy has watched and listened for some time—never having seen such things before—strands of fur string are wound around his head to make a tightly fitting cap, and there is tied about his waist a girdle of twisted hair, such as he has seen the men wear. Three men then lead him through the dancing women to a brake of bushes behind which he is now to remain for a number of days. They paint on him a design and warn him that he has now entered upon a higher stage of young manhood. He must never disclose to any woman or boy any of the secret things that he is about to see and learn. Throughout the coming ceremony he is not to utter a word unless addressed, and then only to answer as briefly as possible. And he is to remain crouching behind his brake until called. Should he attempt to see what he is forbidden to see, the great spirit whose voice he has heard in the sound of the bull-roarers would carry him away. And so he sits alone and silently all night, behind the brake, while the men dance on the ceremonial ground.

The next day the boy's mother arrives, accompanied by the sisters of his father and by the woman whose daughter has been assigned to become his wife. All night the boy's mother has kept a fire burning in her camp, and she now brings in her hands two long sticks lighted from this fire. The men sing a fire-song while the mother hands one stick to the woman who is to become the boy's mother-in-law, and the latter, approaching the boy, ties some bands of fur string around his neck, hands him the fire-stick, and tells him to hold fast to his own fire; that is to say, never to interfere with women assigned to other men. This rite concluded, the boy returns to his brake with the fire-stick, and the women go back with the second fire-stick to their camp.

The boy is now taken into the forest, where he sits quietly for three days and is given little to eat. The great solemnity of the rites that he is about to behold is thus impressed upon his whole mind and he is prepared to receive the impact of their imagery. On the fourth day he is returned to his brake, and that night the men's performances begin. They are to continue for about a week.

The first rite of the particular series observed by Baldwin Spencer and F. J. Gillen, described in their important work on *The Native Tribes of Central Australia,*[56] commenced after dark, with the boy still crouching in his retreat. The old men sang the legend of the ancestors of the Little Hawk totem group, who in the *altjeringa,* "dream time" of the mythological age, introduced the art of circumcising with a stone knife instead of with a fire-stick. We may read in this theme a dim reference to some recent or ancient transformation of the ritual tradition, perhaps following such a fusion of two peoples as the recent studies of Australian culture strata and ancient petroglyphs have begun to indicate.[57] But we must recognize also that the fire-stick that the boy has just received from the two mothers is in the context of the rite an explicit reference to the controlled release of his own sexual fire, which is to be socially authorized through the ritual ordeal of his impending circumcision—the second stick, to which his own is to be directed, being now in the precinct of his selected wife.

The series of remarkable rites, crude as it may seem to the civilized eye, is not to be dismissed as simply a superstitious work of primitive ignorance. On the contrary, it is the functioning implement of a primitive wisdom, which, in some aspects at least, is more sophisticated and effective than much of our own, the chief aim being pedagogical, or, as we might perhaps better say, hermetical: the magical transformation of a psyche. In fact, in a very real sense, it is an example of the early actuality from which the later medieval European idea of homunculus evolved, which Goethe has handled with such subtle psychological and historical understanding in the second part of his *Faust:* the mysterious art through which a little man (*homunculus*) is brought into being from the crude stuff (*materia prima*) supplied by nature.

At midnight the boy undergoing the ordeal was blindfolded, led from his brake, and placed face downward at the edge of the dance ground, then, after a time, was told to sit up and look; whereupon he saw lying before him a decorated man who represented, as he was told, a wild dog. A second decorated man was standing with legs apart at the other end of the dance ground, holding up twigs of eucalyptus in each hand, and having on his head a sacred ornament emblematic of the kangaroo. The kangaroo moved its head from side to side, as though watching for something, and every now and then uttered the call of the kangaroo. The dog looked up, saw the other, began barking, and suddenly, running along on all fours, passed between the other's legs and lay down behind him, the kangaroo watching the dog over his shoulder. The wild dog then ran between the kangaroo's legs once again, but this time was caught and thoroughly shaken. A pretense was made of dashing his head against the ground, whereupon he howled, as if in pain, until, finally, he was supposed to have been killed. He lay still for a while, but then, on all fours, came running to the boy candidate and lay on top of him. The kangaroo hopped over and lay on top of the two, and the boy had to bear their weight for about two minutes; when they got up, he was told that their mime represented an event of the *altjeringa* age, when a wild-dog man attacked a kangaroo man and was killed. He was sent back to his brake, and the men continued singing throughout the night.

This sort of thing went on for the boy's instruction for six days and nights. Kangaroo men, rat men, dog men, little night hawks and big performed their legends, lay on top of him, and went away. But then, on the seventh day, behind his brake, the boy was solemnly rubbed all over with grease and three men carefully painted his back with a design of white pipe-clay, while on the dance ground a number of performances were enacted in which the women had a role. Suddenly the sound was heard of approaching bull-roarers, and the women fled. The lad was lying on his back. The men piled poles on top of him, banging them up and down upon his body, beating time, while they sang, over and over, the following verse:

> Night, twilight, a great clear light:
> A cluster of trees, sky-like, rising red as the sun.

"All," as our observers tell us, "was now excitement."

The fire was giving out a brilliant light and the two men who were to perform the circumcision took their position at the western end of the ceremonial ground.

> With their beards thrust into their mouths, their legs widely extended and their arms stretched forward, the two men stood perfectly still, the actual operator in front and his assistant pressing close up behind him, so that their bodies were in contact with each other. The front man held in his extended right hand the small flint knife with which the operation was to be conducted, and, as soon as they were in position, the boy's future father-in-law, who was to act as shield bearer, came down the lines, carrying the shield on his head and at the same time snapping the thumb and first finger of each hand. Then, facing the fire, he knelt down on one knee just a little in front of the operator, holding his shield above his head. During the whole time the bull-roarers were sounding everywhere so loudly that they could easily be heard by the women and children in their camp, and by them it is supposed that the roaring is the voice of the great spirit *Twanyirika,* who has come to take the boy away.[58]

The legend told to the women and children concerning Twanyirika is not a true myth but a "screening allegory," coined to hide from exoteric view the facts of an esoteric rite, while suggesting symbolically the rite's spiritual sense. Many such screening legends are represented in the history of religion, hermetic philosophy, mysticism, and pedagogy. They are not to be confused with such outright parodies and frauds as those of the old Eskimo shaman Najagneq, which were invented to intimidate his fellow villagers.*

* Cf. supra, p. 53.

They serve a double function. The first is that of excluding those not eligible for initiation from the knowledge of the crucial mystery and thus protecting the force of the rites when properly applied; but the second is that of readying the minds of those to be initiated for the full impact of the shock of a revelation that will not controvert the allegory but disclose its reference. The allegory of Twanyirika tells of a spirit dwelling in wild, inaccessible regions, who arrives at initiation time to enter the body of the boy, after the operation, and bear him away into the wilderness until he is well. The spirit then quits the boy, who returns to the camp an initiated man.[59]

Still believing in Twanyirika, the boy is lying on his back beneath the rising and falling poles. The deep, loud tones of the circumcision song are being thundered out by all the men, when, suddenly, the poles are removed and the boy, lifted by two strong fellows, is carried feet foremost to the shield, upon which he is placed. Quickly the assistant circumciser grasps the foreskin, pulls it out as far as possible, and the operator cuts it off. Immediately, all the men who have acted in any official capacity in the rite disappear, and the boy, in a more or less dazed condition, is told by those who carried him, "You have done well, you have not cried out." He is conducted back to the place where the brake had stood but now is gone, and receives the congratulations of the men. The blood from his wound is allowed to flow into a shield and while he is still bleeding some of the bull-roarers are brought up and pressed against the wound. He is told that it was these, and not Twanyirika, that made the sound—and thus he is forced past the last bogey of childhood. He learns at the same time that the bull-roarers are *tjurunga,* sacred objects deriving from the mythological age and realm. He is introduced to all the functionaries by their ceremonial names and given a packet of *tjurungas* by the eldest.

"Here is Twanyirika, of whom you have heard so much," the old man tells him. "These are *tjurunga.* They will help to heal you quickly. Guard them well and do not lose them, or you and your blood and tribal mothers and sisters will be killed. Do not let them out of your sight. Do not let your blood and tribal mothers and sisters see you. The man in charge will remain with you. Do not eat forbidden food."

The boy, meanwhile, is standing over a fire whose smoke is supposed to heal his wound;[60] but there is a second meaning to this action of the smoke, for in Australia a child is smoked at birth, to purify it: the lad has just undergone at this moment his second birth.

Géza Róheim, in his psychoanalytic studies of Australian ritual and myth, has pointed out that the simulated attitude of the circumcisers in this rite "is that of a furious father attacking his son's penis"; the two men chew their beards to simulate wrath, and their ceremonial name is the "pain makers."[61] Moreover, in the myths of the origin of the rite it is told that originally the boys died, but that the substitution of the flint knife for the fire-stick mitigated the danger of the operation. "The dramatized anger of both the father and the circumciser and the myths of the original initiation in which all the boys were killed," wrote Dr. Róheim, "certainly show the Oedipal aggression of the elder generation as the basic drive behind initiation. In this sense therefore we are perfectly justified in calling circumcision a mitigated form of castration."[62]

"The growing boy," observes Róheim further, "with his increased strength and sexual desire is a dangerous threat to the stability of the horde. Among the Pitjentara tribe [who dwell just to the west of the Aranda], when the lads are beginning to show development (in stature, in the appearance of pubic hair, and in general demeanor) with the approach of puberty, their female kinsfolk arm themselves with digging-sticks and at dusk form a circle around one or more of the youths. They prod and beat the boys about the legs and shoulders unmercifully so that they become half-stupefied. This may happen just before initiation ceremonies are to be held, or weeks or even months before. . . .

"According to the Ngatatara and Western Aranda, if the young men were not subjected to the discipline of the initiation ritual they would become demons (*erintja*), would fly up into the sky, and kill and eat the old men."[63] To keep them down, the old men kill and eat the boys symbolically—or even actually if the boys do not obey, which, if we may judge from what has been learned about the phenomenology of juvenile delinquency in recent years, is perhaps not an excessive threat, after all.

But there is another side to the work of the elders besides that of intimidation. They must woo their sons from the primary infantile attachment to their mothers through an effective conjuration of their sympathy. During the course of the painful rites, therefore, the lads, at times, are given nothing to eat or drink but the men's blood. They take it from bowls, either in liquid form or coagulated and carved like cake. The blood is poured over them, also, as a bath. And so they are literally soaked, inside and out, in the good body content of the fathers, which has been drawn in almost incredibly great quantities from the men's arms and subincision wounds. The men jab the subincision scars of their penises or slash the insides of their arms, and the blood pours forth, which then is used not only as food and drink for the boys, but also as paint for the ceremonials and as a kind of glue, to make the bird-down decorations stick to their bodies when they assume the forms of the ancestors for the sacred rites. Thus the blood is physical food, like mothers' milk, but spiritual food also (which the mothers cannot furnish): no mere children's food, nourishing only the body, but truly man's food, the amniotic fluid and energizing force of the alchemy of this frightening yet fascinating crisis of the second birth.

On the psychological side, then, we may say that the boy is being carried across the difficult threshold, from the sphere of dependency on the mothers to that of participation in the nature of the fathers, not only by means of a decisive physical transformation of his own body (first, in the rite of circumcision, just reviewed, and then, more cruelly, as we shall presently see, in the rite of subincision), but also by means of a series of intense psychological experiences, reawakening but at the same time reorganizing all the primary imprints and fantasies of the infantile unconscious. Or, to use the Freudian jargon, the elders arouse, absorb, and redirect their sons' Oedipal impulses to aggression (*destrudo: thanatos*) and simultaneously their will to live and love (*libido: eros*). As we have just seen, the boy's future father-in-law is the functionary who offers him on a shield to the operation. "What is cut off the boy," writes Dr. Róheim, "is really the mother; as compensation he naturally receives a wife. . . . The glans in the foreskin is the child in the mother." [64]

But there is another aspect to this great world of the men's rites, for which no merely psychological reading of their symbolism can adequately account; namely, the particular mythological field to which the boy's intellect is being introduced. His crude energies of love and aggression are being broken from their primary spheres of reference and reorganized for manhood; but the particular system of imagery through which this psychological transformation is being effected has been determined not exclusively by general psychological laws, but also, and perhaps equally, by the particular social concerns of the local group.

And we may well marvel at the simple, adroit, wonderfully direct manner in which the participation of his interest is elicited. We have already seen how the sacred objects of his tribe were first presented to his awakened imagination. Throughout his childhood the boy had heard the awesome sound of the bull-roarers at the time of the mysteries of the men's camp, and had been told that the curiously whirring hum was the voice of a spirit that at the time of his own initiation would enter his body and support him to manhood. An anxious sense of interest and curiosity had thus been aroused, which, at the time of the revelation, was considerably shocked when it appeared that the actual spirit was a bit of flat wood, about a foot and a half long, bearing a scratched design on its surface, and whirled at the end of a long string. The childhood bogey was abruptly collapsed into this tangible stick—which, however, was declared to have been derived from the mythological realm and to be of the profoundest import both to the boy himself, as representing his own eternal aspect, and to his people, as constituting one of a constellation of sacred objects, known as *tjurunga,* revered in the tribal rites. Pressed to the boy's bleeding circumcision wound, his *tjurunga* turned his mind from a sense of loss to one of gain and directly joined him, both emotionally and in thought, to the realm of myth.

But the reader, meanwhile, must certainly have recalled, perhaps with a touch of wonder, the celebrated Classical myth of the death and second birth (through his father Zeus) of the babe Dionysos.

When the great goddess Demeter—we are told—arrived in Sicily from Crete with her daughter Persephone, whom she had conceived of Zeus, she discovered a cave near the spring of Kyane, where she hid the maiden, setting to guard her the two serpents that were normally harnessed to the maiden's chariot. And Persephone there began weaving a web of wool, a great robe on which there was to be a beautiful picture of the universe; while her mother, Demeter, contrived that the girl's father, Zeus, should learn of her presence. The god approached his daughter in the form of a serpent, and she conceived of him a son, Dionysos, who was born and nurtured in the cave. The infant's toys were a ball, a top, dice, some golden apples, a bit of wool, and a bull-roarer. But he was also given a mirror, and while he was gazing into this, delighted, there approached him stealthily, from behind, two Titans, who had been sent to slay him by the goddess Hera, the jealous wife and queen of his father, Zeus. And they were painted with a white clay or chalk. Pouncing upon the playing child, they tore him into seven parts, boiled the portions in a caldron supported by a tripod, and then roasted them on seven spits. However, when they had consumed their divine sacrifice—all except the heart, which had been rescued by the goddess Athene—Zeus, attracted by the odor of the roasting meat, entered the cave and, when he beheld the scene, slew the white-painted cannibal Titans with a bolt of lightning. The goddess Athene thereupon presented the rescued heart in a covered basket to the father, who accomplished the resurrection—according to one version of the miracle—by swallowing the precious relic and himself then giving birth to his son.[65]

It surely is no mere accident, nor consequence of parallel development, that has brought the bull-roarers on the scene for both the Greek and the Australian occasions, as well as the figures masquerading in white (the Australians wearing bird down, the Greek Titans smeared like clowns with a white clay). For the Titans were divine beings of an earlier generation than the gods. They were the children of the sky and earth, and from two of their number, Kronos and Rhea, the gods themselves—the Olympians—were born. They and their mythology derive from an earlier stratum of thought and religion than the Classical pantheon of the Olympians, and the episodes in which they appear have frequently traits of an extremely primitive tone. A number of recent scholars have pointed to the parallels between these traits and those of the rites of living primitive tribes.[66] From the Greeks, however, we do not learn through what motherly organ Father Zeus could have given birth to his son. In the primitive ritual this now appears.

For the next dramatic series of instructions and ordeals to which the young Australian is subjected are those of his subincision, which follow the rites of circumcision after an interval of some five or six weeks—depending on the time required by the boy for recovery from the first operation. These extremely painful rites commence with a brief series of instructive mimes, which terminate with the planting of a sacred pole in the ground: a pole made of a long spear ensheathed in grass, bound with a string of human hair, and ornamented with alternate rings of red and white birds' down, having a large tuft of eagle-hawk feathers affixed to the top. And when the pole, following a final mime and dance, has been planted, the youth is told to embrace it, for it will prevent the operation from being painful; he need not be afraid. One of the men lies on the ground, face downward, and a second lies on top of him. The boy is led from the pole and placed full length, face upward, on this living table, while the company sets up a great shout. Immediately a third man, sitting astride the boy's body, grasps the penis and holds it ready for the stone knife, while the operator, appearing suddenly, slits the whole length of the urethra from below.

Meanwhile, in the women's camp, the boy's female relatives, having heard the men's shout, are ceremonially slashed across the stomach and shoulders by the boy's mother.

The boy is lifted away and squats over a shield into which the blood is allowed to drain, while one or more of the younger men present, who have been operated on before, stand up and voluntarily undergo a second operation to increase the length of their incisions. These stand, hands behind their backs and legs wide apart, close to the sacred pole, and shout, "Come and slit mine to the root!" They are pinioned from behind, and the operator cuts them to the root. "Most men at some time or other undergo the second operation," write Spencer and Gillen, "and some come forward a third time, though a man is often as old as thirty or thirty-five before he submits to this second operation." [67]

The sexual aspect of the symbolism of this fantastic rite is almost too obvious to require comment. The subincision wound is frequently referred to as a "penis womb or vagina"; [68] so that the male has been intentionally converted by the operation into a male-female. "The 'vaginal father,' " as Dr. Róheim has observed, "replaces the 'phallic mother' of the infantile situation," [69] and the blood that is drawn from the subincision wounds, therefore, corresponds in the men's imagination to the menstrual blood of the women—which in the usages of women's magic is extremely potent. That one of the most pronounced traits of primitive psychology, in many parts of the world, is the savage male's horror of menstruation has long been a commonplace of anthropological knowledge.[70] "It is a well-known fact," states Dr. Róheim, "that the sight of the bleeding vagina produces castration anxiety in the male. . . . The boys must always have been afraid of the castrating vagina; now the fathers have this powerful weapon." [71] But now, too, the lads themselves have been given it. Their traumatic separation from the mother in the rite of circumcision has thus been balanced by an achievement of identification, simultaneously with the mothers and with the fathers. "We are not afraid of the bleeding vagina," they now can say; "we have it ourselves. It does not threaten the penis; it is the penis." And finally: "We are not separated from the mother; for 'we two are one.' " [72]

But there is more to the matter than this psychological theme; for there is a mythological theme consciously associated with the rite, which has to be taken into account also.

The Western world is well acquainted with one version of the associated myth in its biblical tradition. In the Book of Genesis it is written that God caused a deep sleep to fall upon Adam, "and while he slept took one of his ribs and closed up its place with flesh; and the rib which the Lord God had taken from the man he made into a woman and brought her to the man. Then the man said, 'This at last is bone of my bones and flesh of my flesh; and she shall be called Woman, because she was taken out of Man.' Therefore a man leaves his father and his mother and cleaves to his wife and they become one flesh." [73] Before the separation of Eve, Adam was both male and female.

Or consider the allegory in Plato's *Symposium,* where it is said by Aristophanes—playfully, yet in the form of the same myth—that the earliest human beings were "round and had four hands and four feet, back and sides forming a circle, one head with two faces looking opposite ways, set on a round neck and precisely alike; also four ears, two privy members, and the remainder to correspond." According to this Platonic version of the great theme, these original creatures were of three kinds; male-male, male-female, and female-female. They were immensely powerful; and since the gods were in fear of their strength, Zeus decided to cut them in two, like apples halved for pickling,

> or as you might divide an egg with a hair; and as he cut them one after another, he bade Apollo give the face and the half neck a turn. . . . Apollo twisted the face and pulled the skin around over that which in our language is called the belly, like the purses which draw in, and he made one mouth at the center, which he fastened in a knot (this is called the navel); he also moulded the breast and took out most of the wrinkles, much as a shoemaker might smooth out leather upon a last; he left a few, however, in the region of the belly and navel, as a memorial of the primeval change. After the division the two parts of man, each desiring his other half, came together, and threw their arms about one another eager to grow into one, and would have perished from hunger without ever making an effort, because they did not like to do anything apart . . : so ancient is the desire of one another which is implanted in us, reuniting our original nature, making one of two, and healing the state of man. Each of us when separated is but the indenture of a man, having one side only like a flat fish, and he is always looking for his other half.[74]

In China we learn of the Holy Woman, the Great Original, T'ai Yuan, who combined in her person the active-masculine and the passive-feminine powers of nature, the *yang* and the *yin*.[75]

And finally, in the Vedic Indian *Bṛhadāraṇyaka Upaniṣad* we read:

> . . . in the beginning this universe was but the Self in the form of a man. He looked around and saw nothing but himself. Thereupon, his first shout was, "It is I!"; whence the concept "I" arose.—And that is why, even today, when addressed, one answers first, "It is I!" then gives the other name that one bears. . . .
>
> Then he was afraid.—And that is why anyone alone is afraid.—He considered: "Since there is nothing here but myself, what is there to fear?" Whereupon the fear departed; for what should have been feared? it is only to a second that fear refers.
>
> However, he still lacked delight.—Therefore, one lacks delight when alone.—He desired a second. He was just as large as a man and woman embracing. This Self then divided himself in two parts; and with that, there were a master and mistress.—Therefore this body, by itself, as the sage Yajnavalkya declares, is like half of a split pea. And that is why, indeed, this space is filled by a woman.—He united with her, and from that mankind arose.
>
> She, however, reflected: "How can he unite with me, who am produced from himself? Well then, let me hide!" She became a cow, he a bull and united with her; and from that cattle arose. She became a mare, he a stallion; she an ass, he a donkey and united with her; and from that solid-hoofed animals arose. She became a goat, he a buck; she a sheep, he a ram and united with her; and from that goats and sheep arose.—Thus he poured forth all pairing things, down to the ants.
>
> Then he realized: "I, actually, am creation; for I have poured forth all this." Whence arose the concept "Creation" [*sṛṣṭiḥ:* literally, "what is poured forth, projected, sent forth, emanated, generated, let go, or given away"].—One who thus understands becomes, himself, truly a creator in this creation.[76]

The primitive Australian renditions of this mythological motif that has served so well to support some of the most elevated themes of the high civilizations are numerous and give a new dimension to the mystery of the ritual that we have just observed.

In the beginning, we hear, for example, from the Northern Aranda of the Bandicoot Totem, all was darkness: night oppressed the earth like an impenetrable thicket. And the ancestor of the bandicoots, whose name was Karora, lay asleep in the everlasting night, at the bottom of the soak of Ilbalintja, where there was not yet water. Above him the soil was red with flowers and overgrown with many grasses; and a great sacred pole swayed above him, which had sprung from the midst of the bed of flowers. At its root rested the head of Karora, whence it mounted upward toward the sky, as though to strike the vault of the heavens. It was a living creature, covered with a smooth skin, like the skin of a man.

Karora's head lay at the root of this great swaying pole, and had been resting thus from the beginning. But Karora was thinking: wishes and desires flashed through his mind. Bandicoots then began to come out of his navel and from his armpits. They burst through the sod above and sprang into life. Dawn began to break. The sun began to rise. And the bandicoot ancestor rose too: he burst through the crust that had covered him and the gaping hole that he left behind became Ilbalintja Soak, filled with the sweet dark juice of the honeysuckle buds.

The bandicoot ancestor now felt hungry, for the magic had gone out of his body. Feeling dazed, slowly fluttering his eyelids, he opened his eyes a little and, groping about in his dazed state, he felt a moving mass of bandicoots all around him. Seizing two, he cooked them in the white-hot sand close to where the sun stood, the sun's fingers providing him with the needed fire.

Evening approached. The sun, hiding his face with a veil of hair string and his body with hair-string pendants, vanished from sight, and Karora, with his thoughts turning toward a helpmate, fell asleep, stretching his arms out to both sides.

And while he slept there emerged from underneath his armpit something in the shape of a bull-roarer. It assumed human form and grew in one night to the stature of a young man fully grown. Karora, feeling that his arm was being oppressed with the weight of something heavy, awoke; and he saw his first-born son lying at his side, his head resting on his father's shoulder.

Dawn broke. Karora rose and sounded a loud, vibrating call. The son then stirred into life, got up, and danced a ceremonial dance around his father, who was now sitting adorned with full ceremonial designs worked in blood and feather-down. The son tottered and stumbled, being only half awake; but the father put his body and chest into a violent quiver, and the son placed his hands upon him. And when this had been done, the first ceremony came to an end.[77]

Numerous parallels to this primitive origin legend of the Bandicoot Clan exist in the various high mythologies of the world, among the most striking the resemblance of the living pole growing from Karora's head to the Tree of Jesse, in the symbolism of the Middle Ages (for example, as in the Tree-of-Jesse window of Chartres Cathedral), whence the Second Adam, Jesus, was derived; or the cross itself on which Jesus hung, placed on the hill of Golgotha, "Hill of the Skull," so called because it was there that the skull was buried of Adam, the androgynous dawn man of the Hebrew myth. Or again, we think of the curious, somnolent first man, Ymir, of the Icelandic Eddas, who took form in the "yawning void" of the beginning, when the ice-waves pressing down from the north met the heat-waves of the south. "Now it is said that when he slept, a sweat came upon him, and there grew under his left hand a man and a woman, and one of his feet begat a son with the other; and thus the races are come." [78] Ymir's great somnolent body then was cut up to form the world:

> Of Ymir's flesh the earth was fashioned,
>   And of his sweat the sea;
> Crags of his bones, trees of his hair,
>   And of his skull the sky.[79]

In many of the myths of India the cut-up man, the primordial, world-creating sacrifice of whom the visible world was fashioned, is called Purusha, which means simply, "Man." [80] In the ancient Babylonian epic of creation, the figure was a monstrous female, the goddess-mother of the world abyss, Tiamat.[81] In the Australian legend of Karora, this same universal archetype, or elementary idea, of the all-containing primal being has been adjusted to the conditions of the local scene and ceremonial style. There is no glacial cold, as in Iceland; no reference to the Brahmanic sacrifice, as in India; no mention of the female sex, as in all the others. The pattern is exclusively masculine—as in the case of the Hebrew Lord God's unassisted creation of the world and production without female intervention of Adam, his original son. The Australian rituals of the circumcision and subincision, with their emphatically patriarchal bias, find their validation in a myth of this kind, where the whole life stage of the child with the mother is simply disregarded, and the son is born as the full-grown son of the father in one night.

The living, swaying pole, rising from Karora's head, which mounted upward as though to strike the vault of the heavens and was a living creature, covered with a smooth skin like the skin of a man, is represented in the rite by the ceremonial pole that the young initiate embraces immediately before submitting to the operation of the subincision. The pole of the rite, before being planted in the ground, is carried upright on a man's back, paralleling the line of his spine and continuing, like a flagpole, far above his head. Both the pole and the man are decorated with bird-down, stuck on with blood drawn from subincision wounds, and this down, flying off as the man jumps about, is symbolic of the life-generative power that went out in all directions from the ancestors. The cosmic pole and the subincised phallus are the same: they are the male-female, self-sufficient, all-producing ancestor of the beginning. The temporal polarity of past and present, the sexual of male and female, the ritualistic of the ceremonial ground and place of the beginning are all, equally and simultaneously, dissolved. And the phallic operation, which, according to an authentic Freudian reading, enables the men to say to themselves, "We are not separated from the mother, for we two are one," simultaneously and equally enables them to participate in their own way in a mythological image of the metaphysical mystery of the cosmos: the mystery of that cosmogonic sleight-of-hand by which the one became and continues to become the many, and by which the timelessness of eternity is reflected in the changing scene of time.

The enigma of this ultimate mystery, which Schopenhauer aptly termed the "World Knot," is no better explained in the formulas of philosophy or theology than in the image of the ancestor of the bandicoots; nor can we dismiss the Aranda myth as a mere curiosity of the primitive mind if we are going to ponder in a serious way the analogous imagery of the Book of Genesis, the *Bṛhadāraṇyaka Upaniṣad,* or Plato's *Symposium.* The mystery of the universe and the wonder of the temple of the world are what speak to us through all myths and rites—as well as the great effort of man to bring his individual life into concord with the whole. And the imagery by which this mystery, wonder, and effort have been rendered in the recorded traditions of mankind is so marvelously constant—in spite of all the varieties of local life and culture—that we well may wonder whether it may not simply be coeval with the human mind.

But in this section of the present chapter the chief concern is not the problem of the universals, to which the following section returns, but the local, geographically and historically conditioned, various manners of rendering and applying those general themes. And even the brief view already given of the spectrum of the myth of the primordial androgynous giant suffices to afford a preliminary notion of the ways in which one common image can be turned to differing ends. We observe, for example, that whereas in the Greek and Hebrew versions man is split in two by a god, in the Chinese, Hindu, and Australian it is the god itself who divides and multiplies.

In the Hindu version, furthermore, the image of the androgynous ancestor is developed in terms of an essentially psychological reading of the problem of creation. The universal Self becomes divided immediately after conceiving and uttering the pronoun "I" (Sanskirt *aham*). This illustrates the fundamental Indian conviction that a sense of ego is the root of the world illusion. Ego generates fear and desire, and these are the passions that animate all life and even all being; for it is only after the concept "I" has been established that the fear of one's own destruction can develop or any desire for personal enjoyment. The aim of Indian yoga, therefore, is to clear the mind of the concept "I" and therewith dissolve both fear and desire. But this amounts to an undoing of creation—or, at least, of one's psychological participation in its effects. For it leads not only to the knowledge that the seat of anxiety and sorrow is ego, but also to a level of immediate experience, antecedent to all thought, where there is neither hope nor fear but only the rapture of a sheer—and mere—consciousness of being.

In the Hebrew version, on the other hand, the image of the primal androgyne has been applied to a theological reading of the mystery of creation—culminating in a concept of the Jewish people as the agents of God's will, following the failure and disobedience of the divided androgyne in the Garden. To maintain the tension between God and man, the creator is in this mythology held aloof from his creation. It is not the god who falls into a state of exile from his own true nature, but rather his creature; and the exile is not an essentially psychological one, antecedent to and inherent in the concept of the manifold of the universe, but a concrete historical episode occurring in a world already created by a transcendent but not immanent Lord God and universal disciplinarian.

Finally, in the Greek allegory of Plato, the same basic theme has been applied poetically, to give point to a genial, metaphorical interpretation of the mystery of human love, its trials, depth, and delight. And it is worth observing that though the gods are here represented as in a certain sense superior to the beings whom they divide, in a second, ironical sense it is the human beings who are in their love superior. The jealous gods divided them out of fear of their strength.

If we now allow all three of these versions—the Hindu, the Hebrew, and the Greek—to supplement and play against one another in our minds, we shall certainly find it difficult to believe that they have not been derived from a single common tradition; and this probability becomes even more confounding and amazing when the primitive Australian example is considered in relation to the rest. The circumcised boy initiate, embracing the living tree that rises from the head of the first ancestor, before being lanced and therewith identified with the father! Who is he? In this science we must have the courage to compare, so let us not be afraid to draw the obvious parallel (though we may not yet be ready to understand why it should be possible) with Jesus on the cross that rises on the hill of the skull of the first ancestor, whose side is to be opened by a lance in the awesome rite of his at-one-ment with the Father.

There can be little doubt that there is a common tradition back of all these myths. Is it, however, the one and only mythological tradition of our species, so that we may expect to find that its themes and motifs have been coextensive with human thought? If so, then perhaps we should accept without further ado Bastian's theory of the elementary and ethnic ideas.* But if it should appear, on the other hand, that this mythological tradition, though broadly diffused and of prodigious import, is but one of many, or even one of two, completely disparate traditions, then we must inquire when and where it may have originated and what experiences or insights can have brought it forth; likewise, when and where the other traditions originated and from what different experiences or insights. Furthermore, with respect to this particular mythology, are we to think of it as having been diffused, at some remote but determinable period of the past, from the centers of a higher civilization to Australia, where, on flinty soil, a regressive metamorphosis reduced the imagery to its present form; or did a reverse process take place, the material being sublimated from its primitive to the higher forms through centuries of progressive transformation? Or does it represent, rather—as some of the leading theological students of the problem have suggested—the vestiges of a primitive Revelation vouchsafed to man at the commencement of his career on earth?

An early theory of this kind was proposed in the first part of the nineteenth century by the Romantic philosopher Friedrich W. J. von Schelling (1775–1854), who claimed that man was created in the "Center of Godhead," where he beheld all things as they are in God, which is to say, in terms of their essential order; and in this view there was no room or need for myth. But when man had moved from this center to the periphery, his unity in the

* Cf. supra, p. 32.

center being gone, his vision was no longer superior to things, for he had sunk to the level of being a mere thing himself; and it was on this level that the various polytheistic mythologies arose as uncentered man's dreams of his own lost state of being. Schelling believed, however, that man's original unity in God had been imperfect, since in this state he had not yet had the experience of testing his own freedom. Hence, the polytheistic mythologies represent a stage (or rather, series of stages) in a historical progress toward the manifestation of the Second Adam in the ultimate religion of Christ. In the heathen religions Christ is implicit; in the Old Testament, prophesied; and in the New Testament, revealed. Thus Christianity is innate in human life and as old as the world.[82]

Such an idea could have been developed from a reading of certain passages of the early Church Fathers; for example, Tertullian's statement (c. 160–230 A.D.) that "the soul is naturally Christian" (*anima naturaliter christiana*). But Schelling might also have developed his thought independently; for the phenomenology that gave rise to Bastian's theory of elementary ideas has been observed by many throughout the history of the intercourse of the races. Analogies—even minute analogies—exist far too numerously between the mythological traditions of the higher and lower cultures to be dismissed as the mere fall of chance; and those weaving a net of common strands between the Christian liturgy and such barbarous rites as those of our severely shaken Aranda lads are particularly strong. Let us return, therefore, to the mystery of their resurrection.

When the boys have died their death to childhood and survived their painful metamorphosis into incarnations of the original androgynous being, they are told that they have no further operations to fear. There is one more extremely interesting event in store, however, when, following a season of some four full months of continuous dancing and viewing of the world-establishing mythological age of the cosmic "dream time," they will be shown —in a very mysterious way—a particularly important double *tjurunga,* after which they will be roasted on a hot, though smothered, fire, and finally sent back to the women's camp to be received by their waiting brides as fully tested and warranted Aranda males.

The great festival of initiatory rites at the conclusion of which the double *tjurunga* is exposed is known as the Engwura ceremony, and the detailed account of its pantomimes in the work of Spencer and Gillen occupies more than a hundred pages. The ceremonies are conducted by a number of tribal groups, which have come together with some eighteen or twenty young men to be initiated, and the festal spirit, growing greater and greater from week to week, keeps the whole company, by some miracle of the gods, from collapsing in sheer fatigue. The daytime temperature at times reaches a broiling hundred and fifty-six degrees Fahrenheit;[83] nevertheless, the rites go on unabated, and if anyone dies of sunstroke the blame is placed on the black magic of some alien tribe.

A supernatural being called Numbakulla, "Eternal," is supposed to have fashioned the original *tjurungas,* and then, by splitting these, to have made pairs. The pairs were then tied together, one having a man's spirit and one a woman's, the two being mates. And the name of these double *tjurungas* is *ambilyerikirra.*[84]

"The ceremonies," write Spencer and Gillen, "now became very interesting. . . . The leader of the Engwura remained in camp preparing, with the aid of the men of his locality, a special sacred object which consisted of two large wooden *tjurunga,* each three feet in length. They were bound together with human hair string so as to be completely concealed from view, and then the upper three quarters were surrounded with rings of white down, put on with great care, and so closely side by side, that when complete the appearance of rings was quite lost. The top was ornamented with a tuft of owl feathers. When it was made it was carefully hidden in the dry bed of a creek."[85]

The men's camp had been divided from the women's throughout the four months of the ceremony by this dry bed of a stream in which the *tjurunga* now lay buried. There it remained until the candidates for initiation, who had been away from the camp all day on a number of assigned adventures, returned and were made to lie in a row on their backs, while an old man, delegated to watch them, walked back and forth along the line. Perfect silence now fell over the camp. Night had descended; the young men were lying still; their guard was slowly pacing; it was perfectly dark; and the leader of the festival, who had spent the day fashioning the double *tjurunga,* was now squatting with the sacred object in his two hands, having dug it up from its place of hiding in the stream bed. He was holding it upright before his face by the undecorated end, holding it like a bat; and kneeling beside him, at either elbow, was an assistant. These two were supporting his arms, and the man was lifting and lowering the sacred object slowly before his face.

When the boys, returning to camp, had been made to lie down, the solemn trio had been screened from view by a phalanx of old men. Throughout the night, therefore, lying on their backs in the silence, the boys were unaware of what was taking place. The old man with his two assistants, however, was continually lifting and lowering the sacred symbol, as Spencer and Gillen declare, "without any cessation, save for a few seconds at a time, during the whole night." [86]

At a certain moment of the night the older men began chanting, but the boys remained as they were. The guardian still paced before them. And it was not until dawn, when the boys were roused, that the old leader and the two men supporting him ceased from lifting and lowering the *ambilyerikirra.* "There was little wonder," wrote Spencer and Gillen, "that they looked tired and haggard, but even yet their work was not quite done."

> Getting up, they moved to the north end of the ceremonial area, the two sides-men still retaining hold of the leader's arms. The young candidates proceeded to a line of sacred bushes, and having taken boughs, arranged themselves so as to form a solid square behind the leaders. Most of the older men remained on the Engwura ground, from which one of them, the watcher over the candidates, shouted instructions across to the women. The main party, headed by the three men bearing the *ambilyerikirra,* and accompanied by a few of the older men, moved in the form of a solid square out from the Engwura ground, over the river and up the opposite bank

> to where the women stood grouped together. . . . Each woman, with her arms bent at the elbow, moved her open hand, with the palm uppermost, up and down on the wrist as if inviting the men to come on, while she called out *"Kutta, Kutta, Kutta,"* keeping all the while one leg stiff, while she bent the other and gently swayed her body. . . . The party approached slowly and in perfect silence, and when within five yards of the front rank of the women, the men who carried the *ambilyerikirra* threw themselves headlong on the ground, hiding the sacred object from view. No sooner had they done this than the young initiates threw themselves on the top, so that only the heads of the three men could be seen projecting from the pile of bodies. Then, after remaining thus for two minutes, the young men got up and formed into a square facing away from the women, after which the three leaders rapidly jumped up, turned their backs on the women, and were hustled through the square which they then led back to the Engwura ground, and with this the *ambilyerikirra* ceremony came to an end.[87]

Thus were the boys, led by their trinity of mystagogues, introduced as marriageable men to the land of fair women, where the naked sirens who formerly had driven them away were now quaintly beckoning, cooing *"Kutta, Kutta, Kutta";* and we may compare their role to that of Solveig in the poet Ibsen's *Peer Gynt,* who softly sang her cradle song to the spiritual adventurer when he returned to her, following his long man's-madness:

> I will cradle thee, I will watch thee;
> Sleep and dream thou, dear my boy! [88]

I think we shall not be going too far if we also compare the long night of silence, when a deep sleep was allowed to fall upon the young men and the wonderful double *tjurunga* was lifted and lowered, lifted and lowered from nightfall until dawn, with the deep sleep that fell upon Adam when Eve was taken from his side. For after their rite of subincision, the youths, as we have seen, were comparable to Adam as the primordial male-female, fashioned in the image of a god; but, following that night, they were to be shown the Woman. Traversing the river, they passed from the men's dancing ground, the magical land of myth, where the eyes see beings that are eternal and the dream can be lived of "we two are one," to the shore of time, death, and procreation, where the two that are mystically one are to be recognized as practically two: the land, resented by all good Platonists, to which woman leads, as from the Garden Eve. And the way of the young initiate now should be to recognize the wisdom of *"Kutta, Kutta, Kutta"* as well as that of the bull-roarers' thrilling hum, and to let even the subincised penis be a bridge to the toils of life in the world as well as to the garden of the gods.

These rites, then, on the one hand, are certainly particular to Australia, inasmuch as their references to the local animal ancestors—the bandicoot, kangaroo, etc.—are not precisely duplicated anywhere else in the world. Nor shall we find elsewhere anything precisely duplicating the sacred *tjurungas,* to which all Australian mythological themes are systematically referred. In different religions different objects serve as sacra. Yet the idea of regarding as of divine origin a certain specific type of stick or stone, holy wafer, piece of bone, sacred utterance, or what not, is one of those universal traits of the religious life that Bastian termed elementary. Likewise, the motif of the male-female original being, which, as we have seen, has been developed in these Australian rites in considerable detail, from the moment of its first sounding in the ceremony of the two mothers and the two fire-sticks, through the ordeals and related myths of the subincision, to the final night ritual of the supremely sacred double *tjurunga* and the return of the initiates to the women's camp: the richly suggestive symbolism of this powerful motif is certainly duplicated in essence, and often even in detail, in many other traditions of the world. Furthermore, if we consider the underlying hermetic principle of the ritual series we are again on common ground; for in any rite, or system of rites, of initiation the same three stages are to be distinguished as in the rituals of Australia, namely: separation from the community, transformation (usually physical as well as psychological), and return to the community in the new role. The ritual of tossing in the air represented the crisis of separation. The rites of circumcision and subincision effected, irreversibly, the transformation. And the ritual of the double *tjurunga* marked the return.

In sum, then, it may be said that in the education of the young it has been the general custom in traditionally based societies to reorganize the common human inheritance of infantile imprints in such a way as to conduct the energies of the psyche from the primary system of references of infantile dependency into the sphere of the chief concerns of the local groups, but that in this developed reorganization of the primary symbols certain motifs appear that cannot be convincingly described as infantile and yet are not exclusively local either. Throughout the world the rituals of transformation from infancy to manhood are attended with, and effected by, excruciating ordeals. Scourgings, fastings, the knocking out of teeth, scarifications, finger sacrifices, the removal of a testicle, cicatrization, circumcision, subincision, bitings, and burnings are the general rule. These, indeed, make brutally actual a general infantile fantasy of Oedipal aggression; but there is an additional aspect of the situation to be considered, inasmuch as the natural body is transformed by the ordeals into an ever-present sign of a new spiritual state. For even in the gentler, higher societies, where the body is no longer naked and mutilated, new clothes and ornaments are assumed, following initiations, to symbolize and support the new spiritual state. In India the caste marks, tonsure, clothes, etc., represent precisely the individual's social role. In the West we know the military uniform, clerical collar, medical goatee, and judge's wig. But where people are naked, it is the body itself that must be changed. A Marquesan physique fully tattooed was hardly a natural body any more; it was a mythological epiphany, and the consciousness inhabiting it could hardly have wished to behave otherwise than in a manner comporting with the physical form.

One is linked to one's adult role, that is to say, by being identified with a myth—participating actually, physically, oneself, in a manifestation of mythological forms, these being visibly supplied by the roles and patterns of the rite, and the rite, in extension, supporting the form of the society. So that, in sum, we may say that whereas the energies of the psyche in their primary context of infantile concerns are directed to the crude ends of individual pleasure and power, in the rituals of initiation they are reorganized and implicated in a system of social duty, with such effect that the individual thenceforth can be safely trusted as an organ of the group.

Pleasure, power, and duty: these are the systems of reference of all experience on the natural level of the primitive societies. And when such societies are in form, the first two are subordinated to the last, which, in turn, is mythologically supported and ritually enforced. Ritual is mythology made alive, and its effect is to convert men into angels. For archaic man was not a man at all, in the modern, individualistic sense of the term, but the incarnation of a socially determined archetype. And it was precisely in the rites of initiation that his apotheosis was effected—with what cruel imprint of hermetic art we have now seen.

VI. The Impact of Old Age

Death is foreshadowed by the first signals of old age, which appear even today too soon for pleasure. How much sooner in the primitive past! When the woman of forty-five was a hag and the warrior of fifty an arthritic cripple, when, moreover, disease and the accidents of the hunt and of battle were everyone's immediate experience, Death was a mighty presence who had to be faced boldly even within the safest sanctuary, and whose force had to be assimilated.

An East African vision of this great lord of the world emerges from a folktale of the Basumbwa tribe of the Victoria Nyanza district. The tale is of a young man whose dead father appeared to him, driving the cattle of Death, and conducted him along a path going into the ground, as into a burrow. They came to an area with many people, where the father hid his son and left him. In the morning the Great Chief Death appeared. One side of him was beautiful, but the other rotten, with maggots dropping to the ground. Attendants were gathering up the maggots. They washed the sores and, when they had finished, Death said, "The one born today will be robbed if he goes trading. The woman who conceives today will die with the child. The man who works in his garden will lose the crop. The one who goes into the jungle today will be eaten by the lion." But the next morning Death again appeared, and his attendants washed and perfumed the beautiful side, massaging it with oil, and, when they had finished, Death pronounced a blessing. "The one born today: may he become rich! May the woman who conceives today give birth to a child who will live to be old! Let the one born today go into the market: may he strike good bargains; may he trade with the blind! May the man who goes into the jungle slaughter game; may he discover even elephants! For today I pronounce the benediction."

"If you had arrived today," said the father to his son, "many things would have come into your possession, but now poverty has been ordained for you; so much is clear. Tomorrow you had better go." And the son departed, returning to his home.[89]

Very far from Africa, in the mid-Pacific islands of Hawaii, the land of the dead was also thought to be entered through clefts in the earth. These were called "casting-off places,"[90] and there was one for every inhabited district. The soul, arriving, found there a tree with a gathering of little children around it, who gave directions. One side of the tree looked fresh and green, but the other dry and brittle, and, according to one version of the adventure, the soul had to climb to the top by the brittle side and descend by the same to a level where the children would direct it; if a green branch were taken, it would break and the soul fall to annihilation.[91] According to a second version, however, it was a branch of the green side that should be grasped, which then would break and hurl the soul quickly into "the labyrinth that leads to the underworld."[92]

It is a telling image, this of the tree with the deceptive branches, standing at the entrance to a realm where what would seem to be dead must be known to be living and what to be alive, dead. It is an image of the hope that has everywhere enabled the old to enter willingly the dark gate. And yet, not all can pass; only those who understand the secret of death—which is that death is the other side of what we know as life, and that, just as we must leave childhood when entering upon the duties of maturity, so life when going on to death.

The Hawaiians had several images of the afterlife. Many souls had no abiding place, but only wandered over the waste lands of the world and occasionally entered some living person. Others went into the bodies of sharks, eels, lizards, or owls, and might then become guardians or helpers of the living. But for those who were perfectly successful in the transit of the deceptive tree, there were abiding places according to rank (for the Hawaiians were meticulous about rank). And in these privileged realms sports were played, dangerous sports, as they had been in life, and there was food in abundance requiring no cultivation—fish and taro, yams, coconuts and bananas. The highest of these afterworlds was in a flaming crater at the top of the mountain of the volcano-goddess Pele, where there was no pain, only sheer delight.[93]

The atmosphere of this Polynesian warrior-paradise corresponds to that of the warrior-hall of the Germanic god of warriors, Wotan (Odin, Othin), to which the Valkyrs bore the heroic slain. "And what is the sport of the champions, when they are not fighting?" we read in the twelfth-century *Prose Edda* of the Icelandic warrior-poet, Snorri Sturluson. "Every day, as soon as they are clothed, they put on their armor and go out into the court and fight and fell each other. That is their sport; and when the time draws near for their midday meal, they all ride home to Valhall and sit down to drink." [94] The Valkyrs, Odin's daughters, there attend to the flagons and table service, [95] gold illumines the hall, and swords are used instead of fire.[96]

The Hawaiian tree with the deceptive branches, of which one side seems to be alive but the other dead, suggests the Eddic World Ash, Yggdrasil, whose shaft was the pivot of the revolving heavens, with the World Eagle perched on its summit, four stags running among its branches, browsing on its leaves, and the Cosmic Serpent gnawing at its root:

> The ash Yggdrasil suffers anguish,
> More than men can know:
> The stag bites above; on the side it rots;
> And the dragon gnaws from beneath.[97]

It is the greatest of all trees and the best, the ash where the gods give judgment every day. Its limbs spread over the world and stand above heaven. Its roots penetrate the abyss. And its name, Yggdrasil, means "The horse of Ygg," whose other name is Odin; for this great god once hung on that tree nine days, in the way of a sacrifice to himself.

I ween that I hung on the windy tree,
Hung there for nights full nine;
With the spear I was wounded, and offered I was
To Odin, myself to myself,
On that tree that none may ever know
What root beneath it runs.[98]

We have here certainly hit upon a series of images aptly contrived to render certain hopes, fears, and realizations concerning the mystery of death, such as might well have arisen spontaneously in many parts of the world in the minds of those facing the dark gate. Or, since these images of the tree or man that is at once dead and alive do not appear in isolation, but always amid comparable contexts of associated motifs, should we not look for signs of a prehistoric distribution of the syndrome from a single myth-making center to the rest of the world? In the puberty rites we found the imagery of the androgyne associated with a tree or great pole. Here we again have the tree, and again a dual association: not the duality of male and female, but that of life and death. Are these two dualities mythologically related? To realize that they may indeed be linked, one need only think of the Bible story of the First Adam, who became Adam and Eve and fell by the tree, bringing into the world both death and its counterbalance, procreation. Add to this, then, the figure of the Second Adam, Christ, by whose death on the "tree" eternal life was given to man, and a key to the structuring of the many-faceted image will have been found. It is a threshold image, uniting pairs-of-opposites in such a way as to facilitate a passage of the mind beyond anxiety. But then, may it not have emerged independently in many parts of the world as a naturally given poetic inspiration? The associated notion of the underworld as a realm of the dead, entered by a cleft or burrow in the earth, would seem to be natural enough also; likewise, the related themes of the labyrinth and abyss of water. We have already recognized these as possible imprints from the period of the infant's view and experience of the world.* And so, once again, we are brought to the delicate psychological problem of the force of the imprints of infancy, and Bastian's theory of the elementary ideas.

Can it be, that, as old age approaches and the body begins to fail in the manly tasks to which it was long ago assigned in the rites of initiation, the energies of the psyche drop back, regress, or revert to the earlier system of childhood and so reactivate the old context of the dear but frightening mother womb and the terrible father? Are we to say that the old expression, "second childhood," is thus of unexpected depth? Or is it rather that, as age approaches, the mind begins everywhere to withdraw from the local system of interests (having by now, so to say, used them up), moving on, in natural anticipation (since man is the one animal that knows of death's approach), to an anxious brooding on the mystery of the next threshold—which, indeed, can hardly be said to be a function of the local scene, but is the same for all mankind? And can it be said that then, as in the case of the imagery of infancy, an experience of such force and consistency smites the mind that we may speak confidently of an imprint universally struck upon some psychological mechanism open to receive it? Either case may be possible—or both. And either way, the shift is from a local to a generally human system of references. The concerns of house, village, and field boundary fade, and the lineaments of a dark mystery appear gradually from the night that is both without and within. The mind is summoned to a new task; one, however, which, like suffering and rapture, is a grave and constant factor in the experience of the human race. And the force of this factor in the shaping of myths, even among the remotest peoples, surely is to be held in the reckoning of our science.

For in all societies, whether primitive or advanced, the maintenance of the religious forms is in charge, largely, of the old, the younger adults being busy with the physical maintenance not only of themselves and their children, but also of their parents and

* Supra, pp. 61–71.

grandparents. Furthermore, the old in many societies spend a considerable part of their time playing with and taking care of the youngsters, while the parents delve and spin; so that the old are returned to the sphere of eternal things not only within but without. And we may take it also, I should think, that the considerable mutual attraction of the very young and the very old may derive something from their common, secret knowledge that it is they, and not the busy generation between, who are concerned with a poetic play that is eternal and truly wise. Have we not already heard the words of the old, life-pummeled shaman Najagneq concerning the wisdom of Sila, the upholder of the universe, who is "so mighty that his speech to man comes not through ordinary words, but through storms, snowfall, rain showers, the tempests of the sea, through all the forces that man fears, or through sunshine, calm seas, or small, innocent, playing children who understand nothing"?

It is not in the writings of Sigmund Freud but in those of Carl Jung that the most profound analytical consideration has recently been given to the problem confronting all men throughout the long last portion of the human cycle of life: that, namely, of the irresistible approach of King Death. "A human being," Jung once wrote,

> would certainly not grow to be seventy or eighty years old if this longevity had no meaning for the species to which he belongs. The afternoon of human life must have a significance of its own and cannot be merely a pitiful appendage to life's morning. The significance of the morning undoubtedly lies in the development of the individual, our entrenchment in the outer world, the propagation of our kind and the care of our children. But when this purpose has been attained—and even more than attained—shall the earning of money, the extension of conquests, and the expansion of life go steadily on beyond the bounds of all reason and sense? Whoever carries over into the afternoon the law of the morning—that is, the aims of nature—must pay for so doing with damage to his soul just as surely as a growing youth who tries to salvage his childish egoism must pay for this mistake with social failure. Money-making, social existence, family and posterity are nothing but plain nature—not culture. Culture lies beyond the purpose of

> nature. Could by any chance culture be the meaning and purpose of the second half of life?
>
> In primitive tribes, we observe that the old people are almost always the guardians of the mysteries and the laws, and it is in these that the cultural heritage of the tribe is expressed.[99]

"As a physician I am convinced that it is hygienic," Jung declares elsewhere, with an apology for employing such a clinical term with reference to religion, "to discover in death a goal toward which one can strive; and that shrinking away from it is something unhealthy and abnormal which robs the second half of life of its purpose. I therefore consider the religious teaching of a life hereafter consonant with the standpoint of psychic hygiene. When I live in a house that I know will fall about my head within the next two weeks, all my vital functions will be impaired by this thought; but if, on the contrary, I feel myself to be safe, I can dwell there in a normal and comfortable way. From the standpoint of psychotherapy it would therefore be desirable to think of death as only a transition—one part of a life-process whose extent and duration escape our knowledge." And in fact, as Dr. Jung then notes and all of us well know, "a large majority of people have from time immemorial felt the need of believing in a continuance of life. In spite of the fact that by far the larger part of mankind does not know why the body needs salt, everyone demands it none the less because of an instinctive compulsion. It is the same in things of the psyche. The demands of therapy, therefore, do not lead us into any bypaths, but down the middle of the roadway trodden by humankind. And therefore we are thinking correctly with respect to the meaning of life, even though we do not understand what we think." [100]

Observations such as these have earned for Dr. Jung the reputation of being a mystic—though actually they are no more mystical than the recommendation of a hobby to a mind becoming ossified in its office task would be. Jung has here simply said that in the afternoon of life the symbolism of King Death does in fact conduce to a progressive inclination of the energies of the psyche, and hence to maturity. Nor does he think it necessary, or even possible, to "understand" the ultimate secret of the force of such symbolic forms. For, as he asks,

> Do we ever understand what we think? We understand only such thinking as is a mere equation and from which nothing comes out but what we have put in. That is the manner of working of the intellect. But beyond that there is a thinking in primordial images—in symbols that are older than historical man; which have been ingrained in him from earliest times, and, eternally living, outlasting all generations, still make up the groundwork of the human psyche. It is possible to live the fullest life only when we are in harmony with these symbols; wisdom is a return to them. It is a question neither of belief nor knowledge, but of the agreement of our thinking with the primordial images of the unconscious. They are the source of all our conscious thoughts, and one of these primordial images is the idea of life after death.[101]

We may let this statement stand as the most radical to be presented for the point of view of the elementary ideas; the new, important themes here added to the general theory being that of the progressive life-furthering influence of these ideas, and that of the new value they acquire in the second half of life, when, as Dr. Jung has so frequently stated, "man's values and even his body tend to undergo a reversal into opposite." [102] Old men become womanish, old women mannish, the fear of life becomes a fear of death. And so now it is the dry branches, not the green, of the universal tree around which the heavens spin that must be grasped and painfully climbed.

However, there is an important difficulty to be noted before we commit ourselves to any general psychological interpretation of the mythological symbolism of King Death; for, as any seasoned anthropologist can readily show, neither the imprints of experience nor the images associated with the mystery of death are universal.

Leo Frobenius was the first, I believe, to point out that two contrasting attitudes toward death appear among the primitive peoples of the world.[103] Among the hunting tribes, whose life style is based on the art of killing, who live in a world of animals that kill and are killed and hardly know the organic experience of a natural death, all death is a consequence of violence and is generally ascribed not to the natural destiny of temporal beings but to magic. Magic is employed both to defend against it and to deliver it to others, and the dead themselves are regarded as dangerous spirits, resenting their dispatch to the other world and now seeking revenge for their miserable state on those still alive. Indeed, as Frobenius formulates the attitude: "The power exercised by the living individual for good, the dead exercises for evil; so that the better he was, the worse will he become; and the mightier he was in life, the greater must be the restraining weight of bonds and stones upon his corpse. In short: the better and stronger the living, the more dangerous his ghost." [104] Frobenius gives a considerable series of examples from Africa and antiquity of corpses bound in ropes, bandages, or nets to keep their ghosts from roaming, with the orifices of their bodies stopped to keep the ghosts inside, buried under heaps of stones to keep them down, or simply tossed to the wolves and hyenas, with the hope that they will be consumed that very night.

Among the Australian Aranda, according to the detailed account of Spencer and Gillen,[105] the village where a death has occurred is burned to the ground, the person's name is never mentioned, a number of painful and awkward ordeals are imposed on the widow and nearest relatives to ensure that the dead man shall regard himself as properly mourned, and finally, a dance and wild commotion of shouting, ground-beating, and mutual mayhem is enacted by the relatives on the grave itself, so that the deceased may know that he must not come back in such a way as to frighten people any more—though he may still watch over his friends if he likes, visit them gently in dreams, and guard them from evil. We may say that in a cultural atmosphere of this sort death is interpreted as terminal, as far as the relationship of the deceased to his society is concerned, and its mystery is in a sense denied and defied, feared yet challenged, never having been assimilated either psychologically or philosophically. Old age then leads to an attitude of resistance and to a pattern of thought and feeling that may be called that of the plucky old warrior, fighting to the end.

For the planting folk of the fertile steppes and tropical jungles, on the other hand, death is a natural phase of life, comparable to the moment of the planting of the seed, for rebirth. As an example of the attitude, we may take the composite picture presented by Frobenius of the sort of burial and reliquary rites that he observed everywhere among the horticulturalists of South and East Africa.

> When an old kinsman of the sib dies, a cry of joy immediately fills the air. A banquet is arranged, during which the men and women discuss the qualities of the deceased, tell stories of his life, and speak with sorrow of the ills of old age to which he was subject in his last years. Somewhere in the neighborhood—preferably in a shady grove—a hollow has been dug in the earth, covered with a stone. It now is opened and there within lie the bones of earlier times. These are pushed aside to make room for the new arrival. The corpse is carefully bedded in a particular posture, facing a certain way, and left to itself then for a certain season, with the grave again closed. But when time enough has passed for the flesh to have decayed, the old men of the sib open the chamber again, climb down, take up the skull, and carry it to the surface and into the farmstead, where it is cleaned, painted red and, after being hospitably served with grain and beer, placed in a special place along with the crania of other relatives. From now on no spring will pass when the dead will not participate in the offerings of the planting time; no fall when he will not partake of the offerings of thanks brought in at harvest: and in fact, always before the planting commences and before the wealth of the harvest is enjoyed by the living. Moreover, the silent old fellow participates in everything that happens in the farmstead. If a leopard fells a woman, a farmboy is bitten by a snake, a plague strikes, or the blessing of rain is withheld, the relic is always brought into connection with the matter in some way. Should there be a fire, it is the first thing saved; when the puberty rites of the youngsters are to commence, it is the first to enjoy the festival beer and porridge. If a young woman marries into the sib, the oldest member conducts her to the urn or shelf where the earthly remains of the past are preserved and bids her take from the head of an ancestor a few kernels of holy grain to eat. And this, indeed, is a highly significant custom; for when this young, new vessel of the spirit of the sib becomes pregnant, the old people of the community watch to see what similarities will exist between the newly growing and the faded life. . . .[106]

Frobenius terms the attitude of the first order "magical," and the latter "mystical," observing that whereas the plane of reference of the first is physical, the ghost being conceived as physical, the second renders a profound sense of a communion of death and life in the entity of the sib. And anyone trying to express in words the sense or feeling of this mystic communion would soon learn that words are not enough: the best is silence, or the silent rite.

Not all the rites conceived in this spirit of the mystic community are as gentle, however, as those just described. Many are appalling, as will soon be shown. But through all there is rendered, whether gently or brutally, an awesome sense of this dual image, variously turned, of death in life and life in death: as in the form of the Basumbwa Chief Death, one of whose sides was beautiful, but the other rotten, with maggots dropping to the ground; or in the Hawaiian tree with the deceptive branches at the casting-off place to the other world, one side of which looked fresh and green but the other dry and brittle.

When the rites and mythologies even of the most primitive planting villages are compared with those of any tribe of hunters, it is readily seen that they represent a significant deepening both of religious feeling and of the commitment of the individual to communal life; the hunters, comparatively, are rugged individualists. For it is in the rituals and mysteries of the group that the planters not only achieve their sense of the entity of the sib, but also learn the way by which the dangers of the journey to the happy land of the dead are to be overcome and the company joined of the ancestors, who from there work as a continuing presence in the living memory of the rite. The living and the dead are thus, so to say, the matched hemispheres, light and dark, of a single sphere, which is being itself; and the mystery or wonder of this being is the final reference of such symbols as those just seen in the Great Chief and the paradoxical tree.

Moreover, where death and life are joined in a single living round, as in the imagery of the plant and its seed, the passage of the individual from the state of childhood, through maturity, to the period of old age is marked by his graduation through clearly recognized age grades, to each of which particular social duties and functions are assigned. Among the natives of Malekula, for example, where, as already noted, the soul at the entrance to the underworld is challenged by a spirit to complete the design of a labyrinth which the individual during his life was taught in the rites of his society, five age grades are recognized for the male. These are: (1) the male child, (2) the young man, (3) the middle-aged man, (4) the old man (gray-headed), and (5) the very old man (white-headed). These grades, furthermore, continue after death, the ghost remaining in the age grade attained during life. And only the old or the very old man is able to proceed to the end of the journey, the ultimate land of the dead, which, like the paradise of the Hawaiian chiefs, is on the summit of a great volcano. There the dead dance every night among the flames;[107] whereas men of the younger age grades, not having completed the course of their initiation into the mystery of death through life, remain in the entrance cave, in which, as we have seen, there is a tree that has to be climbed, much as in the casting-off places of Hawaii.

Two contrasting images of death, then, have fashioned two contrasting worlds of myth: one deriving from the impact, imprint, or *upādhi* of life and death in the animal sphere; the other from the model of the cycle of death and rebirth in the plant.

In the first domain the paramount object of experience is the beast. Killed and slaughtered, it yields to man its flesh to become his substance, teeth to become his ornaments, hides for clothing and tents, sinews for ropes, bones for tools. The animal life is translated into human life entirely, through the medium of death, slaughter, and the arts of cooking, tanning, sewing. So that, if it be true, as Géza Róheim has suggested, that "whatever is killed becomes father," it should be no cause for wonder that the animals in the mythologies of the Great Hunt are revered as spiritual fathers. The enigma of the totem (the curious dual image, at once animal and human, from which both the clan and the animal species of like name are supposed to be derived and which is the key figure in the social thinking of many hunting tribes) is by this formula perfectly interpreted. For, just as a father is the model for his son, so is the animal for the hunter. And in the way, perhaps, of a wonderful game (Huizinga), or perhaps rather of a seizure (Frobenius),* the whole world of man becomes linked to the world of the animal to an extent that for people whose world-picture, like our own, cleaves to the model of the plant is very difficult to conceive. The history, distribution, and chief structures of the mythologies of this type—the mythologies of the primitive hunters—are discussed in Part Three.

In Part Two, the question, already posed, of the relationship of the high mythologies of the Near East, Europe, and Greater Asia to the primitive imagery of Chief Death and the Cosmic Tree is pursued. This more mystical mythology, in which man finds life and death to be alternating phases in the temporal manifestation "of something far more deeply interfused," is closer than the other to our own; yet the two may be of equal age. Or, at least, as far into the well of the past as the flicker of our little candle of science can reach, signs of the two are to be seen.

And so what shall be said now of Bastian's psychological theory of the elementary and ethnic ideas? Can it be argued that two such contradictory mythologies could have stemmed from a single psychological inheritance?

Indeed it can. For, just as in the earliest stages of every human biography the images of mother and father involve contradictory traits—threatening and protecting, malignant and benign—so also, in the latter years, the image of death. And just as in one biography it is the negative aspect of a parental image, but in another case the positive, that determines the ultimate structuring of the psyche and its dreams, according to local circumstance, so here, in the larger sphere of the adult's attitude toward death, the negative or positive attitude may be taken according to the lessons either of the fierce animals as mystagogue, or of the gentler plant. The elementary idea (*Elementargedanke*) is never itself directly figured in mythology, but always rendered by way of local ethnic ideas or forms (*Völkergedanke*), and these, as we now perceive, are locally conditioned and may reflect attitudes either of resistance or of assimilation.

* Cf. supra, pp. 22–23.

The imagery of myth, therefore, can never be a direct presentation of the total secret of the human species, but only the function of an attitude, the reflex of a stance, a life pose, a way of playing the game. And where the rules or forms of such play are abandoned, mythology dissolves—and, with mythology, life.

Part Two

THE MYTHOLOGY OF THE PRIMITIVE PLANTERS

Chapter 3

THE CULTURE PROVINCE OF THE HIGH CIVILIZATIONS

One of the most interesting of the many recent developments in the field of archaeological research has been the steady progress of the excavations in the Near East, which now are bringing into focus the centers of origin and path of diffusion of the earliest neolithic culture forms. To introduce the main results of the work pertinent to our present theme, it may be noted, first, that the arts of grain agriculture and stockbreeding, which are the basic forms of economy supporting the high civilizations of the world, now seem to have made their first appearance in the Near East somewhere between 7500 and 4500 B.C., and to have spread eastward and westward from this center in a broad band, displacing the earlier, much more precariously supported hunting and food-collecting cultures, until both the Pacific coast of Asia and the Atlantic coasts of Europe and Africa were attained by about 2500 B.C. Meanwhile, in the nuclear zone from which this diffusion originated, a further development took place, circa 3500 to 2500 B.C., which yielded all the basic elements of the archaic high civilizations—writing, the wheel, mathematics, the calendar, kingship, priestcraft, the symbolism of the temple, taxation, etc.—and the mythological themes specific to this second development were then diffused comparatively rapidly, together with the technological effects, along the ways already blazed, until once again the coasts of the Pacific and Atlantic were attained.

I. The Proto-Neolithic: c. 7500–5500 B.C.

The first phase of this crucial transformation of society appears to be represented by a series of discoveries made in the middle nineteen-twenties by Dorothy Garrod at the so-called Mount Carmel caves in Palestine.[1] Artifacts similar to those she found have since been discovered as far south as Helwan, Egypt, as far north as Beirut and Yabrud, and as far east as the Kurdish hills of Iraq. The industry is known to archaeology as the Natufian, and may have flourished anywhere from the eighth to fifth milenniums B.C.; the dating is still extremely obscure.* We may term its vaguely defined era the proto-neolithic and its stage of development "terminal food-gathering." The materials suggest a congeries of nomadic, or semi-nomadic, hunting tribes with a rich variety of flint and bone implements of a late paleo-microlithic type, not yet dwelling in villages yet supplementing their food supply with some variety of grainlike grass; for sickle blades made of stone have been found among the remains, and these suggest a harvest. Numerous bones of the pig, goat, sheep, ox, and of an equid of some sort let us know, furthermore, that if the Natufians were not yet domesticating, they were nevertheless slaughtering, the same beasts that would later constitute the basic barnyard stock of all the higher cultures. Their style of life was transitional, between the stages of food collecting and cultivation.

The real crux of the archaeological problem of the origin of the basic arts of the food-cultivators, however, rests in the question, still unanswered, as to whether such Near Eastern remains actually represent the first steps toward agriculture and stock-breeding taken anywhere in the world, or may not, rather, represent merely an area of peripheral acculturation, the superficial adoption by nomadic hunters of ideas and elements derived from somewhere else.

* "Before 8000 B.C.," according to Walter A. Fairservis, Jr. ("The Ancient East," *Natural History*, November 1958, p. 505), but "within five hundred years either way of about 5000 B.C.," according to Robert J. Braidwood (*Primitive Men*, Chicago Natural History Museum, 3rd edition, 1957, p. 113). A sensible tentative mean would seem to be c. 7500–5500 B.C., as noted here.

According to a view that has been gaining force in recent decades, the latter is the more likely case. The first plantings should be sought, according to this conjecture, in that broad equatorial zone where the vegetable world has supplied not only the food, clothing, and shelter of man since time out of mind, but also his model of the wonder of life—in its cycle of growth and decay, blossom and seed, wherein death and life appear as transformations of a single, superordinated, indestructible force.* Today we find throughout this immense area a well-developed style of village life based on a garden economy of yams, coconuts, bananas, taro, etc., as well as a characteristic cultural assemblage including rectangular gabled huts, drums made of split logs and a way of communicating by drum beats, a galaxy of distinctive musical instruments, secret societies of a particular kind, tattooing, a type of bow and feathered arrow, such forms of burial and skull cult as have just been described for South or East Africa,† bird-, snake-, and crocodile-worship, spirit posts and huts, particular methods of making fire, and a way of fashioning cloth of palm fiber and of bark.[2] Add to these an elaborate ritual lore culminating in communal rites of animal and human sacrifice, a mythology of the journey to the land of the dead in many particulars resembling that of the Malekulan guardian of the labyrinth,‡ an astonishing community of folklore motifs, and the spread of a single linguistic complex (the Malayo-Polynesian) from Madagascar, off the coast of Southeast Africa, to Easter Island,[3] and you have a considerable base from which to argue for a common sphere. Furthermore, when it is observed (and this point is of particular moment) that it was just beyond the eastern finger of this sphere that a highly developed system of agriculture appeared in Peru and Middle America, based largely on maize but including also some fifty-odd other crops and associated with the breeding of llamas and alpacas (in Peru) and turkeys (in Mexico), whereas midway in the same vast zone (the Southeast Asian neighborhood of Indo-China and Indonesia) rice agriculture, the soybean, the water-buffalo,

* Cf. supra, pp. 126–129.
† Supra, p. 127.
‡ Supra, pp. 68–69.

and domestic fowl first appear, it cannot be surprising that a number of scholars have developed the concept of a single culture realm, out of which, or in association with which, three major matrices of grain agriculture matured, namely: Southeast Asia (rice), the Near East (wheat and barley), and Peru and Middle America (maize).

The archaeologists spading up the Near East, stage by stage, however, tend to believe that they are fathoming there the ultimate reach of the problem of the origins of the neolithic village—at least for the Afro-Eurasian hemisphere. In their view, the Southeast Asian complex would represent, then, the local adaptation of a system of arts carried thither by diffusion. And comparably, many of those now exploring the origins of the high civilizations of Peru and Middle America believe that these too developed independently of the primitive gardening complex of the Madagascar-to-Easter-Island axis. The question is extremely complex and, for some reason, tends to involve scholars emotionally. I return to it in the following chapters, and meanwhile focus attention on a brief reconstruction of the Near Eastern chapter of this intricate story.

II. The Basal Neolithic: c. 5500–4500 B.C.*

The second phase of the crucial Near Eastern development can be assigned schematically to the millennium between 5500 and 4500 B.C. and termed the basal neolithic. Settled village life on the basis of an efficient barnyard economy now becomes a well-established pattern in the nuclear region, the chief grains being wheat and barley, and the animals the pig, goat, sheep, and ox (the dog having joined the human family much earlier as an aid to the hunters of the late paleolithic, perhaps c. 15,000 B.C.). Pottery and weaving have been added to the sum of human skills; likewise

* The recent claims of a town-level at Jericho "at a period which must approach the Eighth Millennium," if substantiated, would require us to move the upper date for the basal neolithic back to c. 7000 B.C. However, many authorities doubt the evidence; e.g., Braidwood, op. cit., p. 120, and W. F. Albright, "A Survey of the Archaeological Chronology of Palestine from Neolithic to Middle Bronze," in Robert W. Ehrich, ed., *Relative Chronologies in Old World Archaeology* (Chicago: University of Chicago Press, 1954), p. 29, note 2.

the arts of carpentry and housebuilding. And the role of women has perhaps already been greatly enhanced, both socially and symbolically; for whereas in the hunting period the chief contributors to the sustenance of the tribes had been the men and the role of the women had been largely that of drudges, now the female's economic contributions were of first importance. She participated—perhaps even predominated—in the planting and reaping of the crops, and, as the mother of life and nourisher of life, was thought to assist the earth symbolically in its productivity.

However, no one can speak with certainty of the social and religious place of woman in this period, for the meager evidence of the bones and coarse pottery shards reveals nothing of her lot. One has to read back, hypothetically, from the evidence of the following millennium (4500–3500 B.C.), when a multitude of female figurines appear among the potsherds. These suggest that the obvious analogy of woman's life-giving and nourishing powers with those of the earth must already have led man to associate fertile womanhood with an idea of the motherhood of nature. We have no writing from this pre-literate age and no knowledge, consequently, of its myths or rites. It is therefore not unusual for extremely well-trained archaeologists to pretend that they cannot imagine what services the numerous female figurines might have rendered to the households for which they were designed. However, we know well enough what the services of such images were in the periods immediately following—and what they have remained to the present day. They give magical psychological aid to women in childbirth and conception, stand in house shrines to receive daily prayers and to protect the occupants from physical as well as from spiritual danger, serve to support the mind in its meditations on the mystery of being, and, since they are frequently charming to behold, serve as ornaments in the pious home. They go forth with the farmer into his fields, protect the crops, protect the cattle in the barn. They are the guardians of children. They watch over the sailor at sea and the merchant on the road.

A number of the typical and apparently perennial roles of this mother-goddess can be learned, furthermore, by simply perusing the Roman Catholic "Litany of Loreto," which is addressed to the Virgin Mother Mary. She is there called the Holy Mother of God, the Mother of Divine Grace and Mother of Good Counsel; the Virgin most renowned, Virgin most powerful, Virgin most merciful, Virgin most faithful; and she is praised as the Mirror of Justice, Seat of Wisdom, Cause of our Joy, Gate of Heaven, Morning Star, Health of the Sick, Refuge of Sinners, Comforter of the Afflicted, and Queen of Peace; Tower of David, Tower of Ivory, and House of Gold.

Among the symbols associated with the great goddess in the archaic arts of the Mediterranean we find the mirror, the kingly throne of wisdom, the gate, the morning and evening star, and a column flanked by lions rampant. Moreover, among the numerous neolithic figurines of her we see her standing pregnant, squatting as though in childbirth, holding an infant to her breast, clutching her breasts with her two hands, or one breast while pointing with the other hand to her genitals (the posture modified in the Roman period in the celebrated image of the same goddess found in the porticus of Octavia and now in Florence, the Medicean Venus). Or again, we may see her endowed with the head of a cow, bearing in her arms a bull-headed child; standing naked on the back of a lion; or flanked by animals rampant, lions or goats. Her arms may be opened to the sides, as though to receive us, or extended, holding flowers, holding serpents. She may be crowned with the wall of a city. Or again, she may be seen sitting between the horns, or riding on the back, of a mighty bull.

III. The High Neolithic: C. 4500–3500 B.C.

In the period in which this neolithic constellation of naked female figurines first appears, and which may be called the high neolithic, the pottery becomes suddenly—very suddenly—extraordinarily fine and beautifully decorated; showing, moreover, a totally new concept of ornamental art and of the organization of aesthetic forms, one such as had never before appeared in the history of the world. In the earlier, paleolithic art of the great caves of southern France and northern Spain—of which we treat in Part Three—one finds no evidence of any concept of the *geo-*

metrical organization of an aesthetic field. In fact, the painted or incised surfaces of the cave walls were so little regarded as fields of aesthetic interest that the animals frequently overlap each other in great tangles. Nor do we find anything like a geometrically organized aesthetic field in the works surviving from the later, terminal stages of the paleolithic. Many of the petroglyphs in the later stages of the hunting age have lost their earlier impressionistic beauty and precision; some have even deteriorated into mere geometrical scrawls or abstractions. Furthermore, on certain flat painted pebbles that have been found in what were apparently religious sanctuaries of the hunters, geometrical devices appear: the cross, the circle with a dot in the center, a line with a dot on either side, stripes, meanders, and something resembling the letter E. However, we do not find, even in this latest stage of the hunting period, anything that could be termed a geometrical organization, anything suggesting the concept of a definitely circumscribed field in which a number of disparate elements have been united or fused into one aesthetic whole by a rhythm of beauty. Whereas suddenly—very suddenly—in the period that we are now discussing, which coincides with the appearance in the world of well-established, strongly developing settled villages, there breaks into view an abundance of the most gracefully and consciously organized circular compositions of geometrical and abstract motifs, on the pottery of the so-called Halaf and Samarra styles.

And we find certain symbols in the centers of these designs that have remained characteristic of such organizations to the present day. In the Samarra ware, for example, there occurs the earliest known association of the swastika with the center of a circular composition (there is, in fact, only one earlier known occurrence of the swastika anywhere: on the under-wings of an outstretched flying bird carved of mammoth ivory and found in a paleolithic site not far from Kiev). We find the Maltese cross, too, in the centers of these earliest known geometrical designs—occasionally modified in such a way as to suggest stylized animal forms emerging from the arms; and in several examples the figures of women appear, with their feet or heads coming together in the middle of the circular design, to form a star. Again, the forms of four gazelles may circumambulate a tree. A number of the bowls show lovely wading birds catching fish.

Pottery designs, c. 4000 B.C. Halaf ware (left), Samarra ware (right)

The archaeological site after which this superb series of decorated vessels has been named, Samarra, is located in Iraq, on the river Tigris, some seventy miles above Baghdad; and the area over which the ware has been diffused extends northward to Nineveh, southward to the head of the Persian Gulf, and eastward, across Iran, as far as to the border of Afghanistan. The Halaf ware, on the other hand, is scattered through an area northward of this, with its chief center in northern Syria, just south of the so-called Taurus, or Bull, Mountains of Anatolia (now Turkey), where the river Euphrates and its tributaries descend from the foothills to the plain. And what is most remarkable is the prominence in this beautifully decorated northwestern ware of the bull's head (the so-called bucranium), viewed from the front and with great curving horns. The form is rendered both naturalistically and in variously stylized, very graceful designs. Another prominent device in this series is the double ax. We find the Maltese cross once again, as in Samarra, but no swastika, nor those graceful gazelle designs. Furthermore, in association with the female statuettes (which are numerous in this context) clay figures of the dove appear, as well as of the cow, humped ox, sheep, goat, and pig. One charming fragment represents the goddess standing, clothed, between two goats rampant—that on her left a male, the other a female giving suck to a young kid. And all the symbols are associated in this Halafian culture complex with the so-called beehive tomb.

But this is precisely the complex that appeared a full millennium later in Crete, and from there was carried by sea, through the Gates of Hercules, northward to the British Isles and southward to the Gold Coast, Nigeria, and the Congo. It is the basic complex, also, of the Mycenaean culture, from which the Greeks, and thereby ourselves, derived so many symbols. And when the cult of the dead and resurrected bull-god was carried from Syria to the Nile Delta, in the fourth or third millennium B.C., these symbols went with it. Indeed, I believe that we may claim with a very high degree of certainty that in this Halafian symbology of the bull and goddess, the dove, and the double ax, we have the earliest evidence yet discovered anywhere of the prodigiously influential mythology associated for us with the great names of Ishtar and Tammuz, Venus and Adonis, Isis and Osiris, Mary and Jesus. From the Taurus Mountains, the mountains of the bull-god, who may already have been identified with the horned moon, which dies and is resurrected three days later, the cult was diffused, with the art of cattle-breeding itself, practically to the ends of the earth; and we celebrate the mystery of that mythological death and resurrection to this day, as a promise of our own eternity. But what experience and understanding of eternity, and what of time, gave rise in that early period to this constellation of eloquent forms? And why in the image of the bull?

THE SUMERIANS

An important development, full of meaning and promise for the history of mankind in civilizations to come, took place in the latter part of this same period (c. 4000 B.C.) when certain of the peasant villages began to assume the size and function of market towns and there was an expansion of the culture area southward onto the mud flats of riverine Mesopotamia. This is the period in which the mysterious race of Sumerians first appears on the scene, to establish on the torrid Tigris and Euphrates delta flats sites that were to become presently the kingly cities of Ur, Kish, Lagash, Eridu, Sippar, Shuruppak, Nippur, and Erech. The only natural resources there were mud and reeds. Wood and stone had to be imported from the north, and very soon little copper beads would begin appearing among the imports, for the age of metal was about to dawn. But the mud was fertile, and the fertility annually refreshed. Furthermore, the mud could be fashioned into sun-dried bricks, which now appear for the first time in history, and these could be used for the construction of temples—which likewise now appear for the first time in the history of the world. Their typical form is well known; it was that of the ziggurat in its earliest stages—a little height, artificially constructed, with a sanctuary on its summit for the ritual of the world-generating union of the earth-goddess with the lord of the sky. And if we may judge from the evidence of the following centuries, the queen or princess of each city was in those earliest days identified with the goddess, and the king, her spouse, with the god.

The painted pottery from the earliest level of these south Mesopotamian riverine sites is known to archaeology as Obeid ware, after an excavated mound, Tell el-Obeid, just south of the southern reach of the river Euphrates and not far from the ancient city (soon to rise) of Ur, from which Father Abram and his wife Sarai are supposed to have departed (Genesis 11:31). And this again is a fine, geometrically ornamented ware, somewhat less graceful, perhaps, and less colorful than the products of the rich Halaf and Samarra styles, but remarkably beautiful nevertheless. Its designs, with few exceptions, are not polychromatic, but painted on a light background in one color only, black or brown. And the period is dated circa 4000–3500 B.C.[4]

IV. The Hieratic City State: C. 3500–2500 B.C.

We have taken note of: the proto-neolithic period of the Natufians, which is to be dated somewhere between 7500 and 5500 B.C., when the first signs of an incipient grain agriculture appeared in widely scattered parts of the Near East; the basal neolithic of the earliest settled villages, circa 5500–4500 B.C.,* centered apparently in regions neighboring the upper reaches of the Tigris and Euphrates river systems, but extending eastward into Iran, westward into Anatolia (now Turkey), and southward, along the Mediterranean, into Egypt; and then, finally, the high neolithic of the Halaf and Samarra pottery styles, circa 4500–3500 B.C., and of the Obeid style in the riverine south, circa 4000–3500 B.C., when the abstract concept of a geometrically organized esthetic field and certain abstract and stylized symbols (the Maltese cross, swastika, rosette, double ax, and bucranium) first appear in our documentation of human thought, together with the earliest examples of a neolithic series of naked female figurines, representing functions of the fertility goddess of a well-established, land-rooted peasantry.

This last was the period when the earliest signs of human habitation began appearing in the mud flats of riverine Mesopotamia. Furthermore, over the whole area, from Anatolia to Egypt and from the Mediterranean to Iran, the more strategically situated villages began developing into market towns, while some of the smaller villages seem to have begun specializing in particular crafts: For example, in a small but extremely interesting site known to archaeology as Arpachiya, in northern Iraq, not far from the larger, walled settlement of Nineveh, there was found in the center of the community the large shop of an extraordinarily competent potter, who appears to have been the headman of the village. He had set out many of his bowls on display on shelves around the walls of his comparatively large adobe dwelling; so that we get the impression of a community of peasant potters, tilling their own fields and breeding their cattle, but fashioning their beautiful Halaf ware not for themselves alone but for an elite market somewhere else as well; possibly Nineveh, the nearby larger town. For trade was developing in this period no less than agriculture and the arts—the arts of pottery, stone carving, jewelry, and weaving.[5]

It was, moreover, in the larger market towns of this period, as we have seen, that the earliest ziggurats appeared in the course of

*** But see footnote, supra, p. 138.**

the fourth millennium B.C., symbolizing, apparently, the pivot of the universe, where the life-generating union of the powers of earth and heaven was consummated in a ritual marriage. Perhaps the ritual was enacted by a divine queen and her spouse, if kings and queens can be assumed to have come into being already in this early day. We know exactly nothing of the social and political structure of the high neolithic market town.

However, in the period immediately following—that of the hieratic city state, which may be dated for the south Mesopotamian riverine towns, schematically, circa 3500–2500 B.C.—we encounter a totally new and remarkable situation. For at the level of the archaeological stratum known as Uruk A, which is immediately above the Obeid and can be roughly placed at circa 3500 B.C., the south Mesopotamian temple areas can be seen to have increased notably in size and importance; and then, with stunning abruptness, at a crucial date that can be almost precisely fixed at 3200 B.C. (in the period of the archaeological stratum known as Uruk B), there appears in this little Sumerian mud garden—as though the flowers of its tiny cities were suddenly bursting into bloom—the whole cultural syndrome that has since constituted the germinal unit of all of the high civilizations of the world. And we cannot attribute this event to any achievement of the mentality of simple peasants. Nor was it the mechanical consequence of a simple piling up of material artifacts, economically determined. It was actually and clearly the highly conscious creation (this much can be asserted with complete assurance) of the mind and science of a new order of humanity, which had never before appeared in the history of mankind; namely, the professional, full-time, initiated, strictly regimented temple priest.

The new inspiration of civilized life was based, first, on the discovery, through long and meticulous, carefully checked and rechecked observations, that there were, besides the sun and moon, five other visible or barely visible heavenly spheres (to wit, Mercury, Venus, Mars, Jupiter, and Saturn) which moved in established courses, according to established laws, along the ways followed by the sun and moon, among the fixed stars; and then, second, on the almost insane, playful, yet potentially terrible notion that the laws governing the movements of the seven heavenly spheres should in some mystical way be the same as those governing the life and thought of men on earth. The whole city, not simply the temple area, was now conceived as an imitation on earth of the cosmic order, a sociological "middle cosmos," or mesocosm, established by priestcraft between the macrocosm of the universe and the microcosm of the individual, making visible the one essential form of all. The king was the center, as a human representative of the power made celestially manifest either in the sun or in the moon, according to the focus of the local cult; the walled city was organized architecturally in the design of a quartered circle (like the circles designed on the ceramic ware of the period just preceding), centered around the pivotal sanctum of the palace or ziggurat (as the ceramic designs around the cross, rosette, or swastika); and there was a mathematically structured calendar to regulate the seasons of the city's life according to the passages of the sun and moon among the stars—as well as a highly developed system of liturgical arts, including music, the art rendering audible to human ears the world-ordering harmony of the celestial spheres.

It was at this moment in human destiny that the art of writing first appeared in the world and that scriptorially documented history therefore begins. Also, the wheel appeared. And we have evidence of the development of the two numerical systems still normally employed throughout the civilized world, the decimal and the sexigesimal; the former was used mostly for business accounts in the offices of the temple compounds, where the grain was stored that had been collected as taxes, and the latter for the ritualistic measuring of space and time as well. Three hundred and sixty degrees, then as now, represented the circumference of a circle—the cycle of the horizon—while three hundred and sixty days, plus five, marked the measurement of the circle of the year, the cycle of time. The five intercalated days that bring the total to three hundred and sixty-five were taken to represent a sacred opening through which spiritual energy flowed into the round of the temporal universe from the pleroma of eternity, and they were designated, consequently, days of holy feast and festival. Comparably, the ziggurat, the pivotal point in the center of the sacred circle of space, where the earthly and heavenly powers joined, was also characterized by the number five; for the four sides of the tower, oriented to the points of the compass, came together at the summit, the fifth point, and it was there that the energy of heaven met the earth.

This early Sumerian temple tower with the hieratically organized little city surrounding it, where everyone played his role according to the rules of a celestially inspired divine game, supplied the model of paradise that we find, centuries later, in the Hindu-Buddhist imagery of the world mountain, Sumeru, whose jeweled slopes, facing the four directions, peopled on the west by sacred serpents, on the south by gnomes, on the north by earth giants, and on the east by divine musicians, rose from the mid-point of the earth as the vertical axis of the egg-shaped universe, and bore on its quadrangular summit the palatial mansions of the deathless gods, whose towered city was known as Amaravati, "The Town Immortal." But it was the model also of the Greek Olympus, the Aztec temples of the sun, and Dante's holy mountain of Purgatory, bearing on its summit the Earthly Paradise. For the form and concept of the City of God conceived as a "mesocosm" (an earthly imitation of the celestial order of the macrocosm) which emerged on the threshold of history circa 3200 B.C., at precisely that geographical point where the rivers Tigris and Euphrates reach the Persian Gulf, was disseminated eastward and westward along the ways already blazed by the earlier neolithic. The wonderful life-organizing assemblage of ideas and principles—including those of kingship, writing, mathematics, and calendrical astronomy—reached the Nile, to inspire the civilization of the First Dynasty of Egypt, circa 2800 B.C.; it spread to Crete on the one hand, and, on the other, to the valley of the Indus, circa 2600 B.C.; to Shang China, circa 1600 B.C.; and, according to at least one high authority, Dr. Robert Heine-Geldern, from China across the Pacific, during the prosperous seafaring period of the late Chou Dynasty, between the seventh and fourth centuries B.C., to Peru and Middle America.[6]

If the last fact be true as well as the rest (and its likelihood is considered in the following chapters), then it can be said without exaggeration that all the high civilizations of the world are to be thought of as the limbs of one great tree, whose root is in heaven. And should we now attempt to formulate the sense or meaning of that mythological root—the life-inspiring monad that precipitated the image of man's destiny as an organ of the living cosmos—we might say that the psychological need to bring the parts of a large and socially differentiated settled community, comprising a number of newly developed social classes (priests, kings, merchants, and peasants), into an orderly relationship to each other, and simultaneously to suggest the play through all of a higher, all-suffusing, all-informing, energizing principle—this profoundly felt psychological as well as sociological requirement must have been fulfilled with the recognition, some time in the fourth millennium B.C., of the orderly round-dance of the five visible planets and the sun and moon through the constellations of the zodiac. This celestial order then became the model for mankind in the building of an earthly order of coordinated wills—a model for both kings and philosophers, inasmuch as it seemed to show forth the supporting law not only of the universe but of every particle within it. In our normal earthly way of knowledge, we may become distracted by the multiplicity of the world's effects, as well as by our misdirected desires for personal power and pleasure, and, losing touch with the inward order of our being, go astray. But the law of heaven now shall set us aright; for, as we read—once again—in the words of Plato: "The motions akin to the divine part in us are the thoughts and revolutions of the universe; these, therefore, every man should follow, and correcting those circuits in the head that were deranged at birth, by learning to know the harmonies and revolutions of the world, he should bring the intelligent part, according to its pristine nature, into the likeness of that which intelligence discerns, and thereby win the fulfillment of the best in life set by the gods before mankind both for this present time and for the life to come." [7]

The Egyptian term for this universal order was Ma'at; in India it is Dharma; and in China, Tao.

And if we now try to convey in a sentence the sense and meaning of all the myths and rituals that have sprung from this conception of a universal order, we may say that they are its structuring agents, functioning to bring the human order into accord with the celestial. "Thy will be done on earth, as it is in heaven." The myths and rites constitute a mesocosm—a mediating, middle cosmos, through which the microcosm of the individual is brought into relation to the macrocosm of the all. And this mesocosm is the entire context of the body social, which is thus a kind of living poem, hymn, or icon of mud and reeds, and of flesh and blood, and of dreams, fashioned into the art form of the hieratic city state. Life on earth is to mirror, as nearly perfectly as is possible in human bodies, the almost hidden—yet now discovered—order of the pageant of the spheres.

Chapter 4

THE PROVINCE OF THE IMMOLATED KINGS

1. The Legend of the Destruction of Kash

A legend throwing a beam of light into the past of the now largely Mohammedan Sudan was told in 1912, in the market place of the capital of Kordofan, by a proud graybeard, Arach-ben-Hassul, captain of the camel-boys of the Frobenius Kordofan Expedition. The little city of El Obeid, some 240 miles southwestward of Khartoum,* was teeming with tribesmen from every quarter of the bleak and sparsely populated countryside—Berbers, Arabs, Nubians, forgotten tribesmen from the fastnesses of the outlying hills—who had come streaming in to shout welcome to the new consul general, Lord Kitchener. The period was a delicate one politically. Italy had opened war on Turkey, bombarding Prevaza without warning and occupying Tripoli, Cyrenaica, and the Dodecanese Islands; so that Kitchener, to keep his charges occupied with their own affairs, had instituted a broad program of economic reform: the opening of cotton markets throughout the country, village schools, savings banks, cantonal courts, and a heightening of the Aswan dam. It was a fortunate moment for the science of comparative mythology that set the German pencils to work among the squatting clusters of camel-keepers, cattle nomads, and chivalrous bandits who were listening everywhere to the story-tellers rehearsing the old legends of the great past of Kordofan, of Darfur to the west, Ethiopia eastward, Nubia to the north, and Darnuba

* Not to be confused with the Tell-el-Obeid of Chapter 3, which is in Iraq.

to the south. Arach-ben-Hassul, from the province of Darfur, was a descendant of one of the last surviving families of the old guild of the coppercraftsmen of Kordofan, and he too sat listening. For seven days he sat in silence behind his beard. And when he had listened for seven days, on the eighth day Arach-ben-Hassul stood up, passed his hand across his eyes, down his face, and to his beard, and said, "I speak."

His tale was "The Legend of the Destruction of Kash," of a time—not "once upon a time," but in a period long past—when this region, which today is a cultural as well as a physical desert, was green and great.

"Four kings at that time ruled an empire in this realm," he told the squatting cluster of scions of the great past:

> and the first king dwelt in Nubia, the second in Ethiopia, a third in Kordofan, and the fourth in Darfur; but the richest of the four was the Nap of Napata in Kordofan, whose capital stood near the site of the village now called Hophrat-en-Nahas. The Nap of Napata was the possessor of all the copper and gold of the region. His gold and copper were carried to Nubia, to be sent to the great kings of the West. Also, envoys arrived in his court from eastward, from over sea, by ship. And to the south he held domain over many peoples: these forged for him iron weapons and furnished slaves by the many thousand for his court.
>
> But now, although this king was the richest man on earth, his life was the saddest and shortest of all mankind; for each Nap of Napata could rule but a brief span of years. Throughout his reign the priests every night observed the stars, made offerings, kindled sacred fires; and they were not to miss a night of these prayers and offerings, lest they should lose track of the stars and not know when, according to practice, the king was to be killed. The custom had come down from time out of mind. Night by night, year after year, the priests were to keep watch for the day when the king should be killed.
>
> And so, once again, as so many times before, that day arrived. The hind legs of sacrificial bulls were slashed; the fires of the land were extinguished; women were locked indoors; and the priests kindled the new fire. They summoned the new king. He was the son of the sister of the one just killed, and his name, this time, was Akaf: but Akaf was the king in whose period the ancient customs of the land were changed—and

people say that this change was the cause of the destruction of Napata.

Now the first official act of every Nap of Napata was that of deciding what persons should accompany him on the path of death. They were to be chosen from those dearest to him, and the first named would be the one to lead the rest. A slave named Far-li-mas, celebrated for his story-telling art, had arrived in the court some years before from over sea, sent as a gift by a king of the distant East. And the new Nap of Napata said: "This man shall be my first companion. He will entertain me until the time for my death; and make me happy after death."

When Far-li-mas heard, he was not afraid. He only said to himself: "It is God's will."

And it was, moreover, the custom at that time in Napata that a flame should be kept burning perpetually, just as today in certain secluded places in Darfur; and for its maintenance the priests were to designate a young boy and girl. These should watch the fire, be absolutely chaste throughout their lives, and be killed, not together with the king, but immediately after, at the moment of the kindling of the new flame. And so, now, when the new fire had been established for Akaf, the priests chose as vestal for the coming term the youngest sister of the new king. Her name was Sali—Sali-fu-Hamr. But she was afraid of death and, when she heard how the choice had fallen, was appalled.

The king lived, for a while, happily, in great delight, enjoying the wealth and majesty of his domain. He spent each evening with his friends and with whatever visitors may have come as envoys to the court. But one fateful night God allowed him to realize that with each of these joyous days he was moving one step closer to certain death; and he was filled with fear. He was unable to turn the dreadful thought away and became depressed. Whereupon God sent him a second thought: that of letting Far-li-mas tell a story.

Far-li-mas, therefore, was summoned. He appeared, and the king said: "Far-li-mas, today the day has arrived when you must cheer me. Tell me a story." "The performance is quicker than the command," said Far-li-mas, and began. The king listened; the guests also listened. The king and his guests forgot to drink, forgot to breathe. The slaves forgot to serve. They, too, forgot to breathe. For the art of Far-li-mas was like hashish, and, when he had ended, all were as though enveloped in a delightful swoon. The king had forgotten his thoughts of death. Nor had any realized that they were being held from twilight until dawn; but when the guests departed they found the sun in the sky.

Akaf and his company, that day, could hardly wait till evening; and thereafter, every day, Far-li-mas was summoned to perform. The report of his tales spread throughout the court, the city, the land, and the king presented him, each day, with the gift of a beautiful garment. The guests and envoys gave him gold and jewels. He became rich. And when he now went through the streets he was followed by a troop of slaves. The people loved him. They began to bare their breasts to him, in sign of honor.

Sali, hearing of the wonder, sent a message to her brother. "Let me," she asked, "just once, hear Far-li-mas tell a story!"

"The fulfillment goes before the wish," the king replied.

And Sali came.

Far-li-mas saw Sali and for a moment lost his senses. All that he saw was Sali.

All that Sali saw was Far-li-mas.

The king said: "But why do you not begin your story? Do you not know any more?"

Removing his eyes from Sali, the story-teller began. And his tale was first like the hashish that induces a gentle stupefication, but then like the hashish that carries men through unconsciousness to sleep. After a time the guests were sleeping; the king was sleeping. They were hearing the story only in dream, until they were carried entirely away, and only Sali remained awake. Her eyes were fixed on Far-li-mas. She was filled completely with Far-li-mas. And when he had finished the tale and arose, she, too, arose.

Far-li-mas moved toward Sali: Sali toward Far-li-mas. He embraced her: she embraced him, and she said: "We do not want to die." He laughed into her eyes. "It is yours to command," he said. "Show me the way." And she answered: "Leave me now. I shall think of a way, and when the way has been found, shall call you." They parted. And the king and his guests lay there asleep.

That day, Sali went to the high priest. "Who is it determines the time when the old fire is put out," she asked, "and the new one kindled?"

"That is decided by God," answered the priest.

Sali asked: "But how does God communicate his will to you?"

"Every night we keep watch on the stars," the priest said.

"We do not let them out of our sight. Every night we observe the moon and we know, from night to night, which stars are approaching the moon and which moving away. It is by this that we know."

Sali said: "And you must do that every night? What happens of a night when nothing can be seen?"

The priest said: "On such a night we make many offerings. If a number of nights should pass when nothing could be seen, we should not be able to find our stars again."

Sali said: "Would you then not know when the fire should be extinguished?"

"No," said the priest, "we should not be in a position, then, to fulfill our office."

Whereupon Sali said to him: "God's works are great. The greatest, however, is not his writing in the sky. His greatest work is our life on earth. This I learned last night."

"What do you mean?" said the priest.

And Sali answered: "God gave Far-li-mas the gift of telling tales in a way that has never before been equaled. It is greater than his writing in the sky."

The priest retorted: "You are wrong."

But Sali said to him: "The moon and stars, these you know. But have you heard the tales of Far-li-mas?"

"No," said the priest, "I have not heard them."

She asked: "How, then, can you pronounce a judgment? I assure you that even you priests, when listening, will forget to keep watch of the stars."

"Sister of the king, are you quite sure?"

She answered: "Only prove to me that I am wrong and that the writing in the sky is greater and stronger than this life on earth."

"That is just what I shall prove," said the priest.

And the priest then sent word to the young king. "Allow the priests to come to your palace tonight and listen to the tales of Far-li-mas from the setting to the rising of the sun."

The king consented, and Sali sent word to Far-li-mas: "Tonight you must do as you did before. This will be the way."

And so, when the sun was approaching the hour of its setting and the king, his guests, and the envoys were assembling, they were joined by all the priests, who bared the upper parts of their bodies and prostrated themselves on the ground. The high priest said: "It has been declared that the tales of Far-li-mas are the greatest of God's works." The king said to him: "You may decide for yourselves." "You will pardon us,

O King," prayed the high priest, "if we depart from your palace at the rising of the moon, to fulfill the duties of our office." And the king replied: "Act according to God's will."

Whereupon the priests took their places. The guests and the envoys took their places. The hall was filled with people and Far-li-mas made a way between them. "Begin," said the king. "Begin, my dear Companion in Death." Far-li-mas looked at Sali, Sali at Far-li-mas; and the king said: "But why do you not begin your story? Do you not know any more?"

Removing his eyes from Sali, the story-teller began.

And his tale commenced as the sun was going down. It was like the hashish that beclouds and transports. It was like the hashish that induces faintness. It was like the hashish that sends one into a dead faint. So that when the moon rose, the king, his guests, and the envoys lay asleep, and the priests too lay in a sound sleep. Only Sali was awake, drawing in with her eyes sweet words from the lips of Far-li-mas.

The tale was ended, Far-li-mas rose and moved toward Sali; she toward him, and she said: "Let me kiss these lips, from which come words that are so sweet." She pressed close to his lips, and Far-li-mas said to her: "Let me embrace this form that has given me the power." They embraced, entwining arms and legs, and lay awake among those that slumbered, knowing such happiness as breaks the heart. Rejoicing, Sali asked: "Do you see the way?" "Yes," the other replied, "I do." And they left the hall. So that in the palace there remained only those that slept.

Sali came to the high priest the next morning. "So now tell me," she said, "whether you were right in your condemnation of my judgment."

He answered: "I shall not give my reply today. We must listen once more to Far-li-mas; for yesterday we were not prepared."

And so, the priests attended to their prayers and offerings. The fetlocks of many bullocks were slashed, and throughout the day, without pause, prayers were recited in the temple. When evening came they arrived in the palace.

Sali sat again beside the king, her brother, and Far-li-mas commenced his tale. So that once again, before the dawn had come, all slept—the king, his guests, the envoys, and the priests—enwrapt in rapture. But Sali and Far-li-mas were awake among them and sucked joy from each other's lips. And they embraced again, entwining arms and legs. And thus it continued, from day to day, for many days.

But if there had gone out among the people, at first, the news of Far-li-mas' tales, now there went out among them the rumor that the priests were neglecting their offerings and prayer. Uneasiness began to spread abroad, until, one day, a distinguished gentleman of the city paid a visit to the high priest.

"When do we celebrate the next festival of the season?" he asked. "I am planning a voyage and wish to return for the feast. How long have I got?"

The priest was embarrassed; for it had been many nights since he had seen the moon and stars. He replied: "Wait only one day; then I shall tell you."

"My thanks," said the man. "I shall return tomorrow."

The priests were summoned and their chief inquired: "Which of you, recently, has observed the course of the stars?"

They were silent. Not a single voice replied; for all had been listening to the tales of Far-li-mas.

"Is there not one among you that has observed the course of the stars and position of the moon?"

They sat perfectly still, until one, who was very old, arose and spoke. "We were enchanted," he said, "by Far-li-mas. Not one of us can tell you when the feasts are to be celebrated, when the fire is to be quenched, and when the new fire is to be kindled."

The high priest was terrified. "How can this be?" he cried. "What shall I tell the people?"

The very old priest replied: "It is the will of God. But if Far-li-mas has not been sent by God, let him be killed; for as long as he lives and speaks, everything will listen."

"What, however, shall I tell the man?" the high priest demanded.

Whereat all were silent. And the company, then, silently dispersed.

The high priest went to Sali. "What was it," he asked, "that you said to me on that first day?"

She answered, "I said, 'God's works are great. The greatest, however, is not his writing in the sky, but the life on earth.' You rejected my word as untrue. But now, today, tell me whether I lied."

The priest said to her: "Far-li-mas is against God. He must die."

But Sali answered: "Far-li-mas is the Companion in Death of the king."

The priest said: "I shall speak with the king."

And Sali answered: "God dwells in my brother. Ask him what he thinks."

The high priest proceeded to the palace and addressed himself to the king, whose sister, Sali, now sat beside him. The high priest bared his chest before the king, and, throwing himself on the ground, prayed: "Pardon, Akaf, O my King!"

"Tell me," said the king, "what is in your heart."

"Speak to me," the high priest said, "of Far-li-mas your Companion in Death."

The king said to him: "God sent me, first, the thought of the approaching day of my death, and I was afraid. God sent me, next, the recollection of Far-li-mas, who was sent to me as a gift from the land eastward, beyond the sea. God confused my understanding with the first thought. With the second he enlivened my spirits and made me—and all others—happy. So I gave beautiful garments to Far-li-mas. My friends gave him gold and jewels. He distributed much of this among the people. He is rich, as he deserves to be; and the people love him, as I do."

"Far-li-mas," the high priest said, "must die. Far-li-mas is disrupting the revealed order."

Said the king, "I die before him."

But the priest said: "The will of God will give the decision in this matter."

"So be it! And to this," the king replied, "the whole people shall bear witness."

The priest departed, and Sali spoke to Akaf. "O my King! O my brother! The end of the road is near. The companion of your death will be the awakener of your life. However, I require him for myself, as the fulfillment of my destiny."

"My sister Sali," said Akaf, "then you may take him."

Heralds went out through the city and cried in every quarter that Far-li-mas, that evening, would speak in the great square before all. A veiled throne for the king was erected in the large plaza between the royal palace and the buildings of the priests, and when evening came, the people streamed from all sides and settled everywhere, round about. Thousands upon thousands assembled. The priests arrived and took their places. The guests and the envoys arrived and were seated.

Sali sat beside her brother, Akaf, the veiled king; and Far-li-mas then was called.

He arrived. His entire retinue came behind him, all clothed in dazzling garments, and they placed themselves opposite the priests. Far-li-mas, himself, bowed before the veiled king, and assumed his seat.

The high priest arose. "Far-li-mas has destroyed our established order," he said. "Tonight will show if this was by the will of God." And he resumed his place.

Far-li-mas removed his eyes from Sali, gazed about over the multitude, glanced at the priests, and arose. "I am a servant of God," he said, "and believe that all evil in the human heart is repugnant to God. Tonight," said Far-li-mas, "God will decide." And he commenced his tale.

His words were at first as sweet as honey, his voice penetrating the multitude as the first rain of summer the parched earth. From his tongue there went forth a perfume more exquisite than musk or incense: his head shone like a light, the only luminary in a black night. And his tale in the beginning was like the hashish that makes people happy when awake; then it became like the hashish of a dreamer. Toward morning he raised his voice, however, and his words swelled like the rising Nile in the hearts of the people: they were for some as pacifying as the entrance into Paradise, but as frightening for others as the Angel of Death. Joy filled the spirits of some, horror the hearts of others. And the closer the moment of dawn, the more powerful became his voice, the louder its reverberations within the people, until the hearts of the multitude reared against each other as in a battle; stormed against each other like the clouds in the heavens of a tempestuous night. Lightning bolts of anger and thunderclaps of wrath collided.

But when the sun rose and the tale of Far-li-mas closed, unspeakable astonishment filled the confused minds of all; for when those who remained alive looked about them their glances fell upon the priests—and the priests lay dead upon the ground.

Sali got up and prostrated herself before the veiled king. "O my King!" she said, "O my brother! Akaf! Throw from yourself the veil; show yourself to your people and offer up the offering, now, yourself! For these here have been mowed down by the Angel of Death, Azrail, through God's command."

The servants removed the veil from around the royal

throne and Akaf stood up. He was the first of their line of kings whom the people of Napata had ever seen. He was young, and as beautiful to look upon as the rising sun.

The multitude was jubilant. A white steed was brought, which the king mounted. At his left there walked his sister, at his right, the teller of tales, and he rode to the temple. The young king took up the mattock in the temple and hoed three holes in the holy ground. Far-li-mas tossed three seeds into these. The king then hoed two holes in the holy ground and Sali tossed two seeds into these. Immediately and simultaneously the five seeds sprouted, growing before the eyes of the people, and by noon the heads of grain of all five were ripe. In all the courts of the city the fathers of families slashed the fetlocks of great bulls. The king extinguished the fire in the temple, and all the fathers of the city extinguished the fires of their hearths. Sali kindled the new fire, and all of the young virgins in the city came and took fire from this flame. And since that day, there have been no more human sacrifices in Napata.

Thus Akaf became the first Nap of Napata to remain alive until it pleased God to take him in his old age, and when he died Far-li-mas succeeded to his throne. With that, however, the city of Napata reached the culmination of its fortune and the end. For Akaf's renown as a wise and well-advised prince had spread abroad, through every land, and every king had sent to him men of intelligence, with gifts, to receive the benefit of his advice. Great merchants had settled in his capital and he had had many great ships upon the seas eastward, transporting the products of Napata throughout the world. His mines had not been able to yield gold and copper enough for the demand. And when he was succeeded by Far-li-mas, the fortune of the realm rose even higher, to its climax. The fame of Far-li-mas filled every land, from the sea in the east to that in the west. And with such fame, there came so much envy into men's hearts that, when Far-li-mas died, the neighboring countries broke their treaties, opening war on the kingdom of Napata, and Napata succumbed. Napata was destroyed. The empire fell apart. It was overwhelmed by savages and barbarians. The gold and copper mines were forgotten; the cities disappeared. And nothing remained of the great days but the memory of the tales of Far-li-mas—which he had brought with him from his own land eastward, beyond the sea.

This, then, is the story of the destruction of the land of Kash, the last of whose children now are dwelling in Darfur.[1]

II. A Night of Shehrzad

Leo Frobenius, to whom we owe the recording and publication of this legend from the lips of the old captain of his camel-boys, has pointed out that in the *Historical Library* of the Sicilian analist Diodorus Siculus, who visited Egypt between the years 60 and 57 B.C., there is an account of the practice of ritual regicide among the Nubian Kassites of the Upper Nile, in the province then known as Meroe-Napata.[2] The priests would send a messenger to the king, declaring that the gods had revealed the moment to them through an oracle, and the kings, as Diodorus declares, submitted to this judgment through superstition. However, Diodorus goes on to say, in the period of the Alexandrian pharaoh Ptolemy II Philadelphus (309–246 B.C.), the custom was disregarded by an Ethiopian monarch named Ergamenes, who had received a Greek education. Placing his trust rather in philosophy than in religion, and with a courage worthy of the tenant of a throne, Ergamenes walked with a body of soldiers into the hitherto solemnly feared sanctuary of the Golden Temple, slew the priests to a man, discontinued the tradition derived from the awesome past, and reorganized things according to his own taste.[3]

Arach-ben-Hassul's tale itself, as Frobenius observes, suggests the Arabian Nights, not only in its narrative style and fabulous atmosphere but also in its theme. For, as all recall, in the frame story of that collection the clever bride, Shehrzad, through her fascinating story-telling art rescued from death both herself and all the maidens of her generation; whereas here we have the same art achieving a like result—rescuing now, however, the king too from death, as well as the clever young woman who, like Shehrzad, was the instigator of the whole operation.

The dates of the formation of the main body of the Arabian Nights lie between the eighth and fourteenth centuries A.D., though some of the tales appear to have been composed and added as late as the seventeenth century.[4] The period is one to which the world owes a great many of its most fascinating wonder tales, since it was precisely in those centuries—throughout the Middle Ages, that is to say—that the custom of telling stories flourished most elegantly in the courts of Europe, India, and Persia, as well as in Arabia and Egypt. It must be recognized, therefore, that although our "Legend of the Destruction of Kash" may indeed be founded on some such act as that recorded of Ergamenes in the third century B.C., when the humanism of Greece penetrated to the sanctuaries of ritual regicide in the Sudanese Upper Nile, the incident has been rendered in a style and mood of about the tenth century A.D.

No one who has studied the art of the fairy tale will doubt that such a folk-narrator of the twentieth century as Arach-ben-Hassul might faithfully communicate not only the plot but even the very style of a tale contrived in the Middle Ages. One need only read the folktales gathered by Jeremiah Curtin in the west of Ireland in the 1880s [5] and compare them with Standish H. O'Grady's translations of the tales of the Fianna and Irish saints from a series of fifteenth-century Irish manuscripts [6] to be convinced. The ability of traditional story-tellers to hold their precious tales in mind to the minutest detail had already been noticed by the Brothers Grimm in the course of gathering their German collection. "Anyone believing that traditional materials are easily falsified and carelessly preserved, and hence cannot survive over a long period," they wrote, "should hear how close the old story-teller always keeps to her story and how zealous she is for its accuracy; never does she alter any part in repetition, and she corrects a mistake herself, immediately she notices it. Among people who follow the old life-ways without change, attachment to inherited patterns is stronger than we, impatient for variety, can realize." [7]

It is entirely possible, therefore, that our tale of the destruction of Kash may stem from the period and genius of the great collection of Shehrzad.

But whence the tales of Shehrzad?

"The first who composed tales and made books of them," wrote the tenth-century Arab historian ʻAli Abu-l Hasan ul-Masʻudí (d. c. 956 A.D.), "were the Persians. The Arabs translated them and the learned took them and composed others like them. The first book of the kind made," his account continues, "was that called *Hazār Afsān* ("Thousand Romances"), and its manner was on this wise. One of the kings of the Persians was wont, whenas he took a woman to wife and had lain one night with her, to put her to death on the morrow. Now he married a girl endowed with wit and knowledge, by name Shehrzad, and she fell to telling him tales and used to join the story, at the end of the night, with what should induce the king to spare her alive and question her next night of the ending thereof, till a thousand nights had passed over her. Meanwhile he lay with her, till he was vouchsafed a child by her, when she discovered to him the device she had practiced upon him. Her wit pleased him and he inclined to her and spared her life." [8]

It is usual to regard the nuclear idea of the Arabian *Thousand Nights and One Night* as Persian, even while recognizing that the collection was swollen to its present magnitude through contributions largely from Arabian Syria and Iraq, and Arabian Egypt. Frobenius, however, adds to this view a new and extremely interesting hypothesis based on his own collection of stories from the Sudan; namely, that there may have been a common source from which both the Persian tales and the Sudanese were derived, issuing from South Arabia, Hadramaut, that land "beyond the Eastern Sea" (the Red Sea) from which the fabulous slave Far-limas came to the court of the Nap of Napata.

"Is our Sudanese tale perhaps from an older rendition," Frobenius asks, "not so worn at the edges and over-refined by a series of Indian, Persian, and late Egyptian transformations?" [9]

Do we have, that is to say, in this elegant Sudanese narrative and in the celebrated *Book of a Thousand Nights and One Night* two variants of a single tradition, stemming from a land now largely a wilderness—but a wilderness with the ruins of ancient cities buried in its sands—today called properly *Arabia deserta,* but formerly *Arabia felix?*

"As we moved slowly along through the Red Sea in the year 1915," Frobenius wrote in his account of the collection of his tales from Kordofan, "and I chatted by the hour with the Arab seamen, I learned of an apparently widely spread opinion, which may serve to clarify a number of problems in the present context. My informants maintained, stoutly and firmly, that all the tales of the Arabian Nights had first been told in Hadramaut and from there had been diffused over the earth. And the tale that they particularly stressed was 'Sindbad the Sailor.' " [10]

The question of the relationship of these two traditions has not—as far as I know—been resolved. It leads, however, to a second, no less fascinating question, which we are now able to answer in detail; and this, too, was proposed by Frobenius. It is the question, namely, of a possible historic or prehistoric background for this Sudanese Nights adventure. Can it be that the tale was not a sheer invention, but reflected in the glass of a late story-telling style some actual circumstance of the past?

The passage from Diodorus speaks for the possibility. Moreover, in the vast body of material assembled by Sir James G. Frazer in the twelve volumes of his monumental work *The Golden Bough,* we have evidence enough of the prevalence of a custom of ritual regicide throughout a large portion of the archaic world, associated—just as here—with a pattern of matrilineal descent. Among the Shilluk of the White Nile (a people now inhabiting precisely the region of our tale) the custom of putting their king to death prevailed, according to Frazer, until only a few years ago. "It is said that the chiefs announce his fate to the king," Frazer writes, citing the studies of C. G. Seligman, "and that afterwards he is strangled in a hut which has been specially built for the occasion." [11] Furthermore, in 1926 new evidence attesting to the nature of the destiny of the earliest kings and their courts was unearthed by Sir Leonard Woolley in his excavations of the so-called Royal Tombs of Ur, the city of the moon-god of ancient Sumer. His grim discovery is described in a later chapter. So, from what we now know, it can be said with perfect assurance that in the earliest period of the hieratic city state the king and his court were ritually immolated at the expiration of a span of years determined by the relationship of the planets in the heavens to the moon; and that our legend of Kash is, therefore, certainly an echo from that very deep well of the past, romantically reflected in a late story-teller's art.

III. The King, and the Virgin of the Vestal Fire

The gruesome original sense of the relationship of the vestal virgin Sali's role—as well as of Shehrzad's in the Arabian Nights—to the archaic regicide comes out cruelly the moment we focus on the royal rituals traditionally practiced, until recently, in the Sudan.

Among the Shilluk, the priests, who were the only ones knowing the will of God (whom they called Nyakang), saw to it that the king was killed after a term of seven years, or, if the crops or prosperity of the herds failed before that term, even earlier. The person of the king was sacred and could be seen by none but nobles. Not even his children could enter his dwelling. And when he stepped forth, surrounded closely by the nobles, criers sent the people flying to their huts. When the time arrived for his death, the high priest told the paramount noble, and the latter then assembled the members of his own class and apprised them, in silence, by a motion of his hand. The mystery had to be consummated on one of the dark nights that fall between the last and the first quarters of the moon, in the dry period before the first rain, and before the first seeds were sown. The charge was executed by the chief noble himself; none other should hear of it, know or speak of it; and there should be no weeping. The king was strangled and buried with a living virgin at his side. And, when the two bodies had rotted, their bones were gathered into the hide of a bull. A year later the new king was named, and on his predecessor's grave cattle were speared to death by the hundred.[12]

Of old, such customs were known to many peoples not only of the Upper Nile but of other parts of the Sudan as well; also in Mozambique, Angola, and Rhodesia. India and Indonesia too knew the rites; in fact, the most vivid example on record of an immolation of the sacred king is probably that in Duarte Barbosa's *Description of the Coasts of East Africa and Malabar in the Beginning of the Sixteenth Century*.

The god-king of the south Indian province of Quilacare in Malabar (an area having a strongly matriarchal tradition to this day) had to sacrifice himself at the end of the length of time required by the planet Jupiter for a circuit of the zodiac and return to its moment of retrograde motion in the sign of Cancer—which is to say, twelve years. When his time came, the king had a wooden scaffolding constructed and spread over with hangings of silk. And when he had ritually bathed in a tank, with great ceremonies and to the sound of music, he proceeded to the temple, where he paid worship to the divinity. Then he mounted the scaffolding and, before the people, took some very sharp knives and began to cut off parts of his body—nose, ears, lips, and all his members, and as much of his flesh as he was able—throwing them away and round about, until so much of his blood was spilled that he began to faint, whereupon he slit his throat.[13]

"The essential motif lies in the timing of the death of the god," writes Frobenius in his summary discussion of the archetype of the sacral regicide.

> The great god must die; forfeit his life and be shut up in the underworld, within the mountain. The goddess (and let us call her Ishtar, using her later Babylonian title) follows him into the underworld and after the consummation of his self-immolation, releases him. The supreme mystery was celebrated not only in renowned songs, but also in the ancient new-year festivals, where it was presented dramatically: and this dramatic presentation can be said to represent the acme of the manifestation of the grammar and logic of mythology in the history of the world.
>
> The whole idea was realized, furthermore, in a corresponding organization of the social institutions; the best preserved vestiges and echoes of which are to be found in Africa. Indeed, the ideas have been found preserved to this day in act, in the South African "Eritrean" zone [Mozambique, Angola, and Rhodesia]. There, the king representing the great godhead even bore the name "Moon"; while his second wife was the Moon's beloved, the planet Venus. And when the time arrived for the death of the god, the king and his Venus-spouse were strangled and their remains placed in a burial cave in a mountain, from which they were supposed then to be resurrected as the new, or "renewed," heavenly spheres. And this, surely, must represent the earliest form of the mythological and ritual context. Already in ancient Babylon it had been

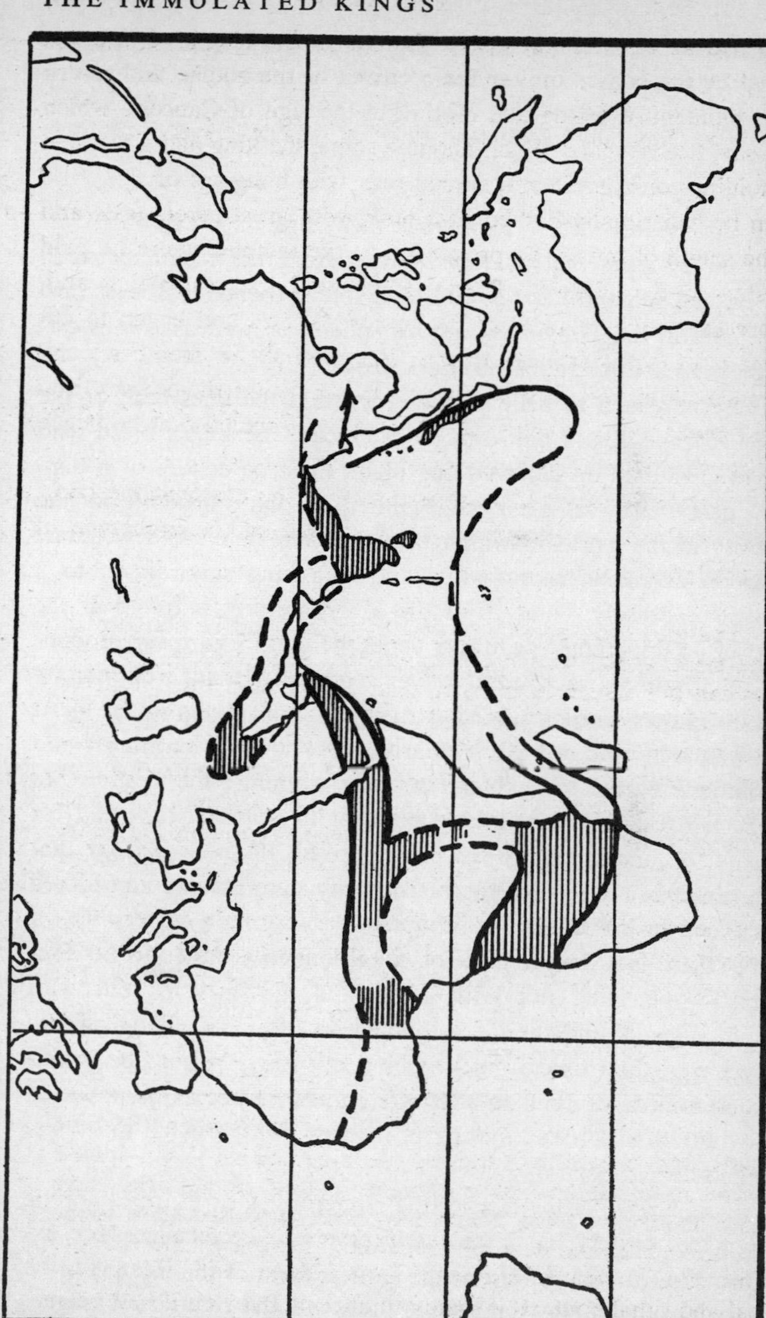

Prevalence of ritual regicide. After Frobenius

> weakened, in as much as the king at the New Year Festival in the temple was only stripped of his garments, humiliated, and struck, while in the marketplace a substitute, who had been ceremonially installed in all glory, was delivered to death by the noose. . . .

"It now seems clear," Frobenius then suggests, "that this constellation of ideas and customs sprang from the region between the Caspian Sea and Persian Gulf and spread thence southeastward into India in the Dravidian culture sphere, as well as southwestward across South Arabia into East Africa." [14]

There is reason to believe, therefore, that the tales both of the king's sister-in-death, Sali, and of Shehrzad, the king's bride who was to have died on her wedding night, must be echoes of a dim, dark past that was, after all, neither so dim nor dark in the memory of the world in which the tales were told. And we must regard it as likely, too, that whenever a king subordinate to a council of priestly dictators of the kingly destiny is found at the head of an apparently primitive tribe, the culture in question cannot be primitive exactly, but rather regressed. Its idea of correcting (in Plato's words, quoted earlier) "those circuits in the head that were deranged at birth by learning to know the harmonies and revolutions of the world" and thereby winning "the best in life set by the gods before mankind both for this present time and for the life to come," must have been derived, ultimately, from that high center of the idea of the hieratic city state that we considered at the conclusion of our last chapter.

Yet there is a deeper level of ritual human sacrifice to be considered—associated not with kings and the heavens, but with simple villagers and their food-plants, in the far-reaching culture province of the tropical gardens; and this may, indeed, be primitive. Before descending to that stratum, however, let us pause to attend the ritual of the kindling of the new fire, to which the vestal virgin Sali had been assigned.

A comparison of the rites of the numerous African tribes among whom the mystery has been lately practiced or recalled (for example, the Mundang, Haussa, Gwari, Nupe, and Mossi of the Sudan; Yoruba of Nigeria; and, in the south, the Ruanda, Wasegue,

Wadoe, Wawemba, Walumbwe, Wahemba, Mambwe, Lunda, Kanioka, Bangala, and Bihe) reveals that when the king was dead all the fires in his domain were extinguished, and that during the period of no rule, between his death and the installation of his successor, there was no holy fire. The latter was ritually rekindled by a designated pubescent boy and virgin, who were required to appear completely naked before the new king, the court, and the people, with their fire-sticks; the two sticks being known, respectively, as the male (the twirling stick) and the female (the base). The two young people had to make the new fire and then perform that other, symbolically analogous act, their first copulation; after which they were tossed into a prepared trench, while a shout went up to drown their cries, and quickly buried alive.[15]

We are entering, indeed, the realm of King Death, the Great Chief Death.

Chapter 5

THE RITUAL LOVE-DEATH

I. The Descent and Return of the Maiden

A rite similar in conception to that of the young couple of the vestal fire, though functioning in the context of a more primitive mythology, is reported from the opposite margin of the Indian Ocean zone, seven or eight thousand miles from East Africa and the Sudan, among the Marind-anim of Dutch South New Guinea. The Swiss ethnologist Paul Wirz, in a two-volume work on the myths and customs of these head-hunting cannibals,[1] tells of their gods—the Dema—who appear in the ceremonies, fabulously costumed, to enact again (or rather, not "again," because time collapses in "ceremonial time" and what was "then" becomes "now") the world-fashioning events of the "time of the beginning of the world." The rites are performed to the tireless chant of many voices, the boom of slit-log drums, and the whirring of the bull-roarers, which are the voices of the Dema themselves, rising from the earth. The ceremonies continue for many nights, many days, uniting the villagers in a fused being that is not biological, essentially, but a living spirit—with numerous heads, many eyes, many voices, numerous feet pounding the earth—lifted even out of temporality and translated into the no-place, no-time, no-when, no-where of the mythological age, which is here and now.

The particular moment of importance to our story occurs at the conclusion of one of the boys' puberty rites, which terminates in a sexual orgy of several days and nights, during which everyone in the village except the initiates makes free with everybody else, amid the tumult of the mythological chants, drums, and the bull-roarers—until the final night, when a fine young girl, painted, oiled, and ceremonially costumed, is led into the dancing ground and made to lie beneath a platform of very heavy logs. With her, in open view of the festival, the initiates cohabit, one after another; and while the youth chosen to be last is embracing her the supports of the logs above are jerked away and the platform drops, to a prodigious boom of drums. A hideous howl goes up and the dead girl and boy are dragged from the logs, cut up, roasted, and eaten.[2]

But what can be the sense of such a cruel game? And who are this annihilated girl and boy? What is the background of such rites, which are not frequent merely, but typical among the cannibal gardeners of the widely dispersed, equatorial villages?

As Professor Adolf Jensen of Frankfurt has pointed out, developing the broadly reaching cross-cultural theory first announced by Leo Frobenius in 1895–97, these rites are but the renditions in act of a mythology inspired by the model of death and life in the plant world. And they are the basal sacrament of a precisely definable prehistoric culture stratum still represented in tropical Africa and America, as well as in India, Indonesia, and Oceania. The unity of the broken field has not been explained; nor is it easy to imagine how it should be. Yet neither was it easy to understand the distribution of the animal known as the tapir (which is found both in the Malay region and in South and Central America, but nowhere between) until fossil forms in Miocene, Pliocene, and Pleistocene formations were found in Europe, China, and the United States of America, which made possible a reconstruction of the history of the animal's diffusion. No biologist, previous to the discovery of these fossils, would have dreamed of suggesting that the New and Old World tapirs might have developed separately through parallel lines of evolution. And in the field of comparative mythology too, perhaps, it would be well not to formulate "scientific" conclusions before a full accounting is made.

The contemporary representatives of the prehistoric culture stratum of the cannibal gardeners dwell in tropical, usually jungle regions, sparsely populated, where the natural abundance of the plant world affords a convenient supply of food: coconuts, the pith of the sago palm, bananas and other fruits, and in California a variety of acorn. In addition, there is generally practiced an orderly, and often highly ritualized, cultivation of tubers: yams, for example, taro, and the sweet potato (rice and the other grains belonging, almost certainly, to a later stratum of culture). In general, the architecture is elaborately developed, usually set on piles, and frequently includes gigantic structures (two hundred yards or more in length) sheltering whole communities—which may number as many as a hundred persons. Bamboo is prominent and variously used. Among the beasts domesticated are the dog, the chicken (turkey, in America), and often the pig (throughout Melanesia and Indonesia) or the goat (in Africa). The arts of metalwork, weaving, and usually pottery are unknown, though imports of these goods are highly prized. And politically there are no great state confederations, kings, professional priests, or significant differentiations of labor (except, of course, along sexual lines); while the village as a cult community usually ranks higher than any tribal organization.

The prehistoric period to which the development of this particular style of life and thought should be assigned cannot be precisely identified. The archaeology of the problem is vague and has not been pressed very far. The characteristic artifacts are of extremely perishable materials: bamboo, pandanus leaves, shell and bone, feathers, palm fronds and logs, withies and beaten bark. Furthermore, the greater part of the region occupied has been the home of man for at least half a million years: the bones of Pithecanthropus erectus (c. 400,000 B.C.) were turned up in Java, and in Africa even earlier remains have been found in abundance. The cultural life of the area stands, indeed, as a kind of enduring though vanishing counterpoise to the more durably registered stone and metal ages of the temperate north. It is a culture-world in which the forms endure but not the materials in which they are rendered, whereas in the world of stone tools and metal it is the materials that last. The prehistoric origin of this primitive gardening syndrome must float enigmatically, therefore, in a loose relationship to the comparatively firm schedule of our various paleolithic, mesolithic, and neolithic ages. Jensen is inclined to refer it to the early neolithic, or perhaps even one step back, to the mesolithic. And if his view is correct, we are viewing here a form of culture not far removed, in time of origin, from the proto-neolithic villages of the Near East.

It was in the course of an expedition to West Ceram (the next major island westward of New Guinea) that Professor Jensen discovered the myth that I present here as our first example from this cannibalistic culture stratum: that of the maiden Hainuwele, whose name means "Frond of the Cocopalm," and who is one of three virgin Dema, highly revered among the tribes of West Ceram. The myth is this:

> Nine families of mankind came forth in the beginning from Mount Nunusaku, where the people had emerged from clusters of bananas. And these families stopped in West Ceram, at a place known as the "Nine Dance Grounds," which is in the jungle between Ahiolo and Varoloin.
>
> Now there was a man among them whose name was Ameta, meaning "Dark," "Black," or "Night"; and neither was he married nor had he children. He went off, one day, hunting with his dog. And after a little, the dog smelt a wild pig, which it traced to a pond into which the animal took flight; but the dog remained on the shore. And the pig, swimming, grew tired and drowned, but the man, who had arrived meanwhile, retrieved it. And he found a coconut on its tusk, though at that time there were no cocopalms in the world.
>
> Returning to his hut, Ameta placed the nut on a stand and covered it with a cloth bearing a snake design, then lay down to sleep. And in the night there appeared to him the figure of a man, who said: "The coconut that you placed upon the stand and covered with a cloth you must plant in the earth; otherwise it won't grow." So Ameta planted the coconut the next morning, and in three days the palm was tall. Again three days and it was bearing blossoms. He climbed the tree to cut the blossoms, from which he wished to prepare himself a drink, but as he cut he slashed his finger and the blood fell on a leaf. He returned home to bandage his finger and in three days came back to the palm to find that where the blood on the leaf had mingled with the sap of the cut blossom the face of someone had appeared. Three days later, the trunk of the person was there, and when he returned again in three days he found that a little girl had developed from his drop

of blood. That night the same figure of a man appeared to him in dream. "Take your cloth with the snake design," he said, "wrap the girl of the cocopalm in the cloth carefully, and carry her home."

So the next morning Ameta went with his cloth to the cocopalm, climbed the tree, and carefully wrapped up the little girl. He descended cautiously, took her home, and named her Hainuwele. She grew quickly and in three days was a nubile maiden. But she was not like an ordinary person; for when she would answer the call of nature her excrement consisted of all sorts of valuable articles, such as Chinese dishes and gongs, so that her father became very rich.

And about that time there was to be celebrated in the place of the Nine Dance Grounds a great Maro Dance, which was to last nine full nights, and the nine families of mankind were to participate. Now when the people dance the Maro, the women sit in the center and from there reach betel nut to the men, who form, in dancing, a large ninefold spiral. Hainuwele stood in the center at this Maro festival, passing out betel nut to the men. And at dawn, when the performance ended, all went home to sleep.

The second night, the nine families of mankind assembled on the second ground; for when the Maro is celebrated it must be performed each night in a different place. And once again, it was Hainuwele who was placed in the center to reach betel nut to the dancers; but when they asked for it she gave them coral instead, which they all found very nice. The dancers and the others, too, then began pressing in to ask for betel and she gave them coral. And so the performance continued until dawn, when they all went home to sleep.

The next night the dance was resumed on a third ground, with Hainuwele again in the center; but this time she gave beautiful Chinese porcelain dishes, and everyone present received such a dish. The fourth night she gave bigger porcelain dishes and the fifth, great bush knives; the sixth, beautifully worked betel boxes of copper; the seventh, golden earrings; and the eighth, glorious gongs. The value of the articles increased, that way, from night to night, and the people thought this thing mysterious. They came together and discussed the matter.

They were all extremely jealous that Hainuwele could distribute such wealth and decided to kill her. The ninth night, therefore, when the girl was again placed in the center of the dance ground, to pass out betel nut, the men dug a deep hole in the area. In the innermost circle of the great ninefold spiral the men of the Lesiela family were dancing, and in the course of the slowly cycling movement of their spiral they pressed the maiden Hainuwele toward the hole and threw her in. A loud, three voiced Maro Song drowned out her cries. They covered her quickly with earth, and the dancers trampled this down firmly with their steps. They danced on till dawn, when the festival ended and the people returned to their huts.

But when the Maro festival ended and Hainuwele failed to return, her father knew that she had been killed. He took nine branches of a certain bushlike plant whose wood is used in the casting of oracles and with these reconstructed in his home the nine circles of the Maro Dancers. Then he knew that Hainuwele had been killed in the Dancing Ground. He took nine fibers of the cocopalm leaf and went with these to the dance place, stuck them one after the other into the earth, and with the ninth came to what had been the innermost circle. When he stuck the ninth fiber into the earth and drew it forth, on it were some of the hairs and blood of Hainuwele. He dug up the corpse and cut it into many pieces, which he buried in the whole area about the Dancing Ground—except for the two arms, which he carried to the maiden Satene: the second of the supreme Dema-virgins of West Ceram. At the time of the coming into being of mankind Satene had emerged from an unripe banana, whereas the rest had come from ripe bananas; and she now was the ruler of them all. But the buried portions of Hainuwele, meanwhile, were already turning into things that up to that time had never existed anywhere on earth—above all, certain tuberous plants that have been the principal food of the people ever since.

Ameta cursed mankind and the maiden Satene was furious at the people for having killed. So she built on one of the dance grounds a great gate, consisting of a ninefold spiral, like the one formed by the men in the dance; and she stood on a great log inside this gate, holding in her two hands the two arms of Hainuwele. Then, summoning the people, she said to them: "Because you have killed, I refuse to live here any more: today I shall leave. And so now you must all try to come to me through this gate. Those who succeed will remain people, but to those who fail something else will happen."

They tried to come through the spiral gate, but not all succeeded, and everyone who failed was turned into either an animal or a spirit. That is how it came about that pigs, deer, birds, fish, and many spirits inhabit the earth. Before that time there had been only people. Those, however, who came through walked to Satene; some to the right of the log on which she was standing, others to the left; and as each passed she struck him with one of Hainuwele's arms. Those going left had to jump across five sticks of bamboo, those to the right, across nine, and from these two groups, respectively, were derived the tribes known as the Fivers and the Niners. Satene said to them: "I am departing today and you will see me no more on earth. Only when you die will you again see me. Yet even then you shall have to accomplish a very difficult journey before you attain me."

And with that, she disappeared from the earth. She now dwells on the mountain of the dead, in the southern part of West Ceram, and whoever desires to go to her must die. But the way to her mountain leads over eight other mountains. And ever since that day there have been not only men but spirits and animals on earth, while the tribes of men have been divided into the Fivers and the Niners.[3]

A related myth tells of the remaining divine maiden, Rabia, who was desired in marriage by the sun-man Tuwale. But when her parents placed a dead pig in her place in the bridal bed, Tuwale claimed his bride in a strangely violent manner, causing her to sink into the earth among the roots of a tree. The efforts of the people to save her were in vain: they could not prevent her from sinking even deeper. And when she had gone down as far as to the neck, she called to her mother: "It is Tuwale, the sun-man, who has come to claim me. Slaughter a pig and celebrate a feast; for I am dying. But in three days, when evening comes, look up at the sky, where I shall be shining upon you as a light." That was how the moon-maiden Rabia instituted the death feast. And when her relatives had killed the pig and celebrated the death feast for three days, they saw for the first time the moon, rising in the east.[4]

II. The Mythological Event

The leading theme of the primitive-village mythology of the Dema is the coming of death into the world, and the particular point is that death comes by way of a murder. The second point is that the plants on which man lives derive from this death. The world lives on death: that is the insight rendered dramatically in this image. Moreover, as we learn from other myths and mythological fragments in this culture sphere, the sexual organs are supposed to have appeared at the time of this coming of death. Reproduction without death would be a calamity, as would death without reproduction.

We may say, then, that the interdependence of death and sex, their import as the complementary aspects of a single state of being, and the necessity of killing—killing and eating—for the continuance of this state of being, which is that of man on earth, and of all things on earth, the animals, birds, and fish, as well as man—this deeply moving, emotionally disturbing glimpse of death as the life of the living is the fundamental motivation supporting the rites around which the social structure of the early planting villages was composed.

As Professor Jensen has observed, "Killing holds a place of paramount significance in the way of life both of animals and of men. Every day men must kill, to maintain life. They kill animals, and, apparently, in the culture here being considered the harvesting of plants also was regarded—quite correctly—as a killing. . . .

"In this culture," he continues,

> killing is not an act of heroism, conceived in a spirit of warlike manliness. All of the details of the headhunt speak to the contrary. In fact, if the actions of the headhunter were to be judged by heroic standards we should have to call him a coward. Nor, on the other hand, is either the mythological first killing that was perpetrated on the holy moon-being or the repetition of that killing in the cult—whether in the village ceremonials or in the actions of the headhunt—"murder," in the sense of a criminal act meriting punishment, as Cain's slaying of Abel would appear to have been. It is true that the first killing brought about a complete transformation of human life in the time of the beginning, and that in the myths this is occasionally represented in terms of a crime and its punishment: for, psychologically, a certain sense of guilt cannot be separated from the act of killing, any more than from that of begetting. Yet the mere fact that a repetition of

the deed is a sacred obligation placed upon mankind makes it impossible to call it murder in the full sense of the word. Guilt and heroism do indeed appear in some of the mythological representations of the episodes, but are certainly not essential to the basic context—which cannot but have been much more elementary. The closest analogy is to be found, according to my opinion [he then suggests], in the world of the beasts of prey. We do not think either of heroism or of murder when considering their manner of killing, but only of the primal force of nature. And there is actually an indication of this parallelism in the appearance of spirits resembling beasts of prey in the ceremonies of the men's secret societies and puberty rites, as well as in the express statement of the people of West Ceram that they derived their ritual of the headhunt from a bird of prey.

But all of this touches only the problem of the psychological attitude toward killing. That killing should have assumed such a prominent position in the total view of the world in this culture sphere, I should like to refer quite specifically to the occupation of these people with the world of the plants. There was here revealed to mankind, in some measure, a new field of illumination. For the plants were continually being killed through the gathering of their fruits, yet the death was extraordinarily quickly overcome by their new life. Thus there was made available to man a synthesizing insight, relating his own destiny to that of the animals, the plants, and the moon.[5]

And so, once again, as in the instance of the cosmic imagery of the hieratic city state, we have an intellectual, emotionally toned insight as the fundamental inspiration of a cult that became basic to a sociology. There is no way, in sheerly economic terms, to account for the phenomenology of a primitive social system in which a tremendous proportion of the time and energy is given to activities of an elaborate ritual nature. The rites are expected to afford economic well-being and social harmony; that is true. Yet their inception cannot be attributed to an economic insight, or even to a social need. Groups of a hundred souls or so do not require the murder of their own finest sons and daughters to enable them to cohere. This flowering of rites derived from a cosmic insight—and one of such force that the whole sense, the formal structuring principle of the universe, seemed for a certain period of human history to have been caught in it.

The rites were representations of this accord, in a way comparable to those formulae of modern physics through which the modes of operation of inscrutable cosmic forces become not only accessible to the mind but also susceptible to control. They function both for man's enlightenment and for the furtherance of his aims. They are physical formulae; written, however, not in the black on white of, say, an $E = mc^2$, but in human flesh. And the individuals rendering it are not individuals any more but epiphanies of a cosmic mystery and, as such, taboo—hence ceremonially decorated, and symbolically, not humanly, regarded and treated.

The harmony and well-being of the community, its coordination with the harmony and ultimate nature of the cosmos of which it is a part, and the integration of the individual, in his thought, feeling, and personal desires, with the sense and essential force of this universal circumstance, can be said, therefore, to be the fundamental aim and nature of the ceremonial. And in a society of the sort here being considered everyone is more or less deeply implicated in the context of the ceremonial in every moment and phase of his life.

Let us say, then, to summarize, that a mythology is an organization of images conceived as a rendition of the sense of life, and that this sense is to be apprehended in two ways, namely: 1) the way of thought, and 2) the way of experience. As thought mythology approaches—or is a primitive prelude to—science; and as experience it is precisely art.

Furthermore, the mythological image, the mythological formula, is rendered present, here and now, in the rite. Just as the written formula, $E = mc^2$, here on this page, is not merely a reference to the formula that Dr. Einstein wrote on another piece of paper somewhere else, but actually that formula itself, so likewise are the motifs of the rite experienced not as references but as presences. They render visible the mythological age itself. For the festival is an extension into the present of the world-creating mythological event through which the force of the ancestors (those eternal ones of the dream) * became discharged into the rolling run of time, and where what then was ever present in the form of a holy being without change now dies and reappears, dies and reappears—like the moon, like the yam, like our animal food, or like the race.

The divine being (the Dema) has become flesh in the living food-substance of the world: which is to say, in all of us, since all of us are to become, in the end, food for other beings. This is the nuclear idea of the killed Dema, who is the source of our good and of our food. A number of infantile motifs have been enlisted in the rendition, but the idea itself cannot be called infantile. It is, in fact, a new insight, fostering not a return to infancy but a willed affirmation of man's fate and of the ruthless nature of being, to which we, today, with our much more sensitive, humanized, and humanistic responses of revulsion, may be said to be reacting in the more childish way. The qualm before the deed of life—which is that of dealing death—is precisely the human crisis here overcome. The beast of prey deals death without knowledge. Man, however, has knowledge, and must overcome it to live. Among the primitive hunting societies the way was to deny death, the reality of death, and to go on killing as willing victims the animals that one required and revered. But in the planting societies a new insight or solution was opened by the lesson of the plant world itself, which is linked somehow to the moon, which also dies and is resurrected and moreover influences, in some mysterious way still unknown, the lunar cycle of the womb.

Through modern science mythology has been refuted in practically all its details; yet in its primary insight into the presence and operation of common laws throughout the fabric of the universe—laws including human life as well as the kingdoms of the animals, plants, and heavenly spheres—it announced not only the main theme but also the chief source of the fascination of science, and perhaps of life itself. Moreover, when the will of the individual to his own immortality has been extinguished—as it is in rites such as these—through an effective realization of the immortality of being itself and of its play through all things, he is united with that being, in experience, in a stunning crisis of release from the psychology of

* Supra, p. 88.

guilt and mortality. Among the tropical planters the rendition of this fundamentally religious experience was effected through rites of the kind that we have observed.

And I think it may be said that if one of the chief problems of man, philosophically, is that of becoming reconciled, in feeling as well as in thought, to the monstrosity of the just-so of the world, no more telling initiatory lesson than that of these rites could have been imagined. As Professor Jensen has pointed out, the number of lives offered up in such rites is far less, proportionately to the population, than that sacrificed in our own cities in traffic accidents. However, among ourselves such deaths are thought of and experienced generally as a consequence of human fallibility, even though their incidence is statistically predictable. In the primitive ritual, on the other hand, which is based on the viewpoint of the species rather than on that of the individual, what for us is "accident" is placed in the center of the system—namely, sudden, monstrous death—and this becomes therewith a revelation of the inhumanity of the order of the universe. And in addition, what is thus revealed is not simply the monstrosity of the just-so of the world, but this just-so as a higher reality than that normally sensed by our unalerted faculties: a god-willed monstrosity in being, and retaining its form of being only because a divinity (a Dema) is actualizing itself in the entire display.[6]

Mythology, we may conclude, therefore, is a verification and validation of the well-known—as monstrous. It is conceived, finally, not as a reference either to history or to the world-texture analyzed by science, but as an epiphany of the monstrosity and wonder of these; so that both they and therewith ourselves may be experienced in depth.

And in the sacrifices through which the major themes of such a mythology are made manifest and present there is no sense of *do ut des:* "I give that thou mayest give." These are not gifts, bribes, or dues rendered to God, but fresh enactments, here and now, of the god's own sacrifice in the beginning, through which he, she, or it became incarnate in the world process. Moreover, all the ritual acts around which the village community is organized, and through which its identity is maintained, are functions and partial revelations of this immortal sacrifice. And finally, it would seem evident that something of this primitive yet profoundly conceived mythology must underlie the larger, celestially oriented constellation that we have already noted in our view of the hieratic city state.

In a mythologically oriented primitive society, such as those of the Marind-anim and West Ceramese, every aspect of life and of the world is linked organically to the pivotal insight rendered in the mythology and rituals of the age of the Dema. Those pre-sexual, pre-mortal ancestral beings of the mythological narrative lived the idyl of the beginning, an age when all things were innocent of the destiny of life in time. But there occurred in that age an event, the "mythological event" *par excellence,* which brought to an end its timeless way of being and effected a transformation of all things. Whereupon death and sex came into the world as the basic correlates of temporality.

Furthermore—and in contrast to our contemporary evolutionary view of the unfolding of forms in time—the mythological notion was of a single, unique, and critical moment of definitive precipitation at the close of the paradisial age and opening of the present, when all things were given precisely the forms in which we see them today: the animals, the fish, the birds, and the plants in their various species, as well as the spirits and the ritual customs of the group. In the Book of Genesis we find much the same idea. But in the primitive version of the mythological event (which is represented in the Book of Genesis in inverted order, Cain's murder of Abel following, instead of preceding, our first parents' eating of the fruit) one does not feel that mankind was cut off as a result of the killing of the Dema Hainuwele. On the contrary, the Dema, through man's act of violence, was made the very substance of his life.

Something of the sort can be felt in the Christian myth of the killed, buried, resurrected, and eaten Jesus, whose mystery is the ritual of the altar and communion rail. But here the ultimate monstrosity of the divine drama is not stressed so much as the guilt of man in having brought it about; and we are asked to look forward to a last day, when the run of this cosmic tragedy of crime and punishment will be terminated and the kingdom of God realized on earth, as it is now in heaven. The Greek rendition of the mythology, on the other hand, remains closer to the primitive view, according to which there is to be no end, or even essential improvement, for this tragedy (as it will seem to some) or play (as it appears to the gods). The sense of it all—or rather, nonsense of it all—is to be made evident forever in the festivals and monstrous customs of the community itself; but is evident also—and forever—in every part and moment of the universe, for those who have been taught by way of the rites to see and to know the world as it truly is.

III. Persephone

The number of details shared by the Greek mythology of Demeter, Hekate, and Persephone with the Indonesian myths and rites of Satene, Rabia, and Hainuwele is too great to have been the consequence either of chance or of what Sir James G. Frazer has plausibly called "the effect of similar causes acting on the similar constitution of the human mind in different countries and under different skies."[7] Like her child, the killed and eaten yet resurrected god of bread and wine, Dionysos (whose mythology we have already compared with the boys' rites of Central Australia),* Persephone—who was known also as Kore, "the maiden"—was conceived of Zeus. Her mother was Demeter, the Cretan goddess of agriculture and the fruitful soil. And the maiden was playing, we are told,[8] in a meadow, culling flowers with the daughters of Okeanos, god of the all-embracing sea, when she spied a glorious plant with a hundred blossoms spreading its fragrance all about, which had been sent up expressly to seduce her by the goddess Earth (Gaia), at the behest of Hades, the lord of the underworld. So that when she hurried to pluck its flowers the earth gaped and a great god appeared in a chariot of gold, who carried her down into his abyss despite her cries. The god was Hades, lord of the underworld, and in the land of the dead she became his queen.

Persephone's cries had been heard only by Demeter, her

* Cf. supra, pp. 100–102.

mother, and Hekate, a goddess of the moon. But when the mother, bereaved, sought to trace her daughter, she found that her footprints had been obliterated by those of a pig. For it had chanced—most curiously—that at the time of Persephone's abduction a herd of pigs had been rooting in the neighborhood; and the swineherd's name, Eubouleus, means "the giver of good counsel" and was in earlier times an appellation of the god of the underworld himself. Furthermore, when the earth opened to receive Persephone those pigs fell into the chasm too, and that, we are told, is why pigs play such a role in the rites of Demeter and Persephone. "Originally, we may conjecture," Frazer comments in his discussion of this matter, "the footprints of the pig were the footprints of Persephone and of Demeter herself." [9]

In a festival celebrated in memory of the sorrows—and later joy—of Demeter and Persephone, suckling pigs were offered in a manner suggestive not only of an earlier human sacrifice but of one precisely of the gruesome kind that we have observed in Africa and among the Marind-anim of Melanesia. The Greek festival, called Thesmophoria, was exclusively for women, and, as Jane Harrison has demonstrated in her *Prolegomena to the Study of Greek Religion,*[10] such women's rites in Greece were pre-Homeric; that is to say, survivals of the earlier, so-called Pelasgian period, when the hieratic bronze-age civilizations of Crete and Troy were in full flower and the warrior gods, Zeus and Apollo, of the later patriarchal Greeks had not yet arrived to reduce the power of the great goddess. The women fasted for nine days in memory of the nine days of sorrow of Demeter as she wandered over the earth, holding a long, staff-like torch in either hand. Demeter met the moon-goddess Hekate, and together they proceeded to the sun-god, Phoebus, who had seen the maid abducted and could tell them where she was; after which Demeter, in wrath and grief, quit the world of the gods. As an old woman, heavily veiled, she sat for days by a well known as the Well of the Virgin. She served as nurse in a kingly household near Eleusis, which city then became the greatest sanctuary of her rites in Greece. And she cursed the earth to bear no fruit, either for man or for the gods, for a full year—until, when Zeus and all the deities of Olympus had come to her in vain, one after another, begging her to relent, Zeus at last caused Persephone to be released. She had eaten, however, a seed of the pomegranate in the world below and, as a consequence, would now have to spend one-third of each year with Hades. Embraced and accompanied by both her mother and the goddess Hekate, she returned to Olympus in glory, and, as though by magic, the fields were covered again with flowers and the life-giving grain.

The seed-time festival of the Thesmophoria lasted three days, and the first day was named the *Kathodos* (downgoing) and *Anodos* (upcoming), the second *Nesteia* (fasting), and the last *Kalligeneia* (fair-born or fair-birth); and it was during the first day that the suckling pigs were thrown, probably alive, into an underground chamber called a *megara,* where they were left to rot for a year, the bones from the year before being carried up to the earth again and placed upon an altar. Figures of serpents and human beings made of flour and wheat were also thrown into the chasm, or "chamber," at this time. "And they say," writes the ancient author to whom we owe our knowledge of this matter,[11] "that in and about the chasms are snakes which consume the most part of what is thrown in; hence a rattling din is made when the women draw up the remains and when they replace the remains by those well-known images, in order that the snakes which they hold to be the guardians of the sanctuaries may go away."

The rites were secret; hence little has been told of them. However, in the widely celebrated and extremely influential mysteries of Eleusis, where the *Kathodos*-and-*Anodos* of the maiden Persephone was again the central theme, pigs were again important offerings. And there, moreover, a new motif appeared; for the culminating episode in the holy pageant performed in the "hall of the mystics" at Eleusis, representing the sorrows of Demeter and the ultimate *Anodos* or return of the maiden, was the showing of an ear of grain: "that great and marvelous mystery of perfect revelation, a cut stalk of grain," as the early Christian bishop Hippolytus described it [12]—forgetting for the nonce, apparently, that the culminating revelation of his own holy mass was a lifted wafer of bread made of the same grain.

What could have been the meaning of such a simple act as the lifting of a cut stalk of grain?

What is the meaning of the elevated host of the mass?

As in the play-logic, or dream-logic, of any traditional religious pageant, the sacred object is to be identified, at least for the moment of the ceremony, with the god. The cut stalk is the returned Persephone, who was dead but now liveth, in the grain itself.

A bronze gong was struck at this moment, a young priestess representing Kore herself appeared, and the pageant terminated with a paean of joy.[13]

Between the primitive Indonesian cycle and this cherished, highly regarded classical mystery, through which the Greek initiate learned (as a grave-inscription lets us know) that "death was not an evil, but a blessing,"[14] the range of accord includes not only a number of surprisingly minute details, but also every one of the major themes. In fact, at every turn a fresh constellation of correspondences appears.

At the heart of both mythologies there is a trinity of goddesses identified with the local food plants, the pig, the underworld, and the moon, whose rites insure both a growth of the plants and a passage of the soul to the land of the dead. In both the marriage of the maiden goddess or Dema is equivalent to her death, which is imaged as a descent into the earth and is followed, after a time, by her metamorphosis into food: in the primitive cycle, the yam; in the classical, the grain. The women of the Greek Thesmophoria, furthermore, placed figures of flour and wheat, representing snakes and human beings, in the *megara,* together with the pigs; the pigs being left until the flesh rotted, when their bones were brought up and revered as relics, while the figures of wheat were consumed by snakes. And a clatter of noise, rationalized as a ruse to drive away the serpents, accompanied the placement of the pigs and cakes underground.

The ritual is related, trait by trait, to that of the youths and maidens murdered amid an uproar of drums, but has been revised to accord with the new attitude toward human sacrifice that in "The Legend of the Destruction of Kash" was seen to have reached from Greece even to the Sudan, by way of the long finger of the

Nile. Frazer, in *The Golden Bough,* supplies many instances of substitutions of just this kind, and shows, moreover, that cakes in human form have been sacramentally consumed at planting and harvest festivals wherever grain has been ground into flour and baked.[15] So that, in addition to the rest, it would now appear that the sacramental cannibalistic meal must have been, at one time, still another element common to the two cycles.

But why, along with the little pigs and the cakes in human form, were there also cakes in the form of a serpent? Why not living serpents? Or why not pigs of flour?

Greek mythology knew many stories of the maiden given to the serpent—or saved by a timely heroic appearance. For example, when Perseus, flying back on his winged sandals from his conquest of Medusa, was speeding through the air over Ethiopia, he spied, below, a lovely princess chained by her arms to a rough cliff beside the sea; "and save that her hair gently stirred in the breeze," we read in Ovid's account of the event, "and that warm tears were trickling down her cheeks, he would have thought her a marble statue."[16] There came, however, a loud roar from the sea, a monstrous serpent loomed, breasting the waves, and the princess shrieked. But when the great beast, coming toward the maiden like a swift ship, was as far from the cliff as the space through which a Balearic sling can send its whizzing bullet, lo! like an eagle Perseus swooped down with his sword and there ensued a prodigious tumult—the monster rearing, striking, plunging, and belching water mixed with purple blood, until the sword dealt, finally, the blow of the matador and the serpent died.

The name of this rescued princess was Andromeda, and her kingly father, Cepheus, governed Ethiopia, which, as we know from "The Legend of the Destruction of Kash," was the kingdom eastward of Napata, not far from the seat of the rescue of the maiden Sali by the magic of the tongue of Far-li-mas; or from the villages of the present Shilluk of the upper Nile, whose kings were ceremonially strangled and buried with living virgins at their sides, and when the flesh of the two bodies rotted, the bones were gathered into the hide of a bull.*

* Cf. supra, p. 165.

Could Persephone ever have been pictured in this manner, as offered to a serpent, so that the figures of wheaten flour might have represented such a version of her tale? Indeed she could, and indeed they might! For have we not already been told that she was playing in a meadow, culling flowers with the daughters of Okeanos, god of the all-embracing sea? But Okeanos, precisely, is the great serpent, Ocean, biting his tail, who surrounds the world. He supports it, also, in the form of the waters of the abyss and consequently is a counterpart of Hades—who, however, in the later, anecdotal developments of Greek mythology has acquired a separate character of his own. The serpent and human figures of wheaten flour not only may have been but simply must have been Hades and Persephone. And we must notice also that since Persephone was the great serpent's bride she must have been able to assume the form of a serpent as well as that of a pig. Such metamorphoses are all part of the game for goddesses. We all know well enough the classical motif of the two serpents intertwined, which has become the symbol of the medical profession, the priesthood of the well-being that is the boon of the waters of the abyss, which waters flow as sap in the health-giving herbs and as the blood of life in our own healthy bodies.

The figures of wheaten flour, therefore, represent the personages of the myth; and the sacrificed pigs, sacrificed instead of human beings, represent the participation of the living in the mystery, which, though it was *one* in the mythological age, in the lives and rites of men is *many*. Consequently the victim is simultaneously one and many: one in its character as Dema, the mythological maiden; but many in the personal life-offerings of each. The logical principle involved is that of the logic of dream and play, where, as we have already remarked, A *is* B and B *is* C: the Dema is the pig and the pig is man, true god and true man.

The legend of Hainuwele too, contains an unmistakable hint of an earlier version, featuring the serpent, in the painted snake on the cloth in which the little girl, "Frond of the Cocopalm," was wrapped when carried from the tree, and in which the coconut taken from the dead boar had earlier been left standing overnight. The incongruous device of the boar's leap into and drowning in the lake, followed by Ameta's discovery of a coconut hooked to its tusk, as well as the unexplained mystery of the voice that spoke to Ameta in his dream, letting him know what he was to do, suggest very strongly that some earlier form of the myth has been adjusted to a secondary reading, in which a sacrificed pig, and not a supernatural snake, should preponderate, very much as in the mythology of Persephone and Demeter.

The structure of the earlier formula is examined in the next section; we may say here only, in summary of the foregoing findings, that the Greek and Indonesian myths examined have revealed not only a shared body of ritualized motifs but also signs of a shared past, an earlier stratum of their common story, in which a snake and not a pig played the animal part. And the fact that (one way or another) the two cycles were not merely linked remotely by a long, tenuous thread, but established on a broad, common base is made evident by a baffling series of further likenesses.

For example, in both mythologies the numbers 3 and 9 were prominent. We know, also, that in the Greek rites of the goddess—and of her dead and resurrected daughter Persephone, as well as of her dead and resurrected grandson Dionysos—the choral chant, the boom of the drum, and the hum of the bull-roarer were used just as in the rites of the cannibals of Indonesia. We recognize the labyrinth theme in both traditions, associated with the underworld and rendered in the figure of a spiral: in Greece, as well as Indonesia, choral dances were performed in this pattern. The reference in the Indonesian myth to Ameta's desire to prepare a drink for himself from the blossoms of the cocopalm suggests a relationship of wine or intoxication to the cult of the maiden-plant-moon-animal complex that would correspond nicely with the formula in the archaic Mediterranean culture. And finally, is not the figure of Demeter, at the time of her departure in wrath from Olympus, bearing in each hand a long, staff-like torch, comparable to Satene standing at the labyrinthine gate, telling the people of the mythological age that she is about to leave them, and holding in each hand an arm of Hainuwele?

There can be no doubt that the two mythologies are derived

from a single base. The fact was recognized some time ago by the classical scholar Carl Kerényi,[17] and his argument has been supported since by Professor Jensen, the ethnologist chiefly responsible for the collection of the Indonesian material.[18]

Are we to think, then, of the early grain-growing, stock-breeding villages of the Near East as adaptations to a temperate climate of a plant and animal economy derived, in principle, from the tropics? Or shall we say that the influence ran the other way: that the myths and rites of Indonesia represent transformations and regressions from a higher, less brutal system of thought originating in the proto- or basal neolithic villages of the Near East?

The argument is not yet closed; nor is all the evidence in. For the present, we can note simply that a continuum has been established, with its earliest firmly dated marker in the basal-neolithic stratum (c. 5500–4500 B.C.) in the Near East; a second field in the myths and rituals of the planting tribes of South and East Africa and the Sudan; a third (possibly) in Hadramaut; a fourth (certainly) in Malabar; and still another in Indonesia and, as we have seen, Melanesia and Australia. We must now range even farther and measure the reach of this mythological zone into the Pacific—and even, perhaps, the New World beyond.

IV. The Monster Eel

East of Indonesia, Melanesia, and Australia, throughout the island-studded triangle of Polynesia—which has Hawaii at its apex, New Zealand at one angle, and Easter Island at the other—the mythological image of the murdered divine being whose body became a food plant has been adjusted to the natural elements of an oceanic environment. Snakes, for example, are unknown in the islands. The role of the serpent has to be played, therefore, by the closest possible counterpart of the serpent, a monster eel. And the force of the role has been greatly increased—or rather, there is further evidence that in the myths of Hainuwele and Persephone the force of the role must have been greatly reduced. Paradoxically, then, it would appear that although we are moving eastward into the Pacific we are also coming closer to the biblical version of the mythological event through which death came into the world;

and something rather startling is beginning to appear, furthermore, concerning the relationship of Mother Eve to the serpent, and of the serpent to the food tree in the Garden. The voluptuous atmosphere of the lush Polynesian adventure will be different, indeed, from the grim holiness of the rabbinical Torah; nevertheless, we are certainly in the same old book—of which, so to say, all the earliest editions have been lost.

The hero of the following version of the origin of the coconut is not the first parent of mankind but the favorite trickster hero of Polynesia, Maui, who is roughly a counterpart of Hercules. He is generally known as the youngest of a company of brothers, who may vary in number from three (in Rarotonga) to six (in some of the versions from New Zealand); and among the best known of his many magical exploits were the fishing up of the islands from the bottom of the sea, snaring of the sun to slow it down in its passage, lifting of the sky to give his friends more room on earth, and theft of fire for his mother's kitchen. Maui's wife, the heroine of our story, is the passionate, completely unashamed beauty Hina (for, indeed, of what should she be ashamed?), who can be seen to this day in the markings of the moon, where she is sitting beneath a big ovava tree, beating out tapa cloth from its bark.[19]

Here is the Tuamotuan version of Hina's adventure: [20]

> Hina was originally the wife of the Monster Eel, Te Tuna [whose name means frankly, the Phallus], and the two lived together in their land beneath the sea until a day when Hina thought she had been there long enough. The place was intensely cold; and besides, she wanted now to be rid of Te Tuna. So she said to him: "You just stay here at home! I am going off to forage for us both."
>
> "And when shall you return?" he asked.
>
> She answered: "I shall be gone for quite a while; because today and tonight will be spent traveling, tomorrow looking for food, and the next day and night cooking the food; but the following day and night will see me on the way home."
>
> "Then go," he told her, "and stay away as long as necessary."
>
> So she set out on her journey. And she never paused to look for food, but went on to forage for a new lover. She went as far as to the land of the Male-principle (Tane) Clan, and

when she had reached their place called out: "The eel-shaped creature dwelling in this inland region rides manfully to passion's consummation: Te Tuna dwelling in the sea out there is but insipid food. I am a woman to be possessed by an eel-shaped lover; a woman come all the long way hither to unite in the struggle of passion upon the shores of Raro-nuku (the Land-below) and of Raro-vai-i-o (the Land-of-penetrating waters); the first woman thus to come utterly without shame seeking the eel-shaped rod of love. I am the dark pubic patch pursuing the assuagement of desire. For the fame of your manly prowess, O men of the Clan of the Male Principle, reached me even in the world below. I have come to you by way of unnumbered shores—along sandy beaches. Arise, O Detumescent Staff! Be plunged in the consummation of love. I am this woman from afar, desiring you ardently, O men of the Male-principle Clan!"

But the men of the clan only shouted at her in answer: "There is the road: follow it, and keep going! We shall never take the woman of the Monster Eel, Te Tuna, lest we be slain. He would be here in less than a day."

She continued on her way, and when she arrived at the land of the Penetrating-embrace (Peka) Clan, called out again, using the same words; but the men replied as had the others. She went on to the land of the Erect (Tu) Clan, and once again all happened as before. She came to the land of the Wonder-worker (Maui) Clan, where the call and response were again repeated. And then she approached the home of Maui's mother, Hua-hega.

When Hua-hega saw Hina approaching, she said to her son, Maui: "Take that woman for yourself!"

And so Maui-tikitiki-a-Ataraga (Wonder-worker, the Tumid, begotten of Ascending Shadow) took Hina to wife; and they all lived in that place together. But very soon, everybody round about realized that Te Tuna's wife had been taken by Maui, and they went to Te Tuna and told him.

"Your wife," they said, "has been carried off by Maui."

"Oh, let him have that woman to lie upon!" Te Tuna answered.

However, they returned to him so often, always harping on the same theme, that finally Te Tuna was roused to anger. He said to the people who kept coming to him with this chatter: "What, then, is this man Maui like?"

"He is actually a very small fellow," they replied, "and the end of his phallus is quite lopsided."

"Well—just let him get one glimpse of the soiled strip of loincloth between my legs," Te Tuna boasted, "and he'll go flying out of the way!" Then he said: "Go tell Maui that I am coming on an expedition of vengeance!" And he chanted a melancholy song of lamentation for his wife.

The people listened to the song and went to Maui. "Te Tuna," they said, "is coming to get you on an expedition of vengeance."

"Just let him come!" Maui said. But then he asked, "What sort of creature is he?"

"Ho!" they said. "A gigantic monster!"

"Is he as sturdy and strong as a tall, straight coconut tree?"

The people, wishing to mislead him, answered: "He is like a leaning coconut tree."

Maui asked: "Is he always weak and bending?"

They answered: "His weakness is inherent."

"Oho!" cried Maui. "Just let him catch one glimpse of the lopsided end of my phallus, and he'll go flying out of the way!"

The days passed, and patiently Maui waited—he and his household, living all together. And on a certain day when the skies grew dark, thunder rolled and lightning flashed, the people were filled with fear; for they knew that this now must be the coming of Te Tuna: and they all blamed Maui. "This," they said, "is the first time that one man has stolen the woman of another. We shall all be slain."

Maui reassured them. "Just keep close together and we shall not be slain."

Te Tuna presently appeared, and there were with him four companions: Pupu-vae-noa (Tuft-in-the-center), Maga-vai-i-e-rire (Noose-existing-in-woman), Porporo-tu-a-huaga (Testicles-set-in-the-scrotum), and Toke-a-kura (Clitoris-continuously-suffused). The Monster Eel stripped off his soiled loincloth and held it up in the sight of all, when at once a vast billowy surge reared up and roared landward from the sea. It came sweeping on, towering above the land, and Hua-hega shouted to her son Maui: "Be quick! Let your phallus be seen!"

Maui obeyed, and immediately the huge wave receded until the bed of the sea was laid bare and the monsters were piled high and dry on a reef. Then he proceeded to the place where they were stranded and struck down three. Toke-a-kura got away with a broken leg, while Te Tuna, himself, Maui spared.

Together, Maui and Te Tuna went to Maui's home, where they lived in harmony until a day when Te Tuna said to Maui: "We shall have to fight a duel, and when one of us has been killed the other will take the woman for himself."

"What sort of duel would you like it to be?" Maui asked.

And Te Tuna said: "We shall first engage in a contest in which each goes completely into the body of the other, and when that is over, I am going to kill you, take my woman, and return with her to my own land."

"Let it be as you wish," Maui agreed. Then he asked: "And who is to be the first?"

"I'll begin," the Monster Eel replied, and when Maui consented, Te Tuna stood up and commenced chanting his incantation:

The Orea-eel swings and sways,
The Orea-eel balances his head lower and lower:
He is a mighty monster who has come hither across the ocean from his distant isle.
Your phallus will urinate from fright!

The monster contracts, becoming smaller and smaller.
It is I, Te Tuna, who now enter, O Maui, into your body!

And Te Tuna disappeared completely into Maui's body, where he disposed himself to remain. However, after a long while, he came out again.

Maui had not been disturbed in the least. "Well, now it is my turn," Maui said.

Te Tuna agreed and the Wonder-worker began to chant his own spell, thus:

The Orea-eel swings and sways,
The Orea balances his head lower and lower—
A small man stands erect upon the land—
Your phallus will urinate from fright!

The man contracts—becoming smaller and smaller.
It is I, Maui, who now enter, O Te Tuna, into your body!

Maui disappeared completely into Te Tuna's body, and at once all the sinews of the Monster Eel were rent apart, so that he died. Whereupon Maui stepped forth and, cutting off Te Tuna's head, bore it away, intending to give it to his grandfather. But his mother, Hua-hega, got hold of it and refused to give it up. She said to Maui: "Take the head and bury it beside the post in the corner of our house." And so he took it, buried it as she had directed, and never gave it another thought.

Maui continued to go about his usual daily tasks and they all went on living together as before, until, one evening, when they were sitting in the corner of the house where the head of Te Tuna had been buried, Maui perceived that a new shoot had sprung up from the sand. He was amazed. Hua-hega, noticing his surprise, said to him: "Why are you surprised?" To which he answered: "The head of Te Tuna that I buried here in this corner of our house: why has it sprouted?"

Hua-hega then told him: "The plant growing beside you is a kind of coconut known as 'husk of the sea-green color from the region of the gods,' because it has arisen from the depths of the sea, to reveal to us the color of its own land. Take care of your precious coconut tree and you will find that it will provide us all with food."

Maui plucked the fruit when it matured. The meat within was eaten by all, and the shell then was fashioned by Maui into a couple of bowls, to serve as drinking cups. And when all was done he danced and sang a boastful song in celebration of his own prowess and of that superiority in magic through which the Monster Eel's head had become transformed into his food:

No more than a woman's belt strap,
No more than a scurrying cockroach,
Was Tuna the Ancient One!

Bewitched with a sprig of *mohio* fern,
A leaf casting its spell upon a mere simpleton in the arts of enchantment!
What, indeed, did he bring against me?

Nothing at all!

"And that," the tale concludes, "is the way the coconut was acquired as food for all the people of this Earth-world here above."

The adventure, as here narrated, was taken down from the lips of Fariua-a-Makitua, an old chieftain of the island of Fagatu in the Tuamotu Archipelago, which is in the very middle of the Pacific, just east of the Society Islands and Tahiti. The old man had been a disciple in his youth of an earlier teacher, Kamake, who in his time had been regarded as the greatest of all the Tuamotuan sages.[21] And I have presented this unadulterated version of the legend of Hina and the monster eel *in extenso,* not only because it renders authentically the moral atmosphere of the ancient Polynesian epics, but also because it may serve as an introduction to our later studies of magic, the force of magic, and the power of erotic elements in primitive conjuring.

The narrative, as here recounted, is translated from a style of Polynesian recitative that suggests very strongly both the form and the atmosphere of the archaic ceremonials from which the Greek tragedy and comedy were developed in the sixth century B.C. Just as the Greek satyr-chorus sang and danced its strophe and antistrophe, turning and whirling in a labyrinthine dance while the legend of the god or hero was being sung—so here. Captain Cook and the other early voyagers in the Pacific have described the great religious festivals where literally hundreds of dancers, in orderly files and rows, performed sacred hulas to the boom of drums, sonorous gourds, and organ-pipe bamboos thumped upon the ground, while the sacred chants of the heroes and the gods were sung in strophe and antistrophe by soloists and choruses of many voices.[22] For example, Te Tuna's melancholy chant of lament for the loss of Hina, when the people had convinced him that he should go to win her back, appeared, in the original, as follows:

I

	First Voice
Kua riro!	My loved one has been stolen from me.
	Second Voice
Te aroha i te hoa ki roto i te manava;	Grieving love for the wife stirs within the heart;
	Chorus
—kua riro.	—for she has become the mistress of another.
Matagi kavea mai e Kua riro. Ho atu. . . .	The winds have brought the word That she has been stolen from me. We now set out. . . .

II

	First Voice
Ho atu matou ki Vavau,	We now set out for Vavau.
	Second Voice
Kia higo i te hoa—	To see the loved one—
	Chorus
—kua riro.	—who has become the mistress of another.
Matagi i aue e	Wailing, the very winds lament
Kua riro.	Her who has been stolen from me.
Te aroha. . . .	Grieving love. . . .

III

	First Voice
Te aroha i te vahine	Grieving love for the wife
ki roto i te manava.	wells within the breast.
	Second Voice
Kia kite taku mata	Would that my eyes
i te ipo—	again beheld the loved one—
	Chorus
—kua riro.	—who has been stolen from me; now clasped in the arms of another.
Matagi i aue e.	Even the winds lament.
Te aroha i-i-i-e!	Bitter is my anguish and despair.

Farther along in this chapter we must look again at the highly complex but gradually clearing problem of the relationship of the early Pacific to the archaic Mediterranean traditions; but first let us enlarge our spectrum of the myths and tales of the Polynesian monster eel. We shall then be in a better position not only to analyze the variant versions of the myth in the Bible, but also to comprehend the reduced role of the serpent in the Greek Persephone and Indonesian Hainuwele versions of the myth, with their stress on the ritual sacrifice of a pig. For one of the most important as well as illuminating aspects of the prehistoric perspective opened by a comparative study of myth rests in the problem of the pig's taking on the role of the serpent as the sacred animal of the labyrinth—and after the pig the bull, and after the bull the horse.

In the course of its long history and longer prehistory of diffusion, the mythologem (or nuclear mythological image) of the origin of the food plant generated a broad series of mutually clarifying, yet strikingly different variants, each seeming to reveal some essential quality or aspect of what must once have been the primal form, yet none being definitely more eligible to be its representative than any of the rest. The picture can perhaps be compared to that of a number of sisters and brothers, all representing a family type, yet none more authentically than the rest. And the more numerous the gathered examples, the more fascinating and tantalizing the comparison.

For instance: In the Friendly Islands (Tonga), it is told that a male child, Eel, was born to a human couple, who had also a pair of human daughters. Eel, living in a pool, sprang toward his sisters in eager affection, but they fled, and when he pursued they jumped into the sea and became two rocks that may be seen to this day off the shore of Tongatabu. Eel went on swimming, to Samoa, where he again took up life in a pool. But when a virgin, bathing there, became pregnant because of his presence, the people decided to kill him. He told the girl to ask the people to give her his head when he had been killed, and to plant it, which she did. And it grew into a new sort of tree, the coconut tree.[23]

In Mangaia, one of the Cook Islands, the maiden's name was Ina (a dialect variant of Hina), and she liked to bathe in a certain pool. But there was a great eel that swam past and touched her; this occurred again and again, and one time he threw off his eel form and stood before her as she bathed, a beautiful youth named Tuna (once again—Te Tuna). Ina accepted Tuna as her lover, and he would always visit her in human form but become an eel when he went away. And then, one day, he told her that the time had come when he would have to depart from her forever. He would make one final visit the next day, in a great flood of water, in the form of an eel; when she should decapitate him and bury the head. Tuna came; Ina did as she had been told. And every day thereafter she visited the place of the buried head, until, at length, a green shoot appeared, which grew into a beautiful tree that in the course of time produced fruits, the first coconuts. And every nut, when husked, still shows the eyes and face of Ina's lover.[24]

Plant-origin stories conforming to this stereotype are common for the other food plants of Polynesia also. The breadfruit tree first appeared, for example, according to a legend told in Hawaii, when a man named Ulu, dwelling near the present city of Hilo, died of famine. He and his wife had a sickly baby boy whose life was endangered by the general scarcity of food, and the man, distracted, had gone in prayer to the temple at Puueo, to learn from the god what should be done.

Now the god of that temple was of a type known in Hawaiian as the *mo'o:* which is a word meaning "lizard," or "reptile." But the only reptile in Hawaii is a harmless, even affectionately regarded little lizard that scurries up and down the walls of people's houses and clings like a fly to ceilings, trapping insects with its quick tongue. The manner in which the mythological system of the islands has magnified this innocuous creature to the proportions of a greatly dangerous divine dragon supplies one of the most graphic illustrations I know of a mythological process—seldom mentioned in the textbooks of our subject but of considerable force and importance nevertheless—to which the late Dr. Ananda K. Coomaraswamy referred as *land-náma,* "land naming" or "land taking."[25] Through *land-náma,* "land naming," or "land taking," the features of a newly entered land are assimilated by an immigrant people to its imported heritage of myth. We have already noted the case of the role of the serpent assumed by an eel. We are now considering that of the same serpent role assumed by a harmless lizard. We might also have considered the manner in which the Pilgrim Fathers and pioneers of America established their New Canaans, Nazareths, Sharons, Bethels, and Bethlehems wherever they went. The new land, and all the features of the new land, are linked back as securely as possible to the archetypes—the spiritually, psychologically, and sociologically significant archetypes—of whatever mythological system the people carry in their hearts. And through this process the land is spiritually validated, sanctified, and assimilated to the image of destiny that is the fashioning dynamism of the people's lives. We shall have plenty of occasion, throughout the following chapters, to observe the force of this principle in the shaping of symbols. The process has now been clearly announced to us by the monster eel and the noble *mo'o* of the mythologies of remote Polynesia.

To proceed, then, with the legend of the origin of the breadfruit: When the man, Ulu, returned to his wife from his visit to the temple at Puueo, he said, "I have heard the voice of the noble Mo'o, and he has told me that tonight, as soon as darkness draws over the sea and the fires of the volcano goddess, Pele, light the clouds over the crater of Mount Kilauea, the black cloth will cover my head. And when the breath has gone from my body and my spirit has departed to the realms of the dead, you are to bury my head carefully near our spring of running water. Plant my heart and entrails near the door of the house. My feet, legs, and arms, hide in the same manner. Then lie down upon the couch where the two of us have reposed so often, listen carefully throughout the night, and do not go forth before the sun has reddened the morning sky. If, in the silence of the night, you should hear noises as of falling leaves and flowers, and afterward as of heavy fruit dropping to the ground, you will know that my prayer has been granted: the life of our little boy will be saved." And having said that, Ulu fell on his face and died.

His wife sang a dirge of lament, but did precisely as she was told, and in the morning she found her house surrounded by a perfect thicket of vegetation.

"Before the door," we are told in Thomas Thrum's rendition of the legend,[26]

> on the very spot where she had buried her husband's heart, there grew a stately tree covered over with broad, green leaves dripping with dew and shining in the early sunlight, while on the grass lay the ripe, round fruit, where it had fallen from the branches above. And this tree she called *Ulu* (breadfruit) in honor of her husband. The little spring was concealed by a succulent growth of strange plants, bearing gigantic leaves and pendant clusters of long yellow fruit, which she named bananas. The intervening space was filled with a luxuriant growth of slender stems and twining vines, of

which she called the former sugar-cane and the latter yams; while all around the house were growing little shrubs and esculent roots, to each one of which she gave an appropriate name. Then summoning her little boy, she bade him gather the breadfruit and bananas, and, reserving the largest and best for the gods, roasted the remainder in the hot coals, telling him that in future this should be his food. With the first mouthful, health returned to the body of the child, and from that time he grew in strength and stature until he attained to the fulness of perfect manhood. He became a mighty warrior in those days, and was known throughout all the island, so that when he died, his name, Mokuola, was given to the islet in the bay of Hilo where his bones were buried; by which name it is called even to the present time.

An important system of such myths and rites, folktales and folk customs, deriving from a nuclear concept of the reciprocities of death and life (both in the way of killing and consuming and in that of propagating and dying) has been identified throughout the broad belt of the tropical equatorial zone, from the West African Sudan, across the Indian Ocean, deep into Polynesia—indeed, all the way to Easter Island, where the concept is rendered in the image of a caught and eaten fish.

"Where is our ancient queen?" we read, for example, in a text supplied by a native informant, who was reading (or at least professing to read) one of the mysterious hieroglyphic tablets of Easter Island that are supposed to have been preserved there for generations. "It is known," the reading continued, "that she was transformed into a fish that was finally caught in the still waters. . . . Away, away, if you cannot name the fish: that lovely fish with the short gills that was brought for food to our Great King and was laid upon a dish that rocked this way and that." [27]

Many variants of the constellation are known, ranging from cannibalistic rites to poetical tales of parental love; but their kinship is clear. Nor is the vast diffusion difficult to credit. The Indian Ocean basin has been the watery highway for millenniums of cultural exchanges, back and forth, while Polynesia received its population largely from the Indonesian zone. A single language family, the Malayo-Polynesian, extends, in fact, all the way from

Madagascar (just off the coast of southeast Africa) eastward to Easter Island (off the coast of Peru), and from New Zealand north to Formosa, and northeast to Hawaii.[28] Such linguistic affinities indicate not only cultural and historical relationship, but also psychological homologies—and to such a degree that not even the most passionate supporter of a theory of parallel development would presume (I should think) to explain according to his cherished principles such a coincidence as that represented by the following ways of naming the numbers from one to ten: [29]

	MADAGASCAR	INDONESIA			POLYNESIA	
	MALAGASY	MALAY	JAVANESE	TAGAL	SAMOAN	MAORI
1	isa	sa	sa	isa	tasi	tahi
2	rua	dua	ru	dalawa	lua	rua
3	telu	tiga	telu	tatlo	tolu	toru
4	efatra	ampat	pat	apat	fa	wha
5	limi	lima	lima	lima	lima	rima
6	eni(na)	anam	(ne)nem	anim	ono	ono
7	fitu	tujuh	pitu	pito	fitu	whitu
8	valu	dulafan	wolu	walo	valu	waru
9	sivi	sambilan	sono	siyam	iva	iwha
10	fulu	puluh	puluh	polo	sefulu	nahuru

The next step in this comparative study is to follow our theme to the shores of Peru and Mexico, the jungles of the Amazon, and the North American plains.

v. Parallelism or Diffusion?

The archaeology and ethnography of the past half-century have made it clear that the ancient civilizations of the Old World—those of Egypt, Mesopotamia, Crete and Greece, India and China—derived from a single base, and that this community of origin suffices to explain the homologous forms of their mythological and ritual structures. As already noted,* the beginnings of this epochal flowering have been traced to a neolithic base in the Near East, the first signs of which have been identified c. 7500–5500 B.C., and to the sudden appearance in approximately the same area, c. 3200 B.C., of a syndrome of priestly discoveries and crafts, including an

* Supra, pp. 135–150.

astronomical calendar, the art of writing, a science of mathematics applied to and attempting to coordinate the measurements of space and time, and the conception of the wheel. Nowhere else in the world have any of the elements either of the neolithic assemblage or of higher civilization been identified at levels of anything like these depths; and the probability of a worldwide diffusion from the Near East of the basic arts, not only of all higher civilization, but also of all village living based on agriculture and stock-breeding, has consequently been argued with bountiful documentation, by a group of scholars of which Professor Robert Heine-Geldern of Vienna is today the leader.

As we have observed, there is still some question, however, as to the ultimate backgrounds of the neolithic. One has certainly to concede that the basic arts of higher civilization were derived, as far as the Afro-Eurasian hemisphere is concerned, from the now well established Near Eastern matrix. Nevertheless, with respect to the arts of planting and stock-breeding, the earliest neolithic villages of the Near East may represent simply one province of a considerably larger zone. The earliest horizon for the domestication of the pig in what may be termed, roughly, the Malayo-Polynesian sphere has not yet been established; nor do we know how far back the primitive cultivation of the coconut, banana, and tuberous food plants should be placed. Therefore, though it may, on one hand, ultimately be found that most of the myths and rituals of the Malayo-Polynesian area should be interpreted as provincial to the Near Eastern proto- or basal neolithic, it may, on the other hand, ultimately appear that the reading should be run the other way. But in either case (and this point, I believe, no one acquainted with the facts now assembled would deny) the two developments were not separate; so that the progress of human culture in the Old World from the level of food-collection (hunting and root-gathering) to that of food-cultivation (planting and stock-breeding) has now to be studied as one very broadly spread, yet single process.

With respect, however, to the New World there is still raging a violent, and even cantankerous scholarly conflict of opinion.

For example, in a firm presentation of the point of view that has been favored by the majority of our North American schools of anthropology, we read:

> In both hemispheres, man started from cultural scratch, as a nomadic hunter, a user of stone tools, a paleolithic savage. In both he spread over great continents and shaped his life to cope with every sort of environment. Then, in both hemispheres, wild plants were brought under cultivation; population increased; concentrations of people brought elaboration of social groupings and rapid progress in the arts. Pottery came into use, fibres and wools were woven into cloth, animals were domesticated, metal working began—first in gold and copper, then in the harder alloy, bronze. Systems of writing were evolved.
>
> Not only in material things do the parallels hold. In the New World as well as in the Old, priesthoods grew and, allying themselves with temporal powers, or becoming rulers in their own right, reared to their gods vast temples adorned with painting and sculpture. The priests and chiefs provided for themselves elaborate tombs richly stocked for the future life. In political history it is the same. In both hemispheres group joined group to form tribes; coalitions and conquests brought pre-eminence; empires grew and assumed the paraphernalia of glory.
>
> These are astonishing similarities. And if we believe, as most modern students do, that the Indians' achievement was made independently, and their progress was not stimulated from overseas, then we reach a very significant conclusion. We can infer that human beings possess an innate urge to take certain definite steps toward what we call civilization. And that men also possess the innate ability, given proper environmental conditions, to put that urge into effect. In other words, we must consider that civilization is an inevitable response to laws governing the growth of culture and controlling the man-culture relationship.[30]

Leo Frobenius, however, as early as 1903 was taking a precisely contrary view, one that has since been represented and developed chiefly by the European and South American scholars of the subject. Believing that the primitive planting villages of equatorial America were extensions eastward from Polynesia of a cultural style that he had already identified from the Sudan to Easter

Island, he argued that the basic American hunting-culture continuum—which had been carried into the continent from northeastern Siberia, across Bering Strait, and had spread downward vertically from Alaska to Cape Horn—must have been struck horizontally by sea voyagers from Polynesia and cut through, as by a wedge. "In our study of Oceania," he wrote, "it can be shown that a bridge existed, and not a chasm, between America and Asia. It would be a contradiction to all the laws of the local culture of Oceania for us to assume that the Polynesians called a halt and turned back at Easter Island. And from Hawaii, furthermore, an often traveled bridge of wind currents leads to the Northwest Coast."[31]

The strongest and usual reply of the isolationists to every argument of the diffusionists was that the Polynesian migrations were late, far too late, to account for the invention of agriculture and the flowering of high civilization in the New World. The period of the great Polynesian migrations they placed between the tenth and fourteenth centuries A.D., and the earliest possible entry of man into that far-flung island world of the South Pacific not earlier than the fifth century A.D.[32] Whereas all sorts of ancient dates were proposed for the earliest agricultural horizon in the New World: Spinden's date, for example, of c. 4000 B.C., or Kroeber's, c. 3000 B.C.[33]

Actually, however, the earliest well-established date for American agriculture is only c. 1016 ± 300 B.C., at a site on the northern coast of Peru called Huaca Prieta.* There, at the mouth of the Chicama Valley, a number of mounds excavated in the late 1940s

* I am not discussing any of the fanciful interpretations that have been suggested for the celebrated "Bat Cave" discovery in western New Mexico, where a series of early C-14 datings on a "primitive pod-corn" misled the argument for a time (cf. Alfonso Caso in *Anthropology Today* [Chicago: University of Chicago Press, 1953], p. 231, and Alex D. Krieger, ibid., p. 251). The discovery since of maize pollen in drill cores in the Valley of Mexico at a depth of over 200 feet, where it would appear to represent an age of not less than 60,000 years, indicates that there was a wild primitive corn in North America (cf. Paul C. Mangelsdorf, "New Evidence on the Origin and Ancestry of Maize," *American Antiquity*, XIX, No. 4 [1954], pp. 409–10). The "Bat Cave" date consequently can no longer be argued as evidence of an antecedent agricultural horizon.

yielded a beautiful series of stratified remains, four extremely significant samplings of which have been dated by the new radiocarbon (C-14) method as follows:

1. Sample No. 598: charcoal from bedrock-level fireplaces, 2348 ± 230 B.C. There was no evidence of agriculture on this level. The associated remains indicated the presence only of a primitive hunting, fishing, and food-gathering community.
2. Sample No. 321: wood associated with agricultural products, 1016 ± 300 B.C. On this level the earliest agricultural products appeared, and they were, to everyone's amazement: a) twined fabrics (nets and woven matting) made of an Asiatic cotton, and b) two small bottle-gourds carved in low relief with highly stylized figures suggesting trans-Pacific themes (a double bird head and the mask of a sort of cat- or jaguar-man)—the bottle-gourd being a plant not native to America. In addition, bits of bark cloth (tapa: an Oceanic, trans-Pacific element) were found in association with these remains.
3. Sample No. 323: rope associated with a coarse ceramic ware: 682 ± 300 B.C.
4. Sample No. 75: house timber associated with cultivated maize: 715 ± 200 B.C.[34]

It is obvious that the dates are far short of the old "early agricultural horizon" of c. 3000 or 4000 B.C. And meanwhile, to settle the balance, a radiocarbon date of 1530 ± 200 B.C. has been established for a settlement of some kind on the island of Saipan in the Marianas, well out in the Pacific, some 1500 miles eastward of the Philippines.[35] So the protest of "far too late" has been rendered null.

The latest position of the argument for independent development is presented in a series of articles by Wendel C. Bennett, Alex D. Krieger, and Gordon R. Willey, in a recent encyclopedic inventory of the anthropological sciences, *Anthropology Today,* which was published in 1953. Briefly stated, a so-called "New World Formative Period" has been postulated, during which the basic neolithic arts of both Peru and Middle America should have been developed, "a center, or centers, of origin," as Professor Willey formulates the idea, "lying anywhere between central Mexico and southern Peru."[36] "The argument runs," states Professor Bennett, "that an agricultural economy, based on plant domestication in South America, spread throughout the entire area of what is now called 'Nuclear America.' It is still undetermined whether this complex was spread by migration or by diffusion, or, for that matter, whether it could not have developed independently. In any case, two major centers of advanced civilization grew out of this Formative basis, one in Mesoamerica, one in the Central Andes, in large part independently of each other . . . but in the intermediate region the Formative complex persisted and spread around the Caribbean area." [37]

No one, however, has yet come out quite clearly with the dates to which the New World Formative Period should be assigned. "Certainly no less than 3000 years ago [i.e., 1000 B.C.], and probably much more," writes Professor Julian H. Steward, for example, in his "Interpretative Summary" at the close of the great six-volume *Handbook of South American Indians,* of which he was the editor, "the Indian began to bring native American plants under domestication." [38] Nor can anyone yet say just where the New World Formative Period took its rise. "The region of its ultimate origin is unknown," writes Professor Steward, "but it might have been in South America." [39]

It might, however, have been somewhere else entirely, as we may judge from the early appearance of those bottle-gourds on the coast of Peru, c. 1016 ± 300 B.C. The bottle gourd is not a wild but a cultivated plant and depends, as Carl O. Sauer points out, on the care of man for its preservation. "It is in no sense a marsh plant," he writes. "The theory of its accidental dissemination involves," he then continues, "in addition to the undamaged transit of an ocean, a waiting agriculturalist who carried it in from the seashore to a suitable spot of cultivation." [40]

But the bottle-gourd is not the only plant that came to America across the Pacific. The Asiatic cotton that entered the New World at the same time and is present in the earliest agricultural, preceramic horizons of both Peru and Chile not only made itself at home here but also mixed with a wild American variety—whereupon the mixed breed was carried back into and through Polynesia, as far as to Fiji.[41] Add the fact that the cocopalm was cultivated in pre-Columbian tropical America "in great groves" and is not a plant that can establish itself by being washed up onto a beach;[42] the further fact that the cultivated amaranth (which is known—perhaps significantly—as pigweed) was used as both a cereal and a potherb in pre-Columbian America, as also in India and other Asiatic monsoon lands;[43] again, the fact that the plantain, which was a common staple of Indian diet and widely distributed in the tropics of the New World, from southern Brazil to Jalisco, Mexico, appears to have been introduced from overseas before the coming of Columbus;[44] still again, the fact that the origin of maize itself is still obscure and may indeed have involved a Southeast Asian contribution;[45] and finally, the fact that a number of plants known to have been first cultivated in America have been found well established in the Southwest Pacific (namely the peanut, jackbean, lima bean, jicama, and sweet potato, the last even having the same name—kumar/kumara—in Peru and in Polynesia)[46]—and the case is made for at least a modicum of American participation in the cultural movements of the Malayo-Polynesian sphere.

Professor Paul Rivet, honorary director of the Musée de l'Homme in Paris, has pointed out that in coastal Chile and Peru, as well as in certain regions of Mexico, the Polynesian style of oven is used;[47] that comparisons can be made between the writing system of Easter Island and the ideographs of certain tribes of Colombia, Venezuela, and the high Peruvian-Bolivian plateau; that twenty-one artifacts of Polynesian design have been found in various points in America, from the Argentine to Vancouver Island, wooden clubs identical to those of the South Sea Islands in Peru and among the Tlinkits of the Northwest Coast; that in Polynesia itself traditions existed of voyages beyond Easter Island, and that both the seaworthy catamarans of the South Seas and the balsas of Peru were capable of trans-Pacific adventures: furthermore, that in Peru there were traditions of expeditions to the West—one, indeed, of four hundred boats and twenty thousand men, sent by one of the last of the Incas of Peru, Tupac-Inca-Yupanqui, which returned after nine months or a year with black prisoners and a brass or copper throne—in Mangareva, reciprocally, there having been the tradition of "a red man who came from the East with a fleet of raft-like ships." The Kon-Tiki Expedition of Thor

Heyerdahl in the summer of 1947, from Peru to the Tuamotus on a Peruvian balsa raft, made evident as vividly as anyone could have desired the possibility of voyages of this kind.

"Would it after all have been surprising," asks Monsieur Rivet, after a consideration of all these matters, "if the Polynesians, the most prodigious navigators on earth, had pursued their travels as far as the shores of America? Perfectly familiar with currents and winds, able to steer a course by the stars, they sailed at night and regularly made trips of 2000 miles, sometimes even 4200 miles, without putting ashore. To find the tiny Polynesian islands lost in the immensity of the Pacific they were guided by the small cloud which forms above each island at a height of over 11,000 feet and which is perceived by a practiced eye from a distance of 120 miles. Their double canoes, pirogues, made seven to eight miles per hour, 75 miles in a ten- to twelve-hour day; thus one of these boats could have covered the distance from Hawaii to California, or from Easter Island to the South American coast in twenty days." [48]

But the voyages of the Polynesians cannot have been the earliest by any means; for we have those carbon-dated calabashes of Huaca Prieta; also the cotton, coconut, and amaranth, all of which would have arrived before the period of the Polynesians. Paul Rivet has argued for a series of Melanesian arrivals, pointing out that a certain American Indian language group (the Hokan languages of Central America, Mexico, and California) is closer to Melanesian even than the Polynesian languages are. And in 1923 Professor A. L. Kroeber of the University of California, whom no one, I think, could then have accused of being a diffusionist, in the following passage conceded recognition to an example of what he clearly hoped would ultimately be shown to be a mere fluke—or at most an extraordinary example of parallel development.

> A startling parallelism has been demonstrated between the Pan's pipes of the Solomon Islands in Melanesia and those of the northwest Brazilian Indians. The odd pipes differ, each from the next, by the interval of a fourth. The even pipes give notes half-way in pitch between the adjacent odd ones, and thus form another "circle of fourths." But the similarity does not end here. The absolute pitch of the examined instruments from Melanesia and Brazil is the same. Thus, the

> vibration rates in successive pipes are 557 and 560.5; 651 and 651; 759 and 749; 880 and 879! This is so close a coincidence as to seem at first sight beyond the bounds of accidental convergence. The data have in fact been offered, and in some quarters accepted, as evidence of a historical connection between the western Pacific and South America. Yet the connection would have had to be ancient, since no memory of it remains nor is it supported by resemblances in race, speech, nor anything obvious in culture. The instruments are perishable. Primitive people, working by rule of thumb, would be unable to produce an instrument of given absolute pitch except by matching it against another, and perhaps not then. Moreover, it is not known that absolute pitch is of the least concern to them. It is therefore incredible that this correspondence rests on any ancient diffusion: there must be an error in the record somewhere, or the one accident in a million has happened in the particular instruments examined.
>
> The identity of scale or intervals however remains, and may be a true case of parallelism. Only, as usual, it boils down to a rather simple matter. The circles of fourths evidently originate in the practice, in both regions, of overblowing the pipes. This produces over-tones; of which the second, the "third partial tone," is the fifth above the octave of the fundamental, so that successive notes in either the odd or even series of pipes, would, on the octave being disallowed, differ by fourths. The basis of the resemblance, then, is a physical law of sound. The cultural similarity shrinks to the facts of pipes in series, the use of overblown tones, and the intercalating odd-even series. Even these resemblances are striking, and more specific than many cited cases of parallelism. In fact, were they supported by enough resemblances in other aspects of culture, they would go far to compel belief in actual connections between Melanesia and Brazil.[49]

Actually, of course, a multitude of resemblances exist: the use of the blowgun with poisoned arrows; the chewing of lime mixed with a narcotic; a certain technique of weaving, known as ikat weaving; the pounding of bark cloth (tapa); the headhunt with its ceremonial preservation of the taken head; the men's secret society with its contrived spooks and devices for intimidating the women; the dwelling of whole communities in a single house; an architecture on piles; cat's cradle games (string-labyrinth figures) comprising many transformations, each with a name; certain types of fish weir and animal trap, as well as a particular way of catching sea turtles by skewering a line through the tail of a sucker fish and allowing it then to swim out and attach itself to the bottom of a turtle; slit-log drums and a considerable battery of characteristic musical instruments; nude female figurines (guess who!); etc., etc. *ad infinitum*—not to mention again the bottle-gourd, the coconut, the amaranth, and the weaving of an Asiatic cotton.

Professor Robert Heine-Geldern has proposed a well-articulated, precisely documented theory, based on the concept of a prehistoric circum-Pacific culture zone, represented by an art style probably native to eastern Asia and perhaps dating from as early as the third millennium B.C. Its characteristic sculptural form is well typified in the totem poles of the American Northwest Coast: combinations of heraldic, genealogical, or mythological human and animal figures arranged in vertical series. Another characteristic motif, also exhibited in the arts of the Northwest Coast, appears in weaving and bark-cloth designs, tattoo motifs, painting, and low relief: the bird, fish, animal, or human form to be represented being split down the back or front, opened out like a book, and displayed thus, as though hinged. Still another motif is the human figure in a broad squat, frequently with its tongue out flat and down over the chin—a form that we recognize immediately as one of the postures of the Greek Medusa, the Gorgon whose head Perseus took in Africa just before his rescue of the maid Andromeda from the serpent. Throughout the circum-Pacific culture zone the great serpent, the cosmic serpent, as spouse of the goddess and as a variously manipulated motif in art, is a prominent feature. As Heine-Geldern has shown, the particular idiosyncrasies of this Old Pacific Style, both compositional and thematic, can be readily identified not only in the arts of the Northwest Coast but in Melanesia (New Ireland and parts of New Guinea), as well as among the Dyaks of Borneo, Bataks of Sumatra, and Igorots of the Philippines—that is to say, precisely in the province of our maiden Dema Hainuwele. And finally, Professor Heine-Geldern has demonstrated that traits of this style entered into the arts of early dynastic China—successively, Shang (1523–1027 B.C.), Early Chou (1027–771 B.C.), and Late Chou (771–221 B.C.)—

where they combined with traits derived by diffusion from the great culture matrix of the Near East, and then were carried by Chinese ships to Indonesia, Melanesia, and Polynesia, and to North and South America, appearing, specifically, in the arts of the Northwest Coast, Middle America, Peru, and the Amazon Basin.[50]

Further, when the patterns of the higher civilizations of the great Maya-Aztec and Peruvian late periods are compared with their counterparts in Egypt and Mesopotamia, India and China, we find, among a multitude of other analogies: a basic neolithic complex, comprising agriculture and stock-breeding (in America, the llama, alpaca, and turkey), matting, basketry, painted pottery, both coarse and fine, loom weaving with elegant patterns, using both wool and an Asiatic cotton, metallurgy in gold, silver, tin, platinum, and smelted copper, with alloys of copper-tin, copper-lead, copper-arsenic, copper-silver, and gold-silver, employing the *cire-perdue* method for the casting of sculptured figures, and fashioning, among other products, golden bells; a highly developed calendric system yielding a pattern of interlocking large and smaller cycles, an assignment of deities to the various heavenly spheres and a notion of the horoscope, the idea of cycles of creation and dissolution, the mythological figure of the Cosmic Tree with an eagle at its summit and a serpent at its root; the guardian gods and four colors of the four directions, the four elements (fire, air, earth, and water), heavens stratified above and hells below, a weaving goddess of the moon, and a god who dies and is resurrected. Furthermore, on the sociological side we find: four social classes—priests, nobles, agriculturalists (common people), and slaves—with insignia of kingship almost precisely duplicating those of the ancient world: fan bearers, scepters, canopies, palanquins, and the blown conch as royal trumpet; the idea of the city as capital of an empire, approached by causeways and embellished by ornamented temples and palaces, the temples atop pyramids, almost precisely as in Mesopotamia, and the architecture including colonnades, spiral staircases, sculptured doorways, lintels, pillars, etc.; arts including mosaics, high and low relief, carved jade, murals in fresco, memorial monuments, and the writing of books.

The crucial dates may be summarized about as follows.

I. Formative Horizon (c. 1500–c. 500 B.C.)
(Compare Old World basal and high neolithic)

1. Earliest known agriculture and pottery strata: from c. 1500 B.C.
   Huaca Prieta bottle gourds, bark cloth, and cotton: c. 1016 ± 300 B.C.
   Guañape ceramic complex (Peru)—early negative pottery, weaving, maize: c. 1250(?)–c. 850 B.C.
   Zacatenco ceramic complex (Mexico)—fine, painted pottery and figurines: c. 1500(?)–c. 1000 B.C.
2. Developed, "Pre-Classic" elite styles: from c. 1000 B.C.
   Chavín complex (Peru)—goldwork, colossal architecture and sculpture, jaguar cult: c. 850–500 B.C.
   Olmec complex (Mexico)—lapidary art in jade, pyramids, and great stone heads, jaguar cult: c. 1000–c. 500 B.C.

II. Classic Horizon (c. 500 B.C.–c. 500 A.D.)
(Compare Old World hieratic city states)

MIDDLE AMERICA

Pre-Maya (*Chicanel*)
(424 B.C.–57 A.D.) *
Calendar, writing, stone and stucco ceremonial architecture.

Early Maya (*Tzukol*)
(57–373 A.D.) *
Great stone temple-cities (Tikal and Uaxactún) with corbeled roofs and arches, carved stone monuments, polychrome ceramic.

Late Maya (*Tepeuh*)
(373–727A.D.) *
Many new temple-cities, climaxing c. 530 A.D.; superlative sculptural achievements (viz., Piedras Negras); diffusion of influence, but then decline: abandonment of many cities (reason unknown). Florescence, also, of *Tajín* (Gulf Coast) and *Ulúa* (Honduras) styles.

PERU

Salinar/Gallinazo
(c. 500–c. 300 B.C.)
Fine ceramic, brick pyramids, domesticated llamas, developed weaving and metallurgy.

Moche, Nazca, and Early Tiahuanaco
(c. 300 B.C.–c. 500 A.D.)
Richly developed agriculture with many crops (maize, beans, peanuts, potatoes, sweet potatoes, chili peppers, manioc, pumpkins, bottle gourds, cotton, coco, quinoa, etc.); irrigation works, enormous temple-pyramids of brick, murals; a hieratically organized society; dwellings of brick or stone; exquisite pottery; metalwork in gold, gold alloys, and copper. Metal in coastal north (Moche), tapestry south (Nazca), stone in highlands.

* See footnote on page 214.

III. Historic Horizon (c. 500–1521/33 A.D.)

MIDDLE AMERICA

League of Mayapan
(727–934 A.D.) *
Advent of a new people from the southwest: introduction of a new religion, new customs, and new architecture (including numerous motifs suggesting a fresh influence from Southeast Asia);[51] revival of older cities (Chichen Itza) and the founding of new (Mayapan, Uxmal); the period closing with a devastating war between Chichen Itza and Mayapan.

Toltec/Mixtec
(908–1168/c.1150–1350 A.D.)
Mixcoatl, a barbarian from the north, founds the Toltec empire, his son being the fabulous Quetzalcoatl, whose age was the Golden Age of Tula, when "the cotton grew naturally in all colors." Tula was destroyed 1168 A.D.; the empire dissolved, and the lead passed for two centuries to the Mixtecs of coastal Oaxaca.

Aztec
(c. 1337–1521 A.D.)
The final empire of native Mexico, conquered by Cortes, 1521.

PERU

Late Tiahuanaco
(c. 500–1000 A.D.)
Expansion of the highland (Tiahuanaco) influence over the coastal areas (Moche, Nazca); enormous megalithic monuments; elegant gold, silver, and copper crafts; gilding, casting, annealing, silverplating; superb pottery (polychrome ware in Nazca area, three-dimensional figures in north), textiles (of wool and cotton), tapestries and stone-carving.

Chimu
(c. 1000–1440 A.D.)
A period of wars and fortified refuge places, alliances and coalitions; new kingdoms and new cities (the "city-builder period"); flowering of the great Chimu metropolis, Chanchan (near present Trujillo): eight square miles of walls, streets, reservoirs, and pyramids of brick; efficient but uninventive industrial arts and crafts.

Inca
(c. 1440–1533 A.D.)
The final empire of native Peru, conquered by Pizarro, 1533.

* The dates from 424 B.C. to 934 A.D. are based on Spinden's correlation of the Mayan calendar with our own. If the Thompson-Goodman correlation is preferred, the dates should be 260 years later. For a justification of the earlier series, see Covarrubias, *Indian Art of Mexico and Central America,* p. 218; also, Willey and Phillips, *Method and Theory in American Archaeology,* p. 185, note 3.

The summary is necessarily rough, for the datings are not yet firm and the authorities differ considerably.[52]

The "classic horizon" here is placed very much later, obviously, than the comparable developments even in China, where, in contrast to Mesopotamia (3200 B.C.), Egypt (2800 B.C.), Crete and India (2600 B.C.), the high culture style with writing, the calendar, and the hieratic heavenly order of the state did not appear until c. 1523 B.C. The powerful Han Empire was in full career from 202 B.C. to 220 A.D., sending its great ships around Indo-China in trade with Rome. The Dong-son of northeastern Indo-China were masters of the southern seas from c. 333 B.C. to c. 50 A.D., as were the merchant mariners of southeast India, Java, Sumatra, and Cambodia, from perhaps the early seventh century to the close of the twelfth century A.D. Not only are the characteristic elements of the Middle American "classic horizon" characteristic also of Asia (stepped pyramids, corbeled vault architecture, certain types of tomb, hieroglyphic writing combined with a mature calendrical and astronomical science, well developed stone sculpture), but also, as Dr. Gordon Eckholm has shown,[53] many motifs of the Mayan "historic horizon" suggest specifically contemporary India, Java, and Cambodia; e.g., the trefoil arch, tiger throne, lotus staff and lotus throne, conch shell associated with plants, cross and sacred tree (often with a monster mask in the center and bird in the upper branches), serpent columns and balustrades, seated lions and tigers, copper bells. . . . And are we still to suppose that America remained inviolate?

If it did, then psychology has a far greater task ahead, comparing the feats of duplication, than archaeology or ethnology would face if it were merely a six-thousand-mile voyage across the Pacific, c. 1500 B.C., that had to be explained.

"Could such feats of duplication take place, guided only by the parallel structure of men's minds and bodies," asks Professor Gordon R. Willey, "or was the cultural germ transplanted across the oceans?" [54]

One well may wonder.

VI. The Ritual Love-Death in Pre-Columbian America

The best-known North American example of the mythologem of the divine being who was killed and planted, to become the food of man, is that of the Ojibway of the Great Lakes region, whose mythology, as recorded in the 1820s by the young United States government agent Henry Rowe Schoolcraft (1793–1864), became the source and inspiration of Longfellow's *The Song of Hiawatha.* Schoolcraft's wife was a Christianized Indian; some of his in-laws were full-fledged savages. The language in which the myths were communicated to him was consequently neither pidgin English nor pidgin Ojibway, but a fluent and natural native prose. We must pardon his style, therefore, if it does not approximate that of our contemporary collectors of Indian lore, whose comparatively brief visits with their "informants" have conduced to the development among them of a curiously choppy, ostensibly primitive, purely anthropological prose style that is actually neither here nor there and serves to underplay the delicacy and sophistication of native thought. Schoolcraft erred, we may say, on the side of literary embroidery; but at least no one is in danger of mistaking his prose for a literal translation.

Here is his rendition of "The Legend of Mondawmin, or The Origin of Indian Corn," which became the source of Longfellow's Chapter V: "Hiawatha's Fasting."

> In times past a poor Indian was living with his wife and children in a beautiful part of the country. He was not only poor, but inexpert in procuring food for his family, and his children were all too young to give him assistance. Although poor, he was a man of a kind and contented disposition. He was always thankful to the Great Spirit for everything he received. The same disposition was inherited by his eldest son, who had now arrived at the proper age to undertake the ceremony of Ke-ig-nish-im-o-win, or fast, to see what kind of spirit would be his guide and guardian through life.
>
> Wunzh, for this was his name, had been an obedient boy from his infancy, and was of a pensive, thoughtful, and mild disposition, so that he was beloved by the whole family. As soon as the first indications of spring appeared, they built him

the customary little lodge, at a retired spot some distance from their own, where he would not be disturbed during this solemn rite. In the meantime he prepared himself, and immediately went into it and commenced his fast.

The first few days he amused himself in the mornings by walking in the woods and over the mountains, examining the early plants and flowers, and in this way prepared himself to enjoy his sleep, and, at the same time, stored his mind with pleasant ideas for his dreams. While he rambled through the woods, he felt a strong desire to know how the plants, herbs, and berries grew, without any aid from man, and why it was that some species were good to eat, and others possessed medicinal or poisonous juices. He recalled these thoughts to mind after he became too languid to walk about, and had confined himself strictly to the lodge; he wished he could dream of something that would prove a benefit to his father and family, and to all others. "True!" he thought, "the Great Spirit made all things, and it is to him that we owe our lives. But could he not make it easier for us to get our food, than by hunting animals and taking fish? I must try to find this out in my visions."

On the third day he became weak and faint, and kept his bed. He fancied, while thus lying, that he saw a handsome young man coming down from the sky and advancing toward him. He was richly and gaily dressed, having on a great many garments of green and yellow colors, but differing in their deeper or lighter shades. He had a plume of waving feathers on his head, and all his motions were graceful.

"I am sent to you, my friend," said the celestial visitor, "by that Great Spirit who made all things in the sky and on earth. He has seen and knows your motives in fasting. He sees that it is from a kind and benevolent wish to do good to your people, and to procure a benefit for them, and that you do not seek for strength in war or the praise of warriors. I am sent to instruct you, and show you how you can do your kindred good."

He then told the young man to arise and prepare to wrestle with him, as it was only by this means that he could hope to succeed in his wishes. Wunzh knew he was weak from fasting, but he felt his courage rising in his heart, and immediately got up, determined to die rather than fail. He commenced the trial, and, after a protracted effort, was almost exhausted, when the beautiful stranger said, "My friend, it is enough for once; I will come again to try you"; and, smiling on him, he ascended in the air in the same direction from which he came.

The next day the celestial visitor reappeared at the same hour and renewed the trial. Wunzh felt that his strength was even less than the day before, but the courage of his mind seemed to increase in proportion, as his body became weaker. Seeing this, the stranger again spoke to him, in the same words he had used before, adding, "Tomorrow will be your last trial. Be strong, my friend, for this is the only way you can overcome me and obtain the boon you seek."

On the third day he again appeared at the same time and renewed the struggle. The poor youth was very faint in body, but grew stronger in mind at every contest, and was determined to prevail or perish in the attempt. He exerted his utmost powers, and after the contest had been continued the usual time, the stranger ceased his efforts and declared himself conquered. For the first time he entered the lodge, and sitting down beside the youth, he began to deliver his instructions to him, telling him in what manner he should proceed to take advantage of the victory.

"You have won your desires of the Great Spirit," said the stranger. "You have wrestled manfully. Tomorrow will be the seventh day of your fasting. Your father will give you food to strengthen you, and as it is the last day of trial, you will prevail. I know this, and now tell you what you must do to benefit your family and your tribe. Tomorrow," he repeated, "I shall meet you and wrestle with you for the last time; and, as soon as you have prevailed against mc, you will strip off my garments and throw me down, clean the earth of roots and weeds, make it soft, and bury me in the spot. When you have done this, leave my body in the earth, and do not disturb it, but come occasionally to visit the place, to see whether I have come to life, and be careful never to let the grass or weeds grow on my grave. Once a month cover me with fresh earth. If you follow my instructions, you will accomplish your object of doing good to your fellow creatures by teaching them the knowledge I now teach you." He then shook him by the hand and disappeared.

In the morning the youth's father came with some slight refreshments, saying, "My son, you have fasted long enough. If the Great Spirit will favor you, he will do it now. It is seven days since you have tasted food, and you must not sacrifice your life. The Master of Life does not require that."

"My father," replied the youth, "wait till the sun goes down.

I have a particular reason for extending my fast to that hour."

"Very well," said the old man, "I shall wait till the hour arrives, and you feel inclined to eat."

At the usual hour of the day the sky visitor returned, and the trial of strength was renewed. Although the youth had not availed himself of his father's offer of food, he felt that new strength had been given to him, and that exertion had renewed his strength and fortified his courage. He grasped his angelic antagonist with supernatural strength, threw him down, took from him his beautiful garments and plume, and finding him dead, immediately buried him on the spot, taking all the precautions he had been told of, and being very confident, at the same time, that his friend would again come to life.

He then returned to his father's lodge, and partook sparingly of the meal that had been prepared for him. But he never for a moment forgot the grave of his friend. He carefully visited it throughout the spring, and weeded out the grass, and kept the ground in a soft and pliant state. Very soon he saw the tops of the green plumes coming through the ground; and the more careful he was to obey his instructions in keeping the ground in order, the faster they grew. He was, however, careful to conceal the exploit from his father.

Days and weeks had passed in this way. The summer was now drawing toward a close, when one day, after a long absence in hunting, Wunzh invited his father to follow him to the quiet and lonesome spot of his former fast. The lodge had been removed, and the weeds kept from growing on the circle where it stood, but in its place stood a tall and graceful plant, with bright-colored silken hair, surmounted with nodding plumes and stately leaves, and golden clusters on each side.

"It is my friend," shouted the lad; "it is the friend of all mankind. It is *Mondawmin* ('maize'). We need no longer rely on hunting alone; for, as long as this gift is cherished and taken care of, the ground itself will give us a living." He then pulled an ear. "See, my father," said he, "this is what I fasted for. The Great Spirit has listened to my voice, and sent us something new, and henceforth our people will not alone depend upon the chase or upon the waters."

He then communicated to his father the instructions given him by the stranger. He told him that the broad husks must be torn away, as he had pulled off the garments in his wrestling; and having done this, showed him how the ear must be held before the fire till the outer skin became brown,

> while all the milk was retained in the grain. The whole family then united in a feast on the newly grown ears, expressing gratitude to the Merciful Spirit who gave it. So corn came into the world, and has ever since been preserved.[55]

An excellent South American example of the same mythologem was recorded by Theodor Koch-Grünberg during his expedition to the jungles of the upper Amazonian basin in the years 1903–1905. Primitive as the people of that almost impenetrable green hell appear and savage as they certainly are, they cultivate a number of food plants, the most important of which is manioc (cassava), a vegetable containing a lethal poison (hydrocyanic acid), which has to be removed by cooking before the nourishing rootstock can be consumed. The women—whose customary costume is their own skin with all body hair removed—plant their manioc in gardens cleared in the jungles by the men, while the latter—whose attire is never more than a meager shred or string of pubic covering or decoration—hunt, fish, and try to ambush the best-looking women of the neighboring tribes. Besides yielding the staple nourishment of these people and the poison for their blowgun darts, manioc renders a weak yet adequate intoxicant as well, which contributes considerably to the spirit of their dancing feasts; and so it is a plant that combines remarkably all the mysteries of the Dema. It is at once life-supporting, death-administering, and spirit-rousing.

However, the art of raising, preparing, and enjoying this wondrous plant (from which we, by the way, derive tapioca) is but one of the wonders of the heritage of these jungle inhabitants (who, surely, cannot be as simple as they seem!); for they play at their festivals a large battery of musical instruments, by no means primitive: trumpets of bark and of wood, both great and small, clarionets, flutes and flageolets, ocarinas, pan pipes, and a kind of "roarer" made of a tube blown into a jar—besides the well-known slit-log drums of Frobenius' "equatorial" zone, and a sort of hollow wooden cylinder, upwards of three feet long, which is struck, end down, like a pestle, upon the ground. In the legend of the wonderful sun-boy Milomaki, which Professor Koch-Grünberg recorded among the cannibalistic Yahuna, who occupy an area on the left bank of the lower Apaporis River that is practically on the equator (latitude 2 degrees south) and about at the border of Colombia and Brazil (longitude 70 degrees west), we learn of the origin not only of the food plants and first-fruits festival of these people, but also of the curious music of the flutes and reeds to the tones of which the rites are celebrated:

> From the great Water House, the Land of the Sun, there came, many years ago, a little boy who sang so beautifully that many people flocked from near and far to see and hear him; and the name of this boy was Milomaki. But when those who had heard him returned to their homes and ate fish, they all died. Hence their relatives seized Milomaki, who meanwhile had grown to young manhood, and because he was so dangerous, having killed their brothers, they cremated him on a great pyre. Nevertheless, the youth continued to sing beautifully to the very end, and even while the flames were licking his body he was singing: "Now I die, now I die, now I die, my Son, now I depart from this world!" And when his body was swelling with the heat, he still was singing in glorious tones: "Now my body breaks, now I am dead!" And his body burst. He died and was consumed by the flames, but his soul ascended to heaven, while from his ashes there grew, that very day, a long, green blade, which became steadily bigger and bigger, spreading out, until the next day it was already a tall tree—the first paxiuba palm in the world. . . .
>
> The people fashioned huge flutes of the wood of this palm and these gave forth the same wonderfully beautiful tones that formerly had been sung by Milomaki himself. Furthermore, the men blow on such flutes to this day when the fruits are ripe, and they dance, while doing so, in memory of Milomaki, who is the creator and giver of all fruits. But the women and children must not see these flutes; for if they did, they would die.[56]

Ultimately—as we now know—the art of cultivating maize was derived by the North American Indians from either Mexico or Peru, the great centers of high civilization in the New World. And so we shall conclude the present brief sampling of the variant forms of our mythologem with an example from the Aztecs. Sir James G. Frazer, in *The Golden Bough,* supplies an instance from the vivid account of Fray Bernardino de Sahagún:

At a great festival in September, which was preceded by a strict fast of seven days, they sanctified a young slave girl of twelve or thirteen years, the prettiest they could find, to represent the Maize Goddess Chicomecohuatl. They invested her with the ornaments of the goddess, putting a mitre on her head and maize-cobs round her neck and in her hands, and fastening a green feather upright on the crown of her head to imitate an ear of maize. This they did, we are told, in order to signify that the maize was almost ripe at the time of the festival, but because it was still tender they chose a girl of tender years to play the part of the Maize Goddess. The whole long day they led the poor child in all her finery, with the green plume nodding on her head, from house to house dancing merrily to cheer people after the dulness and privations of the fast.

In the evening all the people assembled at the temple, the courts of which they lit up by a multitude of lanterns and candles. There they passed the night without sleeping, and at midnight, while the trumpets, flutes, and horns discoursed solemn music, a portable framework or palanquin was brought forth, bedecked with festoons of maize-cobs and peppers and filled with seeds of all sorts. This the bearers set down at the door of the chamber in which the wooden image of the goddess stood. Now the chamber was adorned and wreathed, both outside and inside, with wreaths of maize-cobs, peppers, pumpkins, roses, and seeds of every kind, a wonder to behold; the whole floor was covered deep with these verdant offerings of the pious. When the music ceased, a solemn procession came forth of priests and dignitaries, with flaring lights and smoking censers, leading in their midst the girl who played the part of the goddess. Then they made her mount the framework, where she stood upright on the maize and peppers and pumpkins with which it was strewed, her hands resting on two banisters to keep her from falling. Then the priests swung the smoking censers round her; the music struck up again, and while it played, a great dignitary of the temple suddenly stepped up to her with a razor in his hand and adroitly shore off the green feather she wore on her head, together with the hair in which it was fastened, snipping the lock off by the root. The feather and the hair he then presented to the wooden image of the goddess with great solemnity and elaborate ceremonies, weeping and giving her thanks for the fruits of the earth and the abundant crops which she had bestowed on the people that year; and as he wept and prayed, all the people, standing in the courts of the temple, wept and prayed with him. When that ceremony was over, the girl descended from the framework and was escorted to the place where she was to spend the rest of the night. But all the people kept watch in the courts of the temple by the light of torches till break of day. The morning being come, and the courts of the temple being still crowded by the multitude, who would have deemed it sacrilege to quit the precincts, the priests again brought forth the damsel attired in the costume of the goddess, with the mitre on her head and the cobs of maize about her neck. Again she mounted the portable framework or palanquin and stood on it, supporting herself by her hands on the banisters. Then the elders of the temple lifted it on their shoulders, and while some swung burning censers and others played on instruments or sang, they carried it in procession through the great courtyard to the hall of the god Huitzilopochtli and then back to the chamber, where stood the wooden image of the Maize Goddess, whom the girl personated. There they caused the damsel to descend from the palanquin and to stand on the heaps of corn and vegetables that had been spread in profusion on the floor of the sacred chamber. While she stood there all the elders and nobles came in a line, one behind the other, carrying saucers full of dry and clotted blood which they had drawn from their ears by way of penance during the seven days' fast. One by one they squatted on their haunches before her, which was the equivalent of falling on their knees with us, and scraping the crust of blood from the saucer cast it down before her as an offering in return for the benefits which she, as the embodiment of the Maize Goddess, had conferred upon them. When the men had thus humbly offered their blood to the human representative of the goddess, the women, forming a long line, did so likewise, each of them dropping on her hams before the girl and scraping her blood from the saucer. The ceremony lasted a long time, for great and small, young and old, all without exception had to pass before the incarnate deity and make their offering. When it was over, the people returned home with glad hearts to feast on flesh and viands of every sort as merrily, we are told, as good Christians at Easter partake of meat and other carnal mercies after the long abstinence of Lent. And when they had eaten and drunk their fill and rested after the night watch, they returned quite refreshed to the temple to see the end of the festival. And the end of the festival was this. The multitude being assembled,

> the priests solemnly incensed the girl who personated the goddess; then they threw her on her back on the heap of corn and seeds, cut off her head, caught the gushing blood in a tub, and sprinkled the blood on the wooden image of the goddess, the walls of the chamber, and the offerings of corn, peppers, pumpkins, seeds, and vegetables which cumbered the floor. After that they flayed the headless trunk, and one of the priests made shift to squeeze himself into the bloody skin. Having done so they clad him in all the robes which the girl had worn; they put the mitre on his head, the necklace of golden maize-cobs about his neck, the maize-cobs of feathers and gold in his hands; and thus arrayed they led him forth in public, all of them dancing to the tuck of drum, while he acted as fugleman, skipping and posturing at the head of the procession as briskly as he could be expected to do, incommoded as he was by the tight and clammy skin of the girl and by her clothes, which must have been much too small for a grown man.[57]

No wonder, we may say, if the Spanish padres thought they recognized in the liturgies of the New World a devil's parody of their own high myth and holy mass of the sacrifice and resurrection!

One version of the mythological event at the beginning of time which supplied the model for this rite tells that as the goddess Tlalteutli was walking alone upon the face of the primordial waters —a great and wonderful maiden, with eyes and jaws at every joint that could see and bite like animals—she was spied by the two primary gods Quetzalcoatl (the Plumed Serpent) and Tezcatlipoca (the Smoking Mirror); whereupon, deciding that they should create the world of her, they transformed themselves into mighty serpents and came at her from either side. One seized her from the right hand to the left foot, the other from the left hand to the right foot, and together they ripped her asunder. From the parts they fashioned not only the earth and heavens, but also the gods. And then to comfort the goddess for what had happened to her, all the gods came down and, paying her obeisance, commanded that there should come from her all the fruits that men require for their life. And so, from her hair they made trees, flowers, and grass; from her eyes springs, fountains, and the little caves; from her mouth rivers and the great caves; from her nose valleys, and from her shoulders mountains. But the goddess wept all night, for she had a craving to consume human hearts. And she would not be quiet until they were brought to her. Nor would she bear fruit until she had been drenched with human blood.[58]

Part Three

THE MYTHOLOGY OF THE PRIMITIVE HUNTERS

Chapter 6

SHAMANISM

1. The Shaman and the Priest

Among the Indians of North America two contrasting mythologies appear, according to whether tribes are hunters or planters. Those that are primarily hunters emphasize in their religious life the individual fast for the gaining of visions. The boy of twelve or thirteen is left by his father in some lonesome place, with a little fire to keep the beasts away, and there he fasts and prays, four days or more, until some spiritual visitant comes in dream, in human or animal form, to speak to him and give him power. His later career will be determined by this vision; for his familiar may confer the power to cure people as a shaman, the power to attract and slaughter animals, or the ability to become a warrior. And if the benefits gained are not sufficient for the young man's ambition, he may fast again, as often as he likes. An Old Crow Indian named One Blue Bead told of such a fast. "When I was a boy," he said, "I was poor. I saw war parties come back with leaders in front and having a procession. I used to envy them and I made up my mind to fast and become like them. When I saw the vision I got what I had longed for. . . . I killed eight enemies."[1] If a man has bad luck, he knows that his gift of supernatural power simply is insufficient; while, on the other hand, the great shamans and war leaders have acquired power in abundance from their visionary fasts. Perhaps they have chopped off and offered their finger joints. Such offerings were common among the Indians of the plains, on some of whose old hands there remained only fingers and joints enough to enable them to notch an arrow and draw the bow.

Among the planting tribes—the Hopi, Zuñi, and other Pueblo dwellers—life is organized around the rich and complex ceremonies of their masked gods. These are elaborate rites in which the whole community participates, scheduled according to a religious calendar and conducted by societies of trained priests. As Ruth Benedict observed in her *Patterns of Culture:* "No field of activity competes with ritual for foremost place in their attention. Probably most grown men among the western Pueblos give to it the greater part of their waking life. It requires the memorizing of an amount of word-perfect ritual that our less trained minds find staggering, and the performance of neatly dovetailed ceremonies that are chartered by the calendar and complexly interlock all the different cults and the governing body in endless formal procedure."[2] In such a society there is little room for individual play. There is a rigid relationship not only of the individual to his fellows, but also of village life to the calendric cycle; for the planters are intensely aware of their dependency upon the gods of the elements. One short period of too much or too little rain at the critical moment, and a whole year of labor results in famine. Whereas for the hunter—hunter's luck is a very different thing.

We have already read one typical account of an American Indian's quest for his vision in the legend of the origin of maize. The Ojibway tribe, from whom that version of this widely spread legend was derived, were on a cultural level, when Schoolcraft lived among them, approximately equivalent to that of the Natufians of the archaic Near East, c. 6000 B.C. They were a hunting and fighting people of Algonquin stock, and their main body of myths and tales was of a hunting, not a planting, tradition. Nevertheless, they had recently acquired from the agricultural peoples of the much more highly developed south the arts of planting, reaping, and preparing maize, which they were now using to supplement their gains from the chase. And with the maize had come the old, old myth of the wonderful plant-Dema, which we first encountered among the cannibals of Indonesia and saw as having crossed the Pacific with the cocopalm. In South America it has been applied by hundreds of tribes to the various food plants of that richly fruitful continent, and here, in North America, we have found it again, accommodated not only to the tall green growth and feathered crest of the maize, but also to an alien style of mythological thought, that of the vision. We do not hear in this tale of a great group, the "people" of the mythological age, but of a single youth—just such a boy as each would be in his own visionary quest in that great solitude of which our Eskimo shaman, Igjugarjuk, has already told, which "can open the mind of a man to all that is hidden to others."

The contrast between the two world views may be seen more sharply by comparing the priest and the shaman. The priest is the socially initiated, ceremonially inducted member of a recognized religious organization, where he holds a certain rank and functions as the tenant of an office that was held by others before him, while the shaman is one who, as a consequence of a personal psychological crisis, has gained a certain power of his own. The spiritual visitants who came to him in vision had never been seen before by any other; they were his particular familiars and protectors. The masked gods of the Pueblos, on the other hand, the corn-gods and the cloud-gods, served by societies of strictly organized and very orderly priests, are the well-known patrons of the entire village and have been prayed to and represented in the ceremonial dances since time out of mind.

In the origin legend of the Jicarilla Apache Indians of New Mexico there is an excellent illustration of the capitulation of the style of religiosity represented by the shamanism of a hunting tribe to the greater force of the more stable, socially organized and maintained priestly order of a planting-culture complex. The Apache, like their cousins the Navaho, were a hunting tribe that entered the area of the maize-growing Pueblos in the fourteenth century A.D. and assimilated, with characteristic adaptations, much of the local neolithic ceremonial lore.[3] The myth in question is fundamental to their present concept of the nature and history of the universe and is clearly of southern derivation, associated with the rites and social order of a planting culture, and—as we shall see—concerned rather to integrate the individual in a firmly ordered, well-established communal context than to release him for the flights of his own wild genius, wheresoever they may lead.

"In the beginning," we are told, "nothing was here where the world now stands: no earth—nothing but Darkness, Water, and Cyclone. There were no people living. Only the Hactcin existed. It was a lonely place. There were no fishes, no living things. But all the Hactcin were here from the beginning. They had the material out of which everything was created. They made the world first, the earth, the underworld, and then they made the sky. They made Earth in the form of a living woman and called her Mother. They made Sky in the form of a man and called him Father. He faces downward, and the woman faces up. He is our father and the woman is our mother." [4]

The Hactcin are the Apache counterparts of the masked gods of the Pueblo villages: personifications of the powers that support the spectacle of nature. The most powerful of their number, Black Hactcin—the myth continues—made an animal of clay and then spoke to it. "Let me see how you are going to walk on those four feet," he said. Then it began to walk. "That's pretty good," said the Hactcin. "I can use you." And then he said, "But you are all alone. I shall make it so that you shall have others from your body." And then all sorts of animals came from that one body; for Black Hactcin had power: he could do anything. At that time all those animals could speak, and they spoke the Jicarilla Apache language.

The world creator, Black Hactcin, held out his hand, and a drop of rain fell into the palm. He mixed this with earth and it became mud. Then he fashioned a bird from the mud. "Let me see how you are going to use those wings to fly," he said. The mud turned into a bird and flew around. "Well, that's just fine!" said Black Hactcin, who enjoyed seeing the difference between this one and the ones with four legs. "But," he said, "I think you need companions." Then he took the bird and whirled it around rapidly in a clockwise direction. The bird grew dizzy, and, as one does when dizzy, saw many images round about. He saw all kinds of birds there, eagles, hawks, and small birds too, and when he was himself again, there were all those birds, really therc. And birds love the air, dwell high, and seldom light on the ground, because the drop of water that became the mud out of which the first bird was made fell from the sky.

The clockwise whirling image from which the birds of the air were produced suggests those designs on the earliest Samarra pottery of the Mesopotamian high neolithic (c. 4500–3500 B.C.) * where the forms of animals and birds emerge from a whirling swastika, and it is surely by no mere accident or parallel development that similar designs—as those in the figures below—occur among the prehistoric North American mound-builder remains,

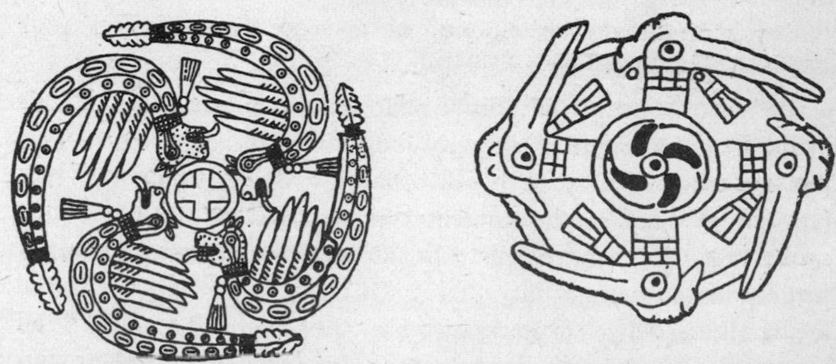

Designs from shell gorgets, Spiro Mound, Oklahoma

or that in the ritual life and symbolism of the present Indians of the Southwest—the Pueblos, Navaho, and Apache—the swastika plays a prominent part. This circumstance, however, may supply us not only with additional evidence of a broad cultural diffusion, but also with a clue to the sense of the swastika in the earliest neolithic art and cult, both in the Old World and in the New.

The creator whirled the bird in a clockwise direction and the result was an emanation of dreamlike forms. But swastikas, counter-clockwise, appear on many Chinese images of the meditating Buddha; and the Buddha, we know, is removing his consciousness from just this field of dreamlike, created forms—reuniting it through yogic exercise with that primordial abyss or "void" from which all springs.

* Cf. supra, pp. 140–143.

Stars, darkness, a lamp, a phantom, dew, a bubble,
A dream, a flash of lightning, or a cloud:
Thus should one look upon the world.[5]

This we read in a celebrated Buddhist text, *The Diamond-Cutter Sutra,* which has had an immense influence on Oriental thought.

Now I am not going to suggest that there has been any Buddhist influence on Apache mythology. There has not! However, the poignant thought that Calderón, the great Spanish playwright, expressed in his work *La Vida es Sueño* ("Life is a Dream"), and that his contemporary, Shakespeare, represented when he wrote

We are such stuff
As dreams are made on, and our little life
Is rounded with a sleep,[6]

was a basic theme of the Hindu philosophers in the earliest phase of their tradition; and if we may judge from the evidence of certain little figures in yoga posture dating from c. 2000 B.C. that have been found in the ancient ruins of the Indus Valley, this trance-inducing exercise must already have been developed in the earliest Indian hieratic city states. One of the best-known forms of the Hindu deity Vishnu shows him sleeping on the coils of the cosmic serpent, floating on the cosmic sea and dreaming the lotus-dream of the universe, of which we all are a part. What I am now suggesting, therefore, is that in this Apache legend of the creation of the bird we have a remote cognate of the Indian forms, which must have proceeded from the same neolithic stock; and that in both cases the symbol of the swastika represents a process of transformation: the conjuring up (in the case of the Hactcin), or conjuring away (in the case of the Buddha), of a universe that because of the fleeting nature of its forms may indeed be compared to the substance of a mirage, or of a dream.

Well, the birds all presently came to their creator, Black Hactcin, and asked, "What shall we eat?" He lifted his hand to each of the four directions, and because he had so much power, all kinds of seeds fell into his hand, and he scattered them. The birds went to pick them up, but the seeds all turned to insects, worms, and grasshoppers, and they moved and hopped around, so that the birds, at first, could not catch them. The Hactcin was trying to tease them. He said, "Oh yes! It's hard work to catch those flies and grasshoppers, but you can do it." And so they all chased the grasshoppers and other insects around; and that is why they are doing that to this day.

Now presently all the birds and animals came to Black Hactcin and told him that they wanted a companion; they wanted man. "You are not going to be with us all the time," they said. And he said, "I guess that will be true. Some day, perhaps, I shall go to a place where no one will see me." And so he told them to gather objects from all directions. They brought pollen from all kinds of plants, and they added red ocher, white clay, white stone, jet, turquoise, red stone, opal, abalone, and assorted valuable stones. And when they had put these before Black Hactcin, he told them to withdraw to a distance. He stood to the east, then to the south, then to the west, then to the north. He took pollen and traced with it the outline of a figure on the ground, an outline just like that of his own body. Then he placed the precious stones and other objects inside this outline, and they became flesh and bones. The veins were of turquoise, the blood of red ocher, the skin of coral, the bones of white rock; the fingernails were of Mexican opal, the pupil of the eye of jet, the whites of the eyes of abalone, the marrow in the bones of white clay, and the teeth too were of opal. He took a dark cloud and out of it fashioned the hair. It becomes a white cloud when you are old.

The Hactcin sent wind into the form that he had formed and made it animate. The whorls at the ends of our fingers indicate the path of the wind at that time of the creation. And at death the wind leaves the body from the soles of the feet, where the whorls at the bottom of the feet represent the path of the wind in its exit. The man was lying down, face downward, with his arms outstretched; and the birds tried to look, but Black Hactcin forbade them to do so. For now the man was coming to life. The man braced himself, leaning on his arms. "Do not look," said Hactcin to the birds, who were now very much excited. And it is because the birds and animals were so eager to see that people are so curious today, just as you are eager to hear the rest of this story.

"Sit up," Hactcin said to the man; and then he taught him to speak, to laugh, to shout, to walk, and to run. And when the birds saw what had been done they burst into song, as they do in the early morning.

But the animals thought this man should have a companion, and so Black Hactcin put him to sleep; and when the man's eyes became heavy he began to dream. He was dreaming that someone, a girl, was sitting beside him. And when he woke up, there was a woman sitting there. He spoke to her, and she answered. He laughed, and she laughed. "Let us both get up," he said, and they rose. "Let us walk," he said, and he led her the first four steps: right, left, right, left. "Run," he said, and they both ran. And then once again the birds burst into song, so that the two should have pleasant music and not be lonesome.

Now all of this took place not on the level of the earth on which we now are living, but below, in the womb of the earth; and it was dark; there was neither sun nor moon at that time. So White and Black Hactcin together took a little sun and a little moon out of their bags, caused them to grow, and then sent them up into the air, where they moved from north to south, shedding light all around. This caused a great deal of excitement among the people—the animals, the birds, and the people. But there were a lot of shamans among them at that time, all kinds of shamans among the people—men and women who claimed to have power from all sorts of things. These saw the sun going from north to south and began to talk.

One said, "I made the sun"; another: "No, I did." They began quarreling, and the Hactcin ordered them not to talk like that. But they kept making claims and fighting. One said, "I think I'll make the sun stop overhead, so that there will be no night. But no, I guess I'll let it go. We need some time to rest and sleep." Another said, "Perhaps I'll get rid of the moon. We really don't require any light at night." But the sun rose the second day and the birds and animals were happy. The next day it was the same. When noon of the fourth day came, however, and the shamans, in spite of what the Hactcin had told them, continued to talk, there was an eclipse. The sun went right up through a hole overhead and the moon followed, and that is why we have eclipses today.

One of the Hactcin said to the boastful shamans, "All right, you people say you have power. Now bring back the sun."

So they all lined up. In one line were the shamans, and in another all the birds and animals. The shamans began to perform, singing songs and making ceremonies. They showed everything they knew. Some would sit singing and then disappear into the earth, leaving only their eyes sticking out, then return. But this did not bring back the sun. It was only to show that they had power. Some swallowed arrows, which would come out of their flesh at their stomachs. Some swallowed feathers; some swallowed whole spruce trees and spat them up again. But they were still without the sun and moon.

Then White Hactcin said, "All you people are doing pretty well, but I don't think you are bringing the sun back. Your time is up." He turned to the birds and animals. "All right," he said, "now it is your turn."

They all began to speak to one another politely, as though they were brothers-in-law; but the Hactcin said: "You must do something more than speak to one another in that polite way. Get up and do something with your power and make the sun come back."

The grasshopper was the first to try. He stretched forth his hand to the four directions, and when he brought it back he was holding bread. The deer stretched out his hand to the four directions, and when he brought it back he was holding yucca fruit. The bear produced choke-cherries in the same way, and the groundhog, berries; the chipmunk, strawberries; the turkey, maize; and so it went with all. But though the Hactcin were pleased with these gifts, the people were still without the sun and moon.

Thereupon, the Hactcin themselves began to do something. They sent for thunder of four colors, from the four directions, and these thunders brought clouds of the four colors, from which rain fell. Then, sending for Rainbow to make it beautiful while the seeds that the people had produced were planted, the Hactcin made a sand-painting with four little colored mounds in a row, into which they put the seeds. The birds and animals sang, and presently the little mounds began to grow, the seeds began to sprout, and the four mounds of colored earth merged and became one mountain, which continued to rise.

The Hactcin then selected twelve shamans who had been particularly spectacular in their magical performances, and, painting six of them blue all over, to represent the summer season, and six white, to represent the winter, called them Tsanati; and that was the origin of the Tsanati dance society of the Jicarilla Apache. After that the Hactcin made six clowns, painting them white with four black horizontal bands, one across the face, one across the chest, one across the upper leg and one across the lower. The Tsanati and clowns then joined the people in their dance, to make the mountain grow.[7]

It would be difficult to find a clearer statement of the process by which the individualistic shamans, in their paleolithic style of magical practice, were discredited by the guardians of the group-oriented, comparatively complex organization of a seed-planting, food-growing community. Lined up, fitted into uniform, they were given a place in the liturgical structure of a larger whole. The episode thus represents the victory of a socially annointed priesthood over the highly dangerous and unpredictable force of individual endowment. And the teller of the Jicarilla Apache story himself explained the necessity for incorporating the shamans in the ceremonial system. "These people," he said, "had ceremonies of their own which they derived from various sources, from animals, from fire, from the turkey, from frogs, and from other things. They could not be left out. They had power, and they had to help too." [8]

I do not know of any myth that represents more clearly than this the crisis that must have faced the societies of the Old World when the neolithic order of the earth-bound villages began to make its power felt in a gradual conquest of the most habitable portions of the earth. The situation in Arizona and New Mexico at the period of the discovery of America was, culturally, much like that which must have prevailed in the Near and Middle East and in Europe from the fourth to second millenniums B.C., when the rigid patterns proper to an orderly settlement were being imposed on peoples used to the freedom and vicissitudes of the hunt. And if we turn our eyes to the mythologies of the Hindus, Persians, Greeks, Celts, and Germans, we immediately recognize, in the well-known, oft-recited tales of the conquest of the titans by the gods, analogies to this legend of the subjugation of the shamans by the Hactcin. The titans, dwarfs, and giants are represented as the powers of an earlier mythological age—crude and loutish, egoistic and lawless, in contrast to the comely gods, whose reign of heavenly order harmoniously governs the worlds of nature and man. The giants were overthrown, pinned beneath mountains, exiled to the rugged regions at the bounds of the earth, and as long as the power of the gods can keep them there the people, the animals, the birds, and all living things will know the blessings of a world ruled by law.

In the Hindu sacred books there is a myth that appears frequently, of the gods and titans cooperating under the supervision of the two supreme deities, Vishnu and Shiva, to churn the Milky Ocean for its butter. They took the World Mountain as a churning stick and the World Serpent as a twirling rope, and wrapped the serpent around the mountain. Then, the gods taking hold of the head end of the snake and the demons of the tail, while Vishnu supported the World Mountain, they churned for a thousand years and produced in the end the Butter of Immortality.[9]

It is almost impossible not to think of this myth when reading of the efforts of the quarrelsome shamans and orderly people, under the supervision of the Apache Hactcin, to make the World Mountain grow and carry them to the world of light. The Tsanati and clowns, we are told, joined the people in their dance, and the mountain grew, until its top nearly reached the hole through which the sun and moon had disappeared; and it remained, then, only to construct four ladders of light of the four colors, up which the people could ascend to the surface of our present earth. The six clowns went ahead with magical whips to chase disease away and were followed by the Hactcin; and then the Tsanati came; after them, the people and animals. "And when they came up onto the earth," said the teller of the story, "it was just like a child being born from its mother. The place of emergence is the womb of the earth." [10]

The highest concern of all the mythologies, ceremonials, ethical systems, and social organizations of the agriculturally based societies has been that of suppressing the manifestations of individualism; and this has been generally achieved by compelling or persuading people to identify themselves not with their own interests, intuitions, or modes of experience, but with the archetypes of behavior and systems of sentiment developed and maintained in the public domain. A world vision derived from the lesson of the plants, representing the individual as a mere cell or moment in a larger process—that of the sib, the race, or, in larger terms, the species—so devaluates even the first signs of personal spontaneity that every impulse to self-discovery is purged away. "Truly, truly, I say to you, unless a grain of wheat falls into the earth and dies, it remains alone; but if it dies, it bears much fruit." [11] This noble maxim represents the binding sentiment of the holy society—that is to say, the church militant, suffering, and triumphant—of those who do not wish to remain alone.

But, on the other hand, there have always been those who have very much wished to remain alone, and have done so, achieving sometimes, indeed, even that solitude in which the Great Spirit, the Power, the Great Mystery that is hidden from the group in its concerns is intuited with the inner impact of an immediate force. And the endless round of the serpent's way, biting its tail, sloughing its old skin, to come forth renewed and slough again, is then itself cast away—often with scorn—for the supernormal experience of an eternity beyond the beat of time. Like an eagle the spirit then soars on its own wings. The dragon "Thou Shalt," as Nietzsche terms the social fiction of the moral law, has been slain by the lion of self-discovery; and the master roars—as the Buddhists phrase it—the lion roar: the roar of the great Shaman of the mountain peaks, of the void beyond all horizons, and of the bottomless abyss.

In the paleolithic hunter's world, where the groups were comparatively small—hardly more than forty or fifty individuals—the social pressures were far less severe than in the later, larger, differentiated and systematically coordinated long-established villages and cities. And the advantages to the group lay rather in the fostering than in the crushing out of impulse. We have already seen the Ojibway father introduce his son to the solitude of the initiatory fast—the shrine, so to say, of self-discovery, sheer emptiness, with no socially guaranteed image or concept of what the god to be found should be, and with the perfect understanding that whatever the boy should find there would be honored and accepted as the boy's own divinely given way. And we have seen also the manner of the masked gods of the planters, binding everything into the compass of their own hieratically organized world-society; offering the power of the group as a principle finally and absolutely superior to any of those "ceremonies of their own" which the shamans had derived from the various sources of their own experience.

This, then, is to be our first distinction between the mythologies of the hunters and those of the planters. The accent of the planting rites is on the group; that of the hunters, rather, on the individual—though even here, of course, the group does not disappear. Even among the hunters we have the people—the dear people—who bow to one another politely, like brothers-in-law, but have comparatively little personal power. And these constitute, even on that level, a group from which the far more potent shamans stand apart. We have read of the Eskimo shaman Najagneq, who carried on a war against his whole village and then faced them out of countenance when they came to accuse him in a court of law. And we have read also of the more primitive Caribou Eskimo shaman Igjugarjuk, who, when he knew the girl he wished to marry, simply took his gun, shot her family from around her, and brought her home. In the villages and towns of the planters, however, it is the group and the archetypal philosophy of the group—the philosophy of the grain of wheat that falls into the earth and dies but therein lives, the philosophy imaged in the rites of the monster serpent and the maiden sacrifice—that preponderate and represent perfectly the system of sentiments most conducive to group survival; in the hunter's world, where the group was never large or strong enough to face down a man who had achieved in his own way his own full stature, it was the philosophy, rather, of the "lion roar" that prevailed.

As we have seen, in some areas (e.g., North America) this shamanistic, individualistic principle prevailed to such an extent that even the puberty rites had as their chief theme the personal quest for a vision. In others (e.g., Central Australia, where a powerful influence from the planting world of Melanesia had been assimilated),* a greater emphasis on the age of the ancestors and disciplines of the men's dancing ground left to the individual very little of his own. Nevertheless, in the main it can be said that in the world of the hunt the shamanistic principle preponderates and that consequently the mythological and ritual life is far less richly developed than among the planters. It has a lighter, more whimsical character, and most of its functioning deities are rather in the nature of personal familiars than of profoundly developed gods. And yet, as we have also seen, there have been depths of insight reached by the mind in the solitude of the tundras that are hardly to be matched in the great group ecstasies of the bull-roarers, borne on the air, heavy with dread.

II. Shamanistic Magic

"From Wakan-Tanka, the Great Mystery, comes all power," said an old chieftain of the Oglalla Sioux, Chief Piece of Flat Iron, to Natalie Curtis when she was collecting material for *The Indians' Book* in the first decade of the present century.

> It is all from Wakan-Tanka that the Holy Man has wisdom and the power to heal and to make holy charms. Man knows that all healing plants are given by Wakan-Tanka; therefore they are holy. So too is the buffalo holy, because it is the gift of Wakan-Tanka. The Great Mystery gave to men all things for their food, their clothing, and their welfare. And to man he gave also the knowledge how to use these gifts—how to find the holy healing plants, how to hunt and surround the buffalo, how to know wisdom. For all comes from Wakan-Tanka—all.

* Cf. supra, pp. 88–115.

> To the Holy Man comes in youth the knowledge that he will be holy. The Great Mystery makes him know this. Sometimes it is the Spirits who tell him. The Spirits come not in sleep always, but also when man is awake. When a Spirit comes it would seem as though a man stood there, but when this man has spoken and goes forth again, none may see whither he goes. Thus the Spirits. With the Spirits the Holy Man may commune always, and they teach him holy things.
>
> The Holy Man goes apart to a lone tipi and fasts and prays. Or he goes into the hills in solitude. When he returns to men, he teaches them and tells them what the Great Mystery has bidden him to tell. He counsels, he heals, and he makes holy charms to protect the people from all evil. Great is his power and greatly is he revered; his place in the tipi is an honored one.[12]

Knud Rasmussen received from the Caribou Eskimo shaman Igjugarjuk a full account of the ordeal through which he had acquired his shamanistic power. When young, he had been visited constantly by dreams that he could not understand.

> Strange unknown beings came and spoke to him, and when he awoke, he saw all the visions of his dream so distinctly that he could tell his fellows all about them. Soon it became evident to all that he was destined to become an *angakoq* [a shaman] and an old man named Perqanaoq was appointed his instructor. In the depth of winter, when the cold was most severe, Igjugarjuk was placed on a small sledge just large enough for him to sit on, and carried far away from his home to the other side of Hikoligjuag. On reaching the appointed spot, he remained seated on the sledge while his instructor built a tiny snow hut, with barely room for him to sit cross-legged. He was not allowed to set foot on the snow, but was lifted from the sledge and carried into the hut, where a piece of skin just large enough for him to sit on served as a carpet. No food or drink was given him; he was exhorted to think only of the Great Spirit and of the helping spirit that should presently appear—and so he was left to himself and his meditations.
>
> After five days had elapsed, the instructor brought him a drink of lukewarm water, and with similar exhortations, left him as before. He fasted now for fifteen days, when he was given another drink of water and a very small piece of meat, which had to last him a further ten days. At the end of this

> period, his instructor came for him and fetched him home. Igjugarjuk declared that the strain of those thirty days of cold and fasting was so severe that he "sometimes died a little." During all that time he thought only of the Great Spirit, and endeavored to keep his mind free from all memory of human beings and everyday things. Toward the end of the thirty days there came to him a helping spirit in the shape of a woman. She came while he was asleep and seemed to hover in the air above him. After that he dreamed no more of her, but she became his helping spirit. For five months following this period of trial, he was kept on the strictest diet, and required to abstain from all intercourse with women. The fasting was then repeated; for such fasts at frequent intervals are the best means of attaining to knowledge of hidden things. As a matter of fact, there is no limit to the period of study; it depends on how much one is willing to suffer and anxious to learn.[13]

Women too became shamans. In the same Eskimo community was Kinalik: "still a young woman," as Dr. Rasmussen describes her, "very intelligent, kind hearted, clean and good looking, who spoke frankly and without reserve."

> Igjugarjuk was her brother-in-law and had himself been her instructor in magic. Her initiation had been severe. She was hung up to some tent poles planted in the snow and left there for five days. It was midwinter, with intense cold and frequent blizzards, but she did not feel the cold, for the spirit protected her. When the five days were at an end, she was taken down and carried into the house, and Igjugarjuk was invited to shoot her, in order that she might attain to intimacy with the supernatural by visions of death. The gun was to be loaded with real powder, but a stone was to be used instead of the leaden bullet, in order that she might still retain connection with earth. Igjugarjuk, in the presence of the assembled villagers, fired the shot, and Kinalik fell to the ground unconscious. On the following morning, just as Igjugarjuk was about to bring her to life again, she awakened from the swoon unaided. Igjugarjuk asserted that he had shot her through the heart, and that the stone had afterward been removed and was in the possession of her old mother.[14]

One gets the impression, however, that, although these Saint Anthonys of the wilderness must truly have suffered in their youthful years of austerity, they have had a tendency to pull the long bow when telling of their trials, or perhaps, rather, to confuse dream reality with daytime events. We have already heard of the ten deaths and resurrections of Rasmussen's other Eskimo shaman, Najagneq.* In the same community with Igjugarjuk there was still another practicing shaman, a young man whose name was Aggjartoq, "who," as Dr. Rasmussen declares, without the hint of a smile, "had also been initiated into the mysteries of the occult with Igjugarjuk as his teacher; and in his case a third form of ordeal had been employed; to wit, that of drowning. He was lashed to a long pole and carried out onto a lake, a hole was cut in the ice, and the pole with its living burden thrust down through the hole, in such a fashion that Aggjartoq actually stood on the bottom of the lake with his head under water. He was left in this position for five days and when at last they hauled him up again, his clothes showed no sign of having been in the water at all and he himself had become a great wizard, having overcome death."[15]

The Caribou Eskimos, dwelling in the cruel arctic wastes west of the northern reaches of Hudson Bay, are among the most primitive people on earth; and their counterparts at the other extreme of the New World, on the no less bleak and difficult rocky tip of the southern continent, Tierra del Fuego, are likewise specimens of a type of life that was already out of fashion in the later millenniums of the paleolithic, 30,000–10,000 B.C. It is not known when the people now inhabiting the southern tip of South America —that "uttermost part of the earth"—first arrived in their rocky refuge, pressed down by the later, more highly developed societies of the north; but their ancestors must have crossed to the New World from Siberia many millenniums ago. When first explored by Europeans, the area was found divided among four tribes: the Yahgans (or Yamanas) of the southern coasts, a short and sturdy people who lived largely on fish and limpets, handled canoes with skill, and could occasionally manage to harpoon a seal, porpoise, or even diminutive whale; a considerably taller and comparatively handsome mountain-dwelling people, known as the Ona, in the inland area north of the Yahgans, who lived by the hunt; and to the west and east of these, respectively, the Alacaloof and the

* Supra. p. 53.

Aush, the former, like the Yahgans, a canoe people, and the latter, like the Ona (to whom they were related), a race of hunters. In the year 1870 a mission was established at the site since known as Ushuaia by a courageous young clergyman, Thomas Bridges, whose son Lucas, born at Ushuaia in 1874, has given an account of his long life among his friends the Yahgans and the Ona.

"Some of these humbugs," he says, describing the medicine men, or *joon,* of the Ona,

> were excellent actors. Standing or kneeling beside the patient, gazing intently at the spot where the pain was situated, the doctor would allow a look of horror to come over his face. Evidently he could see something invisible to the rest of us. His approach might be slow or he might pounce, as though afraid that the evil thing that had caused the trouble would escape. With his hands he would try to gather the malign presence into one part of the patient's body—generally the chest—where he would then apply his mouth and suck violently. Sometimes this struggle went on for an hour, to be repeated later. At other times the *joon* would draw away from his patient with the pretense of holding something in his mouth with his hands. Then, always facing away from the encampment, he would take his hands from his mouth, gripping them tightly together, and, with a guttural shout difficult to describe and impossible to spell, fling this invisible object to the ground and stamp fiercely upon it. Occasionally a little mud, some flint or even a tiny, very young mouse might be produced as the cause of the patient's indisposition. I myself have never seen a mouse figure in one of these performances, but they were quite common. Perhaps when I was there the doctor had failed to find a mouse's nest.[16]

An occasion to observe a considerably more puzzling manifestation of power occurred when a highly celebrated *joon* named Houshken, who had never seen a white man before, was induced to put on a brief performance for Mr. Bridges, who writes:

> Our conversation—as was always the case at such meetings—was slow, with long pauses between sentences, as though for deep thought. I told Houshken that I had heard of his great powers and would like to see some of his magic. He did not refuse my request, but answered modestly that he was disinclined, the Ona way of saying that he might do it by and by.

After allowing a quarter of an hour to elapse, Houshken said he was thirsty and went down to the nearby stream for a drink. It was a bright moonlight night and the snow on the ground helped to make the scene of the exhibition we were about to witness as light as day. On his return, Houshken sat down and broke into a monotonous chant, which went on until suddenly he put his hands to his mouth. When he brought them away, they were palms downward and some inches apart. We saw that a strip of guanaco hide, about the thickness of a leather bootlace, was now held loosely in his hands. It passed over his thumbs, under the palms of his half-closed hands, and was looped over his little fingers so that about three inches of end hung down from each hand. The strip appeared to be not more than eighteen inches long.

Without pulling the strip tight, Houshken now began to shake his hands violently, gradually bringing them farther apart, until the strip, with the two ends still showing, was about four feet long. He then called his brother, Chashkil, who took the end from his right hand and stepped back with it. From four feet, the strip now grew out of Houshken's left hand to double that length. Then, as Chashkil stepped forward, it disappeared back into Houshken's hand, until he was able to take the other end from his brother. With the continued agitation of his hands, the strip got shorter and shorter. Suddenly, when his hands were almost together, he clapped them to his mouth, uttered a prolonged shriek, then held out his hands to us, palms upward and empty.

Even an ostrich could not have swallowed those eight feet of hide at one gulp without visible effort. Where else the coil could have gone to I do not profess to know. It could not have gone up Houshken's sleeve, for he had dropped his robe when the performance began [and, like all male Onas without their robes, was naked]. There were between twenty and thirty men present, but only eight or nine were Houshken's people. The rest were far from being friends of the performer and all had been watching intently. Had they detected some simple trick, the great medicine-man would have lost his influence; they would no longer have believed in any of his magic.

The demonstration was not yet over. Houshken stood up and resumed his robe. Once again he broke into a chant and seemed to go into a trance, possessed by some spirit not his own. Drawing himself up to his full height, he took a step towards me and let his robe, his only garment, fall to the ground. He put his hands to his mouth with a most impressive gesture and brought them away again with fists clenched and thumbs close together. He held them up to the height of my eyes, and when they were less than two feet from my face slowly drew them apart. I saw that there was now a small, almost opaque object between them. It was about an inch in diameter in the middle and tapered away into his hands. It might have been a piece of semi-transparent dough or elastic, but whatever it was it seemed to be alive, revolving at great speed, while Houshken, apparently from muscular tension, was trembling violently.

The moonlight was bright enough to read by as I gazed at this strange object. Houshken brought his hands further apart and the object grew more and more transparent, until, when some three inches separated his hands, I realized that it was not there any more. It did not break or burst like a bubble; it simply disappeared, having been visible to me for less than five seconds. Houshken made no sudden movement, but slowly opened his hands and turned them over for my inspection. They looked clean and dry. He was stark naked and there was no confederate beside him. I glanced down at the snow, and, in spite of his stoicism, Houshken could not resist a chuckle, for nothing was to be seen there.

The others had crowded round us and, as the object disappeared, there was a frightened gasp from among them. Houshken reassured them with the remark:

"Do not let it trouble you. I shall call it back to myself again."

The natives believed this to be an incredibly malignant spirit belonging to, or possibly part of the *joon* from whom it emanated. It might take physical form, as we had just witnessed, or be totally invisible. It had the power to introduce insects, tiny mice, mud, sharp flints or even a jelly-fish or baby octopus, into the anatomy of those who had incurred its master's displeasure. I have seen a strong man shudder involuntarily at the thought of this horror and its evil potentialities. It was a curious fact that, although every magician must have known himself to be a fraud and a trickster, he always believed in and greatly feared the supernatural abilities of other medicine-men.[17]

When this account of the functioning of a *joon* of the Ona is compared with what we have learned of his counterparts in the north, a number of interesting points emerge. Drawn, it will be recalled, from two of the most primitive hunting communities on earth, at opposite poles of the world, and out of touch, certainly for millenniums, with any common point of traditional origin—if such there ever was—the two groups have nevertheless the same notion of the role and character of the shaman, while the shamans themselves have had the same types of experience and face practically the same orders of problem in relation to their practice among their simpler fellows. "He was no humbug," said Dr. Ostermann in the judgment quoted earlier of the Alaskan ten-horse-power Najagneq, "but a solitary man accustomed to hold his own against many and therefore had to have his little tricks." And Mr. Bridges, while retaining the view, suitable to the son of a clergyman, that shamans were indeed humbugs, nevertheless recognized that they feared one another's power. And this element of fear, real fear, is a characteristic reaction wherever men and women of shamanistic power and skill have appeared.

But, reciprocally, the shamans themselves have always lived in fear of their communities. "Medicine men," wrote Mr. Bridges, "ran great dangers. When persons in their prime died from no visible cause, the 'family doctor' would often cast suspicion, in an ambiguous way, on some rival necromancer. Frequently the chief object of a raiding party, in the perpetual clan warfare of the Ona, was to kill the medicine man of an opposing group." [18] The shaman, as he puts it, "was a creature apart from the honest hunters." And we have already seen the signs of this separation, not only in the war of the Eskimo Najagneq with the rest of his community, but also in the way of lining the people and the shamans in two rows in the Jicarilla Apache myth.

The shaman has an occult power over nature, which he can use either to harm or to benefit his fellows. Moreover, the shaman need not appear as a human being. Mr. Bridges tells of a mountain near Ushuaia that was thought to be a witch: to show her ill will, she could conjure up a storm.[19] And he tells also of a solitary guanaco (a kind of wild llama) that he shot high in the mountains, which he and his Indian companions then discovered to have been dwelling, solitary, in a small cave. "These guanaco recluses, braving the long winter in the mountains alone," writes

Mr. Bridges, "were very rare. . . . That night, discussing the matter round our camp-fire, I suggested that the hermit might have remained there alone in the cave to study guanaco magic. Instead of laughing, my companions agreed, with serious expressions on their faces, that this was quite likely." [20]

The shamanistic affinity with nature, which these two anecdotes of the witch-mountain and the shaman-guanaco suggest, is of a deeper, more occult kind than that of the "honest hunters" of the tribe, no matter how skillful and amazing to the white man the woodcraft of the latter may seem to be. Mr. Bridges—himself no mean woodsman—describes with wonder the almost incredible sensitivity of the Ona to the presences around them in the deep forest; but these same Ona hunters observed with wonder the power over nature of their shaman. For, whereas they could function expertly in relation to its outer aspect, he could work in the manner of a cause, reaching behind the veil and touching those hidden centers that break the normal, natural circuits of energy and create transformations. He could cause ectoplasmic emanations to appear between his violently trembling palms; take the form of a mountain; appear as a beast; conjure up or dispel a storm, and tell, as though reciting tales of his own intimate knowledge and experience, the mythological lore and legends of the tribe.

For in every society in which they have been known, the shamans have been the particular guardians and reciters of the chants and traditions of their people. "Being a *joon* of repute," wrote Mr. Bridges of his shaman friend, "Tininisk preferred chanting or instructing us in ancient lore to work and drudgery." [21]

And why not?

The realm of myth, from which, according to primitive belief, the whole spectacle of the world proceeds, and the realm of shamanistic trance are one and the same. Indeed, it is because of the reality of the trance and the profound impression left on the mind of the shaman himself by his experiences that he believes in his craft and its power—even though, for a popular show, he may have to put on a deceptive external performance, imitating for the honest hunters some of the wonders that his spirits have shown him in the magical realm beyond the veil.

This relationship of the shaman's inner experiences to myth is a supremely important theme and problem of our subject. For if the shaman was the guardian of the mythological lore of mankind during the period of some five or six hundred thousand years when the chief source of sustenance was the hunt, then the inner world of the shaman must be assumed to have played a considerable role in the formation of whatever portion of our spiritual inheritance may have descended from the period of the paleolithic hunt. We must consider, therefore, what the visions within, and springing from, the shamanistic world of experience may have been.

III. The Shamanistic Vision

The inward experiences through which the power of the shaman is attained and from which the motifs of his shamanistic rites derive may be surmised from a survey of autobiographies gathered in recent years from the Buriat, Yakut, Ostyak, Vogul, and Tungus shamans of that vast quadrangle of Siberia—bounded on the west by the Yenisei River, east by the Lena River, south by Lake Baikal, and north by the Taimyr Peninsula—which has been from paleolithic times a classical academy of shamanism and is today its strongest surviving center.

"A person cannot become a shaman if there have been no shamans in his sib," the Tungus shaman Semyonov Semyon declared, when questioned at his home on the Lower Tunguska River, in the spring of 1925, by the Russian folklorist G. V. Ksenofontov, who was himself a full-blooded Yakut. "Only those who have shaman ancestors in their past receive the shamanistic gift," said the shaman; "whence the gift descends from generation to generation. My oldest brother, Ilya Semyonov, was a shaman. He died three years ago. My grandfather on my mother's side was a shaman too. My grandmother on the mother's side was a Yakut from Chirindi, of the Yessei Yakut sib, Jakdakar."

"It is to be understood," Ksenofontov comments, "that these

shamans, in their turn, received their shamanistic gift from further representatives of the family line, whose names they knew; so that an unbroken chain of shamanistic tradition has come down from the depth of the centuries. The Yessei Yakut," he adds, "are most probably Yakutized Tungus."

"When I shamanize," the shaman continued,

> the spirit of my deceased brother Ilya comes and speaks through my mouth. My shaman forefathers, too, have forced me to walk the path of shamanism. Before I commenced to shamanize, I lay sick for a whole year: I became a shaman at the age of fifteen. The sickness that forced me to this path showed itself in a swelling of my body and frequent spells of fainting. When I began to sing, however, the sickness usually disappeared.
>
> After that, my ancestors began to shamanize with me. They stood me up like a block of wood and shot at me with their bows until I lost consciousness. They cut up my flesh, separated my bones, counted them, and ate my flesh raw. When they counted the bones they found one too many; had there been too few, I could not have become a shaman. And while they were performing this rite, I ate and drank nothing for the whole summer. But at the end the shaman spirits drank the blood of a reindeer and gave me some to drink, too. After these events, the shaman has less blood and looks pale.
>
> The same thing happens to every Tungus shaman. Only after his shaman ancestors have cut up his body in this way and separated his bones can he begin to practice.[22]

As Professor Mircea Eliade has shown in his cross-cultural study of shamanism,[23] the overpowering mental crisis here described is a generally recognized feature of the vocational summons. Its counterparts have been registered wherever shamans have appeared and practiced; which is to say, in every primitive society of the world. And though the temporary unbalance precipitated by such a crisis may resemble a nervous breakdown, it cannot be dismissed as such. For it is a phenomenon *sui generis;* not a pathological but a normal event for the gifted mind in these societies, when struck by and absorbing the force of what for lack of a better term we may call a hierophantic realization: the realization of "something far more deeply interfused," inhabiting both the round earth and one's own interior, which gives to the world a sacred character; an intuition of depth, absolutely inaccessible to the "tough minded" honest hunters (whether it be dollars, guanaco pelts, or working hypotheses they are after), but which may present itself spontaneously to such as William James has termed the "tender minded" of our species,[24] and who, as Paul Radin shows in his work on *Primitive Man as Philosopher,* exist no less in primitive than in higher societies.[25]

The force of such a hierophantic realization is the more compelling for the mind dwelling in a primitive society, inasmuch as the whole social structure, as well as the rationalization of its relationship to the surrounding world of nature, is there mythologically based. The crisis, consequently, cannot be analyzed as a rupture with society and the world. It is, on the contrary, an overpowering realization of their depth, and the rupture is rather with the comparatively trivial attitude toward both the human spirit and the world that appears to satisfy the great majority.

It has been remarked by sensitive observers that, in contrast to the life-maiming psychology of a neurosis (which is recognized in primitive societies as well as in our own, but not confused there with shamanism), the shamanistic crisis, when properly fostered, yields an adult not only of superior intelligence and refinement, but also of greater physical stamina and vitality of spirit than is normal to the members of his group.[26] The crisis, consequently, has the value of a superior threshold initiation: superior, in the first place, because spontaneous, not tribally enforced, and in the second place, because the shift of reference of the psychologically potent symbols has been not from the family to the tribe * but from the family to the universe. The energies of the psyche summoned into play by such an immediately recognized magnification of the field of life are of greater force than those released and directed by the group-oriented, group-contrived, visionary masquerades of the puberty rites and men's dancing ground. They give a steadier base and larger format to the character of the individual concerned, and have tended, also, to endow the phenomenology of shamanism itself with a quality of general human validity, which

* Cf. supra, pp. 90–92.

the local rites—of whatever community—simply do not share. And finally, since the group rites of the hunting societies are, *au fond,* precipitations into the public field of images first experienced in shamanistic vision, rendering myths best known to shamans and best interpreted by shamans, the painful crisis of the deeply forced vocational call carries the young adept to the root not only of his cultural structure, but also of the psychological structures of every member of his tribe.

In a profound sense, then, the shaman stands against the group and necessarily so, since the whole realm of interests and anxieties of the group is for him secondary. And yet, because he has gone through—in some way, in some sense—to the heart of the world of which the group and its ranges of concern are but manifestations, he can help and harm his fellows in ways that amaze them.

But how, then, does he come to such power?

We note first that, just as in the puberty rites, so also in Semyonov's vision, the structuring theme was an adventure of death and resurrection. We have already mentioned the infantile image of the parent as a cannibal ogre. The point of the shamanistic vision is that, though the victim indeed was eaten, there was a power of restitution inherent in his bones that brought him back to life. He is stronger than death.

Spencer and Gillen have described the corresponding event in the lives of the medicine men of the Aranda. When a man of this Australian tribe feels that he has the power to become a shaman, he leaves the camp alone and proceeds to the mouth of a certain cave, where, with considerable trepidation, not venturing to go inside, he lies down to sleep. At the break of day a spirit comes to the mouth of the cave and, finding the man asleep, throws at him an invisible lance, which pierces his neck from behind, passes through his tongue, and emerges from his mouth. The tongue remains throughout life perforated in the center with a hole large enough to admit the little finger; and, when all is over, this hole is the only visible and outward sign remaining of the treatment. A second lance then thrown by the spirit pierces his head from ear to ear, and the victim, falling dead, is immediately carried into the depths of the cave, within which the spirits live in perpetual sunshine, among streams of running water. The cave in question is supposed to extend far under the plain, terminating at a spot beneath what is called the Edith Range, ten miles away. The spirits there remove all of the man's internal organs and provide him with a completely new set, after which he presently returns to life, but in a condition of insanity. This does not last very long, however. When he has become sufficiently rational, the spirits of the cave—who are invisible to all except a few highly gifted medicine men and to dogs—conduct him back to his own people. He continues to look and behave queerly until, one morning, it is noticed that he has painted with powdered charcoal and fat a broad band across the bridge of his nose. Every sign of insanity has now disappeared, and the new medicine man has graduated. But he must not practice for another year, and if, during this period of probation, the hole in his tongue closes, he will know that his power has departed and will not practice at all. Meanwhile, consorting with the local masters of his profession, he learns the secrets of his craft, "which consist," as Spencer and Gillen declare, "principally in the ability to hide about his person and to produce at will small quartz pebbles and bits of stick; and, of hardly less importance than this sleight of hand, the power of looking preternaturally solemn, as if he were the possessor of knowledge quite hidden from ordinary men." [27]

The new intestines of the shaman are composed of quartz crystals, which he is now able to project into people, either for good or for ill.[28] And so here again we see a theme of death and restitution, but with a new body that is adamantine. The Oriental counterpart, which plays a considerable role in both Hindu and Buddhist mystical literature, is the "diamond" or "thunderbolt" body (*vajra*), which the yogi achieves. On the primitive level it may be proper to read such an idea psychoanalytically, as a reparation fantasy defending the infantile psyche against its own body-destruction anxieties.[29] I do not think, however, that such a reading quite does justice to the reach of Hindu and Buddhist thought, or, indeed, to the generally known metaphysical concept of a principle of permanence underlying the phenomenology of temporal change. It is not easy to know how far back into the primitive situation one can press the idea, universal to all the higher traditions of mysticism, of the changing of "our lowly bodies to be like His glorious body" (Philippians 3:21); but I should say, judging from what we have already been told by our Eskimo shamans, that it should be possible to run it back all the way. Nor do I know how tenaciously the reader is going to cling to the idea, advertised by Dr. Freud, that all higher thought, except psychoanalysis, is a function of infantile anxiety. But either way, we have certainly struck here a level or point of experience that would seem to represent precisely what Bastian was referring to when he wrote of elementary ideas. The introversion of the shamanistic crisis and the break, temporarily, from the local system of practical life lead to a field of experience that in the deepest sense transcends provincialism and opens the way at least to a premonition of something else. Indeed, I suspect that we are approaching here the ultimate sanctuary and wellspring of the whole world and wonder —all the magic—of the gods.

Said the Tungus shaman, Semyonov Semyon:

> Up above there is a certain tree where the souls of the shamans are reared, before they attain their powers. And on the boughs of this tree are nests in which the souls lie and are attended. The name of the tree is "Tuuru." The higher the nest in this tree, the stronger will the shaman be who is raised in it, the more will hc know, and the farther will he see.
>
> The rim of a shaman's drum is cut from a living larch. The larch is left alive and standing in recollection and honor of the tree Tuuru, where the soul of the shaman was raised. Furthermore, in memory of the great tree Tuuru, at each seance the shaman plants a tree with one or more cross-sticks in the tent where the ceremony takes place, and this tree too is called Tuuru. This is done both among us here on the Lower Tunguska and among the Angara Tungus. The Tungus who are connected with the Yakuts call this planted tree "Sarga." It is made of a long pole of larch. White cloths are hung on the cross-sticks. Among the Angara Tungus they hang the pelt of a sacrificed animal on the tree. The Tungus of the Middle Tunguska make a Tuuru that is just like ours.
>
> According to our belief, the soul of the shaman climbs up this tree to God when he shamanizes. For the tree grows

during the rite and invisibly reaches the summit of heaven.
God created two trees when he created the earth and man: a male, the larch; and a female, the fir.[30]

The vision of the tree is a characteristic feature of the shamanism of Siberia. The image can have been derived from the great traditions of the south; it is applied, however, to a distinctly shamanistic system of experience. Like the tree of Wotan, Yggdrasil, it is the world axis, reaching to the zenith. The shaman has been nurtured in this tree, and his drum, fashioned of its wood, bears him back to it in his trance of ecstasy. As Eliade has pointed out, the shaman's power rests in his ability to throw himself into a trance at will. Nor is he the victim of his trance: he commands it, as a bird the air in its flight. The magic of his drum carries him away on the wings of its rhythm, the wings of spiritual transport. The drum and dance simultaneously elevate his spirit and conjure to him his familiars—the beasts and birds, invisible to others, that have supplied him with his power and assist him in his flight. And it is while in his trance of rapture that he performs his miraculous deeds. While in this trance he is flying as a bird to the upper world, or descending as a reindeer, bull, or bear to the world beneath.

Among the Buriat, the animal or bird that protects the shaman is called *khubilgan,* meaning "metamorphosis," from the verb *khubilku,* "to change oneself, to take another form." [31] The early Russian missionaries and voyagers in Siberia in the first part of the eighteenth century noted that the shamans spoke to their spirits in a strange, squeaky voice.[32] They also found among the tribes numerous images of geese with extended wings, sometimes of brass.[33] And as we shall soon see,* in a highly interesting paleolithic hunting station known as Mal'ta, in the Lake Baikal area, a number of flying geese or ducks were found, carved in mammoth ivory. Such flying birds, in fact, have been found in many paleolithic stations; and on the under-wings of an important example found near Kiev, in the Ukraine, in a site called Mezin, there appears the earliest swastika of which we have record—a symbol associated (as we have already remarked) in the later Buddhist art of nearby China and Tibet with the spiritual flight of the Buddha. Further-

* Infra, p. 330.

more, in the great paleolithic cavern of Lascaux, in southern France, there is the picture of a shaman dressed in bird costume, lying prostrate in a trance and with the figure of a bird perched on his shaman staff beside him. The shamans of Siberia wear bird costumes to this day, and many are believed to have been conceived by their mothers from the descent of a bird. In India, a term of honor addressed to the master yogi is Paramahamsa: paramount or supreme (*parama*) wild gander (*haṁsa*). In China the so-called "mountain men" or "immortals" (*hsien*) are pictured as feathered, like birds, or as floating through the air on soaring beasts. The German legend of Lohengrin, the swan knight, and the tales, told wherever shamanism has flourished, of the swan maiden, are likewise evidence of the force of the image of the bird as an adequate sign of spiritual power. And shall we not think, also, of the dove that descended upon Mary, and the swan that begot Helen of Troy? In many lands the soul has been pictured as a bird, and birds commonly are spiritual messengers. Angels are but modified birds. But the bird of the shaman is one of particular character and power, endowing him with an ability to fly in trance beyond the bounds of life, and yet return.

Something of the world in which these wonder-workers move and dwell may be gathered from the legend of the Yakut shaman Aadja. His fabulous triple-phased biography commences with a tale of two brothers, whose parents had died when they were very young; and when the elder was thirty and the younger twenty, the latter married. "In the same year," we then are told,

> a red piebald stallion foal was born, and the signs all pointed to this foal's becoming a beautiful steed. But that same fall the younger of the two brothers—the one who had married—fell sick and died. And although he lay there dead, he could hear everything that was said around him. He felt as though he had fallen asleep. He could neither move a limb nor speak, yet could distinctly hear them making his coffin and digging his grave. And so there he lay, as though alive, and he was unhappy that they should be getting together to bury him when he might very well have come back to life. They placed him in the coffin, put the coffin in the grave, and shoveled in the dirt.

He lay in the grave, and his soul, his heart, cried and sobbed. But suddenly, then, he heard that someone up there had begun to dig. He was glad to think that his elder brother, believing that he might still be alive, wished to disinter him. However, when at last the cover of his coffin was removed, he saw four black people whom he did not know. They took up his body and stood him upright on his coffin with his face turned toward his house. Through the window he could see a fire burning and smoke was coming from the chimney.

But then he heard, from somewhere, far in the depths of the earth, the bellowing of a bull. The bellowing came nearer, nearer; the earth began to tremble, and he was terribly afraid. From the bottom of the grave the bull emerged. It was completely black and its horns were close together. The animal took the man, sitting between its horns, and went down again through the opening from which it had just emerged. And they reached a place where there was a house, from within which there came the voice of what seemed to be an old man, who said: "Boys, it is true! Our little son has brought a man. Go out and relieve him of his load!" A number of black, withered men came hopping out, grabbed the arrival, carried him into the house and set him on the flat of the old man's hand. The old man held him to estimate his weight; then said: "Take him back! His fate predestines him to be reborn up there!" Whereupon the bull again took him on its horns, bore him back along the old way, and set him down where he had been before.

When the living corpse came to his senses, night had descended and it was dark. Shortly thereafter, a black raven appeared. It shoved its head between the man's legs, lifted him, and flew with him directly upward. In the zenith he saw an opening. They went through this to a place where both the sun and moon were shining and the houses and barns were of iron. All the people up there had the heads of ravens, yet their bodies were like those of human beings. And there could be heard inside the largest house something like the voice of an old man: "Boys! Look! Our little son has brought us a man. Go out and bring him in!" A number of young men dashed out and, seizing the newcomer, bore him into the house, where they set him on the flat of the hand of a gray-haired old man, who first tested his weight and then said: "Boys, take him along and place him in the highest nest!"

For there was a great larch up there, whose size can hardly be compared to anything we know. Its top surely reached heaven. And on every branch there was a nest, as large as a haystack covered with snow. The young men laid their charge in the highest of these, and when they had set him down, there came flying a winged white reindeer, which settled on the nest, and its teats entering his mouth, he began to suck. There he lay three years. And the more he sucked from the reindeer the smaller his body became, until finally he was no bigger than a thimble.

Thus reposing in his lofty nest, he one day heard the voice of the same old man, who now was saying to one of his seven raven-headed sons: "My boy, go down to the Middle World, seize a woman, and bring her back!" The son descended, and presently returned with a brown-faced woman by the hair. They were all delighted, and arranging for a celebration, danced. But the one lying in the nest then heard a voice that said: "Shut this woman in an iron barn, so that our son, who lives in the Middle World, may not come up and carry her away!"

They locked the woman in a barn, and from his nest, in a little while, the nestling heard the sound of a shaman drum coming up from the Middle World; also, the sound of a shaman's song. These sounds gradually grew, coming nearer—nearer—till finally, from below, there appeared, in the exit-opening, a head, and from the nest could then be seen a man of moderate stature and nimble mien, with hair already gray. Hardly had he fully appeared, however, when, pressing the drumstick, crosswise, to his forehead, he was immediately transformed into a bull with a single horn that grew forward from the middle of his forehead. Thc bull shattered with a single blow the door of the barn in which the woman was locked and galloped off with her, down, and away.[34]

What is being witnessed here—the reader may need to be told—is the arrival in the upper world of an earthly shaman, coming to rescue the soul of a woman who has passed away. For sickness, according to a shamanistic theory, can be caused either by the entrance of an alien element into the body, as in Mr. Bridges' account of the magic of the Ona (a little mouse, pebble, worm, or some less substantial shamanistic projectile), or by the departure of the soul from the body and its imprisonment in one of the spirit regions: above, below, or beyond the rim of the world. The shaman called to a sickbed must first decide, therefore, what sort of disease is to be treated. And if what is required is massage, purgative herbal treatment, or the sucking away of some intrusive element, he will set to work in appropriate style; but if the soul has flown his clairvoyant vision must discover its lurking place. Then, riding —as they say—on the sound of his drum, he must sail away, on the wings of trance, to whatever spiritual realm may harbor the soul in question, overwhelm the guardians of that celestial, infernal, or tramontane place, and work swiftly his shamanistic deed of rescue. This latter is the classic shamanistic miracle and, particularly when the patient is already dead, it is an act requiring the greatest physical stamina and spiritual courage.

We shall presently view these affairs from a terrestrial standpoint, but for the present, let us return to the celestial region of our tale. A master shaman has arrived, transformed himself into a bull, shattered the bolts of an iron storage house, and galloped away with his prize, the soul of a woman whom the gods had thought to let die.

> Following him, there went up cries and shouts, laments and mourning, and the son of the old man went down again to the Middle World. He returned with another, a white-faced woman, who was first transformed into a little insect and then perfectly hidden in the main, or middle, structural pole of the yurt; but soon again, the drum and song of a shaman could be heard. And this time, again, the one who arrived discovered his patient. He broke the pole in which she was hidden and carried her off.
>
> Whereupon the son of the old man went his way a third time, returning with the same white-faced woman as before. But now the raven-headed spirit-people in the upper world made better arrangements for her protection. They set fire to a pile of wood at the exit hole, took glowing brands in their hands, and stood about the aperture, alert and waiting. Then, when the shaman appeared, they struck him with the firebrands and drove him back to the earth.
>
> At last, the little watcher in the nest, at the end of his three years, once again heard the voice of the old man. "His years are up," the voice said. "Throw our child down to the Middle Earth. He is to go into a woman, to be born. And

with the name, Shaman Aadja, which we have given him, he shall become famous: no one shall take this name in vain in the holy month!"

Intoning songs and blessings, the seven hurled him down to the Middle World, where he immediately lost consciousness and could not recall by what means he had come to be where he was. It was only when he was five that this recollection returned—and then he knew how he had been born before; how he had lived on the earth; and how he had been born above and there had seen with his own eyes the arrival of a shaman.

Seven years after his new birth he was seized by the spirits, forced to sing, and cut to pieces. At eight he began to shamanize and to perform the ritual dance. At nine he was already famous. And at twelve he was a great shaman.

It turned out that he had come into the world this time, fifteen versts [about ten miles] from the place of his former residence. And when he paid a visit to his former brother he found that his wife had married again and that the colorful stallion foal, born the year of his death, was now a famous steed. But his relatives failed to recognize him and he told them nothing. One summer day, however, when a man of property was celebrating the so-called Isyach Festival—the blessing of the sacred kumiss *—which is accompanied by a ritual called the Lifting Up of the Soul of the Horse, the young shaman there met the same shaman whom he had seen entering the Upper World while he had been lying in his nest. The older man immediately recognized him and said in a voice loud enough for others to hear: "When I once was helping another shaman recover the soul of a sick woman, I saw you in the nest on the ninth, the uppermost, bough, sucking the teats of your animal mother. You were looking out of the nest." And the younger shaman, Aadja, hearing these words, immediately became furious. "Why do you bring out before everybody the secret of my birth?" he asked. To which the other answered: "If you are planning evil against me, destroy me, eat me! I formerly was nurtured on the eighth bough of the same larch on which you were nurtured. I am to be born again and nurtured by the black Raven, Chara-Suorun."

"And they say," concluded the Yakut narrator, Popov Ivan, "that the young shaman, that same night, killed the elder. The

* An intoxicant fermented or distilled from mare's milk.

shaman spirits swallowed him and thus committed him to death—and no one saw. —This ancient tale was told to me by a very old man." [35]

Spirits initiate the shamans of Australia in a cave; those of Siberia in a tree. Yet do we doubt that the sense of the two experiences is the same? In Siberia the shaman's flesh is eaten and restored; in Australia his intestines are removed and replaced by quartz crystals. But are these not two versions of the same event? We note that in both cases two inductions are required: one by the spirits; one by living masters. But these two are characteristic of shamanism wherever it appears. In the various provinces the visions differ, likewise the techniques of ecstasy and magic traditionally taught; for the cultural patterns through which the shamanistic crisis moves and is realized have local histories and are locally conditioned. Yet the morphology of the crisis (it can no longer be doubted) remains the same wherever the shamanistic vocation has been experienced and cultivated.

The main point that has here been so vividly illustrated is that in the phenomenology of mythology and religion two factors are to be distinguished: the non-historical and the historical. In the religious lives of the "tough minded," too busy, or simply untalented majority of mankind, the historical factor preponderates. The whole reach of their experience is in the local, public domain and can be historically studied. In the spiritual crises and realizations of the "tender minded" personalities with mystical proclivities, however, it is the non-historical factor that preponderates, and for them the imagery of the local tradition—no matter how highly developed it may be—is merely a vehicle, more or less adequate, to render an experience sprung from beyond its reach, as an immediate impact. For, in the final analysis, the religious experience is psychological and in the deepest sense spontaneous; it moves within, and is helped, or hindered, by historical circumstance, but is to such a degree constant for mankind that we may jump from Hudson Bay to Australia, Tierra del Fuego to Lake Baikal, and find ourselves well at home.

In the present chapter on shamanism, that is to say, we are touching lightly the problem of the mystical experience—which is non-historical and yet, wherever it appears, gives sense and depth to whatever imagery may be cherished in the local tradition, cultivated by the local priests, and more or less crudely utilized for social ends and a bit of spiritual comfort by the local populace. The shaman represents this principle on the primitive level, as do the mystic, the poet, and the artist in the higher reaches of the culture scale.

I should like to suggest, as a basic hypothesis, therefore, a correlation of the elementary idea with the mystical and of the ethnic idea with the historical factors just described. The elementary idea is never rendered or experienced except through the medium of the ethnic, and so it *looks* as though mythology and religion could be studied and discussed on the historical plane. Actually, however, there is a formative force spontaneously working, like a magnetic field, to precipitate and organize the ethnic structures from behind, or within, so that they cannot finally be interpreted economically, sociologically, politically, or historically. Psychology lurks beneath and within the entire historical composition, as an invisible controller.

But, on the other hand, all mythological imagery and ritual forms, both in their bearing on philosophy and in their impact on society, can and must be studied historically. As Professor Jensen has well said in his strongest criticism of a purely psychological approach to mythology, "A myth is not a sequence of independent images, but a meaningful whole, in which a particular aspect of the actual world is reflected." [36] In Part Two of the present study, the aspect represented to man's imagination by the model of death and birth afforded by the plant world was reviewed; in the remaining chapters of Part Three, we consider the response to the aspect represented by the animal world. Within each of these contexts, men and women are linked to each other and to their world—"engaged," that is to say, in the local ways of life; and the myths serve primarily a social end. However in the phase of our subject we are now considering—shamanism and the techniques of ecstasy—the same symbols work for "disengagement."

The subjects of our present study may be summarized as follows:

A. The non-historical, spontaneous factor of the shaministic-mystical rapture, released and rendered by way of
   (1) the imagery of the hunting societies
   (2) the imagery of the primitive planters
   (3) the imagery of the hieratic city state

B. The historical, conditioned, and conditioning factor of the local, socially oriented traditon, as represented in
   (1) the imagery of the hunting societies
   (2) the imagery of the primitive planters
   (3) the imagery of the hieratic city state

Moreover, the basic form of the shamanistic crisis can be summarized as follows:

A. A spontaneously precipitated rupture with the world of common day, revealed in symptoms analogous to those of a serious nervous breakdown: visions of dismemberment, fosterage in the world of the spirits, and restitution

B. A course of shamanistic, mythological instruction under a master, through which an actual restitution of a superior level is achieved

C. A career of magical practice in the service of the community, defended from the natural resentment of the assisted community by various tricks and parodies of power

The healing of the shaman is achieved through art: i.e., mythology and song. "When I began to sing," said the shaman Semyonov Semyon, "my sickness usually disappeared." And the practice of the shaman also is by way of art: an imitation or presentation in the field of time and space of the visionary world of his spiritual "seizure." A pole is placed in the center of the yurt, with cleats by which he climbs—imitating the magical ascent of his soul, "for the tree," as we are told, "grows during the rite and invisibly reaches the summit of heaven."

"I remember how, in the old days," said Alexejev Michail, an old Yakut dwelling near the Lena River, "the shamans bellowed during the seance like bulls. And there would grow on their heads pure, opaque horns. I once saw such a thing myself. There used to live in our village a shaman whose name was Konnor. When his older sister died, he shamanized. When he did so, horns grew on his head. He stirred up the dry clay floor with them and ran about on all fours, as children do when they play 'bull.' He mooed loudly and bellowed like a bull." [37]

"Every shaman," said another informant, Pavlov Kapiton, "must have an animal-mother or origin-animal. It is usually pictured in the form of an elk, less often as a bear. This animal lives independently, separated from the shaman. Perhaps it can best be imagined as the fiery force of the shaman that flies over the earth." [38] "It is the embodiment of the prophetic gift of the shaman," adds G. V. Ksenofontov; "it is the shaman's visionary power, which is able to penetrate both the past and the future." [39]

The shaman, furthermore, has bird and animal familiars who assist him in his task. "The shamans tell us," said Samsonov Spiridon, "that they have two dogs who are their invisible assistants. In the seance they call them by their names, 'Chardas' and 'Botos.' The dogs of a blood-thirsty shaman possessed by evil spirits will kill cattle and people: grown up people, however, they do not kill.

"It is also said," this informant continued, "that some shamans have a bear and a wolf and that these appear at seances." [40]

But not all who would like to practice the shaman's art can do so. Danilov Pyotr described an attempt that gently failed:

> In the Bertun area there was a man, two summers ago, who said that he was soon to become a shaman. He ordered a hut built for himself in a clearing in the neighborhood. The little house was placed right against the tallest larch; and on this there were a lot of shamanistic idols that had been hung there after seances. Young, unmarried boys had to build the hut of unpeeled branches, according to his instructions. The man's name was Michail Savvitch Nikitin, and he was about forty years old.
>
> When the hut that he had built was finished, he went into it and remained three days. He had said: "I am to lie there like a dead man for three days and shall be cut to pieces. On the third day I shall rise again." For the day of his resurrection he had ordered a shaman to be brought by the name of Botshukka, the son of Taappyn, who should perform over him the ceremony of the "Lifting-up of the Body" and "In-

structive Ordination." And they say also that a man named Dimitri Saba-Uktuur was with him as an attendant.

Well, when the shaman who had been summoned arrived, a lot of people gathered around the hut to watch the ceremony, and I joined them. The shaman had come with his drum and the candidate had donned his shaman costume. I was close enough to hear the ordaining shaman, when he had summoned his spirits, given them praise, and asked them for help. "It is mid-summer," he said. "When the leaves and blades of the trees and grasses have already come out, one should not perform the ordination of a shaman. The right times for that are spring and fall!" And with that, he broke off the ceremony.

The other shamanizes to this day in a half-baked way. He does so without wearing a shaman costume, performs only the preliminary summonses, and can take into himself only minor illnesses.[41]

"It is said," declared Alexeyev Ivan, "that the really good shamans are cut up three times in their life, the poor only once. The spirit of an exceptional shaman is born again after his death. They say that great shamans are reborn three times."[42]

IV. The Fire-Bringer

One day, runs a North American tale, as Old Man was walking in the woods, he chanced upon something very queer. There was a bird sitting on the limb of a tree, making a strange noise, and every time it made this noise, its eyes would go out of its head and fasten to the tree. Then the bird would make another kind of noise, and the eyes would come flying back to their places.

"Little Brother," said Old Man, "teach me how to do that."

"If I show you," the bird replied, "you must not let your eyes go out of your head more than three times a day. You will be sorry if you do."

"Little Brother, just as you say! The trick is yours, and I will listen."

The bird taught him how to do it and Old Man was so pleased that he did it three times, right away. Then he stopped. But presently he felt very much that he wanted to do it again, and after hesitating for some time but still feeling that he wanted to do it, he said to himself: "Why did he tell me to do it only three times? That bird has no sense. I will do it again." And so he made his eyes go out a fourth time; but now they would not come back. Then he called to the bird, "Oh, Little Brother, come and help me get back my eyes." But the bird did not respond; it had flown away. Old Man felt over the tree with his hands, but could not find his eyes; and he wandered about that way for a long time, crying and calling to the animals for help.

Now a certain wolf, perceiving that Old Man was blind, began to tease him and to make fun of him. The wolf had found a dead buffalo and, taking a piece of the meat, which had begun to rot and smelled badly, he would hold it close to Old Man. "I smell something dead," Old Man would say. "I wish I could find it; I am nearly dead with hunger." And he would feel around for the meat and the wolf then would jerk it away. Once, however, when the wolf was up to this trick, Old Man chanced to catch hold of him and, plucking out one of his eyes, put it into his own head. Whereupon he could see, and he recovered his eyes. But he never again could do the trick the little bird had taught him.[43]

Another day, as Old Man was traveling about the prairie, he overheard some very queer singing. He had never heard anything like it before and looked around to learn where it came from. At last he spied a circle of cottontail rabbits, singing and making medicine; they had built a fire and, having collected a lot of red-hot ashes, would lie down in these and sing, while one of their number covered them up. And then, after a while, the other would uncover them and they would all jump out. And apparently this was a great deal of fun.

"Little Brothers," said Old Man, "it is very wonderful how you lie in those hot ashes and coals without burning. I wish you would teach me how to do it."

"Come on, Old Man," said the rabbits. "We'll show you how. You must sing our song, and stay in the ashes only a short time." So Old Man began to sing, and he lay down, and they covered him with coals and ashes, and the heat did not burn him at all.

"This is very nice," he said. "You have powerful medicine indeed. Now I want to know it all, so you lie down and let me cover you up."

All the rabbits lay down in the ashes, and then he put the whole fire over them. Only one old rabbit got out, and when Old Man was about to put her back, she said, "Pity me, my children are about to be born." "All right," he said. "I shall let you go, so that there will continue to be rabbits; but I shall roast these others nicely and have my feast."

He put more wood on the fire and, when the rabbits were cooked, cut some red-willow brush and laid them on it to cool. The grease soaked into the branches, so that even today, if you hold red willow over a fire, you will see the grease on the bark. And you can see, too, that, ever since, the rabbits have a burnt place on their backs where the one that got away was singed.[44]

One day the trickster, in the form of a coyote, killed a buffalo and while his right arm was skinning it with a knife his left suddenly grabbed the animal. "Give that back to me," the right arm shouted. "This is mine!" The left arm grabbed again, and the right drove it off with the knife. The left grabbed again and the quarrel became a vicious fight. And when the left arm was all cut up and bleeding, Trickster cried, "Oh, why did I do this? Why did I let this happen? How I suffer!"[45]

Another day, he took an elk's liver and made a vagina of it, took the elk's kidneys and made breasts, donned a woman's dress that was too tight for him, and thus transformed himself into a very pretty woman. He let the fox have intercourse with him and make him pregnant, then the jaybird, and finally the nit. Then he walked to a village, married the chief's son, and gave birth to four handsome little boys.[46]

When he was one day wandering about aimlessly, he heard someone say, "Anyone who chews me will defecate; he will defecate." "Well," said Trickster, "why is this person talking in this manner?" He moved in the direction from which the voice had come and then he heard it again. Looking around, he saw a bulb on a bush. "I know very well," he said to himself, "that if I chew this I will not defecate." So he took it, put it into his mouth, chewed, swallowed it, and went on.

"Well," he said, "where is the bulb that talked so much? How could such an object influence me in the least? When I feel like defecating I shall do so, and no sooner." But while he was speaking he began to break a little wind. "Well," he thought, "I guess this is what it meant. It said, though, that I would defecate and I'm just breaking a little wind. In any case, I am a great man even if I do expel a little gas." Then it happened again, and this time it was really strong. "Well indeed! How foolish I was! Perhaps this is why they call me the Fool!" It happened again, very loudly, and this time his rectum began to smart. Next time he was propelled forward. "Well, well," he thought defiantly, "it may give me a little push but it will never make me defecate." It happened again and this time the hind part of his body was lifted into the air and he landed on his knees and hands. "Well, just go ahead, do it again!" he cried. "Do it again!" It did, and he went far up into the air, landing flat on his stomach. He began to take the matter seriously. He grabbed a log, and both he and the log were sent into the air. Coming down, the log was on top and he was nearly killed. He grabbed a poplar tree; it held, but his feet flew into the air and nearly broke his back. Next, the tree came up by the roots. He grabbed a large oak tree; this held, but again his feet flew into the air. Trickster ran to a village and contrived to have all the lodges piled on top of him, together with the people, dogs, and everything else. His explosion scattered the camp in all directions and the people, coming down, shouted angrily at each other, while the dogs howled. Trickster just laughed at them until his insides were sore. But then he began to defecate. At first it was only a little, but then a good deal, and then so much that he had to begin climbing a tree to keep above his excrement. He went on up, higher, higher, and reached the top, where he slipped, fell, and came out of the bottom of the pile covered and blinded by his own filth.[47]

Anyone used to the concept of God the Creator, as that image is rendered in the higher mythologies and religions of the agriculturally based civilizations, will surely be surprised to learn that this figure of whom we have been reading was the creator of man and all the animals.

Another of his tales—just another of the many that are told of his curious adventures—tells of his coming up to the country of the Blackfeet from the south, traveling north, and making the birds and animals as he passed along. He made the mountains, prairies, timber, and the brush first, putting rivers here and there, and waterfalls upon them, putting red paint here and there in the ground—fixing up the world as we see it today. And he covered the plains with grass, so that it might furnish food for the animals. He put trees in the ground, and all kinds of animals on the ground. And when he made the bighorn with its great head and horns, he set it out on the prairie. It did not seem to travel easily on the prairie; so he took it by one of its horns, and led it up into the mountains where he turned it loose; and it skipped about among the rocks, and went up fearful places with ease. So he said, "This is the place that suits you; this is what you are fitted for, the rocks and mountains." And while he was there in the mountains, he made the antelope out of dirt, and turned it loose, to see how it would do. But it ran so fast that it fell over the rocks and hurt itself. Seeing that this would not do, he took the antelope down onto the prairie and turned it loose. It ran away gracefully, and he said, "This is what you are suited for."

Then one day he decided that he would make a woman and a child, and so he formed them both of clay. And after he had molded the clay in human shape he said to it, "You shall be people." Then he covered it up and went away. The next morning, returning, he took the covering off and saw that the clay shapes had changed a little. The second morning there was still more change, and the third still more. The fourth morning he took the covering off, looked at the images, and told them to rise and walk; and they did so. They walked down to the river with their maker, and then he told them that his name was Old Man.

As they were standing by the river, the woman asked Old Man, "How is it? Shall we always live, shall there be no end to it?" And he said, "I have never thought of that. We must decide. I shall take this chip of dried buffalo dung and throw it into the river. If it floats, people will die but in four days become alive again; they will die for only four days. But if it sinks, there will be an end of them." He tossed the chip into the river and it floated. The woman turned and picked up a stone and said, "No, it is not to be like that. I shall throw this stone into the river and if it floats we shall always live, but if it sinks people must die, so that they shall feel pity for each other and feel sorrow for each other." The woman threw the stone into the water and it sank. "There!" said Old Man. "You have chosen. And so that is the way it shall be."

The first people were poor and naked and did not know how to live; but Old Man showed them the roots and berries and told them how to eat them; and he showed them that in a certain month of the year they could peel the bark off certain trees and eat it, and that it would be good. He told them that the animals should be their food. He made all the birds that fly and told the people that their flesh could be eaten. And of a certain plant he would say, "The root of this plant, if gathered in a certain month of the year, is good for a certain sickness." And thus they learned the powers of all the herbs.

Old Man taught the people how to make hunting weapons and to kill and slaughter buffalo, and, since it is not healthful to eat the meat raw, gathered soft, dry, rotten wood and made punk of it, and then got a piece of hard wood and, drilling a hole in it with an arrow point, taught them how to make fire with fire-sticks, and to cook the flesh of the animals and eat it.

And then he said to them, "Now, if you are overcome, you may go to sleep and get power. Something will come to you in your dream, and that will help you. Whatever those animals who appear to you in your sleep tell you to do, you must obey them. Be guided by them. If you want help, are alone and traveling, and cry aloud for aid, your prayer will be answered—perhaps by the eagles, or by the buffalo, or by the bears. Whatever animal answers your prayer you must listen." And that was how the first people got through the world, by the power of their dreams.[48]

When Trickster, at the end of his wandering, left the earth, he made a kettle and dish of stone, boiled a meal, and said, "Now, for the last time, I shall eat a meal on earth." He sat on a rock and his seat is visible there to the present day. You can see the imprint of his buttocks, the imprint of his testicles, the imprints of the kettle and the dish. The rock is not far from where the Missouri enters the Mississippi. Then he left, first entering the ocean and then the heavens. He is now under the earth, in charge of the lowest of the four worlds. Bladder is in charge of the second, Turtle of the third, and Hare of the world in which we live.[49]

This ambiguous, curiously fascinating figure of the trickster appears to have been the chief mythological character of the paleolithic world of story. A fool, and a cruel, lecherous cheat, an epitome of the principle of disorder, he is nevertheless the culture-bringer also. And he appeared under many guises, both animal and human. Among the North American Plains Indians his usual form was Coyote. Among the woodland tribes of the north and east, he was the Great Hare, the Master Rabbit, some of whose deeds were assimilated by the Negroes of America to an African rabbit-trickster whom we know in the folktales of Br'er Rabbit. The tribes of the Northwest Coast knew him as Raven. Blue Jay is another of his forms. In Europe he is known as Reynard the Fox; but also, on a more serious plane, he appears as the devil.

Here is a tale told by the Christianized Yakuts of Siberia:

> Satan was the older brother of Christ, but wicked, whereas Christ was good. And when God wished to create the earth he said to Satan: "You boast of being able to do everything and say that you are greater than I; well then, bring up some sand from the bottom of the ocean." Satan dove to the bottom, but when he returned to the surface saw that the water had washed the sand out of his hand. He dove twice again, without success, but the fourth time changed himself into a swallow and managed to bring up a little mud on his beak. Christ blessed the morsel, which then became the earth. And the earth was nice and flat and smooth. But Satan, planning to create a world of his own, had deceitfully hidden a portion of the mud in his throat. Christ understood the wile and struck him on the back of the neck. Whereupon the mud squirted from his mouth and formed the mountains; whereas originally everything had been as smooth as a plate.[50]

In the carnival customs of Europe this figure survives in the numerous clowns, buffoons, devils, Pulcinellas, and imps who play the roles, precisely, of the clowns in the rites of the Indian Pueblos and give the character of topsy-turvy day to the feast. They represent, from the point of view of the masters of decorum, the chaos principle, the principle of disorder, the force careless of taboos and shattering bounds. But from the point of view of the deeper realms of being from which the energies of life ultimately spring, this principle is not to be despised. Indeed, in a most amazing manner, in the period of the building of the cathedrals of the high Middle Ages—as Dr. Jung has reminded us in his article "On the Psychology of the Trickster Figure" [51]—there were some strange ecclesiastical customs reflecting the grimace of this master of chaos: most notably the *festum asinorum,* which Nietzsche parodied in his chapter on the "Ass Festival" in *Thus Spake Zarathustra.* The occasion honored in this whimsical feast was the flight of the Holy Family into Egypt, and in the cathedral of Beauvais the girl playing the role of Mary, together with the ass, went right up to the altar, where she stationed herself at the Gospel side, and at the conclusion of each section of the high mass that followed, the whole congregation brayed. An eleventh century codex states that "at the end of the mass, instead of the words *Ite missa est* ("Go, the mass is ended"), the priest shall bray three times, and instead of the words *Deo gratias* ("God be thanked"), the congregation shall bray three times." [52]

Dr. Jung's view is that "the trickster is a collective shadow figure, an epitome of all the inferior traits of character in individuals." [53] Such a view, however, is presented from the ground of our later "bounded" style of thought. In the paleolithic sphere from which this figure derives, he was the archetype of the hero, the giver of all great boons—the fire-bringer and the teacher of mankind.

The Buriats in the area of Lake Baikal tell of the Great Spirit, Sombol-Burkhan, who, when moving over the waters, saw a waterfowl swimming with its twelve young. "Water-bird," he said, "dive down and bring me earth—black soil in your beak and red clay in your feet." The bird dove, and Sombol-Burkhan scattered first the red clay on the water and then upon it the black soil; after which he thanked the bird. "You shall ever live," he said, "and dive in the water." [54]

This is a more primitive version of the earth-diver theme than the Christianized Yakut tale presented. Relieved of the ethical dualism of god and devil, it shows the creative force in its primary innocence. But the Ostyaks of the Yenisei River area depict the creator still more simply, as a shaman. The Great Shaman Doh—they say—was hovering over the waters with a company of swans, loons, and other water-fowl, finding nowhere to come down and rest, when he asked one of his diving birds to plunge and fetch a bit of earth from the bottom. The bird dove twice before it brought up even a grain; yet the Great Shaman Doh was able to make of this bit of mud an island in the sea.[55]

The hunting tribes of North America attribute the same shamanistic earth-fashioning deed to their paleolithic hero-trickster. At the time of a great flood we find this ambiguous figure floating on a raft full of animals, bidding them dive to bring up some earth. Three go down but return exhausted; but then some exceedingly powerful swimmer descends—a loon, muskrat, or turtle—and after a long time (in some of the tales even days), he comes floating to the surface, belly up, practically dead, but with a bit of dirt caught in his paw. And then Old Man, Coyote, Raven, or the Great Hare—in whichever character the trickster is represented—removes the bit of mud and, reciting a charm, places it on the surface of the water. The particle increases, growing in four days to the present size of the earth, the animals step ashore, and all begins anew.[56]

It is hardly proper to call such a figure a god, or even to think of him as supernatural. He is a super-shaman. And we find his counterparts in myth and legend throughout the world, wherever shamanism has left its mark: in Oceania and Africa, as well as in Siberia and Europe. In Polynesia, Maui is the trickster. We have already witnessed a couple of his feats.* Br'er Rabbit has taught

* Supra, pp. 191–195.

us something of his African form, where he is also Anansi, the spider. Among the Greeks he was Hermes (Mercury), the shape-shifter and master of the way to the land of the dead, as well as Prometheus, the fire-bringer. In Germanic myth he appeared as the mischief-maker Loki, whose very character was fire and who, at the time of Ragnarök, the Twilight of the Gods, will be the leader of the hosts of Hel.

We may imagine this trickster-hero in his character as Coyote, standing one evening on the top of a mountain, looking south. And far away he thought he saw a light. Not knowing, at first, what it was, by a process of divination he learned that he was seeing fire; and so, making up his mind to procure this wonder for mankind, he gathered a company of companions: Fox, Wolf, Antelope —all the good runners went along. And after traveling a very great way, they all reached the house of the Fire People, to whom they said: "We have come to visit you, to dance, to play and to gamble." And so, in their honor, preparations were made for a dance, to be held that night.

Coyote prepared a headdress for himself, made of pitchy yellow-pine shavings, with long fringes of cedar bark, reaching to the ground. The Fire People danced first, and the fire was very low. Then Coyote and his people began to dance around the flame, and they complained that they could not see. The Fire People made a larger fire, and Coyote complained four times, until finally they let it blaze up high. Coyote's people then pretended to be very hot and went out to cool themselves: they took up positions for running and only Coyote was left inside. He capered about wildly until his headdress caught fire, and then, pretending to be afraid, he asked the Fire People to put it out. They warned him not to dance so close to the blaze. But when he came near the door, he swung the long fringes of his headdress across the fire and ran out. The Fire People pursued him and he gave his headdress to Antelope, who ran and passed it on to the next runner; and so it went in relay. One by one, the Fire People caught up with the animals and killed them, until the only one left was Coyote; and they nearly caught him too, but he ran behind a tree and gave the fire to the tree. Since then, men have been able to draw fire with fire-sticks from the wood of trees.[57]

This version of the great event is from the Thompson River Indians of British Columbia. The Creek Indians of Georgia and Alabama, some three thousand miles away, present their trickster Rabbit in precisely the same adventure, dance and all, cap afire and animal relay,[58] while among the Chilcotin, who are considerably north of the Thompson tribes, the hero of the same adventure is Raven, again with the fire-cap, the dance, and the animal relay.[59]

Still farther north, however, among the Kaska, a primitive Athapascan tribe dwelling on the arctic slopes of the Rocky Mountains in the farthest reach of British Columbia, the myth takes another turn.

Fire, these people say, was held in possession, long ago, by Bear, who had a fire-stone, from which he could draw sparks any time he wanted. But the people had no fire; for Bear guarded the fire-stone jealously, always keeping it tied to his belt.

One day, in his lodge, he was lying quietly by his fire when a little bird, coming in, approached him. The bear said gruffly, "What do you want?"

The little bird replied, "I am nearly frozen. I have come to warm myself."

"All right," said the bear, "come in. But while getting warm, come over here and pick my lice."

The guest assented. He began to hop all over the bear, picking his lice and, while doing so, occasionally picked at the string that fastened the fire-stone to Bear's belt. And when the string was picked through, the little bird suddenly snatched the stone and flew away.

Now all the animals were outside; for they had arranged for this stealing of the fire. And they were all waiting in a line, one behind the other. Bear chased the bird and caught up just as it reached the first animal of the line, to whom the fire-stone had already been passed. And Bear caught this animal just as it tossed the fire-stone to the next. And so it went, right along the line, until at last the fire was passed to Fox, who scampered up a high mountain. But the bear was so tired by now that he could no longer run. And so Fox, on top of the mountain, broke up the fire-stone and threw a fragment of it to each tribe. That is how the many tribes all over the earth got fire. And that is why there is now fire everywhere, in the rocks and in the woods.[60]

A glance at the myths of the Andamanese, a race of extremely primitive pygmoid Negritos dwelling in a chain of remote islands in the Bay of Bengal, reveals a number of versions of the same legend, one of the most widespread of which assigns the deed to the kingfisher. The fire, here, was in the possession of the most powerful and important figure of the local pantheon, Biliku—a temperamental, feminine personification of the power of the north-east monsoon, alternately malignant and benign, to whom the fashioning of the earth is attributed. And the ancestors having determined to steal her fire at a time when she was known to be asleep, the kingfisher flew silently into her hut one night and took it. But she woke just as he was making away, and, hurling a pearl shell, cut off his wings and tail. He dove into the sea and swam to a place called Bet-'ra-kudu, where he gave the fire to one of the animals, who passed it on to the bronze-winged dove, and the dove turned it over to all the rest. The kingfisher, as a consequence of his accident, however, became a man, while Biliku, in a rage, withdrew her residence from the earth and has lived, ever since, somewhere in the sky.[61]

The young Nietzsche, in *The Birth of Tragedy,* contrasted the biblical myth of the Fall in the Garden unfavorably with what he took to be the typically Greek heroic and tragic myth of Prometheus. The whole mythology of the Fall with its concept of disobedience to a higher power, its serpent's lying misrepresentation, its seduction, greed, and concupiscence—in short, its constellation of what he termed "feminine affects"—represented for Nietzsche an interpretation of human values that could be termed only contemptuous and contemptible; whereas in the bold impiety of the Greek Titan—representing man's courageous achievement of his own cultural and spiritual stature in defiance of the jealous gods—he saw an essentially masculine worth.

Since Nietzsche's day we have learned that the fire-theft is not a specifically Indo-European mythological motif; nor the idea of the Fall specifically biblical. However, it is still true that these two represent the poles of the Western World's mythological inheritance. The Greek Titan, a sublimation of the image of the self-reliant, shamanistic trickster, who frequently comes off badly at the end of an adventure, is neither condemned in his intransigent defiance of Zeus nor mocked as a fool by the Greek playwright, but offered, rather, as a tragic pattern of man's relationship to the governing powers of the natural universe. Whereas the Bible, in its spirit of priestly piety, recognizing equally the tension between God and man, stands on the side of God and breaks not only man's will but the serpent's too.

Prometheus knows what he has done for mankind, and shouts it in God's teeth. Men, before he taught them, knew no arts but in the dark earth burrowed and housed, like ants in caves. They had no calendar until he taught them to know the rising and setting of the stars. He gave them numbers, the arts of writing, farming and the harnessing of the horse; metallurgy, medicine, divination; yes, and the art, even, of making sacrifice to Zeus. In the bold play of Aeschylus, *Prometheus Bound,* we hear the ring of that great Titan's defiant challenge:

> In one round sentence, every god I hate
> That injures me who never injured him.
>
> Deem not that I, to win a smile from Jove,
> Will spread a maiden smoothness o'er my soul,
> And importune the foe whom most I hate
> With womanish upliftings of the hands.[62]

In contrast, however, we admire no less the proud though humble piety of Job, who, when shown the wonder of the power that had dealt with him unjustly, yet made the world, poured ashes on his head. "I had heard of thee by the hearing of the ear, but now my eyes see thee," Job confessed before his God, "therefore I despise myself and repent in dust and ashes." [63]

These two traditions are mixed in the inheritance not only of the West but of all civilizations and represent the poles of man's spiritual tension: that of the priestly representation of the power that shaped the universe as a force beyond human criticism or challenge, the power that made the sun and moon, the seas, Leviathan, Behemoth, and the mountains, before whom man's proper attitude is awe; and, on the other hand, that of the intransigency of the self-sufficient magician, the titan power of the shaman, the builder of Babel, careless of God's wrath, who knows that he is older, greater, and stronger than the gods. For indeed, it is man that has created the gods, whereas the power that created the universe is none other than the will that operates in man himself and in man alone has achieved the consciousness of its kingdom, power, and glory.

Zeus, it may be recalled, had taken offense when Prometheus had tricked him at the time of the offering of a sacrifice. The Titan, having slain a sacrificial bull, filled the stomach of the beast with meat for himself and his people, wrapping the bones deceptively and attractively in juicy fat; and when he presented these two packaged portions to the king of the gods, bidding him choose the one he desired, Zeus, deceived, took the portion wrapped in fat. Opening which, and finding nothing but bones, Zeus became a god of wrath, and to such an absurd degree that he withheld from mankind the precious gift of fire. Whereupon Prometheus, man's savior, stole it—according to one version, from the workshop of the lame god of fire and metalwork, Hephaistos; but, according to another, from the hearth of Zeus himself, on the summit of Olympus. Prometheus carried with him a hollow stalk of narthex, which he ignited at the blaze, and then, waving the stalk to keep it burning, came running back. Still another version relates that Prometheus plucked his fire from the sun.[64] But in any case, Zeus took upon him an extreme revenge. For he caused Hephaistos to nail the boon-bringer to the highest summit of the Caucasus, drove a pillar through his middle in the way of a stake, and sent an eagle to eat his liver. What is torn away of the liver in the day grows back at night, so that the torture goes on and on. And yet, the punishment, presently, will end; for, as Prometheus knows, there is a prophecy that one day his chains will fall away of themselves and the world-eon of Zeus dissolve.

The prophecy is the same as that of the Eddic Twilight of the Gods, when Loki will lead forth the rugged hosts of Hel:

> Then shall happen what seems great tidings: the Wolf shall swallow the sun; and this shall seem to men a great harm. Then the other wolf shall seize the moon, and he also shall work great ruin; the stars shall vanish from the heavens. Then shall come to pass these tidings also: all the earth shall tremble so, and the crags, that trees shall be torn up from the earth, and the crags fall to ruin; and all fetters and bonds shall be broken and rent. . . . The Fenris-Wolf shall advance with gaping mouth, and his lower jaw shall be against the earth, but the upper against heaven,—he would gape yet more if there were room for it; fires blaze forth from his eyes and nostrils. The Midgard Serpent shall blow venom so that he shall sprinkle all the air and water; and he is very terrible, and shall be on one side of the Wolf. . . . Then shall the Ash of Yggdrasil tremble, and nothing then shall be without fear in heaven or on earth.[65]

The binding of the shamans by the Hactcin, by the gods and their priests, which commenced with the victory of the neolithic over the paleolithic way of life, may perhaps be already terminating —today—in this period of the irreversible transition of society from an agricultural to industrial base, when not the piety of the planter, bowing humbly before the will of the calendar and the gods of rain and sun, but the magic of the laboratory, flying rocket ships where the gods once sat, holds the promise of the boons of the future.

"Could it be possible! This old saint in the forest has not heard that God is dead!" [66]

Nietzsche's word was the first pronouncement of the Promethean Titan that is now coming unbound within us—for the next world age. And the priests of the chains of Zeus may well tremble; for the bonds are disintegrating of themselves.

Chapter 7

THE ANIMAL MASTER

I. The Legend of the Buffalo Dance

The lives of the Blackfoot Indians of Montana were bound up entirely with the comings and goings of the great buffalo herds; and one of their best devices for slaughtering a large number was to lure the animals over a cliff and butcher them when they fell on the rocks below. This same device was used on the buffalo plains of Europe in the period of the great caves, c. 30,000–10,000 B.C.; and no one who has seen the paintings in those caves of the masked shamans luring bison with a lively dancing step will fail to marvel at the reaches of time and space implied in George Bird Grinnell's descriptions of the hunts and drives in which he participated in the "Wild West" of the early '70s—while the scholarship of that same Europe was trying to reconstruct the long-lost Aryan past of only 1500 B.C., and Wagner was building his cycle of *The Ring*.

> In the evening of the day preceding a drive of buffalo into the pis'kun (the buffalo trap), a medicine man, usually one who was the possessor of a buffalo rock, In-is'-kim, unrolled his pipe and prayed to the Sun for success. Next morning the man who was to call the buffalo arose very early, and told his wives that they must not leave the lodge, nor even look out, until he returned; that they should keep burning sweet grass, and should pray to the Sun for his success and safety. Without eating or drinking, he then went up on the prairie, and the people followed him, and concealed themselves behind the rocks and bushes which formed the V, or chute. The medicine man put on a head-dress made of the head of a buffalo, and a robe, and then started out to ap-

proach the animals. When he had come near to the herd, he moved about until he had attracted the attention of some of the buffalo, and when they began to look at him, he walked slowly away toward the entrance of the chute. Usually the buffalo followed, and, as they did so, he gradually increased his pace. The buffalo followed more rapidly, and the man continually went a little faster. Finally, when the buffalo were fairly within the chute, the people began to rise up from behind the rock piles which the herd had passed, and to shout and wave their robes. This frightened the hindermost buffalo, which pushed forward on the others, and before long the whole herd was running at headlong speed toward the precipice, the rock piles directing them to the point over the enclosure below. When they reached it, most of the animals were pushed over, and usually even the last of the band plunged blindly down into the pis'kun. Many were killed outright by the fall; others had broken legs or broken backs, while some perhaps were uninjured. A barricade, however, prevented them from escaping, and all were soon killed by the arrows of the Indians.

It is said that there was another way to get the buffalo into this chute. A man who was very skilful in arousing the buffalo's curiosity, might go out without disguise, and by wheeling round and round in front of the herd, appearing and disappearing, would induce them to move toward him, when it was easy to entice them into the chute.[1]

Once upon a time—so a certain Blackfoot story goes—the hunters, for some reason, could not induce the animals to the fall, and the people were starving. When driven toward the cliff the beasts would run nearly to the edge, but then, swerving to right or left, go down the sloping hills and cross the valley in safety. So the people were hungry, and their case was becoming dangerous.

And so it was that, one early morning, when a young woman went to get water and saw a herd of buffalo feeding on the prairie, right at the edge of the cliff above the fall, she cried out, "Oh! if you will only jump into the corral, I shall marry one of you."

This was said in fun, of course; not seriously. Hence, her wonder was great when she saw the animals begin to come jumping, tumbling, falling over the cliff. And then she was terrified, because a big bull with a single bound cleared the walls of the corral and approached her. "Come!" he said, and he took her by the arm.

"Oh no!" she cried, pulling back.

"But you said that if the buffalo would jump, you would marry one. See! The corral is filled." And without further ado he led her up over the cliff and out onto the prairie.

When the people had finished killing the buffalo and cutting up the meat, they missed the young woman. Then her relatives were very sad, and her father took his bow and quiver. "I shall go find her," he said; and he went up the cliff and over, out across the prairie.

When he had traveled a considerable distance he came to a buffalo wallow—a place where the buffalo come for water and to lie and roll. And there, a little way off, he saw a herd. Being tired, and considering what he should do, he sat down by the wallow; and while he was thinking, a beautiful black and white bird with a long, graceful tail, a magpie, came and lighted on the ground close by.

"Ha!" said the man. "You are a handsome bird! Help me! As you fly about, look everywhere for my daughter, and if you see her, say to her, 'Your father is waiting by the wallow.' "

The magpie flew directly to the herd, and, seeing a young woman among the buffalo, he lit on the ground not far from her and began picking around, turning his head this way and that, and when close to her said, "Your father is waiting by the wallow."

"Sh-h-h! Sh-h-h!" whispered the girl, frightened, and she glanced around; for her bull husband was sleeping close by. "Don't speak so loudly! Go back and tell him to wait."

Presently the bull woke and said to his wife, "Go and get me some water."

The woman was glad and, taking a horn from his head, went to the wallow. "Father!" she said. "Why did you come? You will surely be killed."

"I came to take my daughter home," the man replied. "Come, let us hurry! Let us go!"

"No, no! Not now!" she said. "They would pursue and kill us. Let us wait until he sleeps again; then I shall try to slip away."

She returned to the bull, having filled his horn with water. He drank a swallow. "Ha!" said he. "There is a person close by here."

"No! No! No one!" the woman said. But her heart rose up.

The bull drank a little more; then got up and bellowed. What a fearful sound! Up stood the bulls, raised their short tails and shook them, tossed their great heads, and bellowed back. Then they pawed the dirt, rushed about in all directions, and, coming to the wallow, found the poor man who had come to seek his daughter. They trampled him with their hoofs, hooked him with their horns and trampled him again, so that soon not even a small piece of his body could be seen. Then his daughter wailed, "Oh, my father, my father!"

"Aha!" said the bull. "You are mourning for your father. And so, perhaps, you can now see how it is with us. We have seen our mothers, fathers, many of our relatives, hurled over the rock walls and slaughtered by your people. But I shall pity you; I shall give you just one chance. If you can bring your father to life again, you and he may go back to your people."

The woman turned to the magpie. "Pity me! Help me now!" she said. "Go and search in the trampled mud. Try to find some little piece of my father's body and bring it back to me."

The magpie quickly flew to the wallow, looked in every hole and tore up the mud with his sharp beak, and then, at last, found something white. He picked the mud from around it and, pulling hard, brought out a joint of the backbone. And with this he returned to the young woman.

She placed the particle of bone on the ground and, covering it with her robe, sang a certain song. Removing the robe, she saw her father's body lying there, as though dead. Covering it with her robe again, she resumed her song, and when she next took the robe away her father was breathing; then he stood up. The buffalo were amazed. The magpie was delighted and, flying round and round, set up a clatter.

"We have seen strange things today," the bull husband said to the others of his herd. "The man we trampled to death, into small pieces, is again alive. The people's holy power is strong."

He turned to the young woman. "Now," he said, "before you and your father go, we shall teach you our dance and song. You must not forget them."

For these would be the magical means by which the buffalo

killed by the people for their food should be restored to life, just as the man killed by the buffalo has been restored.

All the buffalo danced; and, as befitted the dance of such great beasts, the song was slow and solemn, the step ponderous and deliberate. And when the dance was over, the bull said, "Now go to your home and do not forget what you have seen. Teach this dance and song to your people. The sacred object of the rite is to be a bull's head and buffalo robe. All those who dance the bulls are to wear a bull's head and buffalo robe when they perform."

The father and daughter returned to their camp. The people were glad when they beheld them and called a council of the chiefs. The man then told them what had happened and the chiefs selected a number of young men, who were taught the dance and song of the bulls.

And that was the way the Blackfoot association of men's societies called I-kun-uh'-kah-tsi (All Comrades) first was organized. Its function was to regulate the ceremonial life and to punish offenses against the community.[2] And it remained in force until the "iron horse" cut across the prairie, the buffalo disappeared, and the old hunters turned to farming and to various laboring jobs.

II. Paleolithic Mythology

The picture in the huge paleothic temple-cave known as Trois Frères, in southern France, of a buffalo-dancer wearing precisely the ceremonial garb established in this legend, and functioning, apparently, in the way of the brave shaman whose power it was to lure the animals to their fall, gives a clue—or more than a clue, I should say, a very strong suggestion—to the antiquity of the legend just told; or, at least, of its theme. Furthermore, in the neighboring cave, known as Tuc d'Audoubert, there is a chamber in which two bison are represented in bas-relief on a raised prominence, around which the footsteps of a dancer have been found. Thc bison represent a cow being mounted by a bull; and the dance was performed not on the full soles of the feet, but on the heels, in imitation of the hoofs of a beast. We have already said that Persephone and Demeter in their animal aspects were to

Figures in the sanctuary of Trois Frères

be seen as pigs, and that Persephone as the bride of the monster serpent was a serpent. Here, comparably, as the bull's wife, the maiden was, surely, a buffalo cow—so that this may well be an early representation of that same divine connubium by which the buffalo dance was given to mankind.

We are reminded, also, of the famous paleolithic figure of a naked female known as the Venus of Laussel, which was carved in bas-relief on the wall of a rock shelter in southern France as the central figure of what was apparently a hunting shrine. She has the great hips and breasts typical of the female figures of the early Stone Age art, and is holding in her right hand a bison's horn, lifted to the level of her shoulder. The left is placed upon her protruding belly. And sufficient traces of ocher remained when she was found to show that she had once been painted red. A number of other figures lay about on broken bits of rock within the shelter: two females holding in their right hands objects that have not been identified; a fourth in a curious attitude, with the head and shoulders of another person upside down beneath her, in such a position as to have sugested to Dr. G. Lalanne, its discoverer, a birth scene; [3] a lithe male figure, head and arms gone, but in an attitude suggesting the throwing of a javelin; and finally, the fragments of a hyena and a horse, besides a number of slabs and blocks incised with feminine genital symbols. The Abbé Breuil, who is the world's chief authority on the art of the French caves, assigns these manifestations of the mythology of the hunt to an extremely early period, namely Aurignacian and Perigordian, which, according to the datings now generally recognized for this art, would be c. 30,000 B.C. We do not know the significance of the bison's horn in the woman's hand; but it surely was a bison's horn and surely, too, the sanctuary served the covenant of man and beast in connection with the hunting rites—precisely such a relationship

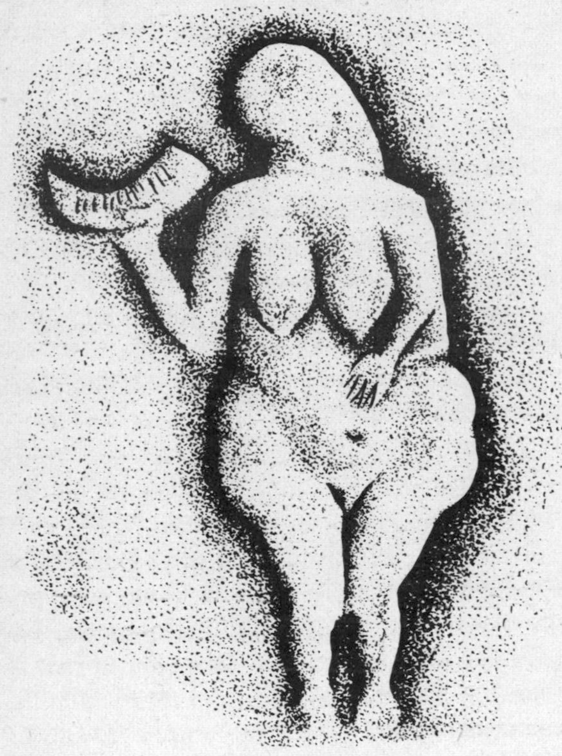

The Venus of Laussel

as that established by the episode of our story. So that while I am not suggesting that these findings in southern France from c. 30,000 B.C. are the illustration of a legend collected c. 1870 A.D. on the buffalo plains of the Wild West, it is worth remarking that a constellation of shared motifs has begun definitely to emerge.

On the walls of many of the paleolithic caves, furthermore, the silhouetted handprints of participants in the rites have been discovered, and many of these show the same loss of finger joints that we have already remarked among the Indians of the plains.

"Old-woman's Grandson," ran the words of a Crow Indian's prayer to the Morning Star, "I give you this joint [of my finger], give me something good in exchange. . . . I am poor, give me a good horse. I want to strike one of the enemy and I want to marry a good-natured woman. I want a tent of my own to live in." [4] "During the period of my visits to the Crow (1907–1916)," wrote Professor Lowie, to whom we owe the recording of this pitiful prayer, "I saw few old men with left hands intact." [5]

These are the maimed hands, then, of the "honest hunters," not the shamans; for the shamans' bodies are indestructible and their great offerings are of the spirit, not the flesh. We are on the trail of the popular rites and myths of the earliest periods of human society of which we have record—myths and rites of an age far greater, apparently, than that of the sacrifice of the maiden, and no less great, surely, in their reach across the barriers of space. We have already remarked the vast span of the shamanistic tradition from pole to pole of the Americas, from Tierra del Fuego to the Yenisei, and from Australia to Hudson Bay. We must now begin to follow the forms of the general, exoteric hunting rites of the paleolithic sanctuaries, down into the dimmest, darkest reaches of the well of the past. The clues become fewer and more widely spaced as we proceed; and yet, throughout, we may readily recognize those that remain as suggesting at least the possibility, or even probability, of such rites as those of the buffalo dance, on back to the very beginnings of the race.

Before commencing the voyage, however, let us pause to examine the clues that our Blackfoot legend of the buffalo dance affords to the mythological atmosphere in which the paleolithic hunt was carried out. We have seven clues of particular importance.

1. As in the Ojibway legend of the origin of maize, so here, the action is not placed in the mythological age, but in a world like the present. For let us not be deceived by the speech and magic of the birds and beasts: such speech and magic are still possible to shamans, and all the chief characters in this legend are endowed with shaman power. The myths and rites of the Australians, to

which we were introduced in Part One, Chapter 2, Section v, referred to a mythological time fundamentally different from our own, when the ancestors shaped the world. Such myths occur also in America. It is probable, however, that they represent a stage in the development of mythology later than do these personal adventure stories of men and women, animals and birds, endowed with shamanistic power. For where shamanism is involved, the mythological age and realm are here and now: the man or woman, animal, tree, or rock possessing shamanistic magic has immediate access to that background of dreamlike reality which for most others is crusted over.

Myths and rites referring to the mythological age, when the great mythological event took place that brought both death and reproduction into play and fixed the destiny of life-in-time through a chain reaction of significantly interlocked transformations, belong rather to the world system of the planters than to the shamanistically dominated hunting sphere. Whenever such myths are found in a hunting society, acculturation from some horticultural or agricultural center can be supposed. In the case of the Australians, the influence came from neighboring Melanesia. Likewise, among the North American tribes there were massive influences, both from the high civilizations of Middle America and from neolithic and post-neolithic China (after c. 2500 B.C.), whose influences can be traced not only south of the Yellow River into Indonesia, and from there westward to Madagascar and eastward to Brazil,* but also north of the River Amur, into the very zones of northeastern Siberia from which the later North American migrations sprang.[6] We are dealing, therefore, in these American myths, with an extremely complex and not a purely paleolithic inheritance. Yet many clues, as we have just observed, point to at least one important strain running back even to the period of the Aurignacian caves.

2. The rescuing hero and central figure of the legend was the magpie, without whose work as intermediary nothing could have been accomplished, and we readily recognize in him the bird form

* Cf. infra, pp. 441–443.

or metamorphosis (*khubilgan*) of the shaman-trickster. For the social function of the shaman was to serve as interpreter and intermediary between man and the powers behind the veil of nature; and this, precisely, is the function of the magpie in this tale.

3. The dead man's return to life was made possible by the finding of a particle of bone. Without this, nothing could have been accomplished. He would have passed into some other form, living for a time as a troublesome spirit, perhaps, and then returning as a buffalo, bird, or something else; but the particle of bone made it possible to bring him back just as he had been before.

We can regard this particle as our sign of the hunters' way of thought in these matters, just as for the planting context we took the seed. The bone does not disintegrate and germinate into something else, but is the undestroyed base from which the same individual that was there before becomes magically reconstructed, to pick up life where he left it. The same man comes back; that is the point. Immortality is not thought of as a function of the group, the race, the species, but of the individual. The planter's view is based on a sense of group participation; the hunter's, on that sense of an immortal inhabitant within the individual which is announced in every mystical tradition, and which it has been one of the chief tasks of ontology to rationalize and define. The two views are complementary and mutually exclusive, and in their higher stages of development, in the higher religions, have yielded radically contrary views of the destiny and righteousness of man on earth.

For example, in the Hebrew cult, where the myths and rites of the earthbound, ancient civilizations of the Near East have been assimilated to a profoundly group-conscious tribal unit, the participation of the individual in the destiny of the group is stressed to such a degree that for any valid act of public worship not less than ten males above the age of thirteen are required, and the whole reference of the ceremonial system is to the holy history of the tribe; whereas in the yoga of India, where a powerful shamanistic influence from the great steppe-lands of the north has done its work, precisely the opposite is the case, and the proper place for a full experience of the ultimate reach of the mystery of being is the utter solitude of a Himalayan peak.

4. The game animals of the legend, refusing the fall and then going over it, were acting under the influence of the great bull, who represents a type of being that plays a prominent role in hunting myths, namely, the animal archetype or animal master. We may think of him as comparable to the first bird, whirled clockwise around the head of the Apache Hactcin, or the first quadruped, from which the others came. Or again, using a philosophical term not as remote from primitive thought as it may seem, we might say that the great bull represents the Platonic Idea of the species. He is a figure of one more dimension than the others of his herd: timeless and indestructible, whereas they are mere shadows (like ourselves), subject to the laws of time and space. They fell and were killed, whereas he was unharmed. He is a manifestation of that point, principle, or aspect of the realm of essence from which the creatures of his species spring.

For the fact that the animal species, in contrast to man, are comparatively stereotyped in their innate releasing mechanisms has made them excellent representatives of the mystery of permanence in change. Each kind has, so to say, its own group soul. No matter how many individual animals may be shot down, others keep pouring forth and are ever the same. The biblical notion, the Platonic-Aristotelean notion, for which conservative Christians have fought a valiant though losing battle, the notion of "fixed species"—with all of its pseudo-philosophical implications about the timeless will and plan of some master mind, some master puppeteer, and about fixed laws and realms of essence within or supporting this phantasmagoria of apparent change—we can regard as of paleolithic antiquity. For it holds a prominent place in all primitive thought.

5. Since it appears that when the animals went over the fall they did so according to the will of their animal master, their flesh is to be regarded as the willed gift of that master to the people, according to the magical order of nature. And this was the primary lesson of the legend for the Blackfeet themselves. Killing buffalo is not against the way of nature. On the contrary, according to the

way of nature, life eats life; and the animal is a willing victim, giving its flesh to be the food of the people.

6. But there is a right and a wrong way to kill. The girl revived her father by means of the magic of the rescued piece of bone, and when the great bull saw that the people's magic was strong enough to bring back to life those apparently dead, he communicated to them the magical dance and ritual chant of the buffalo, by which the animals killed in the buffalo drives might be returned to life. For where there is magic there is no death. And where the animal rites are properly celebrated by the people, there is a magical, wonderful accord between the beasts and those who have to hunt them. The buffalo dance, properly performed, insures that the creatures slaughtered shall be giving only their bodies, not their essence, not their lives. And so they will live again, or rather, live on; and will be there to return the following season.

The hunt itself, therefore, is a rite of sacrifice, sacred, and not a rawly secular affair. And the dance and chant received from the buffalo themselves are no less a part of the technique of the hunt than the buffalo drive and acts of slaughter. Human sacrifice, such as we found in the plant-dominated, equatorial domain, where an identification of human destiny with the model of the vegetable world conduced to rites of death, decay, and fruitful metamorphosis, we do not find among hunters unless there has been some very strong influence from the other zone (as, for example, in certain rituals of the Pawnee). The proper sacrifice for the hunter is the animal itself, which through its death and return represents the play of the permanent substance or essence in the shadow-world of accident and chance. One may hear in the chant of the dancing buffalo, therefore—slow and solemn, ponderous and deliberate, as is fitting to such great beasts—a paleolithic prelude to the great theme of the Hindu *Bhagavad Gītā,* the mystical song of the lord Vishnu, the cosmic dreamer of the cosmic dream: "Know that by which all of this is pervaded to be imperishable. Only the bodies, of which this eternal, imperishable, incomprehensible Self is the indweller, can be said to have an end"; [7] or the words of the Greek sage Pythagoras: "All things are changing; nothing dies. The spirit wanders, comes now here, now there, and occupies whatever frame it pleases. From beasts it passes into human bodies, and from our bodies into beasts, but never perishes." [8]

Compare the Caribou Eskimo Igjugarjuk. "Pinga," he said, naming the female guardian of the animals, to whose realm the powerful shamans go when they seek to increase a failing food supply, "looks after the souls of animals and does not like to see too many of them killed. Nothing is lost; the blood and entrails must be covered up after a caribou has been killed. So we see that life is endless. Only we do not know in what form we shall reappear after death." [9]

7. It is to be noted, finally, that the social organization of the Blackfoot tribe itself was based on the hierarchy of the All Comrades Society, which is supposed to have been founded following this adventure. Grinnell has given a list of the orders of this hierarchy, as they were known at the time of his visit:

Little Birds	boys from 15 to 20 years old
Pigeons	men who have been several times to war
Mosquitoes	men who are constantly going to war
Braves	tried warriors
All Crazy Dogs	men about forty years old
Raven Bearers	(not described)
Dogs; Tails	old men: two societies, but they dress alike and dance together
Horns; Bloods	societies with peculiar secret ceremonies
Soldiers	(not described)
Bulls	a society wearing the bull's heads and robes.[10]

And so it appears that, just as in the great creative period of the hieratic city state a game of identification with the round dance of the planets in the heavens led to an organization of society in which the notion of a macrocosmic, calendrically rendered, celestial order supplied the mythology according to which the "mesocosm" of the state was composed; and as in the tropical areas, where the plant world supplied the chief sustenance for mankind and the chief model of the mystery of life, a game in which young men and women, identified with the first victim of the mythological age, supplied the base and focal episode of a group-coordinating ceremonial structure; so here, the game of identification was played in relation to the animals—and in particular those upon which the life of the human society depended. And the game was that of a mutual understanding, supposed to exist between the two worlds, realized and represented in rites, upon the proper performance of which depended the well-being of both the animals and their companions and co-players, men. This game provided the basis for the idea of the totem, to which so much attention was given by anthropologists in the last years of the nineteenth century that every appearance of an animal anywhere in myth or rite was interpreted as a vestige of totemism—whereas, actually, totemism is but one aspect or inflection of a larger principle, which is represented equally well in the "animal master" and in the "animal guardian" or personal patron.

In a totemistically conceived society the various clans or groups are regarded as having semi-animal, semi-human ancestors, from which the animal species of like name is likewise descended; and the members of the clan are prohibited both from killing and eating the beasts who are their cousins and from marrying within their totem group. Many North American Indian tribes and most Australian are totemistic, and there is reason to believe that the idea goes far back into the past. However, it does not exhaust by any means the modes of relationship of the hunting world to that of their neighbors and companions in life, the beasts. For the animals are great shamans and great teachers, as well as co-descendants of the totem ancestors. They fill the world of the hunter, inside and out. And any beast that may pass, whether flying as a bird, trotting as a quadruped, or wriggling in the way of a snake, may be a messenger signaling some wonder—perhaps the transformation of a shaman, or one's personal guardian come to bestow its warning or protection.

III. The Ritual of the Returned Blood

One of the most illuminating glimpses into the very deep well of past into which we are about to plunge, where in the long ages before mankind was struck by the principle of destiny of the vegetable kingdom it was the mystery of the deathless animal herd and the laws of the hunt that ruled his spirit, Frobenius records in one of his accounts of his journeys in Africa:

> In the year 1905, in the jungle area between Kasai and Luebo [in the Belgian Congo], I encountered some representatives of those hunting tribes, driven from the plateau to the refuge of the Congo jungle, who have become known to the literature of Africa as "Pygmies." Four of their number, three men and a woman, then accompanied the expedition for about a week. One day—it was toward evening and we had already begun to get along with each other famously—there was again a pressing need for replenishments in the camp kitchen and I asked the three little men if they would get us an antelope, which for them, as hunters, would be an easy task. They looked at me, however, in amazement, and one of them finally came out with the answer that, surely, they would be glad to do that little thing for us, but today it would of course be impossible, since no preparations had been made. The conclusion of what turned out to be the very long transaction was that the hunters declared themselves ready to make their preparations next morning at dawn. And with that, we parted. The men then began scouting about and finally settled upon a high place on a nearby hill.
>
> Since I was very curious to know whereof the preparations of these people might consist, I got up before sunrise and hid in some bushes near the clearing that the little fellows had chosen the night before for their preparations. When it was still dark the men arrived; but not alone. They were accompanied by the woman. The men crouched on the ground and cleared the area of all bits of growth, after which they smoothed it flat. One of them then drew something in the sand with his finger, while the other men and the woman muttered formulae of some kind and prayers; after which silence fell, while they waited for something. The sun appeared on the horizon. One of the men, with an arrow in his drawn bow, stepped over to the cleared ground. In a couple of moments the rays of the sun struck the drawing and at the same instant the following took place at lightning speed: the woman lifted her hands as though reaching for the sun and uttered loudly some unintelligible syllables; the man released his arrow; the woman cried out again; then the men dashed into the forest with their weapons. The woman remained standing a few minutes and then returned to the camp. When she had

left, I came out of my hiding and saw that what had been drawn on the ground was an antelope, some four feet long: and the arrow was stuck in its neck.

While the men were gone I wanted to return to the place to try to take a photograph, but the woman, who stayed close to me, kept me from doing so, and begged me earnestly to give up my plan. And so, the expedition went on. The hunters caught up with us that afternoon with a beautiful buck. It had been shot with an arrow through the neck. The little people delivered their quarry and went, then, with a few tufts of its hair and a calabash full of its blood back to their place on the hill. They caught up with us again only two days later and that evening, to the froth of palm wine, I brought myself to speak about the matter with the most trusting of my little trio. He was the oldest of the three. And he told me simply that he and the others had run back to plaster the hair and blood on their drawing of the antelope, pull out the arrow, and then erase the picture. As to the sense of the operation, nothing could be learned, except that he said that if they did not do this the "blood" of the antelope would be destroyed. And the erasure had to be effected at sunrise too.

He pleaded earnestly that I should not let the woman know that he had talked to me about these things. And he seemed, indeed, to be greatly worried about the consequences of his talk; for the next day our Pygmies left us without saying as much as good-bye—undoubtedly at his request, who had been the leader of the little team.[11]

We need only recall the words of the Caribou Eskimo Igjugarjuk to understand the meaning, and therewith, also, the antiquity and durability of this ideology which is found to be the same, fundamentally, whether in the jungles of the Congo or on the tundras of Hudson Bay: "The blood and entrails must be covered up after a caribou has been killed. So we see that life is endless."

"It takes a powerful magic," is the comment of Frobenius, "to spill blood and not be overtaken by the blood-revenge." [12]

One thing more: The crucial point of the Pygmy ceremony was that the rite should take place at dawn, the arrow flying into the antelope precisely when it was struck by a ray of the sun. For the sun is in all hunting mythologies a great hunter. He is the lion whose roar scatters the herds, whose pounce at the neck of the antelope slays it; the great eagle whose plunge traps the lamb; he is the luminous orb whose rays at dawn scatter the herds of the night sky, the stars. One sees the evidence of this primitive hunting myth in the motif, so common in paleolithic art, of the lion pouncing on the neck of the antelope that has just turned its head to look behind it, as well as in that other motif, which is one of the first to appear in ancient Sumerian art, of the solar eagle, clutching an antelope in each claw.

The lesson reads, by analogy: The sun is the hunter, the sun's ray is the arrow, the antelope is one of the herd of the stars; ergo, as tomorrow night will see the star return, so will tomorrow the antelope. Nor has the hunter killed the beast as a personal, willful act, but according to the provisions of the Great Spirit. And in this way "nothing is lost."

Chapter 8

THE PALEOLITHIC CAVES

1. The Shamans of the Great Hunt

It is a profoundly moving human experience to visit the vast underground natural temples of the paleolithic hunters that abound in the beautiful region of the Dordogne, in southern France. One drives over the highways of the most recent period of man's self-transformation so comfortably that even when one tries very hard to imagine what human life must have been during the closing millenniums of the Ice Age—when sturdy tribesmen, not yet possessing even the bow and arrow, ran down and slaughtered with pointed sticks and chipped stones the musk ox, reindeer, woolly rhinoceros, and mammoth that ranged in this region over a frozen arctic tundra—the contrast of that fabulous vision of the past with the gentle humanity of the present is so great that the likelihood of its ever having actually existed on this earth seems remote indeed. One has perhaps paused on the way southward from Paris at the cathedral of Chartres, where the sculptured portals and glowing twelfth- and thirteenth-century stained glass bear into the present the iconography of the remote Middle Ages. Or perhaps one has come around by way of the cities of the Rhone—Avignon, Orange, Nîmes, and Arles—where temples, aqueducts, and colosseums in a totally different style, of the most durably cemented brick, testify to a period of European civilization older than that of cathedrals: that of Rome, two thousand years ago, when Ovid was composing his mythological history of the world, the *Metamorphoses,* and Christ, a Roman subject, was born in Bethlehem—according to tradition, in a cave associated by the local pagans with the mythological birth of their annually sacrificed-and-resurrected deity Adonis. One is not prepared in any way by such touristic, literary, and archaeological experiences of the comparatively recent past, however, for the great leap, the real leap backward that the mind and heart must take, and do take, in the sacred caverns of the Dordogne.

In the vast, multi-chambered hunting-age sanctuary of Lascaux —which has been termed "the Sistine Chapel of the paleolithic"— an experience of divinity has been made manifest, not, as at Chartres or in the Vatican, in human (anthropomorphic) figurations, but in animal (theriomorphic). Overhead, on the domed ceilings, are wondrous leaping bulls, and the rough walls abound

The wizard-beast of Lascaux

in animal scenes that transmute the huge grotto into the vision of a teaming happy hunting ground: a herd of stags, apparently swimming a stream; droves of trotting ponies of a chunky, woolly sort, their females pregnant, full of movement and life; bisons of a kind that has been extinct in Europe for thousands of years. And among these magnificent herds there is one very curious, arresting figure: an animal form such as cannot have lived in the world even in the paleolithic age. Two long, straight horns point directly forward from its head, like the antennae of an insect or a pair of poised banderillas; and the gravid belly hangs nearly to the ground. It is a wizard-beast, the dominant manifestation of this whole miraculous vision.[1]

Moreover, there is another uncanny painting, even more suggestive of the mystery of this Stone Age cathedral of hunting magic, at the bottom of a deep natural shaft or crypt, below the main level of the floor of the cave—a most difficult and awkward place to reach. Down there a large bison bull, eviscerated by a spear that has transfixed its anus and emerged through its sexual organ, stands before a prostrate man. The latter (the only crudely drawn figure, and the only human figure in the cave) is rapt in a shamanistic trance. He wears a bird mask; his phallus, erect, is pointing at the pierced bull; a throwing-stick lies on the ground at his feet; and beside him stands a wand or staff, bearing on its tip the image of a bird. And then, behind this prostrate shaman, is a large rhinoceros, apparently defecating as it walks away.[2]

Figures in the crypt of Lascaux

There has been a good deal of discussion of this painting among the scholars, and the usual suggestion is that it may represent the scene of a hunting accident. No less an authority than the Abbé Breuil himself has supported this opinion, suggesting that the rhino may have been the cause of the disaster.[3] It seems to me certain, however, that, in a cave where the pictures are magical and consequently were expected to bring to pass such situations as they represent, a scene of disaster would not have been placed in the crypt, the holy of holies. The man wears a bird mask and has birdlike instead of human hands. He is certainly a shaman, the bird costume and bird transformation being characteristic, as we have already seen, of the lore of shamanism to this day throughout Siberia and North America. Furthermore, in our Polynesian story of Maui and the monster eel we have learned

Ceremonial mask: the horns are pointing sticks.
After Spencer and Gillen.

something of the power of a magician's phallus; and there is still practiced in Australia a lethal phallic rite of magic known as the "pointing bone," one variety of which has been described by Géza Róheim, who writes:

> Black or hostile magic is predominantly phallic in Australia. . . . If a man has been "boned," his dream will show it. First he sees a crack, an opening in the ground, and then two or three men walking toward him within the opening. When they are near they draw a bone out of their own body. It comes from the flesh between the scrotum and the rectum. The sorcerer, before he actually "bones" his victim, makes him fall asleep by strewing in the air some semen or excrement which he has taken from his own penis or rectum. The man who uses the bone holds it under his penis, as if a second penis were protruding from him.
>
> The Pindupi refer to black magic in general as *erati,* and a special type is described as *kujur-punganyi* ("bad-make"). Several men hold a string or pointing bone with both hands and, bending down, point backward, passing the magical bone just beside the penis. The victim is asleep, and the bone goes straight into his scrotum.

Australians in ceremonial attire with pointing-stick horns. After Spencer and Gillen

"Women also make evil magic," Dr. Róheim continues, "through the agency of their imaginary penis. Luritja women cut their pubic hair and make thereof a long string. They take a kangaroo bone and draw blood from their vagina. The string becomes a snake which penetrates into the heart of their victims." [4] A further example comes from the women of the Pindupi tribe. "They cut the hair from their pubes and make a string. Then they send the string from one woman to another till it gets to the medicine woman. First she dances with the string (*tultujananyi*) and then she swallows it. In her stomach it is transformed into a snake. Then she vomits it and puts it into water. In the water the snake grows till it is *wanapu puntu* ('big dragon'). The dragon undergoes another transformation, becoming a long cloud flying in the air with many women seated on it. The cloud becomes a snake again, it catches the woman's soul while she is asleep." [5]

These examples suffice to suggest a plausible symbolic context for the pointing penis of the prostrate shaman of Lascaux—as well as for the defecation of the passing rhino, who may well be the shaman's animal familiar. The position of the lance, furthermore, piercing the anus of the bull and emerging at the penis, spills the bowels from the area between—which is precisely the region effected by the "pointing bone" of the Australians. And finally it should be noted that the curious horns of the weird wizard beast in the upper chamber of the great cave, among the wonderful animals of that happy hunting ground, are exactly the same in form as the pointing sticks worn in the manner of horns by the performers in many of the Australian ceremonies of the men's dancing ground.[6]

Frobenius in North Africa, years before the discovery of Lascaux in 1940, noted three late paleolithic wall paintings that bear comparison with that in the crypt of Lascaux. One, from the face of a rock wall at Ksar Amar, in the Sahara-Atlas Mountains, shows a man with upraised arms before a buffalo; the second, from Fezzan, in southwest Libya, shows a couple dancing before a bull (two more dancing couples have been added in a later style); and a third, from the Nubian desert, shows three figures with upraised arms before a great ram. "It is to be noted," writes Frobenius, "that in almost all pictures of this kind the representation of the animals has been carried out with great care, while the human figures are exceptionally sketchy." But this observation holds true for the picture at Lascaux as well as for those that Frobenius had seen. "I think that what is shown in these pictures is on no account a ceremony," states Frobenius; "for we have pictures of similar postures of adoration before elephants and giraffes. It is much more likely that, as in the Luebo Pygmy rite * and rock pictures in general, what was undertaken was a consecration of the animal, effected not through any real confrontation of man and beast but by a depiction of a concept in the mind." [7]

Adding up the evidence of the Pygmy rite, the paleolithic North African pictures, the concepts of the willing victim, animal master, ritual of the returned blood, magic of the pointing bone, and signs of shaman power on the sketchily rendered human figure, we can surely say that we know, in general, what the function of the Lascaux picture must have been, and why, of all in the cave, this is the one in the holy of holies.

* Cf. supra, pp. 296–297.

The prostrate figure with the bird's head and the curious questing beast of the upper cave, furthermore, are by no means the only evidences of the presence and importance of shamans in the paleolithic period of the great caves. In Lascaux itself there is a third figure, which the Abbé Breuil has compared to an African practitioner of magic.[8] Indeed, no less than fifty-five figures of the kind have been identified among the teeming herds and grazing beasts of the various caves. These make it practically certain that in that remote period of our species the arts of the wizard, shaman, or magician were already well developed. In fact, the paintings themselves clearly were an adjunct of those arts, perhaps even the central sacrament; for it is certain that they were associated with the magic of the hunt, and that, in the spirit of that dreamlike principle of mystic participation—or, to use Piaget's term, "indissociation"—which we have already discussed,* their appearance on the walls amounted to a conjuration of the timeless principle, essence, noumenal image, or idea of the herd into the sanctuary, where it might be acted upon by a rite.

A number of the animals are shown with darts in their sides or as though struck by boomerangs and clubs. Others, engraved on softer walls, are actually pitted with the holes made by javelins that must have been hurled at them with force.[9] One thinks of the wax images of popular witchcraft, into which a name is conjured, and which then are pierced by needles or set to melt by a fire, so that the person may die.

It is also interesting to note that in most of the caves the animals are inscribed one on top of the other, with no regard for aesthetic effect. Obviously the aim was not art, as we understand it, but magic. And for reasons that we now cannot guess, the necromantic pictures were thought to be effective only in certain caves and in certain parts of those caves. They were renewed there, year after year, for hundreds of centuries. And without exception these magical spots occur far from the natural entrances of the grottos, deep within the dark, wandering, chill corridors and vast chambers; so that before reaching them one has to experience the

* Supra, pp. 80–87.

full force of the mystery of the cave itself. Some of the labyrinths are more than half a mile in depth; all abound in deceptive and blind passages, and dangerous, sudden drops. Their absolute, cosmic dark, their silence, their unmeasured inner reaches, and their timeless remoteness from every concern and requirement of the normal, waking field of human consciousness can be felt even today—when the light of the guide goes out. The senses, suddenly, are wiped out; the millenniums drop away; and the mind is stilled in a recognition of the mystery beyond thought that asks for no comment and was always known (and feared) though never quite so solidly experienced before. And then, suddenly, a surprise, a visual shock, a never-to-be-forgotten imprint—as follows.

Let us enter the great system of initiatory passages and chambers, discovered a few days before the outbreak of the First World War, sixty feet below the surface soil of the property of Count Henri Bégouën and his three sons, at Montesquieu-Avantes (Ariège), in the Pyrenees. The count has named the labyrinth "Trois Frères" (Three Brothers), in honor of his boys, who found it. The corridors, drops, ascents, and vast halls contain some four or five hundred rock paintings and engravings, reproductions of many of which have not yet been published. But the patient work, year after year, of the Abbé Breuil, tracing, deciphering, and disentangling the figures, interpreting and photographing them, has already brought forth such a gallery that we may think of this cave as the richest single treasury of clues to the ritual experience and mythological lore of the late paleolithic period yet broached. It is cut off by a fall of rock underground from the adjoining grotto of Tuc d'Audoubert, whose sanctuary of the bull and cow of the buffalo dance we have already described.* Tuc d'Audoubert the count and his sons had discovered only two years before they entered the Alice's Wonderland of Trois Frères; and these two underground systems together, comprising at least a mile of labyrinthine ways, must have constituted, in the very long period of their use, one of the most important centers of magic and religion—if not, indeed, the greatest—in the world. The period of their use, by the way, was at least some twenty thousand years.

* Supra, p. 287.

The count and his sons, on July 20, 1914, were on their way across a broad meadow to pay a visit to the cave that they had discovered two years before, when they sought the shade of a tree, to rest from the heat; and a passing peasant, noticing their distress, suggested that they should go to the *trou souffleur,* where a cool wind came out of the ground even on the hottest day. With caves in mind, they followed his direction and found the "blow hole" behind a clump of bushes. The boys enlarged it, and one descended, tied to a rope that they had brought for their other adventure. Down, down he went, and some sixty feet were paid out before he stopped. He had brought a ball of twine, which he let out behind him, like Theseus in the labyrinth of the Minotaur, and a miner's lamp to illuminate the corridors, which had not been entered for more than ten thousand years. His father and two brothers, waiting, became nervous when he had been gone for over an hour; but then there was a tug at the rope and they hauled him up, bursting with excitement. "A completely new cave! With hundreds of pictures!" he told them. However, the war came within a month, and it was not until 1918 that the exploration of the cave could be completed and the Abbé Breuil invited to commence his study.[10]

"The ground is damp and slimy," wrote Dr. Herbert Kühn, describing his visit to the cave in the summer of 1926;

> we have to be very careful not to slip off the rocky way. It goes up and down, then comes a very narrow passage about ten yards long through which you have to creep on all fours. And then again there come great halls and more narrow passages. In one large gallery are a lot of red and black dots, just these dots.
>
> How magnificent the stalactites are! The soft drop of the water can be heard, dripping from the ceiling. There is no other sound and nothing moves. . . . The silence is eerie. . . . The gallery is large and long and then there comes a very low tunnel. We placed our lamp on the ground and pushed it into the hole. Louis [the count's eldest son] went ahead, then Professor van Giffen [of Groningen, Holland], next Rita [Mrs. Kühn], and finally myself. The tunnel is not much broader than my shoulders, nor higher. I can hear the others before me groaning and see how very slowly their lamps push on. With our arms pressed close to our sides

> we wriggle forward on our stomachs, like snakes. The passage, in places, is hardly a foot high, so that you have to lay your face right on the earth. I felt as though I were creeping through a coffin. You cannot lift your head; you cannot breathe. And then, finally, the burrow becomes slightly higher. One can at last rest on one's forearms. But not for long; the way again grows narrow. And so, yard by yard, one struggles on: some forty-odd yards in all. Nobody talks. The lamps are inched along and we push after. I hear the others groaning, my own heart is pounding, and it is difficult to breathe. It is terrible to have the roof so close to one's head. And it is very hard: I bump it, time and again. Will this thing never end? Then, suddenly, we are through, and everybody breathes. It is like a redemption.
>
> The hall in which we are now standing is gigantic. We let the light of the lamps run along the ceiling and walls: a majestic room—and there, finally, are the pictures. From top to bottom a whole wall is covered with engravings. The surface had been worked with tools of stone, and there we see marshaled the beasts that lived at that time in southern France: the mammoth, rhinoceros, bison, wild horse, bear, wild ass, reindeer, wolverine, musk ox; also, the smaller animals appear: snowy owls, hares, and fish. And one sees darts everywhere, flying at the game. Several pictures of bears attract us in particular; for they have holes where the images were struck and blood is shown spouting from their mouths. Truly a picture of the hunt: the picture of the magic of the hunt! [11]

The Abbé Breuil has published a beautiful series of tracings and photographs from this important sanctuary.[12] The style is everywhere firm and full of life—with a spirit, as Professor Kühn has remarked, comparable to the best Impressionist sketches. Actually and most amazingly (and, of course, this was one of the features that made the discovery of this art so momentous) they seem very much closer to us than the hieratic, stiffly stylized masterworks of archaic Egypt and Mesopotamia, which are so much closer to us in time.

In this awesome subterranean chamber of Trois Frères the beasts are not painted on the walls, but engraved—fixing for millenniums the momentary turns, leaps, and flashes of the animal kingdom in a teeming tumult of eternal life. And above them all, predominant—at the far end of the sanctuary, some fifteen feet above the level of the floor, in a craggy, rocky apse—watching,

The "Sorcerer of Trois Frères"

peering at the visitor with penetrating eyes, is the now famous "Sorcerer of Trois Frères." Presiding impressively over the animals collected there in incredible numbers, he is poised in profile in a dancing movement that is similar, as the Abbé Breuil has suggested, to a step in the cakewalk; but the antlered head is turned to face the room. The pricked ears are those of a stag; the round eyes suggest an owl; the full beard descending to the deep animal chest is that of a man, as are likewise the dancing legs; the apparition has the bushy tail of a wolf or wild horse, and the position of the prominent sexual organ, placed beneath the tail, is that of the feline species—perhaps a lion. The hands are the paws of a bear. The figure is two and a half feet high, fifteen inches across. "An eerie, thrilling picture," wrote Professor Kühn.[13] Moreover, it is the only picture in the whole sanctuary bearing paint—black paint—which gives it an accent stronger than all the rest.

But who or what is this man—if man he is—whose image is now impressed upon us in a way that we shall not forget?

The Count Bégouën and the Abbé Breuil first supposed it to represent a "sorcerer," but the Abbé now believes it to be the presiding "god" or "spirit" controlling the hunting expeditions and the multiplication of game.[14] Professor Kühn suggests the artist-magician himself.[15] To the anthropologically practiced eye of Professor Carleton S. Coon of the University of Pennsylvania, on the other hand, "this is just a man ready to hunt deer. Perhaps he is practicing. Perhaps he is trying to induce the spirit of the forest that controls the deer to make a fat buck walk his way." And Professor Coon concludes: "Whatever the artist's overt motive in painting it, he did it because he felt a creative urge and liked to express himself, as every artist does, whether he is painting a bison on the wall of a cave or a mural in the main hall of a bank." [16]

There must be some scientific way of supporting the romantic hypothesis of a man crawling on his belly through a tube forty or fifty yards long to relieve a creative urge; otherwise, I am sure, the professor would not have made this suggestion. But for myself, I prefer the simpler course of assuming that this chamber, and the whole cave, was an important center of hunting magic; that these pictures served a magical purpose; that the people in charge here must have been high-ranking highly skilled magicians (powerful by repute, at least, if not in actual fact); and that whatever was done in this cave had as little to do with an urge to self-expression as the activity of the Pope in Rome celebrating a Pontifical Mass.

Between the two guesses of the Abbé Breuil, however, it is extremely difficult to decide—but perhaps not as important to make a choice as a modern man might suppose: for if the vivid, unforgettable lord of the animals in the hunters' sanctuary of Trois Frères is a god, then he is certainly a god of sorcerers, and if a sorcerer, he is one who has donned the costume of a god; and, as we know, and see amply illustrated in the ritual lore of modern savages, when the sacred regalia has been assumed the individual has become an epiphany of the divine being itself. He is taboo. He is a conduit of divine power. He does not merely *represent* the god, he *is* the god; he is a *manifestation* of the god, not a representation.

But a picture, too, is such a manifestation. And so, perhaps, the most likely interpretation is, after all, the second by the Abbé Breuil, namely, that the so-called "Sorcerer of Trois Frères" is actually a god, the manifestation of a god—who, indeed, may also have been embodied in some of the shamans themselves, during the course of the rites, but here is embodied for us, forever, in this wonderful icon.

First among the features of the great caves that are of paramount importance to our study is the fact that these deep, labyrinthine grottos were not dwellings but sanctuaries, comparable in function to the men's dancing grounds of the Aranda; and there is evidence enough to assure us that they were used for similar purposes: the boys' puberty rites and the magical increase of the game. And just as every shrine and ceremony in the ancient world, as well as among the primitive tribes whose customs we know, had its origin legend, so must these sanctuaries of the Old Stone Age have had theirs. The enigmatic figures painted into the crypts and deepest recesses of the caves almost certainly hold in their silence the myths of the ultimate source of the magical efficacy of these magnificent shrines.

The dwellings of the people, on the other hand, were either in shallow caves and under ledges, or out on the open plains, in various kinds of shelter. A number of the paintings suggest the forms of their shacks or houses, while under many ledges abundant remains have been found of Old Stone Age life. In fact, in the beautiful valleys of the Dordogne people are dwelling under those same ledges to this day. They are great ledges, left by the wash of mighty glacial rivers; and the same rivers now being much smaller and lower than they were, they have left a beautiful grassy area between their present banks and the tall cliffs into which the ledges curve. One has to climb a little to reach the comfortable French homes that nestle against the overhanging walls. And just beneath the earth of these modern homes there is to be found a stratum of Gallo-Roman remains, from the period of Vercingetorix and Julius Caesar; below that, remains of the earlier Gallic culture world; still lower, the neolithic of c. 2500–1000 B.C.—and then the paleolithic, level after level: Azilian, Magdalenien, Solutrean, Aurignacian, even Mousterian; some fifty thousand years of human living in one amazing cross-sectional view. On the topmost level you may find a broken bicycle chain; on the bottom a cave-bear tooth two inches long. And the concierge who is showing you the cut is herself living in a house with the solid rock of the cliff for its back wall, and she will tell you what the advantages are of a a building with such a wall: it is cool in summer and warm in winter. The rock, sheer mother rock, affords good protection. Meanwhile, out in front, there is to be seen the graceful sweep of grass down to the lovely river, and one cannot but recognize and feel that for millenniums this has been a fine place for the raising of children. Paleolithic men hunted for their food instead of growing it, and they walked or ran from place to place instead of bicycling or riding in a car. But otherwise? They had their youngsters, and their wives sewed clothes—not of cloth, but of leather. The men had their workshops for the chipping of flint, and their men's clubs in their secret caves. They were living, in the main, just about as people do now. And so it has been for some fifty thousand years. The tick of time in such a situation does not sound quite as loudly as it once did.

II. Our Lady of the Mammoths

Now whereas in the mural paintings of the paleolithic caves animal forms preponderate, the chief subject of interest among the sculptured remains of the same period was the human female; and whereas the comparatively rare figures of men appearing among the painted animals are masked or otherwise modified in such a way as to suggest mythological beings and magical enterprises, the female figurines, carved in bone, stone, or mammoth ivory, are nude, and simply standing. Many are extremely obese, and of these some are radically stylized in a remarkably "modern" manner to give dramatic—and, no doubt, symbolically intended—emphasis to the great loins, the pubic triangle, and the nourishing breasts. In contrast to the male forms in the paintings, they are never masked or otherwise modified to suggest animals, while of the hundred and thirty-odd that have been found, only two appear to be clothed in anything like a shamanistic attire. The others simply *are*. Indeed, a few scholars have interpreted the bold little "Venuses" as paleolithic erotica.[17] But since several have been found set up in shrines, it is now certain that they were the objects of a cult. Without exception, they lack feet, for they were stuck in the ground upright; a few have been discovered actually *in situ*. And so we can say that in the paleolithic period, just as in the much later age of the early agricultural societies of the Near East, the female body was experienced in its own character as a focus of divine force, and a system of rites was dedicated to its mystery.

Were these the rites, however, of a women's cult, of a men's cult, or of both? Were they complementary to, incompatible with, or simply dissociated from, the rites of the grottos? Were they derived from the same province or stratum of Old Stone Age life as the rituals of the caves, or did they represent some totally alien system?

Leo Frobenius was the first, I believe, to suggest—on the basis of his fundamental distinction between the provinces of the tropical forest, where every kind of wood abounds and the art of wood sculpture flourishes in strength to this day, and the temperate steppe and desert lands, where the chief material is stone and the normal art that of lines engraved or scratched on two-dimensional surfaces—that the Aurignacian glyptic art of the figurines must have received its original impulse from the wood- and ivory-carving areas of the south.[18] Professor Menghin too, in his *World History of the Stone Age,*[19] sees a probable relationship between these female figurines and the realm of the tropical planters. They represent, he suggests, that same mother-goddess who was to become so conspicuous in the later agricultural civilizations of the Near East and has been everywhere celebrated as the Magna Mater and Mother Earth. Should it be shown that there is indeed ground for such suggestions, then the beginnings of that mythological system of the planting world at which we glanced in our study of the sacrifice of the maiden are of much greater age than any dating from the proto- or basal neolithic would allow, and we may perhaps think of these Aurignacian statuettes as a prelude or up-beat to the symphony of hymns that we have already heard, and shall hear again, to the great goddess.

But there is another approach to the same elementary idea, which does not invoke the ethnic ideology of the planters. For are mothers not mothers on the banks of the Yenisei as well as on the Congo? As Franz Hančar has pointed out in his article "On the Problem of the Venus Statuettes in the Eurasian Upper Paleolithic,"[20] human figures of larch and aspen wood are carved to this day among the Siberian reindeer hunters—the Ostyaks, Yakuts, Goldi, etc.—to represent the ancestral point of origin of the whole people, and they are always female. The hut is entrusted to the little figure when its occupants leave for the hunt; and when they return they feed her with groats and fat, praying, "Help us to keep healthy! Help us to kill much game!" "The psychological background of the idea," Dr. Hančar suggests, "derives from the feeling and recognition of woman, especially during her periods of pregnancy, as the center and source of an effective magical force."[21] "And from the point of view of the history of thought," he then observes, "these Late Paleolithic Venus figurines come to us as the earliest detectable expression of that undying ritual idea which sees in Woman the embodiment of the beginning and continuance of life, as well as the symbol of the immortality of that earthly matter which is in itself without form, yet clothes all forms." [22]

There can be no doubt that in the very earliest ages of human history the magical force and wonder of the female was no less a marvel than the universe itself; and this gave to woman a prodigious power, which it has been one of the chief concerns of the masculine part of the population to break, control, and employ to its own ends. It is, in fact, most remarkable how many primitive hunting races have the legend of a still more primitive age than their own, in which the women were the sole possessors of the magical art. Among the Ona of Tierra del Fuego, for example, the idea is fundamental to the origin legend of the lodge or *Hain* of the men's secret society. Here is Mr. Lucas Bridges' summary of the legend:

> In the days when all the forest was evergreen, before *Kerrhprrh* the parakeet painted the autumn leaves red with the color from his breast, before the giants *Kwonyipe* and *Chashkilchesh* wandered through the woods with their heads above the tree-tops; in the days when *Krren* (the sun) and *Kreeh* (the moon) walked the earth as man and wife, and many of the great sleeping mountains were human beings: in those far-off days witchcraft was known only to the women of Ona-land. They kept their own particular Lodge, which no man dared approach. The girls, as they neared womanhood, were instructed in the magic arts, learning how to bring sickness and even death to all those who displeased them.
>
> The men lived in abject fear and subjection. Certainly they had bows and arrows with which to supply the camp with meat, yet, they asked, what use were such weapons against witchcraft and sickness? This tyranny of the women grew from bad to worse until it occurred to the men that a dead witch was less dangerous than a live one. They conspired together to kill off all the women; and there ensued a great massacre, from which not one woman escaped in human form.
>
> Even the young girls only just beginning their studies in witchcraft were killed with the rest, so the men now found themselves without wives. For these they must wait until the little girls grew into women. Meanwhile the great question arose: How could men keep the upper hand now they had

got it? One day, when these girl children reached maturity, they might band together and regain their old ascendancy. To forestall this, the men inaugurated a secret society of their own and banished for ever the women's Lodge in which so many wicked plots had been hatched against them. No woman was allowed to come near the *Hain,* under penalty of death. To make quite certain that this decree was respected by their womenfolk, the men invented a new branch of Ona demonology: a collection of strange beings—drawn partly from their own imaginations and partly from folk-lore and ancient legends—who would take visible shape by being impersonated by members of the Lodge and thus scare the women away from the secret councils of the *Hain.* It was given out that these creatures hated women, but were well-disposed towards men, even supplying them with mysterious food during the often protracted proceedings of the Lodge. Sometimes, however, these beings were short-tempered and hasty. Their irritability was manifested to the women of the encampment by the shouts and uncanny cries arising from the *Hain,* and, it might be, the scratched faces and bleeding noses with which the men returned home when some especially exciting session was over.

Most direful of the supernatural visitors to the *Hain* were the horned man and two fierce sisters. . . . The name of the horned man was *Halahachish* or, more usually, *Hachai.* He came out of the lichen-covered rocks and was as gray in appearance as his lurking-place. The white sister was *Halpen.* She came from the white cumulus clouds and shared a terrible reputation for cruelty with her sister, *Tanu,* who came from the red clay.

A fourth monster of the *Hain* was *Short.* He was a much more frequent participator in Lodge proceedings than the other three. Like *Hachai,* he came from the gray rocks. His only garment was a whitish piece of parchment-like skin over his face and head. This had holes in it for eyes and mouth and was drawn tight round the head and tied behind. There were many *Shorts,* and more than one could be seen at the same time. There was a great variation in coloring and pattern of the make-up. One arm and the opposite leg might be white or red, with spots or stripes (or both) of the other color superimposed. The application to the body of gray down from young birds gave *Short* a certain resemblance to his lichen-covered haunts. Unlike *Hachai, Halpen* and *Tanu,* he was to be found far from the *Hain* and was sometimes seen by women when they were out in the woods gathering firewood or berries. On such occasions they would hasten home with the exciting news, for *Short* was said to be very dangerous to women and inclined to kill them. When he appeared near the encampment, the women would bolt for their shelters, where, together with their children, they would lie face downward on the ground, covering their heads with any loose garments they could lay their hands on.

Besides those four, there were many other creatures of the *Hain,* some of whom had not appeared, possibly, for a generation. There was, for instance, *Kmantah,* who was dressed in beech bark and was said to come out of, and return to, his mother *Kualchink,* the deciduous beech tree. Another was *Kterrnen.* He was small, very young and reputed to be the son of *Short.* He was highly painted and covered with patches of down; and was the only one of all the creatures of the Lodge to be kindly disposed towards the women, who were even allowed to look up when he passed.

"I wondered sometimes," states Mr. Bridges, who was himself an initiated member of the *Hain,* "whether these strange appearances might be the remains of a dying religion, but came to the conclusion that this could not be so. There was no vestige of any legend to suggest that any of these creatures impersonated by the Indians had ever walked the earth in any form but fantasy." [23]

Among the Yahgans (or Yamana) too—the southern neighbors of the Ona, but a very different folk, much shorter in stature and devoted not to hunting guanaco in the hills but to fishing and sealing along the dangerous shores—there was the legend that formerly their women had ruled by witchcraft and cunning. "According to their story," states Mr. Bridges, "it was not so very long ago that the men assumed control. This was apparently done by mutual consent; there is no indication of a wholesale massacre of the women such as took place—judging from that tribe's mythology—among the Ona. There is, not far from Ushuaia, every sign of a once vast village where, it is said, a great gathering of natives took place. Such a concourse was never seen before or since, canoes arriving from the farthest frontiers of Yahgan-land. It was at that momentous conference that the Yahgan men took authority into their own hands." And Mr. Bridges concludes:

"This legend of leadership being wrested from the women, either by force or coercion, is too widely spread throughout the world to be lightly ignored." [24]

Among the Australians, as Spencer and Gillen have noted,[25] "in past times the position of women in regard to their association with sacred objects and ceremonies was very different from that which they occupy at the present day." At Emily Gap, one of the most important sacred spots of the Aranda, for example, there is a drawing on the rocks that is supposed to have sprung up spontaneously to mark the place where the *altjeringa* women of the mythological age adorned themselves with ceremonial paint and stood peering up, watching, while the men performed those ceremonies of animal increase (*intichiuma*)* from which the women today are absolutely excluded. "One of the drawings is supposed to represent a woman leaning on her elbow against the rocks and gazing upwards." [26] Other observers, also, have noted evidences in Australia of an age when the role of women in the mythological lore and ceremonial life was more prominent than that accorded them today. Father E. F. Worms, of Broome, for example, has described a cluster of archaic petroglyphs in the northwestern desert, at a site in the upper Yule River area known as Mangulagura, "Woman Island," where all the engravings are representations of women. From their prominent vulvas three lines proceed, which may represent magical emanations of some kind, and above them is a curving picture of the Rainbow Snake.[27]

One is tempted to surmise that there may have taken place in the human past either some crisis of which these legends would be the widely distributed report, or a number of such crises in various parts of the world; and according to the view of the culture-historical school represented by the monumental, twelve-volume work of Father W. Schmidt on *The Origin of the Idea of God*,[28] there is actually evidence enough to justify a historical hypothesis of this kind. Father Schmidt and his colleagues have found it necessary to distinguish three basic types or stages of primitive society. The first is that of the simplest peoples known to the science

* Cf. supra, pp. 95 and 106–109.

of ethnology: the little Yahgans (or Yamana) of the southernmost channels and coves of rugged Tierra del Fuego, a number of extremely primitive, scattered tribes of Patagonia and Central California, the Caribou Eskimo of northern Canada, the Pygmies of the Congo and of the Andaman Islands, and the Kurnai of Southeastern Australia. The ethnological circumstances of these humble hunting, fishing, and collecting peoples do not give rise to either a strong patriarchal or a strong matriarchal emphasis; rather, an essential equality prevails between the sexes, each performing its appropriate tasks without arrogating to itself any special privileges or peculiar rights to command. The ceremonies of initiation at puberty are not confined to the boys and men, nor separated into male and female rites, but are nearly identical for the two sexes. Nor do the rites involve any physical deformation or the communication of mystical secrets. They are simply concentrated courses of education for adolescents, to the end of making good fathers and mothers of the initiates. Special tribal or group interests do not stand in the foreground of the teaching, since the tribal feeling in such groups is not greatly developed—the typical social unit being merely a cluster of twenty to forty parents and children, whose main social problem is hardly more than that of living harmoniously together, gathering food enough to eat during the day, and inventing pleasant games to play together after dark.

The second stage or type of primitive society recognized by this culture-historical school of ethnology is that of the large, totemistic hunting groups, with their elaborately developed clan systems, age classes, and tribal traditions of ritual and myth. Examples of such peoples are abundant on the plains of North America and the pampas of South America, as well as in the deserts of Australia. Their rites of initiation, as we have seen, are secret. Women are excluded; physical mutilations and ordeals are carried sometimes to almost incredible extremes, and they culminate generally in circumcision. Moreover, there is considerable emphasis placed on the role and authority of the men, both in the religious and in the political organization of the symbolically articulated community. Not infrequently, the circumcision of the boys is matched by comparable operations on the girls (artificial or ceremonial defloration, enlargement of the vagina, removal of the labia minora, partial or complete clitoridectomy, etc.), but in such cases the two systems of ceremonial—the male and the female—are kept separate, and the women do not gain through their rites any social advantage over the men. On the contrary, there is a distinct one-sidedness in favor of the male in these highly organized hunting societies, the influence of the women being confined—when it exists at all—to the domestic sphere.

According to the hypothesis of Father Schmidt and his colleagues, the puberty initiations of this second stage or type of primitive society have stemmed from those of the first, with, however, a bias in favor of the males and therewith an emphasis on the sexual aspect of the rites and particularly on circumcision. A very different course of development is to be traced, however, in the sphere of the tropical gardening cultures, where a third type or stage of social organization matured that was almost completely antithetical to that of the hunting peoples. For in these areas it was the women, not the men, who enjoyed the magico-religious and social advantage, they having been the ones to effect the transition from plant-collecting to plant-cultivation.[29] In the simple societies of the first sort, the males, in general, are the hunters and the women the collectors of roots, berries, grubs of various kinds, frogs, lizards, bugs, and other delicacies. Societies of the second type evolved in areas where an abundance of large game occasioned a herculean development of the dangerous art of the hunt; while those of type three took form where the chief sources of nutriment were the plants. Here it was the women who showed themselves supreme: they were not only the bearers of children but also the chief producers of food. By realizing that it was possible to cultivate, as well as to gather, vegetables, they had made the earth valuable and they became, consequently, its possessors. Thus they won both economic and social power and prestige, and the complex of the matriarchy took form.

The men, in societies of this third type, were within one jot of being completely superfluous, and if, as some authorities claim,[30] they can have had no knowledge of the relationship of the sexual act to pregnancy and birth, we may well imagine the utter abyss of their inferiority complex. Small wonder, furthermore, if, in reaction, their revengeful imaginations ran amok and developed secret lodges and societies, the mysteries and terrors of which were directed primarily against the women! According to the view of Father Schmidt, the ceremonials of these secret lodges are to be distinguished radically from those of the hunting-tribe initiations, their psychological function being different and their history different too. Admission to them is through election and is generally limited: they are not for all. Moreover, they tend to be propagandistic, reaching beyond the local tribe, seeking friends and members among alien peoples, and thus bringing it about that, for example, in both West Africa and Melanesia the chapters of certain lodges are to be found dispersed among greatly differing tribes. As already noted,* a particular stress is given in these secret men's societies to a skull cult that is often associated with the headhunt. Ritual cannibalism and pederasty are commonly practiced, and there is a highly elaborated use made of symbolic drums and masks. Ironically (yet by no means illogically), the most prominent divinities of these lodges are frequently female, even the Supreme Being itself being imagined as a Great Mother; and in the mythology and ritual lore of this goddess a lunar imagery is developed—as we have also already seen.

In considering such extreme initiation rites among hunters as those of the Central Australians, which we reviewed briefly in Part One, Father Schmidt calls attention to the secondary influences that can readily be shown to have entered the hunting areas of Australia from the gardening cultures of Melanesia and New Guinea; and comparably, when dealing with Mr. Lucas Bridges' friends, the Yahgans and Ona of Tierra del Fuego, he explains the *Hain,* with its anti-feminine antics, as an alien institution, ultimately derived, through Patagonia, from the planting cultures of the South American tropical zone.

"Whereas the aim of their puberty initiations," he writes in his discussion of the primitive hunting tribes of Tierra del Fuego,

* Supra, p. 177.

was that of turning boys and girls into competent human beings, parents, and tribal members—their teachings and examples being based on the firm foundation of a Supreme Being, both powerful and good, reposing in eternity—the men's festivals not only were addressed to an ignoble, immoral aim, but strove for it through ignoble and immoral means. The aim was to undo the harmonious state of equal privilege and mutual reliance of the two sexes that originally had prevailed in their simple society, supported by economic circumstance, and to establish through intimidation and the subjection of the women, a cruel ascendancy of the males. The means were Hallowe'en burlesques, in which the players themselves did not believe, and which, consequently, were lies and impostures from beginning to end. And the ill effects that issued from all this were not only disturbances of the social balance of the sexes, but also a coarsening and self-centering of the males, who were striving for such ends by such means.

The exoneration of their action, which the men felt called upon to advance in their myth, namely that it was the women who had done these things first and that, consequently, the performances of the men's lodge were justified, was actually an indefensible plea; for there had never been any such practice of agriculture in their community as could have given rise to the matriarchal supremacy reported in the myth. The whole story must have been imported from some other region, where a matriarchy based on horticulture had incited a reaction of the males and their development of men's societies, which then, together with their system of men's festivals, were carried to Tierra del Fuego.[31]

The mythological *apologia* offered by the men of the Ona tribe for their outrageous lodge was marvelously close, as the reader may have noted, to that attributed to Adam by the patriarchal Hebrews in their Book of Genesis; namely, that, if he had sinned, it was the woman who had done so first. And the angry Lord of Israel—conceived in a purely masculine form—is supposed to have allowed a certain value to this excuse; for he then promptly made the whole race of woman subject to the male. "I will greatly multiply your pain in childbearing," the Lord God is declared to have announced; "in pain you shall bring forth children, yet your desire shall be for your husband, and he shall rule over you." [32]

This curious mythological idea, and the still more curious fact that for nearly two thousand years it was accepted throughout the Western World as the absolutely dependable account of an event supposed to have taken place about a fortnight after the creation of the universe, poses forcefully the highly interesting question of the influence of consciously contrived, counterfeit mythologies and inflections of mythology upon the structure of human belief and the consequent course of civilization. We have already noted the role of chicanery in shamanism. It may well be that a good deal of what has been advertised as representing the will of "Old Man" actually is but the heritage of a lot of old men, and that the main idea has been not so much to honor God as to simplify life by keeping woman in the kitchen.

Some such flowery battle in the continuing war of the sexes, translated into and supported by mythology, must underlie the complete disappearance of the female figurines from the European scene at the close of the Aurignacian. We have already remarked that in the mural art of the men's temple-caves, which developed during the Aurignacian and reached its height in the almost incredibly wonderful happy-hunting-ground visions of the Magdalenian age, animals preponderate and the human figures are male, costumed as shamans, whereas in the Aurignacian cult of the figurines, whatever its reference and function may have been, the central form was the female nude, with great emphasis placed on the sexual parts. Was the revolution the consequence of an invasion of some kind—a new race, or one of those missionizing "men's society" movements of which Father Schmidt has written? Or was it the consequence of a natural transformation of the social conditions with a transfer of power and prestige naturally to the male?

The climate of Europe and the great sweep of plains to Lake Baikal was moist and extremely cold during the Aurignacian, when the vast icefields of the fourth glaciation (Würm), though in recession, still held a line at about the latitude of Oslo (60 degrees north). The landscape was arctic tundra, and the animals foraging upon it were the musk ox, woolly rhinoceros, reindeer, and woolly mammoth. The arctic fox, hare, wolverine and ptarmigan were also present.[33] However, with the further retreat of the ice, the climate, though remaining cold, became dry, and steppe conditions began to preponderate over tundra. This brought, in addition to the animals just named, the great grazing herds of the bison, wild cattle, steppe horse, antelope, wild ass, and kiang. The alpine chamois, ibex, and argali sheep also challenged the masters of the hunt.[34] As a result, the modes and conditions of human life greatly changed. In the earlier period of the mammoth, the hunting stations appear to have been widely scattered but comparatively stationary; within the protection of the dwellings the force and value of the feminine part of the community had a sphere in which to make itself felt. In the later period of the great herds, however, a shift to a more continuously ranging style of nomadism took place, and this reduced the domestic role of woman largely to the packing, bearing, and unpacking of luggage, while the men developed that fine sense of their own superiority that always redounds to their advantage when the jobs to be done require more of the running-muscles than of the sitting-fat. In the western portions of the broad hunting range of which we have been speaking, this more mobile style of the hunt developed along with the mural art of the men's temple-caves. Eastward, however, in the colder reaches of southern Russia and Siberia, the mammoth remained, and therewith also the little figurines of Our Lady of the Mammoth, until a much later day. And with this contrast in the historical development of the two areas during the late paleolithic, we have perhaps touched the first level of the profound psychological as well as cultural contrast of East and West.

We have already taken note of the Venus of Laussel and have suggested that the Blackfoot legend of the buffalo dance may be a remote outrider of the late Aurignacian tradition of which she is a representative. In her day the bison had already supplanted the mammoth as the main object of the hunt, but among the tribes for whom she was carved the naked female had apparently not yet been supplanted, in her magical role, by the costumed shaman. We have observed that in the same sanctuary of Laussel, in southern France, three other female forms were found (one, apparently, in the act of giving birth), as well as a number of representations of the female organs. The rock shelter, furthermore, was a habitable retreat. The cult involved was not that of the great, deep temple-caves; and the fact that most of the figures at the site were shattered to such a degree that they could not be reconstructed may point to an actual attack designed to break their power. Other examples have been found of such attacks on the magical objects of paleolithic camps; the suggestion is not fanciful in the least. But whether by some milder process of cultural transformation, or by such violence as the Ona legend of the massacre that broke up the age of women's magic would suggest, the fact remains that at the western pole of the broad paleolithic domain of the Great Hunt, which stretched from the Cantabrian hills of northern Spain to Lake Baikal in southeast Siberia, the earliest races of the species Homo sapiens of which we have any record made a shift from the vagina to the phallus in their magic, and therewith, perhaps too, from an essentially plant-oriented to a purely animal-oriented mythology.

The female figurines are the earliest examples of the "graven image" that we possess, and were, apparently, the first objects of worship of the species Homo sapiens; for on the level below theirs we break into the field of an earlier stage in the evolution of our species—that of Homo neanderthalensis, a short-legged, short-armed, barrel-chested brute, short-necked, chinless, and heavy browed, with highly arched, broad nose and protruding muzzle, who walked with bent knees on the outer edges of his feet.[35] In contrast, the women represented in our figurines, for all their bulk, are definitely of the species Homo sapiens, and are such, indeed, as may well be met to this day, opening another box of candy, in Polynesia, Moscow, Timbuktu, or New York.

The celebrated Venus of Willendorf (Lower Austria) is an extremely corpulent little female, about 4⅜ inches high, standing on pitifully inadequate legs, with her thin, ribbonlike arms resting lightly on ballooning breasts. An equally celebrated example of the subject is an elegantly carved, highly stylized figure from the Grottes de Grimaldi, near Menton (on the Mediterranean shore, about five miles west of Monaco), whose form suggests the modern work of Archipenko or Brancusi; while a fabulous little masterpiece in mammoth ivory, 5¾ inches high, from Lespugue, Haute-Garonne, still bolder in its stylization, presents a figure with trimly sloping shoulders but extravagant breasts reaching even to the

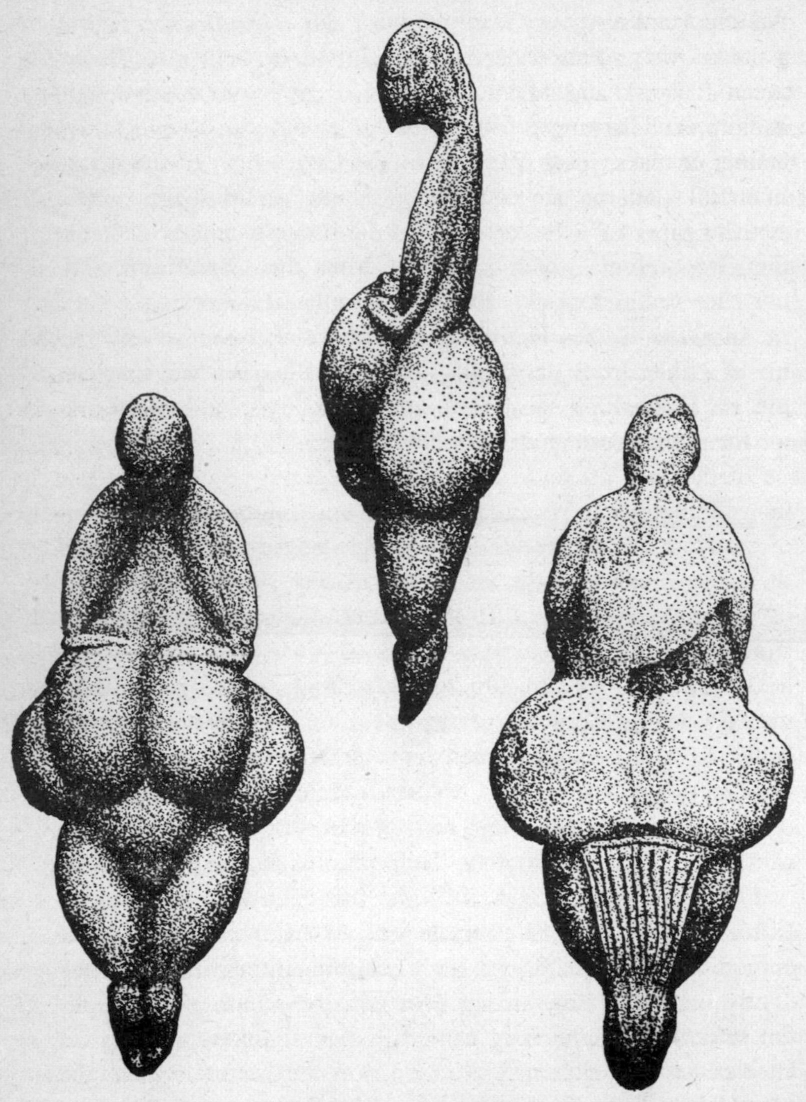

The Venus of Lespugue

groins. A second example from the Grottes de Grimaldi, again carved in the "modern" style, is both steatopygous and prominently pregnant. However, as already noted, not all the figurines are of the portly type. Some are little better than splinters of mammoth tusk with the signs of their feminine gender scratched upon them.

An important discovery was made in 1930 in the Dnieper region, at a site known as Yeliseevici, on the right bank of the river Desna, between Bryansk and Mglin. It consisted of an accumulation of mammoth skulls arranged in the form of a circle, and among them a number of tusks, some plaques of mammoth ivory scratched with geometrical patterns suggesting the forms of dwellings, others with the figures of fish and symbolic signs, and finally a Venus statuette, which, even without its lost head, was about six inches tall: [36] Our Lady of the Mammoths, actually *in situ*.

At another site nearby—Timovka—about two and a half miles south of Bryansk and on a high terrace overlooking the river, where six large dwelling sites, four storage bins, and two workshops for the fashioning of flints were clustered, there was found a piece of the tusk of a young mammoth shaped as a phallus and bearing the figure of a geometrically stylized fish. Another bit of the tusk carried a rhomboid design.[37] And once again, still farther south and still on the right bank of the Desna, about halfway between Bryansk and Kiev, an exceptionally rich excavation known as Mezin yielded, besides some mammoth ivory bracelets engraved with meander and zigzag designs and a pendant of mammoth ivory in the form of a tooth, two roughly carved little sitting animals, six extraordinarily beautiful mammoth-ivory birds, ranging from 1½ to 4 inches long, and ten curiously stylized figurines, also of mammoth ivory, that have been variously identified as female nudes (Abbé Breuil), the heads of long-beaked birds (V. A. Gorodcov), and phalli (F. K. Volkov, the discoverer of the site).

It is impossible not to feel, when reviewing the material of these mammoth-hunting stations on the loess plains north of the Black and Caspian Seas, that we are in a province fundamentally different in style and mythology from that of the hunters of the great painted caves. The richest center of this more easterly style would appear to have been the area between the Dnieper and Don river systems—at least as far as indicated by the discoveries made up to the present. The art was not, like that of the caves, impressionistic, but geometrically stylized, and the chief figure was not the costumed shaman, at once animal and man, master of the mysteries of the temple-caves, but the perfectly naked, fertile female, standing as guardian of the hearth. And I think it most remarkable that we detect in her surroundings a constellation of motifs that remained closely associated with the goddess in the later epoch of the neolithic and on into the periods of the high civilizations: the meander (as a reference to the labyrinth), the bird (in the dovecotes of the temples of Aphrodite), the fish (in the fish ponds of the same temples), the sitting animals, and the phallus. Who, furthermore, reading of the figure amid the mammoth skulls, does not think of Artemis as the huntress, the lady of the wild things; or of the Hindu protectress of the home and goddess of good fortune, Lakshmi, in her manifestation as Lakshmi of the Elephants (*gājā-lakṣmī*), where she is shown sitting on the circular corolla of a lotus, flanked by two mighty elephants that are pouring water upon her, either directly from their trunks or from water jars that they have lifted above her head?

But we must now observe, also, that on the underwings of one of the six beautiful birds of mammoth ivory discovered in this site appears the engraved swastika of which I have already spoken,* the earliest swastika yet found anywhere in the world. Moreover, it is no mere crudely scratched affair, but an elaborately organized form suggesting a reference to the labyrinth, the organization, furthermore, being counter-clockwise. C. von den Steinen, long before the discovery of this site, suggested that the swastika might have been developed from the stylization of a bird in flight, above all of the stork, the enemy of the serpent, and therewith the victorious representative of the principle of light and warmth.[38] And V. A. Gorodcov, developing this idea in connection with the context of Mezin, suggests that in the geometrical motifs of the swastika, rhombus, and zigzag band or meander we may recognize a mythological constellation of "bird (specifically stork), nest, and serpent." [39]

* Supra, p. 141.

The same motifs, it will be recalled, appeared as a fully developed ornamental syndrome in the much later ceramic art of the Samarra style, c. 4500–3500 B.C., which was developed in one of the chief areas of the high neolithic—directly southward of the Ukraine and just across the Black Sea.

And was it merely by chance that when, finally, in 1932, a household shrine was found containing female images, the number present within the shrine was precisely three? The site of this important discovery was on the right bank of the river Don, at Kostyenki, some twenty miles south of Voronesh. And in all, there were found in the same station seven fairly well preserved female figurines made of mammoth ivory, limestone, and marl, besides a large number shattered to bits; a plaque of stone engraved with the figure of a woman; a few medallions bearing representations of the female genitals; and some little animals made of marl. The figurines in the niche were: a badly preserved figure in mammoth ivory, without its head, but with well-engraved indications of a large necklace hanging from the shoulders to the breast; a large, perhaps unfinished figurine (the largest of the Russian series, we are told, but its precise dimensions were not given in the rough and ready Russian report; [40] H. Kühn has estimated its height to be about one foot), [41] made of limestone, but intentionally broken and the four pieces then apparently thrown into the niche; and an ill-made figure with a round head, either of mammoth tusk or of bone. The niche itself was in the northeastern corner of a dwelling, about six feet away from the fireplace, a rounded area, about two feet, eight inches across, one foot, eight inches high, and some five feet deep, within which there was nothing but these three enigmatic statuettes.[42]

The most fascinating and tantalizing site of all, however (which suggests more questions than I can even enumerate in the present chapter) is at Mal'ta, in the Lake Baikal region, about fifty-five miles northwest of Irkutsk, on the Byelaya River. Just here, we recall, are the chief centers of shamanism today—whence we have already learned of the animal mother, by whom the shaman is nourished during his mysterious period of initiation. Here, too, is the center from which a considerable part of the arts and some of the races of pre-Columbian North America were derived—including the Algonquins, of whom both the Blackfeet and Ojibway are representative examples. One Soviet school of anthropology has classified the Vogul and Ostiak of the nearby Yenisei River basin as Americanoid;[43] and the former Curator of Primitive and Prehistoric Art at the Brooklyn Institute of Arts and Sciences, Dr. Herbert Spinden, placed precisely here the mesolithic-neolithic culture center from which he derived what he termed "the American Indian Culture Complex" (c. 2500–2000 B.C.),[44] a complex the main traits of which would now seem best represented by the recently studied mound-builder remains of the so-called Adena People (fl. c. 800 B.C.–700 A.D.) of the Ohio Valley[45] and to the earliest signs of which—in the Red Lake Site, New York—a C-14 dating of 2450 ± 260 B.C. has just been tentatively assigned.[46] We are surely, therefore, one way or another, at the crucial center of an archaic cultural continuum, running, on the one hand, back to the Aurignacian rock shelter of Laussel, on the other, forward to the Blackfoot buffalo dance of the nineteenth century A.D., and then again to the modern shamanism of the Tungus, Buriats, Ostyaks, Voguls, Tatars, even Lapps and Finns.

Here were found no less than twenty female statuettes of mammoth ivory, from 1¼ inches to 5¼ inches tall, one represented as though clothed in a cave-lion's skin, the others nude. But in India and the Near East the usual animal-mount of the goddess was the lion; in Egypt, Sekhmet was a lioness; and in the arts both of the Hittites and of the modern Yoruba of Nigeria the goddess stands poised on the lion, nursing her child.

Some fourteen animal burials were found in Mal'ta: six of the arctic fox (do we think of Reynard and Coyote?); six of deer, in each case with the hindquarters and antlers missing (suggesting that the animals must have been flayed before burial, perhaps to furnish shamanistic attire); one of the head and neck of a large bird; and one of the foot of a mammoth. Six flying birds, and one swimming, of mammoth ivory—all representing either geese or ducks—were also found, along with an ivory fish with a spiral labyrinth stippled upon its side; an ivory baton, suggesting a shaman's staff; and finally—most remarkably—the skeleton of a rickety four-year-old child with a copious accompaniment of mammoth-ivory ornamentation.

The little skeleton was found lying on its back in the crouch or fetus posture, but with its head turned to the left and facing the east, the point of the rising, or rebirth, of the sun. Over the grave was curved a large mammoth tusk, and within were many signs of a highly ceremonious burial. There was a great deal of red coloring matter in the grave—a common finding in paleolithic sites, as well as in the burial mounds of the North American Adena complex—and encircling the head was a delicate crown or forehead band of mammoth ivory. The child had worn, also, a bracelet of the same material and a fine necklace of six octagonal and one hundred and twenty flat ivory beads, from which a birdlike ornamental pendant hung. A second pendant, also in the form of a flying bird, lay in the grave, as well as two decorated medallions. One of the latter seems to have served as a buckle; the other, somewhat larger, showed on one side three cobralike wavy serpents, scratched or engraved, and on the other a stippled design showing a spiral of seven turns, with three spiraling S-forms enclosing it—the earliest spirals known to the history of art.

We are clearly in a paleolithic province where the serpent, labyrinth, and rebirth themes already constitute a symbolic constellation, joined to the imagery of the sunbird and the shaman flight, with the goddess in her classic role of protectress of the hearth, mother of man's second birth, and lady of the wild things and of the food supply. She is here a patroness of the hunt, just as among planters she is the patroness of fields and crops. We cannot yet tell from the evidence whether we are to think, with Frobenius and Menghin, of a plant-oriented people that had moved up into a difficult but rewarding northern terrain of the hunt, or vice versa, of a northern hunting race, some of whose symbols were later to penetrate to the south. But what is surely clear is that a firm continuum has been established from Lake Baikal to the Pyrenees of a mythology of the mammoth-hunters in which the paramount image was the naked goddess.

Moreover, an idea can be gained of the possible relationship of the shamanistic imagery of the mammoth-ivory birds to the character of this goddess from a glance at the Eskimo mythology of the "old woman of the seals."

Whence the earliest Eskimos came, or when they reached their circumpolar habitat, we do not know, but some part of northeast Siberia, strongly colored by the culture of the Lake Baikal zone, would now seem to have been their likely homeland, and circa 300 B.C. would be about the earliest possible date for their arrival. In the walrus-ivory carving of the Punuk period of the Bering Strait and Alaskan Eskimo (c. 500–1500 A.D.), where the naked female form and a fine sense of geometric ornamentation are prominent features, likewise in the shamanism of the Eskimos, their stone lamps, bone harpoons, tailoring of skins, and half-subterranean lodges, we recognize what must have been a more or less direct inheritance of the arts and mythologies of the paleolithic Great Hunt.

The old woman of the seals (*arnarkuagssak*) sits in her dwelling, in front of a lamp, beneath which there is a vessel to receive the dripping oil. She is known also as Pinga, Sedna, and the "food dish" (*nerrivik*). And it is either from the lamp or from the dark interior of her dwelling that she sends forth the food animals of the people: the fish, the seals, the walruses, and the whales; but when it happens that a certain filthy kind of parasite begins to fasten itself in numbers about her head, she becomes angry and withholds her boons. The word for the parasite is *agdlerutt,* which also means abortion or still-born child. Pinga is offended, it is said, by the Eskimo practice of abortion; but also, as Igjugarjuk has told us, "she looks after the souls of animals and does not like to see too many of them killed. . . . The blood and entrails must be covered up after a caribou has been killed." A seal or caribou not returned to life through proper attention to the hunting ritual is no less an "abortion," a "still-born child" of the old woman herself, than a human baby prematurely delivered. And so, when these *agdlerutt* begin to afflict her, the people presently notice that their food supply has begun to fail, and it becomes the task of some highly competent shaman to undertake in trance the very dangerous journey to her dwelling, to relieve the old woman, the "food dish," of her pain.

On the way, the shaman first must traverse the land of the happy dead, *arsissut,* the land of "those who live in abundance," after which he must cross an abyss, in which, according to the earliest authors, there is a wheel, as slippery as ice, which is always turning. Next he must traverse a great boiling kettle, full of dangerous seals; after which he arrives at the old woman's dwelling, which, however, is guarded by terrible beasts, ravenous dogs, or ravenously biting seals. And finally, when he has entered the house itself, he must cross an abyss by means of a bridge as narrow as the edge of a knife.[47]

We are not told by what art his deed of assuaging the old woman is accomplished, but in the end she is relieved both of the parasites and of her wrath; the shaman returns and, presently, so do the seals.

The title of W. Somerset Maugham's novel, *The Razor's Edge,* which is drawn from a verse of the Hindu *Katha Upanishad,* wherein the mind is exhorted to enter upon the path to liberation from death, yet warned of the dangers and difficulties of the way:

> Arise! Awake!
> Approach the high boons and comprehend them:
> The sharpened edge of a razor, hard to traverse,
> A difficult path is this: so say the wise! [48]

should suffice to suggest something of the general context of spiritual experience to which the Eskimo figure of a shaman crossing an abyss on the blade of a knife refers.

We may think, also, of the gallant Sir Lancelot, in Chrêtien de Troyes' courtly twelfth-century romance, *Le Chevalier de la charrette,* "The Knight of the Cart," crossing the very painful "Sword Bridge" to the rescue of his Lady Guinevere, the Queen, from the land of death. "And if anyone asks of me the truth," says Chrêtien, "there never was such a bad bridge, nor one whose flooring was so bad: a polished, gleaming sword across the cold stream, stout and firm, and as long as two lances." The water cascading beneath, furthermore, was a "wicked-looking stream, as swift and raging, black and turgid, fierce and terrible, as if it were the devil's stream; and it is so dangerous and bottomless that anything falling into it would be as completely lost as if it fell into the salt sea." Two lions or leopards were tied to a great rock at the farther end of this bridge; and the water and the bridge and the lions were so terrible to behold that anyone standing before them all would tremble with fear.[49]

We have noticed that among the earliest remains in India of the culture complex of the hieratic city state, dating from c. 2000 B.C.,* representations have been found of figures in yoga posture. There is also a little scene from that period showing an apparition of the goddess among the boughs of a tree. And in the much later monuments of Indian Buddhist art, these same two themes of "the path of yoga" and "the goddess" are presented in the Great Gates of the Sanchi stupas (c. 200 A.D.), where they are represented, respectively, by "the Sun-wheel of the Buddha's Law" and "the Goddess of the Elephants," Gaja Lakshmi.

But we have here broached another abyss, which lures us beyond even our longest archaeological fathom-line. For the goddess who now has shown herself at the very dawn of the first day of our own species, already attended by her well-known court (her serpents and her doves and swans; the lion, the fish ponds, and the razor's edge by which her shaman-lover is to come to her to relieve her of her sterile wrath and make her fruitful again; the little child in its confirmation clothes, in the grave-womb, well prepared for rebirth and watching for the sun-day of unquenched *Sol invictus,* arising from the mother womb), is still the one who can truly say *οὐδεὶς ἐμὸν πέπλον ἀνεῖλε,* "No one has lifted my veil."

III. The Master Bear

The Ainus of the northern islands of Japan—Hokkaido, Sakhalin, and the Kuriles—who once also occupied the northern part of the main island of Honshu, constitute for the science of anthropology a fascinating problem; for, although their body form resembles the Japanese and five thousand miles of Mongolians

* Supra, p. 234.

separate them from the nearest native white population, their skins are white, their eyes caucasoid, and their hair wavy and abundant. They have been termed the hairiest people on earth, yet they are not more so than many a Russian muzhik. Indeed, their proud and sturdy old chieftains, copiously bearded, with their broad noses, bushy brows, and spirited eyes, look very much like the author of *War and Peace,* or a child's vision of Santa Claus, while their women, many of whom are shamans, have had their natural charms embellished with natty slate-blue mustaches, tattooed upon their upper lips at the age of thirteen to make them elegible for marriage. Professor A. L. Kroeber classifies this race, who now number about sixteen thousand, as "a generalized Caucasian or divergent Mongoloid type"—if such a statement can be called a classification; [50] but A. C. Haddon more confidently tells us that "they undoubtedly are the relics of the eastward movement of an ancient mesocephalic [round-headed] group of white cymotrichi [wavy-haired people, in contrast to leiotrichi, straight-haired, and ulotrichi, woolly-haired], who have not left any other representatives in Asia." [51] Their language is unclassified and apparently unique, though one of the archaic components of Japanese must have been a dialect of the same stock. Furthermore a number of their basic mythological and ritual forms bear a close comparison with Shinto.

The Ainus are a semi-nomadic, paleo-Siberian fishing and hunting people, but at the same time a neolithic planting people, with the wonderful idea that the world of men is so much more beautiful than that of the gods that deities like to come here to pay us visits. On all such occasions they are in disguise. Animals, birds, insects, and fish are such visiting gods: the bear is a visiting mountain god, the owl a village god, the dolphin a god of the sea. Trees, too, are gods on earth; and even the tools that men make become gods if properly wrought. Swords and weapons, for example, may be gods; and to wear such a one as guardian gives strength. But of all these, the most important divine visitor is the bear.[52]

When a very young black bearcub is caught in the mountains, it is brought in triumph to the village, where it is suckled by one of the women, plays about in the lodge with her children, and is treated with great affection. As soon as it becomes big enough to hurt and scratch when it hugs, however, it is put into a strong wooden cage and kept there for about two years, fed on fish and millet porridge, until one fine September day, when the time is judged to have come to release it from its body and speed it happily back to its mountain home. The festival of this important sacrifice is called *iyomande,* which means "to send away," and though a certain cruelty and baiting is involved, the whole spirit of the feast is of a joyous send-off, and the bear is supposed to be extremely happy—though perhaps surprised, if this should happen to be the first time that he has visited the Ainus—to be thus entertained.

The man who is to give the feast calls out to the people of his village, "I, so-and-so [perhaps, for example, Kawamura Monokute], am about to sacrifice the dear little divine thing from among the mountains. My friends and masters, come to the feast! Let us enjoy together the delights of the 'sending away'! Come! Come all!"

The guests arrive and a number of prayer-sticks (*inao:* "message-bearers") are fashioned, some two to five feet long, whittled in such a way as to leave shavings clustered at the top in a kind of head. These are stuck beside the hearth, where the fire-goddess, Fuji ("grandmother, ancestress"), is ever present, guarding the house; and, after having been revered there, the prayer-sticks are brought to the place outside where the bear is to be killed, and again stuck in the ground. Two long, thick poles, known as *ok-numba-ni,* "the poles for strangling," are then laid at their base. The men approach the bear cage; the women and children follow, dancing and singing; and the whole company sits in a circle before the bear, while one of their number, moving very close to the cage, lets the little visiting god know what is about to happen.

"O Divine One, you were sent into this world for us to hunt.

When you come to them, please speak well of us and tell them how kind we have been. Please come to us again and we shall again do you the honor of a sacrifice."

The bear, secured with ropes, then is taken from the cage and made to walk around in the circle of the people. Blunt little bamboo arrows, bearing a black and white geometrical design and a compact clump of shavings at the tip (called *hepere-ai,* "cub arrows"), are let fly at him, and he is teased until he becomes furious. Then he is tied to a decorated stake, two strong young fellows seize him, a third thrusts a kind of long wooden bit between his jaws, two more take his back legs, two his front, one of the "poles for strangling" is held under his throat, the other above the nape of his neck, a perfect marksman sends an arrow into his heart in such a way that no blood spills to the earth, the poles are squeezed together, and the little guest is gone.

The bear's head is removed with the whole hide attached, carried into the house, and arranged among prayer-sticks and valuable gifts by the east window, where it is to share the parting feast. A succulent morsel of its own flesh is placed beneath its snout, along with a hearty helping of dried fish, some millet dumplings, a cup of *sake* or beer, and a bowl of its own stew. And then it is honored with another speech.

"O Little Cub, we give you these prayer-sticks, dumplings, and dried fish; take them to your parents. Go straight to your parents without hanging about on your way, or some devils will snatch away the souvenirs. And when you arrive, say to your parents, 'I have been nourished for a long time by an Ainu father and mother and have been kept from all trouble and harm. Since I am now grown up, I have returned. And I have brought these prayer-sticks, cakes, and dried fish. Please rejoice!' If you say this to them, Little Cub, they will be very happy."

A feast is celebrated, there is dancing, while the woman who suckled the bear alternately weeps and laughs, along with some of the older women, who have suckled many young bears and know something of the mixed feelings of waving good-by. More prayer-sticks are made and placed upon the bear's head; another bowl of its own stew is placed before it, and when time has been allowed for it to finish, the man presiding at the feast calls out, "The little god is finished; come, let us worship!" He takes the bowl, salutes it, and divides the contents among the guests, a small portion for each. The other parts of the beast are then eaten also, while some of the men drink the blood for strength and smear a portion upon their clothes.

The head of the bear is then separated from the rest of the skin and, being set upon a pole called *ke-omande-ni,* "the pole for sending away," it is placed among a number of other skulls remaining from earlier feasts. And for the next few days the festival continues, until every bit of the little god has been consumed.[53]

When a wild bear is killed in the mountains it is carried into the hunter's house with honor, by way not of the door but of the so-called "god's window"; and such an entry is known as a "god's arrival." The old goddess of the fire, guarding the fire in the center of the house, is thought to have welcomed the guest invisibly from afar, and the god and goddess now talk together by the fireside all night. The people sing and play music, meanwhile, to entertain them while they chat, and the next day cook and eat the bear with gusto. Offerings are made to the bear's head, which is placed in a seat of honor, and the divinity, given presents, is ceremonially dismissed, to return to his mountain home.[54]

In this goddess of fire, Fuji, the "ancestress and protectress" of the house, we have a counterpart, in some way, of the goddess-figurines found in the dwellings of the mammoth hunters; for they too, apparently, were the guardians of the hearth. In the Ainu household there is a place in the sacred northeast corner of the lodge, behind the family heirlooms, where a special prayer-stick is kept, with a little gash at the top to represent the mouth, which is known as *chisei koro inan,* "ancestral caretaker of the house"; and he is addressed as the husband of the fire.[55] The Kostyenki niche in which three broken female figurines were found was likewise, it will be recalled, in the northeast corner of the house.*

Furthermore, we cannot but note that beautiful Mount Fuji, the

* Supra, p. 329.

sacred mountain of Japan, is an extinct volcano and that its name, though reinterpreted in Japanese to mean, variously, "The Mountain of Wealth," "Peerless," and "Unmatched," is almost certainly of Ainu origin and a reference to the goddess Fire.[56] As goddess of the hearth, she and the visiting bear-god of the mountain, therefore, must have memories to share in their ceremonial conversation. We also recall the Kaska Indian tale from British Columbia, of the bird who stole the fire-stone from Bear.*

Vestiges of a circumpolar paleolithic cult of the bear have been identified throughout the arctic, from Finland and Northern Russia, across Siberia and Alaska, to Labrador and Hudson Bay: among the Finns and Lapps, Ostyaks and Vogul, Orotchi of the Amur river region, Gilyaks, Goldi, and peoples of Kamchatka; the Nootka, Tlingit, Kwakiutl, and others of the Northwest American Coast; and the Algonquins of the Northeast.[57] And so here is a northern circumpolar hunting continuum in counterpoise to that broad equatorial planting belt which we traced from the Sudan to the Amazon in Part Two. And just as there a certain depth in time was indicated, going back to perhaps c. 7500 B.C., the dawn of the proto-neolithic, so here too there is a depth in time—but how very much greater! For in the high Alps, in the neighborhood of St. Gallen, and again in Germany, some thirty miles northwest of Nürnberg, near Velden, a series of caves containing the ceremonially arranged skulls of a number of cave bears have been discovered, dating from the period (it is almost incredible!) of Neanderthal Man.

Ever since 1856, when the remains of a strangely brutish yet manlike skeleton were found in a limestone quarry not far from Düsseldorf, in the valley of the Neander, it has been known that our fair species was preceded by a coarser, heavier type of human being, which now appears to have flourished close to the freezing breath of the glaciers for well over a hundred thousand years. Professor Hans Weinert estimates the period of Neanderthal Man (Homo neanderthalensis) to have commenced about 200,000

* Supra, pp. 277–278.

years ago, during the last (Riss-Würm) interglacial period, and to have closed not earlier than 75,000 years ago, during the centuries of the Würm glaciation.[58] Henry Fairfield Osborn, on the other hand, suggested a much later date for the disappearance:

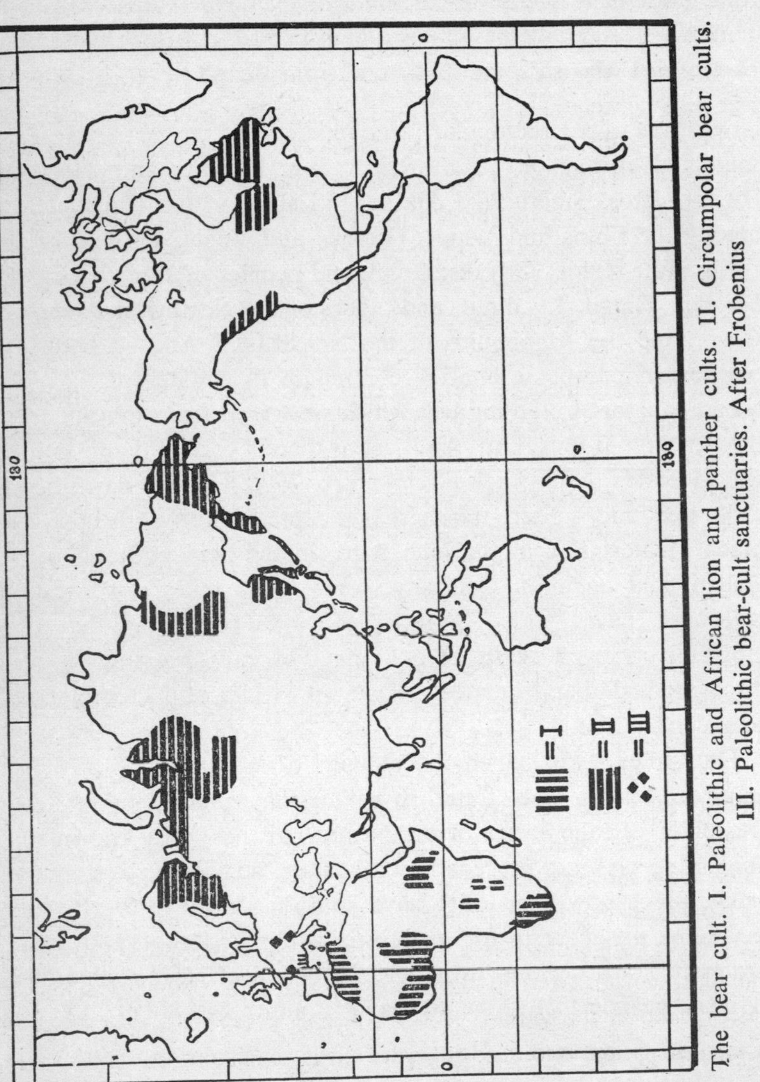

The bear cult. I. Paleolithic and African lion and panther cults. II. Circumpolar bear cults. III. Paleolithic bear-cult sanctuaries. After Frobenius

sometime between 25,000 and 20,000 B.C., which is to say, the terminus of the Würm.[59] Either way, what is certain is that the species disappeared toward the close of the Glacial Age, when it was superseded—definitely and definitively—from the Atlantic to the Pacific, by those earliest races of Homo sapiens, whose cults of the goddess and of the cave we have already viewed.

Emil Bächler, between 1903 and 1927, excavated three caves in the high Alps: the first, Wildkirchi, between 1903 and 1908; the second, Drachenloch, between 1917 and 1922; and the last, Wildermannlisloch, from 1923 to 1927. The first and third were about seven thousand feet and the second over eight thousand above sea level, and they could not have been entered during the period of the Würm glaciation. Hence their remains have been judged to belong to the interglacial period (Riss-Würm) at the latest; which is to say, not later than 75,000 B.C.

And what was found?

Charcoal, flints of pre-Mousterian style, flagstone flooring, benches, work tables, and altars for the ritual of the bear—the earliest altars of any kind yet found, or known of, anywhere in the world.

In Drachenloch and Wildermannlisloch little walls of stone, up to 32 inches high, formed a kind of bin, within which a number of cave-bear skulls had been carefully arranged. Some of these skulls had little stones arranged around them; others were set on slabs; one, very carefuly placed, had the long bones of a cave bear (no doubt its own) placed beneath its snout; another had the long bones pushed through the orbits of its eyes.[60]

The cave in Germany, Petershöhle, near Velden, which was explored by Konrad Hörmann from 1916 to 1922, had closetlike niches in the walls, which contained five cave-bear skulls—and once again the leg bones.[61]

Now the cave bear, it must be told, for all its size, was not an extremely dangerous beast. In the first place, it was not carnivorous but herbivorous, and in the second place, like all bears it had to go to sleep in the winter. But during the ice age the winters were long. The bears would go into the caves to sleep and, while there, could be readily killed. In fact, a tribe of men living in the front part of a cave with a couple of sleeping bears in the rear would have had there a kind of living deep freeze.*

And so now, and finally, at this prodigious depth of the past, let us visit a number of human graves, which are, like the altars, the earliest of their kind yet found.

In southern France, in a cave at La Ferrassie, in the Dordogne, the remains were unearthed of two Neanderthal adults and two children who had been ceremonially buried. One of the elders, probably a woman, had been placed in a crouched or flexed position in a cavity dug into the floor, legs pressed against her body and arms folded upon her breast. The other adult, also lying on his back, with legs flexed, was not in a containing cavity but on the floor, head and shoulders protected, however, by slabs of stone. The two children, lying supine, were in shallow graves. And close by was a hole filled with the bones and ashes of a wild ox, the remains of an offering of some kind.[62]

Again in the Dordogne, at Le Moustier, a youth of sixteen had been buried in a sleeping posture, with his head resting on his right forearm, pillowed on a neat pile of flint fragments. Placed around him were the charred and split bones of wild cattle, while beside his hand was an exceptionally fine Early Mousterian or Late Acheulean fist ax.[63]

And once again in the Dordogne, at La Chapelle-aux-Saints, an individual of about fifty or fifty-five was discovered, placed in a small natural depression, oriented east-and-west and accompanied by a number of shells, some Mousterian flints, and the remains of a woolly rhinoceros, horse, reindeer, and bison.[64]

The mystery of death, then, had been met and faced, both for the beasts killed in the hunt and for man. And the answer found was one that has been giving comfort to those who wish comfort ever since, namely: "Nothing dies; death and birth are but a threshold crossing, back and forth, as it were, through a veil."

The same idea spontaneously occurs to children when they reach

* See Herbert Wendt's amusing discussion of this circumstance in his lively review of man's quest for the origins of his kind, *In Search of Adam* (Boston: Houghton Mifflin Company, 1956), pp. 501 ff.

the age of about five. "Do people turn back into babies when they get very old?" asked a little Swiss boy of that age.

And another, when his uncle's death was announced to him: "Will he grow up again?"

"When you die," asked an infant of four, "do you grow up again?"

"And then I'll die," said another, "and you too, Mamma, and then we'll come back again." [65]

We do not know into what mythological structure this elementary idea was incorporated in the remote Mousterian-Neanderthal period of the Dordogne; but the burial at La Chapelle-aux-Saints, with its orientation to the rising and setting sun, surely shows that a solar symbolism of some kind had already been developed, while the sacrificed animals suggest that something like a difficult journey was to be faced; or perhaps, like the gifts to the departing Ainu bear, they were, rather, souvenirs to be taken along as honorable gifts.

For among the Ainus, we are told, when a funeral ceremony is performed, the master of the family becomes the celebrant. "You are a god now," he says to the corpse. "And without hankering after this world, you are to go now to the world of the gods, where your ancestors abide. They will thank you for the presents that you bring. And now go on quickly! Do not pause to look back." The celebrant puts a pair of leggings on the voyager's legs, a pair of mittens on his hands. "Take care," he tells him, "not to lose your way. The old Goddess of the Fire will guide you aright. I have already asked her to do so. Rely on her, and go your way with care. Farewell!"

A rich dinner is prepared for both the spirit of the departed and the people at the wake; and when they are about to carry away the coffin, the celebrant again has a word for their departing friend. "We have made a fine staff to help you on your way. Take hold of it firmly at the top, and walk securely, minding your feet, lifting and lowering them as you raise and lower the staff. You have plenty of food and drink as souvenirs. Look neither to right, now, nor to left, but go on quickly and delight your ancestors with your presents. Do not keep remembering your brothers, sisters, and other relatives in this world. Go your way and do not yearn to see those that are here. They are safe and sound, under the care of the old Goddess of Fire. If you go on yearning for them, the folks there will laugh. This you must understand. You must not behave in such a foolish manner."

The coffin is not carried out through the door, but a part of the side of the house is taken away and repaired before the mourners return. The ghost, then, will not know how to get back in. Or if the one who has died is the mistress of the house, the whole dwelling is burned. Into the grave go jewels, earrings, kitchen knives, pots, pans, and ladles, weaving looms and other such, if the departed was a woman; swords, bows, and quivers, if a man. And when the burial, or "throwing away," as it is called (*osura*), has been completed, the mourners leave the grave walking backward, lest, turning, they should be possessed by the ghost of the deceased; and they are holding weapons in their hands—the woman sticks, the men their swords—which they wave back and forth for their defense.[66]

One may question the propriety of interpreting by way of the Ainus of contemporary Japan a series of prehistoric remains at the opposite bound of the Eurasian continent, dating from circa 200,000 to 50,000 B.C. Both space and time would seem to argue against the likelihood of a common tradition. Furthermore, the race of Neanderthal has disappeared from the face of the earth, and no one has yet suggested that the Ainus are their descendants; nor the Gilyaks, Goldi, peoples of Kamchatka, Ostyaks, Vogul, Orotchi of the Amur river, Lapps, or Finns. All who have written on the subject express amazement; and yet the facts remain. As Herbert Kühn states the problem in a highly suggestive monograph:

> The location of the sites in remote caves, where they would be most readily concealed, indicated their reference to a cult; and so it immediately occurred to their excavators that they were uncovering the evidences of a sacrificial offering, storage places of the cave-bear skulls used in a primitive service honoring a divinity of the hunt, to whom the offerings were rendered.
>
> Menghin took up the idea in a paper on the evidence of a sacrificial offering in the Lower Paleolithic,[67] where he com-

pared the evidence with that of the hunting peoples of East Asia, the Ainus and the Gilyaks, among whom the offering is traditional, in the same form, to this day. Bächler himself had already indicated parallels among the Caucasian Chevsur, and on the ethnological side the find became the starting point of an intensive study of skull offerings among the reindeer peoples in the work of A. Gahs.[68] Gahs brings a great mass of comparative material to bear on the problem, establishing connections with the studies of bear ceremonials by Hallowell[69] and Uno Holmberg.[70]

All of these works make use of a great fund of factual material from the contemporary hunting peoples of the northern hemisphere. And it becomes evident therewith that the usages and customs of the Interglacial Period have been retained up to the very present in these peripheral regions of the earth, where the same living conditions exist to this day, and where man to this day remains only a hunter and collector on the simplest level. The economic pattern has not greatly altered in these parts, nor the way of thinking; man has remained inwardly the same, even though millenniums, indeed perhaps centuries of millenniums, lie between the hunters of those earlier days and now. The same offering is still made today. The bear skulls still are flayed and preserved in sacred places, offering places. They are covered and set round with slabs of stone, even today. Special ceremonies still are celebrated at the offering places. Even today two vertebrae of the neck are allowed to remain attached to the skull, just as then. And even today we often find that the large molar of the bear has been ground down, precisely as Zotz found the case to be in the course of an excavation of a series of caves in the glacial mountain heights of Silesia.[71]

Such details among the contemporary Asiatic hunters as the grinding down of the teeth of the bear and leaving of two vertebrae attached to the skull, just as in the European Interglacial period, proves that the continuity has actually remained unbroken for tens of thousands of years.[72]

Leo Frobenius, also recognizing the continuity, adds the following observation:

Count Bégouën and N. Casteret discovered a cave near Montespan, Haute-Garonne, where, in a great chamber at the end of a passage, there was the form of a beast made of clay. It was roughly fashioned, without concern for details, but was in a crouching position with outstretched front paws, and was furthermore distinguished by the fact that it lacked a head. The whole thing was clumsy and made about as children make their snowmen. It showed none of the elegance of, for example, the two bisons in the cave Tuc d'Audoubert, which likewise are fashioned of clay. And yet not even the coarseness of the work could explain the lack of a head. It could not have fallen off; for the neck showed a smooth, slightly sloping, sliced-off surface that had the same patine of age as the rest of the form. Furthermore, a hole went in through the center of this surface, like a channel going into the neck, curved in such a way as to suggest that a stick bearing some weight at the further end might have been stuck in. And to this there was added the further fact that the whole form in its general outline, and in particular in the formation of the limbs, the high, strong, rounded withers, suggested the representation of a bear, while between the forepaws there was found lying—a bear's skull.

The discoverers of this extraordinarily important find indicated in their first report (1923) [73] that here we had evidence of a bear cult in the Upper Paleolithic [i.e., the period of the Magdalenian paintings]; that under certain conditions the actual head of a slain bear must have been affixed to the torso; that the skull discovered between the forepaws was obviously the evidence of such a custom; and finally, that the coarse, mushy form of the whole thing pointed to one specific conclusion, namely that the piece had served as supporting form for a freshly flayed bear pelt with the head still attached.[74]

Moreover, in the Volta river area of the Gold Coast, West Africa, Frobenius's collaborator, Dr. Hugershof, discovered a precisely comparable form in use among the Bamana of Tula, which, however, was used for the support not of a bear skin but of a leopard skin.[75] And Frobenius himself, in the French Sudan, among the Kulluballi of Bafulabe, learned that "when a lion or leopard has killed and eaten a man, a jungle offering is prepared and the beast is killed. A place called 'Kulikorra Nyama' is arranged in the forest, consisting of a circular enclosure of thorns, in the center of which the clay form of a beast of prey is set up, *without a head*. The pelt is then removed from the killed lion or leopard, together with the head, still containing its skull; the skin is arranged on the clay form; and then all the warriors surround the enclosure of thorns and the one who killed the beast goes dancing about the figure within, while the remains of the beast are buried." [76]

In western Morocco, when such a panther is killed, the hunter must immediately creep up on the dead beast from behind, with closed eyes, and try to blindfold the dead panther as quickly as possible, so that it may no longer see—to avert the danger of the evil eye.[77] And here, possibly, we have our clue to the long bones pushed through the eye-holes of the cave-bear skulls in the sacred bin of the Drachenloch cave.

IV. The Mythologies of the Two Worlds

In short, then, a prodigious continuum has been identified, deriving in time at least from the period of the Riss-Würm interglacial, about 200,000 B.C. It is represented in its earliest known forms in the high-mountain Neanderthal caves of Germany and Switzerland, but then also, milenniums later, in the caves of Homo sapiens of southern France. Its range in space extends, on the one hand, northeastward throughout the circumpolar sphere of the primitive arctic hunters and collectors, where its ritual of the Master Bear is continued to the present day, and, on the other hand, southward into Africa, where the great felines—lion, leopard, panther, etc.—are in the role that is played by the bear in the north. In the survey of the main outlines of the archaeology of our subject, in Part Four, we must ask whether, actually, the African forms of the cult may not go back even further in time than the bear cult of Neanderthal, so that the shift of role would have been rather from lion to bear than from bear to lion—according to the principle of *land-náma,* described earlier.* For the present, however, our concern can be only: (1) to identify in the broadest terms the cultural zone of the cult of the animal master; (2) to see it in contrast to the younger mythological zone of the maiden sacrifice; and (3) to distinguish both primitive (or relatively primitive) contexts, as far as possible, from the much more securely documented prehistoric assemblages of the basal and

* Supra, pp. 199–200.

high neolithic, from which emerged the great civilizations of the hieratic city state.

1a. With an identified center in central Europe dating from the third interglacial period and a range extending, on the one hand, eastward to Labrador and, on the other, southward to Rhodesia (see map, p. 340), an abundantly documented mythology of the hunt has flourished, of such consistent character that we may well speak—indeed have to speak—of an area of diffusion. It is impossible to name with certainty the basic traits of this mythology in its earliest phase. In such contemporary manifestations as the Ainu bear sacrifice and burial rite, one has to recognize, besides the earliest paleo-Siberian strain of tradition, the probability of very much later neolithic, Sino-Mongolian, Japanese, and even recent Russian influences. Nevertheless, certain patterns of thought and ritual appear in these traditions that can be readily matched in other parts of the great continuum, and these—if we do not try to press them too far—can be taken to represent in the main a general stance of the mind in this domain, which has fundamentally colored the web of whatever culture has come into form within its sphere of force.

The main idea would seem to be that there is no such thing as death, but simply, as we have said, a passing back and forth of an immortal individual through a veil. The idea was well expressed in the words of the Caribou Eskimo shaman Igjugarjuk: "Life is endless. Only we do not know in what form we shall reappear after death." This idea is apparent also in the Ainu prayers both at the bear sacrifice and at the funeral rite. To the bear: "Precious little divinity . . . please come to us again and we shall again do you the honor of a sacrifice"; and to the man: "Take hold of [your staff] firmly at the top, and walk securely, minding your feet." The grave gear and sacrificed animals found in the graves in the Dordogne, at La Ferrassie, Le Moustier, and La Chapelle-aux-Saints, surely indicate something of the kind for the period of Neanderthal. And though we do not know whether burials of such a type were usual or unusual at that time, the fact remains that in these cases, at least, a life beyond death was envisioned. Was the handsome hand ax in the grave at Le Moustier a souvenir to be presented to the gods or ancestors in the other world? We do not know. And would the dead return at will, or remain with the ancestors? This we do not know either. But that there was another world, there can be no doubt.

Several other themes also emerge from the evidence reviewed. The orientation east-and-west of the skeleton at La Chapelle-aux-Saints points to a solar reference; as does likewise the position of the handsomely buried rickety four-year-old in the much later grave at Mal'ta. The crouch position of the two adult skeletons at La Ferrassie, as well as of the child at Mal'ta, suggest the fetal posture for rebirth; though, on the other hand, they may represent an attempt so to bind the ghost that it should not return to terrify those left behind. For the burial rites of the Ainus, as well as those of the more primitive Aranda of Central Australia,* illustrate vividly a primitive fear of the dead, which, as we have already said, is in radical contrast to the attitude expressed in the rites of the primitive planters of the Sudan.† The North African hunter's ritual of defense against the killed panther's evil eye, and the curious thrusting of the bones through the eyes of the paleolithic bear, suggest, by analogy, that in that remote period, too, fear was felt of the revengeful magic of the slain beast. And finally, we note that as the animals of the hunt changed, so too did the focal figure of the rites. The earliest animal master, apparently, was the cave bear, whose counterpart in Africa was the lion, leopard, or panther; whereas in what was perhaps a later context we find the mammoth; and then the bison.

It has been suggested that the daily task and serious concern of dealing death, spilling blood, in order to live, created a situation of anxiety that had to be resolved, on the one hand by a system of defenses against revenge, and on the other by a diminishment of the importance of death. Immediately available, furthermore, was that primary, spontaneous notion of the child that death is not an end, nor birth a beginning.

"Mamma, where did you find me?"

"Mamma, where did I come from?" [78]

* Supra, pp. 125–126.

† Supra, pp. 126–128.

These may not be "inherited ideas," precisely, but they are certainly general, spontaneous ideas, and the raw materials of myth. As we have seen, furthermore, they have been organized in a distinctive system, which has served primitive hunting societies for a period of some two hundred thousand years, both to alleviate the fear of blood revenge and to carry the mind across the ultimate threshold. And perhaps the best summation of the ultimate import of these myths and rites for the courageous men and women whose very difficult lives they served is expressed in the sentiment, reported by Dr. Rasmussen, of our little old friend Najagneq of north Alaska: Silam or Silam inua, "the inhabitant or soul (*inua*) of the universe," is never seen; its voice alone is heard. "All we know is that it has a gentle voice like a woman, a voice 'so fine and gentle that even children cannot become afraid.' What it says is: *sila ersinarsinivdluge,* 'be not afraid of the universe.' "[79]

1b. Within the field of the hunting mythologies, however, a second force appears in the phenomenology of shamanism. This cannot be tritely dismissed as "mere neurosis, self-hypnosis, or schizophrenia," because, even if this were true, it does not explain the universality of the imagery of "neurosis, schizophrenia, and self-hypnosis." The phenomenology of shamanism is locally conditioned only in a secondary sense—as I believe we have well enough seen. And since it has been precisely the shamans that have taken the lead in the formation of mythology and rites throughout the primitive world, the primary problem of our subject would seem to be not historical or ethnological, but psychological, even biological; that is to say, precedent to the phenomenology of the culture styles. This opens again the question of the relationship of ethnic to elementary ideas, which, as we have seen, has not been resolved and remains the chief bone of contention of this entire subject. We return to it in the concluding chapter.

2. In contrast to the childlike spirit of the mythology of the paleolithic hunt, a new depth of realization is achieved in the horrendous myths and rites of the planting cultures. The cultural continuum in which these are at home would appear to extend in a broad equatorial band from the Sudan, eastward through East Africa and Arabia, India, Indo-China, and Oceania, to Brazil.

Death, here, is not simply the blithe passage of an immortal individual once again through a door through which he has already gone many times and back through which he will again return. A fundamental complementarity is vividly recognized between not simply birth and death, but sex and murder. A mythological age is supposed to have anteceded the precipitation of this pair-of-opposites, when there was neither birth nor death but a dreamlike state of essentially timeless being. And the precipitating mythological event by which this age was terminated is renewed in the festivals, in rites such as we have reviewed and studied in Part Two.

The contrast with the hunting mythology could not be greater. Yet one may ask whether the later mythology does not represent simply a deepening, an enrichment, and a systematization of ideas already inherent in the earlier. Is this an "opposite" mythology, or simply a "more mature"? Are the underlying ideas so different that we cannot speak of a common psychological substratum?

The answer, I think, is obvious: namely, that the same ideas have been given a fresh turn and organization, which amounts, indeed, to a new, and certainly magnificent, though somewhat horrifying, crisis of spiritual growth. We should consider seriously, I think, the suggestion of Father Schmidt, already described,* that in the hunting world the masculine psyche prevails and in the planting world the feminine. In the first the feminine principle is comparatively mute, and with the masculine virtues a certain boyish innocence prevails—except in the area of black magic, where the witch and a kind of cloacal mania (which again is rather boyish) come into their own. In the second, on the other hand, the whole mystery of the woman's range of life experience comes into play—and is rendered, tragically yet joyfully, in the mystery of the maiden.

"How can a man know what a woman's life is?" said an Abyssinian woman quoted by Frobenius.[80]

> A woman's life is quite different from a man's. God has ordered it so. A man is the same from the time of his circumcision to the time of his withering. He is the same before he

* Supra, pp. 318–322.

has sought out a woman for the first time, and afterwards. But the day when a woman enjoys her first love cuts her in two. She becomes another woman on that day. The man is the same after his first love as he was before. The woman is from the day of her first love another. That continues so all through life. The man spends a night by a woman and goes away. His life and body are always the same. The woman conceives. As a mother she is another person than the woman without child. She carries the print of the night nine months long in her body. Something grows. Something grows into her life that never again departs from it. She is a mother. She is and remains a mother even though her child die, though all her children die. For at one time she carried the child under her heart. And it does not go out of her heart ever again. Not even when it is dead. And this the man does not know; he knows nothing. He does not know the difference before love and after love, before motherhood and after motherhood. He can know nothing. Only a woman can know that and speak of that. That is why we won't be told what to do by our husbands. A woman can only do one thing. She can respect herself. She can keep herself decent. She must always be as her nature is. She must always be maiden and always be mother. Before every love she is a maiden, after every love she is a mother. In this you can see whether she is a good woman or not.

It is surely in the interplay and mutual spiritual fertilization of the sexes, no less than in the lessons learned of the animal, plant, and celestial kingdoms of the gods or in the profundities of the shamanistic trance experience, that the motivations of the metamorphoses of myth are to be sought. In Part Four, diagraming sketchily the main blocks of the prehistoric periods of myth, from the first we know of man's appearance on earth to the dawn of the ages of writing when the literary record of mythology begins, we must try to bear in mind the force of this dialogue. For it is one of the curiosities and difficulties of our subject that its materials come to us for the most part through the agency of the male. The masters of the rites, the sages and prophets, and lastly our contemporary scholars of the subject, have usually been men; whereas, obviously, there has always been a feminine side to the picture also. The symbols have been experienced and read from the two poles; but also shaped from the force of the two poles in their antagonistic cooperation. So that even where the woman may seem to have disappeared from the scene—as, for example, in the patriarchal Aranda and Hebrew images of the first days of creation*—we must realize that she is there, even so, and watch for the ripple of her presence behind the curtain.

3. The dawn of history, as we know it, has now been securely placed in the Near East in the early hieratic city states. And the powerful diffusion of the great syndrome of the higher civilizations from those early centers to the bounds of the earth has now been traced clearly enough to let us know that most of what used to be regarded as evidence of, in Frazer's words, "the effect of similar causes acting on the similar constitution of the human mind in different countries and under different skies," is actually evidence, rather, of diffusion. Many of the culture forms, furthermore, that formerly were thought to be primitive are actually—as we now know—regressed: regressed neolithic, regressed Bronze, or even regressed Iron Age configurations.

For example, even the pygmoid Negritos of the Andaman Islands, who are certainly among the most primitive peoples now living on earth, cannot be studied simply as primitives; for there is a good deal of evidence, not only in their kitchen middens, which have been piling up for thousands of years, but also in their myths and folkways, of an important cultural influence that arrived from the southeast Asian mainland perhaps three or four thousand years ago, and which brought to them not only pottery and the pig but also a new method of cooking and the art of smoking pipes.[81] They have, besides, an extremely beautiful type of bow, which is not by any means a primitive weapon but one that appears only as late as the mesolithic—that is to say, in the critical culture period of the dawn of the arts of food cultivation.

The most delicate and difficult, as well as crucial, question within the ranges of the ethnological and archaeological phases of our study, indeed, is this of the relative force of the paleolithic and

* Cf. supra, pp. 106–111.

neolithic influences both in the vaguely defined transitional period known variously as mesolithic, proto-neolithic, epi-paleolithic, and, in America, New World Formative, and throughout the field of ethnological research. It is to this question that we turn our regard particularly in Part Four.

Part Four

THE ARCHAEOLOGY OF MYTH

Chapter 9

MYTHOLOGICAL THRESHOLDS OF THE PALEOLITHIC

I. The Stage of Plesianthropus (←— 600,000 B.C. —→)

"The quest for Adam," as Herbert Wendt has termed the long search of science for the homeland of the human race,[1] has led now to Africa—and recently with spectacular results. Three types of theory hold the field with regard to the way in which the family tree of our race should be construed. Most of the authorities believe that mankind emerged from the stage of the higher primates along one line of evolution. Those holding this view are known as "monophyletists": advocates of one (*mono*) line of descent (*phyletikos:* "tribe"). A second group, however, the "polyphyletists"—advocates of many (*poly*) lines of descent (*phyletikoi*)—believe that our race is constituted of a number of independently developed strains which, in the course of the millenniums, became fused. And finally a third group, of recent origin (dating from c. 1925),[2] which as far as I know has not yet received its Greek appellation, stands for the probability of what they term a "zone of hominization," i.e., a limited yet sufficiently broad area of the earth's surface, relatively uniform in character, where a large population of closely related individuals (some Tertiary species of higher primate) became affected simultaneously by a series of genetic mutations conducing to the appearance of a considerable variety of manlike forms.[3] Both the evidence of modern genetics and the recent discoveries in South and East Africa of an astonishing variety of early manlike creatures, ranging in stature from pygmies (Plesianthropus) to giants (Paranthropus robustus), tend to support this latest view. And so the primates that we have now to accept as our first cousins are the higher apes of Africa, the gorilla and chimpanzee, not the orangutan and gibbon of Southeast Asia, who are more remote from the human line, or zone, of hominization.[4]

There are two amusing reports of the behavior of chimpanzees that seem to me worth noting at this point. They appear in Dr. Wolfgang Köhler's volume on *The Mentality of Apes*.

Köhler found that his chimpanzees would conceive inexplicable attachments for objects of no use to them whatsoever and carry these for days in a kind of natural pocket between the lower abdomen and upper thigh. An adult female named Tschengo became attached in this way to a round stone that had been polished by the sea. "On no pretext could you get the stone away," says Köhler, "and in the evening the animal took it with it to its room and its nest." [5]

Köhler's second observation is of a social nature. Tschengo and another chimpanzee named Grande invented a game of spinning round and round like dervishes, which was then taken up by all the rest. "Any game of two together," Dr. Köhler writes,

> was apt to turn into this "spinning-top" play, which appeared to express a climax of friendly and amicable *joie de vivre*. The resemblance to a human dance became truly striking when the rotations were rapid, or when Tschengo, for instance, stretched her arms out horizontally as she spun round. Tschengo and Chica—whose favorite fashion during 1916 was this "spinning"—sometimes combined a forward movement with the rotations, and so they revolved slowly round their own axes and along the playground.
>
> The whole *group* of chimpanzees sometimes combined in more elaborate *motion-patterns*. For instance, two would wrestle and tumble near a post; soon their movements would become more regular and tend to describe a circle round the post as a center. One after another, the rest of the group approach, join the two, and finally march in an orderly fashion round and round the post. The character of their movements changes; they no longer walk, they trot, and as a rule with

special emphasis on one foot, while the other steps lightly, thus a rough approximate rhythm develops, and they tend to "keep time" with one another. . . .

"It seems to me extraordinary," Köhler concludes, "that there should arise quite spontaneously, among chimpanzees, anything that so strongly suggests the dancing of some primitive tribes." [6]

These two notations will suffice to suggest a spiritual plane for the history of our subject lower than which we need not go in imagining the ritual activities of the first societies. The psychological crisis that we have termed "seizure" * is already present, and the joy in group motion patterns that underlies both public ritual and the art of the dance is also in evidence. We note, furthermore, the surprising detail of the central pole, which in the higher mythologies becomes interpreted as the world-uniting and supporting Cosmic Tree, World Mountain, *axis mundi,* or sacred sanctuary, to which both the social order and the meditations of the individual are to be directed. And finally, we have that wonderful sense of play, without which no mythological or ritual game of "make believe" whatsoever could ever have come into being. One can see already that in play fascinating new energy-evoking stimulae are discovered, which unite groups in the way not of economics but of freely patterned action—that is to say, of art. The observation is worth noting because no actual objects of human art have been found earlier than the Aurignacian period, when the female figurines abruptly appear.

The African finds that have most recently stirred the halls of science are roughly (very roughly) dated at the commencement of the Pleistocene or Ice Age, circa 600,000 B.C.; and at the Fifth International Congress of Anthropological and Ethnological Sciences, held at the University of Pennsylvania in 1956, Dr. Raymond Dart of Witwatersrand University, Johannesburg, South Africa, showed a convincing series of slides in which the implements of this pre-lithic (pre-Stone Age) culture were illustrated. These included the lower jaws of large antelopes, which had been cut in half to be used as saws and knives; gazelle horns with part of the skull attached, which showed distinct signs of wear and

* Supra, p. 23.

use, possibly as digging tools; and a great number of ape-man palates with the teeth worn down—human palates being used to this day as scrapers by some of the natives of the area. But the really sensational slides were those showing a number of baboon and ape-man skulls that had been fractured by the blow of a bludgeon of a certain specific type. All the fractures showed that they had been caused by an instrument having two nubs or processes at the hitting end; and it had required only a little thought on the part of Professor Dart and his collaborators for them to surmise that the probable cause of this double dent was the knob at the end of the leg bone of a gazelle. But apes do not use weapons; *ergo,* the culprit was a man—or at least some kind of proto-man.

The animal remains found among the bones of these little fellows of about 600,000 B.C. have been chiefly antelopes, horses, gazelles, hyenas, and other beasts of the plains—swift runners, so that the art of the hunt must have been considerably developed. Professor Dart, furthermore, has found abundant evidence of a practice of removing the heads and tails of certain of the animals killed, and suggests that the tails may have been used for signaling in the chase. Perhaps so! But what of the removal of the heads? Were the animals flayed, perhaps, and their whole skins, with heads and tails attached, then used in some magical rite to avert the danger of blood revenge? Do we hear an echo at the bottom of the well?

II. The Stage of Pithecanthropus (←— 400,000 B.C. —→)

The first evidence of the use of fire was found about as far from South Africa as one could wish, in the now famous Choukoutien Cave, some thirty-seven miles from Peiping. Here, through a series of excavations extending from 1921 to 1939, there was unearthed an impressive assortment of stone tools, cracked skulls, split bones, and fireplaces in what had been the haunt of a sort of ape-man with a brain capacity of about 900 cubic centimeters; that is to say, midway between the men of today (1400–1500 cc. average) and the brainiest ape (600 cc.). The way some of the skulls were opened showed that someone had been knocking holes in them and lapping out the brains. In the cave were the remains, furthermore, of thousands of animals that had also been eaten by the inhabitant, or inhabitants; and the tools of stone were crude choppers and large flakes, such as must have been used for knives.

The unwholesome cannibal of this chilly, fire-heated den, Sinanthropus Pekinensis, Peking Man (or, as we may term him, Prometheus the Great), was a contemporary of the celebrated Pithecanthropus erectus of Java—"the ape-man (*pithecanthropus*) who walks erect (*erectus*)," otherwise known as Java Man and Trinil Man—who, when his remains were found in 1891, was hailed by Haeckel and the other nineteenth-century prophets of evolution as the very figure of Darwin's "Missing Link." But the remarkable thing about the Chinese find was the evidence of fire in the cave. For although a number of proto-human remains of this general period have been found elsewhere in the world, Choukoutien is unique in its evidence of fire.

We have to think of the period in the vast terms of geological reckoning as falling somewhere in the Middle Pleistocene—about 500,000–200,000 B.C., in the great ranges of the second glacial period (Mindel) and second interglacial (Mindel-Riss). The chief remains now assigned to this stage in the development of mankind are those, firstly, of Pithecanthropus and his like in Java, which now include, in addition to the original find, a massive, brutal skull discovered by Ralph von Koenigswald in the 1930s, which is named Pithecanthropus robustus, as well as a huge lower jaw, also found in Java by the same researcher, which is now called Meganthropus palaeojavanicus. Likewise to be classed in this period are the remains of a skull from East Africa that has been dubbed Africanthropus. And then, of course, we have the classic relics of the early paleolithic in Europe, with which every schoolboy is now familiar; most notably Heidelberg Man (Homo heidelbergensis), whose mighty jaw was discovered in 1907 in a deposit that is now assigned to the first interglacial period (Günz-Mindel) —an age in which the bear, lion, wildcat, wolf, and bison shared with man the fields and forests, along with the wild boar, the Mosbach horse, the broad-faced moose, Etruscan rhinoceros, and straight-toothed ancient elephant. Perhaps also from this period are the interesting Swanscombe skull from the Thames, which was found in 1935 and is probably to be dated in the second interglacial; the Fontéchevade skull, found in France in 1947, which appears to belong to the early part of the third interglacial (Riss-Würm); and the skull of a young woman found in a cave at Steinheim, Germany, in 1933, which likewise appears to be from the third interglacial. These latter three, however, have aroused considerable controversy, since they approach far more closely than the Oriental finds the figure of modern man. One side of the argument holds that skulls of this advanced type belong to later periods than those to which their position when found appeared to assign them. The other side contends that two separate strains of evolution are indicated: one developing in the less favorable Pleistocene climates of southeast and far eastern Asia, and the other in the milder spheres of North Africa and Europe. This argument is still unresolved.

What is perfectly clear, however, is that the race of man, by the middle of the second interglacial period (Mindel-Riss), had spread from Africa both northward, into Europe, and eastward (remaining south of the Elburz-Himalayan mountain line) into Southeast Asia, turning then northward up the far eastern coast. Father Wilhelm Schmidt has even suggested the possibility of a continuation of this migration into America. For, as he points out, during the glacial ages the level of the sea was so much lower than now that a land bridge as wide as the nation of France stretched from Siberia to Alaska, across which grazing animals passed—herds of horses, cattle, elephants, and camels. But if animals, then why not their hunters? The land bridge, holding back the icy waters of the Arctic, permitted the warmer currents of the south to flow unhindered up the coast, so that the climate both of Northeast Asia and of Northwest America must have been considerably warmer than today. And Father Schmidt cites to this effect the geologist Dr. W. Krickeberg: "An abundant forest and steppe flora flourished then, where today barren grounds give to the landscape the basic character of a hopeless desert; and this we know since the immigrating Asiatic animal world of the second half of the Ice Age—in whose train, according to this hypothesis, men also came—consisted only to a minor degree of arctic types. The greatest number were the beasts of the northern forests and steppes; among others, the mammoth, whose contemporary, man, must likewise have entered the North American sphere." [7]

No evidence yet found of paleolithic man in America can be dated, even recklessly, earlier than the third interglacial period (Riss-Würm); but new discoveries during the past few years have been pressing the date line steadily back. In 1925 Dr. Aleš Hrdlička was suggesting something like 1000 B.C. as a likely date for man's arrival in the New World. Now we have a date of 6688 ± 450 B.C. for man in Tierra del Fuego. In 1926 a paleolithic type of spear point (the Folsom Point) was discovered in New Mexico in association with an extinct species of bison. The favored date for this point is c. 10,000 B.C. But two earlier types of point (Sandia and Clovis Flutes) have been found associated with mammoth remains, calling for a date of at least c. 15,000 B.C. The conservative estimates now run up to 35,000 B.C.,[8] and some are even prophesying "that the next few years will show the presence of man on this continent long before 'the end of the Pleistocene.'" [9]

All of which, of course, is still a long way indeed from the 400,000 B.C. of Peking; and I am not trying to suggest that the gap will ever be bridged. But what is of interest to our study is the opening, in Father Schmidt's suggestion, of a possible channel of paleolithic influence from Southeast Asia and the Austro-Melanesian zone, up the coast into the New World. A number of careful scholars of the subject have pointed to signs of an extremely early continuity uniting, not only culturally but also racially, certain peoples of the Southeast Asian area and the most primitive groups in America. The Argentinian anthropologist José Imbelloni, for example, recognizes a Tasmanoid (Tasmanian-like) strain in the Yahgans and Alacaloof of Tierra del Fuego; a Melanesian strain among the Indians of the Matto of the Amazon forest; and a semi-Australoid among the nomadic huntsmen of both North and South America.[10] Harold S. Gladwin writes of Australoid skulls discovered all the way from Lower California to the Texas Gulf coast, as well as in Ecuador and Brazil.[11] And

Paul Rivet even suggests the possibility of an Australoid migration by way of the ice of Antarctica to Tierra del Fuego.[12] The point to be noticed here is that if any such early paleolithic Southeast Asia-to-Tierra del Fuego continuity should ever be demonstrated, then the last possibility of anything like a pure case for parallel development, even on the simplest level of culture, will have been removed.

On the face of the evidence, it would surely seem that our ponderous Prometheus with the heavy brows was the world's perfect model of an economic materialist (which is about what one should have expected, considering the size of the brain); for there is not the sign or hint of an artwork to be found in the whole three hundred thousand years of his existence. He was Homo faber, man the tool-maker, *par excellence*. And the manner in which his skill increased in the not too easy task of chipping flints, from the days of his first crude pebble tools to those of his finest fist axes, reveals that, for all his rude and even ghoulish habits, he was no unmitigated lout. The high center of human culture was still Africa. Here an incredible abundance of paleolithic tools have been found. Indeed, some excavations (for example, those of L. S. B. Leakey at Olduvai Gorge in the north of Tanganyika) have revealed in perfect sequence every stage of the evolution of the hand ax from the pebble tools of man's first beginnings to the finely finished, really elegant axes of the period of Neanderthal.[13] And if the view into the depth of the well of time that we obtained in the South of France was great, this of Olduvai is simply beyond speech. But what is even more amazing than the profundity of the prehistoric past here illustrated is the broad diffusion over the face of the earth of exactly the same ax forms as those of paleolithic East Africa. As Dr. Carleton S. Coon has remarked: "During the quarter of a million years when man made these tools, the styles changed very little, but what changes were made are to be seen everywhere. . . . This means that human beings who lived half a million years ago were able to teach their young skills that they had learned from their fathers in most minute detail, as living Australians and Bushmen do. Such teaching requires both speech and a firm discipline, and the uniformity of hand-ax styles over wide areas means that members of neighboring groups must have met together at stated intervals to perform together acts that required the use of these objects. In short, human society was already a reality when the hand-ax choppers of the world had begun to turn out a uniform product." [14]

All of which speaks volumes for the force and reach of diffusion in the primitive world.

Moreover, what is perhaps more remarkable still is that some of the most beautiful of the symmetrically chipped hand axes of this period are as much as two feet long, a size too cumbersome for practical use; the only possible conclusion being that they must have served some ceremonial function. Professor Coon has suggested that such axes were not practical tools but sacred objects, comparable to the ceremonial tools and weapons of later days, "used only seasonally, when wild food was abundant enough to support hundreds of persons at one place and one time. Then the old men," he supposes, "would cut the meat for the assembled multitude with some of these heavy and magnificent tools," after which, like the magically powerful *tjurungas* of the Australians, the sacred implements would be stored in some holy place.[15]

III. The Stage of Neanderthal Man (c. 200,000–75,000/25,000 B.C.)

The pygmoid Negritos inhabiting the Andaman archipelago in the Bay of Bengal, some 250 miles south of the last headlands of Burma, had such a reputation for savagery that they were studiously avoided by the sea captains of the Arab, Chinese, and Indian fleets. Unfortunates shipwrecked on their coasts were killed, sliced up, and incinerated. The report was that they were eaten. And since the wealth of the islands was hardly worth appropriating anyhow—consisting of a species of pig, a civet cat, a few kinds of bat and rat, a tree shrew, and a prolific monitor lizard that could swim in the water, walk on land, and climb trees, and so supplied an excellent theriomorphic prototype of the mythological "master of the three worlds" but was of little use for anything else—the inhabitants survived into the twentieth century A.D. on the cultural level of about the two hundredth B.C.

The eight or ten open-fronted thatch shelters of a local group of some forty or fifty men, women, and children are still placed around an elliptical cleanly swept dance area, with a sounding log at one end to be struck by the foot, where, at night, when the daily chores are done, the women sit on the ground and sing, clapping their thighs, while their little men dance round and round.

"In the dance of the Southern tribes," writes Dr. Radcliffe-Brown, whose fine monograph on this society is a classic of modern anthropological research, "each dancer dances alternately on the right foot or on the left. When dancing on the right foot, the first movement is a slight hop with the right foot, then the left foot is raised and brought down with a backward scrape along the ground, then another hop on the right foot. These three movements, which occupy the time of two beats of the song, are repeated until the right leg is tired, and the dancer then changes the movement to a hop with the left foot, followed by a scrape with the right and another hop with the left." [16] If the reader will now test himself, first with the dance step of Köhler's apes and then with that of Radcliffe-Brown's Andamanese, he will agree, I think, that we are not being overbold in suggesting that something about of this order can have served to express mankind's "amicable *joie de vivre*" through the millenniums of those first and hardest 400,000 years.

Among the Andamanese there is no organized government of any kind. The affairs of the community are regulated by the elder men and women. But in each local group there was usually found also one younger man who by his genial character, skill in the hunt, kindness, and generosity had won the regard of his friends to such a degree that they looked up to him for leadership and advice. And finally, there were those men and women who exerted an influence because they were credited with supernatural powers; such powers, according to Radcliffe-Brown, having been acquired through converse with the spirits, either through death and recovery, through meeting spirits in the jungle, or through dreams. The myths, furthermore, were in the particular charge of these supernaturally endowed men and women.

And so, once again, we find in this living museum of the Andaman archipelago a circumstance that must represent—at least approximately—the elementary level of the order of human life: the force of the wisdom of the elders; the tact, grace, and competence of socially oriented individuals; and the interior depth-experiences of the "tender minded." Add the inevitable "child's concept of the world," represented in such a society by the considerable fraction of its population under seven years of age, and you will have an elementary diagram of the structuring force centers from which the constellations of the mythological kaleidoscope have everywhere been constituted—showing shifts of emphasis, indeed, according to circumstance; showing, also, greatly differing ranges and powers of amplification; but always playing out of these four inevitable, ever-present centers of creative force. Furthermore, since there is no excessive emphasis among the Andamanese either on the male or on the female, the contributions from both poles flow freely into the common fund and there is little of the negative, compensatory, and malignant in their mythology and folklore, save where it has been derived from experiences of the malignancies of nature itself in cyclones, sudden death, disease, and other "acts of God."

The chief personage in the mythology of these little people is the northwest monsoon, Biliku, who is sometimes pictured as a spider and whose character, in keeping with that of the monsoon itself, is tricky and temperamental, being both beneficent and dangerous. Biliku is usually said to be a female, and we cannot but recognize in this hardly surprising designation a probable projection of the infantile "mother imprint" as well as a comment on *das Ewig-Weiblich.* For, according to what we know of the workings of the modern psyche, such a projection would be perfectly natural—indeed, inevitable—and need anyone doubt that the same basic psychological laws apply to the Andamanese? The southwest monsoon, Tarai, which is milder than Biliku, is pictured as her husband, and their children are the sun, the moon, and the birds. The sun, furthermore, is the moon's wife, and their children are the stars; the moon can sometimes turn into a pig.

The mythology has not been systematized, and so a number of versions can be accepted of one event. For example, Biliku, either in a male or in a female form, made the world and then made a man named Tomo, the first of the human race, who was black, like the present Andamanese, but much taller and bearded. Biliku taught Tomo how to live and what to eat. And then Tomo had a wife, Lady Crab. According to one view, Biliku created Lady Crab after teaching Tomo how to live. According to another, Tomo saw her swimming near his home and called to her; she came ashore and became his wife. According to still another account, Lady Crab, already pregnant, came ashore and gave birth to several children who became progenitors of the present race. A different series gives us Lady Dove as Tomo's wife; another, the moon—who, it will be recalled, is also the husband of the sun. Tomo himself is sometimes the sun. But the reader may recall, too, that in the Andamanese myth already given of Kingfisher's theft of fire,* Biliku caused Kingfisher, the fire-bringer, to lose his wings, so that it was he who became the first man.

Sir Monitor Lizard also is the first man; and his wife is Lady Civet Cat. In the days before his marriage, and when he had just completed his initiation ceremonies, he went into the jungle to hunt pig, climbed up a Dipterocarpus tree, and got caught up there in some way by his genitals. Lady Civet Cat, seeing him in that sorry plight, released him and the two then married and became the progenitors of the Andamanese.[17]

Now the dying and resurrected god of the archaic high civilizations of the Near East, Tammuz-Adonis, for whom the women wept in the Temple of Jerusalem (Ezekiel 8:14) and whose Egyptian counterpart was Osiris, was actually out hunting a wild boar when he was gored in the loin and rendered impotent; he descended in death then to the lower world, and was resurrected only when the goddess, Ishtar-Aphrodite, whose animal is not indeed the civet cat but the lion, descended to the underworld and released him. How are we to explain this correspondence? The answer is to be found in the kitchen middens. Lidio Cipriani in 1952 excavated a series of huge Andamanese kitchen middens, which must have been accumulating for a period of some five or six thousand years. And he found: (1) to a depth of about six

* Supra, p. 278.

inches from the top, European imports, chips of broken bottles, rifle-bullets, pieces of iron, etc.; (2) going deeper for many feet, crab legs that had been used as smoking pipes, the bones of pigs, pottery shards, and well-preserved clam shells; (3) within about three feet from the bottom, no crab-leg pipes, no pig bones, no pottery, and clamshells heavily calcinated, showing that they had been exposed directly to the fire. Conclusion: "The Andamanese," writes Cipriani, "on their arrival, did not know pottery. Previous to its introduction, food was roasted in the fire or in hot ashes; later, it was boiled in pots. . . . The first Andamanese pottery is of good make, with clay well worked and well burned in the fire. The more we approach the upper strata, the more it undergoes a degeneration. . . . Bones of *Sus andamanensis* [the Andamanese pig] begin to appear later than pottery. They become more frequent, the more we approach the top levels. The inevitable conclusion would seem to be that the ancient Andamanese knew neither pottery nor the hunting of pigs. It is likely that both pottery and a domesticated *Sus* were introduced by one and the same people." [18] Thus, once again, diffusion even here, and regression: regressed neolithic, along with the great neolithic myth of Venus and Adonis, Ishtar and Tammuz, now transformed by the principle of *land-náma* * into Lady Civet Cat and Sir Monitor Lizard.

The animals most prominent in the tales of the Andamanese have no social value whatsoever. They are the little neighbors in the forest, and during the mythological age, when Biliku lived on the earth, they were of the company of the ancestors. But they were separated from man by the discovery of fire—which is true enough, since man is protected from the animals at night by his fires, which they fear. Some of their markings, in fact, were caused by painful contact with the first fire.

Pleasant little animal tales of this kind are known to all the hunting and food-gathering peoples of the world, and are, in fact, spontaneously invented even by children. I should think it safe to assume, therefore, that the category is of immense antiquity. The plots, however, enacted by the various local stock-companies of familiar beasts and birds, greatly vary; and so, if we are to take

* Cf. supra, pp. 199–200.

seriously the warning in the case just cited of the rescue of Sir Monitor Lizard by Lady Civet Cat, we shall have to remember that though the genre of the animal tale is certainly of paleolithic age, the cultural influences represented in the plots may be derived from centers of civilization of a very much higher order than anything visible in the local scene would have led one to expect.

Among the Andamanese a number of the animals used for food are represented as having originally been men. A canoe upset and its occupants became turtles; Lady Civet Cat turned some of the ancestors into pigs; some of the pigs jumped into the sea and became dugongs. The animals killed and eaten, clearly, have a different psychological import for the islanders from those that are simply man's neighbors in the woods. One thinks of Róheim's observation, quoted earlier, that "whatever is killed becomes the father." The Andamanese rites of initiation are concerned largely with protecting the initiate against the powers of these food animals. The youngster, whether boy or girl, must abstain from eating the animal for a certain time, and then take his first meal under ceremonial protection. The girl's initiation begins with her first menstruation, when she must spend three days sitting in a hut, again under ceremonial protection. Other crises requiring protection are the usual ones of birth, marriage, and death. On all such occasions the individuals involved are defended from the powers of the moment by various types of ceremonial ornamentation—red paint, white clay, incised (scarified) designs, decorative plant fibers, shells, etc.—as well as by ceremonial dancing, ceremonial weeping, and the recitation of myths.

And so here we are given our primary view of the force and function of myths and rites. At moments of psychological danger they magically conjure forth the life energies of the individual and his group to meet and surpass the dangers. These may be such as are met by all in the course of their lives at the various inevitable thresholds, or they may be such as are met only occasionally or by very few. A man who has killed another has to be decorated and ceremonially protected. A man who has met ghosts in the forest, in dreams, or in death, requires the protection of myth. The chief sources of danger to an Andamanese, according to

Professor Radcliffe-Brown, are spirits: the ghosts of the dead and the hidden powers animating nature. And the chief sources of protection to the individual against these dangers are the rites and folkways, the ceremonials, of the group.[19] "The function of the myths and legends of the Andamanese," he writes, "is exactly parallel to that of the ritual and ceremonial";[20] they are "the means by which the individual is made to feel the moral force of the society acting upon him."[21] But the ultimate origin of all these folkways, ceremonials, myths, and rites, by which the moral force of the society is expressed? Here the authorities differ. I have saved my own ruminations on the problem for my final chapter.

The picture of the Andamanese can be taken as a likely norm for the social situation of the early, semi-nomadic, food-gathering and small-game-hunting societies of the tropical and semi-tropical areas of the primary paleolithic diffusion. A new situation developed, however, when the northern, bitterly cold regions north of the Elburz-Himalayan mountain line were entered, about 200,000 B.C., by our sturdy friends of the Neanderthal race. Apparently the possession of fire and the idea of wearing animal skins to keep out the cold made it possible for the tribes of men to brave in number the rigors of the lands of the north, which offered to those who could enter them the advantage of abundant meat. Moreover, the brain power of the species had considerably increased; for, whereas the range in the period of Pithecanthropus had been from about 900 to about 1200 cc., that of Neanderthal was from 1250 to about 1725—considerably greater at the upper range, that is to say, than the norm for man today, which, as we have said, is a mere 1400 to 1500 cc. The picture is no longer that of a lot of scattered families of moronic ape-men, but of an extraordinarily sturdy race of human beings, perhaps of a slightly higher mental order than ourselves, fighting it out, at the dawn of what may be considered to be our properly human history, in a landscape calling for every bit of wit and spunk at their disposal.

We do not know what the hunting methods of these Neanderthalers can have been. There was a great disparity between the size of their weapons and the animals that were their prey. The bow and arrow had not yet been invented, but the boomerang, or throwing stick, apparently had. The chase was pursued with wooden, flint-pointed spears, throwing stones, and boomerangs, while the animals sought and slain were the mammoth, rhinoceros, wild horse, bison, wild cattle, reindeer and deer, the brown bear, and the cave bear. These beasts were pursued afoot and met face to face, at close quarters. It is not difficult to see why the courage and stamina of the male in these circumstances should have redounded to his considerable advantage.

However, it is likely, too, that the power of woman's magic was recognized and accorded something of its due. We have seen how, in the Pygmy rite reported by Frobenius from Africa, the woman's lifted arms and cry to the sun were essential. And we know that among the circumpolar hunters to this day female shamans are numerous and highly regarded. For, as Ruth Underhill has pointed out, the mysteries of childbirth and menstruation are *natural* manifestations of power. The rites of protective isolation, defending both the woman herself and the group to which she belongs, are rooted in a sense and idea of mysterious danger, whereas the boys' and men's rites are, rather, a *social* affair. The latter become rationalized in systems of theology. But the natural mysteries of birth and menstruation are as directly convincing as death itself, and remain to this day what they must also have been in the beginning, primary sources of a rcligious awe.[22]

It would have been toward the close of the period of Neanderthal Man that the first migrations into America occurred, if the earliest dates now being suggested are correct; i.e., about 35,000 B.C. Contemporaries of Neanderthal in the south were the so-called Solo Man of Java (Homo soloensis) and Rhodesian Man of South Africa (Homo rhodesiensis). The former—also known as Ngandong Man—has been tentatively suggested as representing a step intermediate in a family line between the earlier Java Man, Pithecanthropus erectus, and the modern natives of Australia.[23] But Rhodesian Man, (Homo rhodesiensis), on the other hand, cannot be linked genetically with any of the modern races of Negro Africa. These, like the Mongolian and Caucasian races, belong to a very much later stage of human evolution.[24]

We have already viewed the earliest unmistakable archaeological evidences of man's religious thought, in the burials and bear sanctuaries of Homo neanderthalensis. We now add, to complete the picture, the observation that a number of the Neanderthal skulls found at Krapina and Ehringsdorf provide evidence also of his ritual cannibalism. They had been opened in a certain interesting way. Furthermore, every one of the unearthed skulls of Neanderthal's Javanese contemporary, Solo Man (Ngangdong Man), had also been opened. And finally, when skulls opened by the modern headhunters of Borneo for the purpose of lapping up the brains are compared with those of Solo and Neanderthal—the skulls having served, handily, as the bowls for their own contents—they are found to have been opened in precisely the same way.[25]

Remarkable indeed—we might observe in passing—how far cultural patterns can survive beyond the periods of the races among whom they first appear!

What rites were associated with the early headhunt we do not know; but that its spirit was comparable to the head-worship of the bear is likely—particularly in view of the fact that at the five-chambered grotto of Guattari, near San Felice Circeo, on the coast of Italy, some eighty miles southeast of Rome, a Neanderthal skull was recently discovered that had been treated much like the skull of a sacrificed bear. The head having been removed, a hole had been tapped in it for the removal of the brain; the remains of sacrificed animals were preserved in receptacles round about the grotto, and the skull itself, placed on the floor of the cave, was surrounded by a circle of stones.

"O noble Divinity!" We can almost hear the prayer: "Precious Divinity, we adore you. We are about to send you back to your father and mother. When you come to them, please speak well of us and tell them how kind we have been. Please come to us again and we shall again do you the honor of a sacrifice."

Of interest, furthermore, is the fact that on the summit of Monte Circeo itself stand the ruins of a Roman temple supposed to have been dedicated to Circe, the sorceress who not only transformed Odysseus' men into swine but also introduced the great voyager himself to the cavernous entrance to the Land of the Dead. And the name of the promontory is itself a reference to this belief; for the folk memory has it that the vivid headland—high and beautiful, and nearly surrounded by the sea—was Circe's Isle.

IV. The Stage of Crô-Magnon Man (c. 30,000–10,000 B.C.)

The dating of the Aurignacian period varies dramatically according to whether the new Carbon-14 estimates are accepted or rejected. The Abbé Breuil rejects them, declaring that they lead to "absurd results" and spans of time "notoriously insufficient." "We must still wait," he writes, "until we learn the limits of this technique, which seems less accurate when the material is more than fifteen or twenty thousand years old." [26] Herbert Kühn holds to a date for the period of c. 60,000 B.C.; [27] the Abbé Breuil, c. 40,000 B.C. Carleton S. Coon, on the other hand, accepting the new evidence, suggests c. 20,000 B.C.[28] A fair norm, considering the fact that the Würm Glaciation was at its peak about 35,000 B.C., whereas the Aurignacian almost certainly followed this peak, would seem to be about 30,000 B.C.

The typical figure of the time—the "signature" of the time, as Weinert terms him—is Crô-Magnon man, straight and tall, with a brain capacity of from 1590 cc. to something like 1880 (somewhat greater than the modern average); [29] but a number of other racial strains also appear. Some of these (Chancelade Man, Combe Capelle Man) have been said to resemble the modern Eskimo; others (Grimaldi) suggest types of Italian. In the continent of Africa, where Crô-Magnon remains have been discovered down the whole east coast as far as the Cape, other forms suggest the Bushman.[30]

Four major divisions of the upper paleolithic, the culminating age of the Great Hunt, have been generally recognized: the Aurignacian, the Solutrean, the Magdalenian, and the Capsian.

THE AURIGNACIAN

This is the high period of the paleolithic female figurines and of the earliest rock-engraving and painting styles. The mural art is linear and somewhat stiff, though by no means crude or incompetent: one thinks of the tension of the archaic. The bone, ivory, and stone figurines, on the other hand, are boldly stylized—some, indeed, with consummate elegance and in a manner remarkably "modern."

On the walls of a number of the caves claw marks of the cave bear have been found, and it has been observed that engravings and paintings usually appear near these spots. Thus we may say that the Master Bear was the first teacher of this animal art and where he touched was a proper place for animal magic. The stenciled or colored imprints of human hands likewise appear on the walls, many with mutilated fingers. Thus finger-joint offerings are indicated, like those of the North American buffalo plains. The hand imprints were perhaps placed on the walls in imitation of the imprints of the bear.

The caves were the sites of animal magic and of the men's rites. They are the underworld itself, the realm of the herds of the underworld, from which the herds of the upper world proceed and back to which they return. They are of the realm and substance of night, of darkness, and of the night sky, their animals being comparable to the stars, which are slain by the sun yet reappear. The mythologies of the animal masters and shamanism, the journey to the other world by way of a ceremonial burial, men's threshold rites, rebirth, and the masked dance inspired the liturgies of this brilliant age.

The female figurines indicate, furthermore, that a mythology of the goddess existed also, which can have been either complementary or alien to the finger-chopping system of the men's dancing rites. The goddess suggests a context more closely associated than that of the caves, however, with the tropical areas of the primary diffusion, where a planter's mythology—or at least the prelude to a planter's mythology—must by now have come into form.

The classical area of the cavern art is southwestern France and northern Spain; that of the figurines extends, on the other hand, from the Pyrenees to Lake Baikal. Moreover, migrations to America in pursuit of game—roughly, from the Baikal region—were almost certainly in progress before the close of this age.

THE SOLUTREAN

The Solutrean was a cold, dry period, when the protecting grottos and rock shelters were abandoned for the grassy plains, which now, replacing the tundra, became the scene of a broadly ranging world of grazing herds and nomadic hunting bands. From the Dordogne to the Mississippi the mammoth hunt was at its peak.

We no longer find images of the goddess in the West European sites, but she is prominent still in the hunting stations of the broad loess lands from eastern Europe to the Baikal zone. Moreover, it has been noted that the female figurines of Předmost in Moravia, Mezin in the Ukraine, and Mal'ta in remote Siberia—which some authorities assign to this period, others, however, to the Aurignacian—bear close comparison with one another.[31] The common hunting ground, by this time, was enormous in extent and freely traversed.

Among the skeletal remains a new race of men, arriving apparently from the east, through Hungary and the Danube basin, and pressing as far as to the Dordogne, is revealed in a series of remains well represented at Brünn, Brüx, and Předmost; and the particular talent of these new arrivals was for the fashioning of beautiful spear points. Their skulls, however, suggest a certain drop in the mental *niveau,* going down as low as to a capacity of about 1350 cc. Animal figurines in mammoth ivory, as well as figurines of the goddess, and a particular clarity of decorative geometrical design, distinguish many of the sites associated with this race. One of the Brünn skeletons was lavishly adorned with cowrie shells and perforated stone disks, bone ornaments from the ribs of the rhinoceros or mammoth, and mammoth teeth. (A badly damaged ivory figurine, apparently of a male, was also found in this grave, and many of the objects were tinted red.) [32] The race was surely one of vigorous hunting nomads and appears to have continued the cult of the goddess into Solutrean times.

In the type station of the period, at Solutré, in central France, near the Saône, a great open-air camp site has been found, sheltered on the north by a steep ridge and having a fine sunny exposure toward the south, with immense fireplaces and the remains of abundant feasts. Wild cattle and horses, the woolly mammoth, the reindeer, and the stag were abundant; likewise the cave and brown bear, badger, rabbit, wolf, hyena, and fox. The jackal, too, now appears—which in form and character is a precise counterpart of America's coyote.

All these beasts must have figured prominently in the animal tales of the period, told at night around the fires—some perhaps already in the roles that they are playing to this day, not only in the folklore of hunting tribes but also in our children's nursery lore and dreams.

THE MAGDALENIAN

Another cold, wet period arrived, and the grassy steppes began to give place in Europe to forests of pine. The great herds of the hoofed animals therewith moved toward northern Asia, and with them went many of the hunters; yet in the temple-caves of southern France and northern Spain a firm continuity can be recognized, uniting the Magdalenian with the Aurignacian, as though the intervening Solutrean had been but a passing episode.

The animal forms of the mural art now are masterfully rendered in a powerful, painterly style, with fluent lines and rich coloration, through eyes that had looked at animals in a way that has not been known since, and by hands perfectly trained. This art was magic. And its herds are the herds of eternity, not of time—yet even more vividly real and alive than the animals of time, because their ever-living source. At Altamira the great bulls—which are almost breathing, they are so alive—are on the ceiling, reminding us of their nature; for they are stars. And we recall the mythology of Frobenius's Congo Pygmies: how the rays of the rising sun slew the herds of the sky.* The hunter is identified with the sun, his javelin with its rays, and the herds of the field with the herds of the sky. The hunt itself is a heavenly adventure, rendering in time eternal forms. And the ritual of the cave is, so to say, its transubstantiating sacrament.

And so here they are, these heavenly herds, in the primal abyss of the night sky. For according to the logic of this sort of dream,

* Supra, pp. 296–298.

this game of myth, where A is B and B is C, this cave is the timeless abyss of the night, and these paintings are the prototypes, Platonic Ideas, or master forms of those temporal herds of earth, which—together with the people—are to play the play of the animal master, the willing death, and the sacramental hunt.

The Magdalenian is the period of the male and female bison of the sanctuary of Tuc d'Audoubert, the dancing shaman of Trois Frères, the shamanistic trance and bison sacrifice of Lascaux, and the bear sacrifice of Montespan. The mythology of the Great Hunt is in perfect flower.

But the new animals of an encroaching forest have already begun to appear among the remains—the red deer, the forest horse, the moose, and the fallow deer—so that the great days of the plains are passing. The hunters are turning to the rivers and the sea; harpoons of bone are made for whale and seal. Curiously, too, the stature of the Crô-Magnon hunters themselves has now considerably diminished: 5 feet 1 inch and 5 feet 3 inches are their typical measurements; no longer 6 feet and 6 feet 4. And the brain is down to the capacity of our own today, 1500 cc.[33]

A number of interesting motifs discovered in the graves deserve remark. At the Grotto of Les Hôteaux, Ain: a skeleton overlaid with Magdalenian implements, resting on its back, covered with red ochre, and with its thigh bones inverted. At the Grotto of Placard, Charente: seven skulls separated from their bodies for burial; a woman's skull surrounded by snail shells, many of which were perforated; and two skull tops, fashioned into bowls. At the Grotto of Duruthy, at Sorde, Landes: a skeleton with a necklace and girdle of lion teeth and bear teeth. At Chancelade: the Eskimo-like skeleton already mentioned, legs comparatively short, height not more than 4 feet 7 inches, covered with several layers of Magdalenian artifacts, and the limbs so tightly flexed that they must have been enveloped in bandages. And, then, finally, at Oberkassel, near Bonn: two skeletons a yard apart, one female, about twenty years old, and the other male, about forty or fifty; respectively 5 feet 2 and 5 feet 3. They were covered with great slabs of basalt, and red coloring matter extended completely over the skeletons and surrounding stones. The bones of animals were present, also a finely carved small bone horse head and a polished bone tool of beautiful workmanship carved with the head of some small animal resembling a marten.

We may recognize in these, besides honor and sacrifice, the hope that the ghost will stay abroad and leave the living alone: the reversed thighs, the separated skulls, the bandaged crouch, and the heavy basalt slabs. The bear and lion teeth are interesting, because these two animals, in the northern bear and African lion-panther rites, respectively, are, as we have seen, equivalent in form.* Both animals have their eyes in front, they look ahead, as men do, whereas the other animals have their eyes at the side. The shaman of Trois Frères is shown staring full face at the viewer. And in North Africa, in the Sahara-Atlas range, there is again a lion staring full-face at the viewer, in a posture suggesting that of the shaman dancer of the French cave and placed in such a way as to be struck by the first rays of the rising sun. Like the dancer, furthermore, he is in a position of mastery over a great field of engraved grazing herds.[34] A mythological association is thus suggested of the bear and lion with the sun, solar eye, slaying eye, and evil eye, as well as with the animal master and the shaman. This must have been for millenniums one of the dominant mythological equations underlying the magic of the paleolithic hunt.

V. The Capsian-Microlithic Style (c. 30,000/10,000–4000 B.C.)

A hurly-burly of folk movements, new technologies, mythological orientations, and vivid art forms now breaks upon the scene, and we are at the opening of a new age. The bow and arrow have appeared, the hunting dog, and an art of rock painting alive with vivid little forms: bowmen hunting and fighting, ritual scenes, dancers, sacrificial scenes. Whereas the paintings of the caves specialized in the forms of the animals of the hunt, here we discover a lively dance of human figures in a wonderfully vivid stickman style, developed with a sense for the composition of scenes and the rendition of movement. And whereas the art of the caves gave the magical, timeless atmosphere of the realm of myth, the

* Supra, pp. 344–347.

Capsian hunting scene, Castellón

happy hunting ground of eternity, and the operations therein of the archetypal shamans, here we have an atmosphere of life on earth and the ritual acts of living communities. We note, too, that

Three women, Castellón

women are prominent in the scenes, with elegantly rendered ample hips and legs, and willowy bodies, gracefully poised. The scenes are vibrant with the rhythms of the concerted action of groups. Not the shaman now, but the group is the vehicle of the holy power.

The heartland of this new style was the grassy hunting ground of North Africa, where today there is only desert, and the type station is Capsa (Gafsa) in Tunisia. From there a diffusion westward, turning north into Spain, is to be imagined: Europe's monuments of the period are in eastern Spain. But the field extends across the whole of North Africa to the Nile, the Jordan, Mesopotamia, India, and Ceylon. Its characteristic artifact is a tiny geometric flint, chiefly in trapezoid, rhomboid, and triangular forms, commonly known as a microlith, which has been found distributed from Morocco to the Vindhya Hills in India, and from South Africa to Northern Europe. In contrast to this broad diffusion of the tools and weapons, however, the chief reported sites of the art, besides those of eastern Spain, are confined to the Sahara, which of old was a great park and pasture land, full of game. In the rock pictures we see herds of elephants and giraffes, rhinos and running ostriches, monkeys, wild cattle, sheep and gazelles, giant human forms with the heads of jackals or of asses, the lion high on the cliff, struck by the sun, and then, also, men standing in postures

Man with a dart, Castellón

The "White Lady," Rhodesia

of adoration, with uplifted arms, before great bulls or before a standing ram with the sign of the sun-disk between its horns.[35]

We know practically nothing of the early history of this culture; not even how far into the past it should be traced. But the earliest forms, known as Lower Capsian, take us back at least as far, it would appear, as the Aurignacian. The break-through into Spain and thence into northern Europe did not occur, however, until about 10,000 B.C., where it is termed, variously, Final Capsian, Tardenoisian, Azilian, microlithic, mesolithic, proto-neolithic, or epipaleolithic. Let us not become confused, however, by names!

The Capsians of North Africa appear to have been a folk of

moderate stature, averaging about five to five and a half feet tall, having long heads with retreating foreheads. They hunted with boomerangs, clubs, and bows, speared fish with delicate harpoons, collected berries and roots, and made a great thing of snails and shellfish. They wore beads, disk-shaped, of ostrich-egg shell, feathers, bracelets and girdles of perforated shells. The males—like many innocents of the woman-dominated equatorial zone—instead of concealing, decorated their genitals, while the women wore long stylish skirts. The Natufians of the Mount Carmel caves, on whose appearance, c. 6000 B.C., we based our dating of the proto-neolithic,* were a people of this Capsian culture style. Furthermore, with the progressive desiccation of the Sahara and departure of the teeming game, during the fourth millennium B.C., the Capsians and their painting art moved south, where their influence can be seen in the various styles of South Rhodesia: the graceful hunting scenes of the Bushmen of Basutoland; the now famous, more mysterious "White Lady" of Damaraland (who, it appears, however, is actually a man—"a king," they say, but no doubt, then, a god-king); and finally, the curious murals of Rusafe, where the sacred regicide and resurrection of the moon-king are celebrated.

And so we are brought back, once more, to our problems of the ritual sacrifice, the dawn of the neolithic, and the mysteries of the monster serpent and the maiden.

* Supra, pp. 136–138.

Chapter 10

MYTHOLOGICAL THRESHOLDS OF THE NEOLITHIC

I. The Great Serpent of the Earliest Planters (c. 7500 B.C.?)

A young woman—we are told—went into the forest. The serpent saw her. "Come!" he said. But the young woman answered, "Who would have you for a husband? You are a serpent. I will not marry you." He said, "My body is indeed that of a serpent, but my speech is that of a man. Come!" And she went with him, married him, and presently bore a boy and girl; after which the serpent husband put her away, saying, "Go! I shall take care of them and give them food."

The serpent fed the children and they grew. One day the serpent said to them, "Go, catch some fish!" They did so and returned, and he said, "Cook the fish!" but they replied, "The sun has not yet risen." When the sun rose and warmed the fish with its rays, they consumed the food, still raw and bloody.

And the serpent said, "You two are spirits; for you eat your food raw. Perhaps you will eat me. You, girl, stay here! You, boy, crawl into my belly!" The boy was afraid and said, "What shall I do?" But the snake said, "Come!" and he crept into the serpent's belly. The serpent said to him, "Take the fire and bring it out to your sister! Come out and gather coconuts, yams, taro, and bananas!" So the boy crept out again, bringing the fire from the belly of the serpent.

Then, having gathered roots and fruit, as told, they lit a fire with the brand the boy had brought forth, and cooked their food; and when they had eaten, the serpent asked, "Is my kind of food or yours the better?" To which they answered, "Yours! Our kind is bad." [1]

Here is a legend of the planting world such as might have been told practically anywhere along the tropical arc of the primary migration, from Africa eastward (south of the Elburz-Himalayan mountain line) to southeast Asia, Indonesia, and Melanesia; whereas, actually, its place along the arc was a primitive enclave at the remote eastern end of this great tropical province: the Admiralty Islands, just off the northern coast of New Guinea.

Now the archaeology of the paleolithic periods of Southeast Asia has, unfortunately, hardly been broached; but the bit that we know indicates that the region was far behind Africa in its development of Stone Age tools. Furthermore, as Professor Robert Heine-Geldern has observed: "The paleolithic seems to have lasted here into a very late period. Apparently paleolithic cultures maintained themselves in large parts of the area, particularly in western Indonesia, well into the second millennium B.C., and in places even into much later times." [2]

Of the mythologies open to study in that extremely interesting area, many are undoubtedly of great age. But, as we have seen in the Andaman Island legend of Sir Monitor Lizard and Lady Civet Cat playing the roles of Tammuz and Ishtar, traits from the higher culture spheres can be absorbed even by the most primitive traditions. And yet, on the other hand, as we have seen in the case of the Solo (Ngandong) skulls from c. 200,000 B.C. treated in the manner of the modern Borneo headhunt, the most amazing conservatism can also be represented in these societies. Coming across such a trait, therefore, as that of the serpent and the maiden among primitive Papuans, are we to think it a regressed, or a primitive, form of the Fall in the Garden? Or does anyone know, indeed, where this mythological theme first arose?

It is reasonably clear that the widely known mythological theme of the serpent and the maiden first appeared somewhere along the arc of the primary tropical diffusion from Africa, through Arabia and the Near East, to India, Southeast Asia, Indonesia, and

Melanesia. As we have learned from the evidence of the paleolithic tools,* a broad and even fairly rapid diffusion along this arc can be readily demonstrated; however, two major provinces are to be distinguished: (*a*) that from Africa to India; and (*b*) that from North-Central India, through Southeast Asia, to Indonesia and Melanesia. In the first, a number of developed varieties of the paleolithic hand ax have been found as well as earlier and cruder "pebble tools"; but in the second, only relatively crude types of chopping tool. Furthermore, in the first we have found the vigorous microlithic-Capsian diffusion, which did not extend into the second. So that Province *a* would appear not only to have been the earlier of the two, but also to have retained the cultural lead at least until the end of the paleolithic.

No one has yet determined where the first steps were taken toward plant cultivation. Menghin has suggested tropical South Asia;[3] Heine-Geldern has termed this idea unlikely, without suggesting an alternative.[4] The only possible alternative, however, is some more westerly part of Province *a;* which, indeed, would seem to have been the sector—and therewith the likely sector also for our myth of the serpent and the maiden, which, as we have seen, is linked to the idea of the cultivated plant.

We have already spoken of the biological theory of a "zone of hominization": a limited yet sufficiently broad area of the earth's surface, relatively uniform in character, where a large population of closely related individuals became affected simultaneously by a series of genetic mutations conducing to the appearance of a considerable variety of manlike forms.† I should like now to propose a comparable theory for the origin both of our myth and of the art of cultivating plants, with which it is affiliated. For we can be certain that from one end to the other of Province *a* there was an effective communication of thought and techniques; slow, indeed, according to modern standards—requiring centuries instead of seconds—yet eventually effective, nevertheless. And so we may think of this broad area as a continuum in which a fairly uniform state of human affairs prevailed and which, consequently, was characterized

* Supra, pp. 364–365.

† Supra, pp. 357–358.

by a fairly uniform state of psychological readiness for the reception of an imprint—a readiness, that is to say, for precisely such "seizures" as that described in our account of the professor's little girl and the witch.* The whole province might therefore be described as a limited yet sufficiently broad area of the earth's surface, relatively uniform in character, where a large population of closely related individuals (to wit, the members of the relatively recent species Homo sapiens) became affected simultaneously by roughly comparable imprints, and where, consequently, "seizures" of like kind were everywhere impending and, in fact, became precipitated in a ritualized procedure and related myth. We may term such a zone a "mythogenetic zone," and it should be the task of our science to identify such zones and clearly distinguish them from "zones of diffusion," as well as from zones of later development and further crisis.

In the case of our present myth, we do not know where, on the great arc of Province *a,* the idea occurred to some of the women grubbing for edible roots that it would be sensible to concentrate their food plants in gardens; nor do we know whether the idea stemmed from a concept of economy or from some "seizure" and related ritual play. All that is certain is that the functions of planting and of this myth are related and that the myth flourishes among gardeners; moreover, that it can have appeared spontaneously within a broad zone of readiness in more than one place at once; and finally, that within a period which in terms of paleolithic reckoning need not have been long (say, a thousand years) the myths and rites, together with their associated gardening techniques, can have filled the arc. We may guess the date, therefore, to have been somewhere in the neighborhood of 7500 B.C.

But since we know that a mythology of the goddess was already flourishing earlier than this—having shown itself in the Aurignacian figurines, practically with the first appearance of Homo sapiens on the prehistoric scene—we must recognize that the myth of the serpent and the maiden represents only a development from an earlier base. In the rickety child's grave at the Mal'ta site, where some twenty female figurines were found, there was an ivory

* Supra, pp. 22–23.

plaque bearing on one side a spiral design and on the other three cobralike snakes. Another spiral was stippled on the side of an ivory fish. The child was in the fetal position, facing east. And there were some ivory birds in the grave.

Now an extremely primitive Papuan tribe, the Baining of New Britain, declare that the sun one day called all things together and asked which desired to live forever. Unfortunately, man disobeyed the summons, and that is why the stones and snakes now live forever, but not man. Had man obeyed the sun, he would have been able to change his skin, from time to time, like a snake.[5]

This symbolism of the serpent of eternal life appearing in the paleolithic period on the reverse of a plaque bearing on its obverse the labyrinth of death; a fish in the same assemblage bearing the labyrinth on its side; the birds, suggesting a flight of the soul in death, as in shamanistic trance; the orientation to the rising sun; and the fetal posture of the little skeleton—these, in a single grave in a site where twenty statuettes of the goddess were discovered as well as a number of ceremonially buried beasts,* speak for the presence of a developed mythology in the late paleolithic, in which the goddess of spiritual rebirth was already associated with the symbols of the very much later neolithic cult of Ishtar-Aphrodite: the bird, the fish, the serpent, and the labyrinth.

And so we are brought, once again, as always through myth, to the problem of permanence in change, or, as James Joyce says, to what is "ever the same yet changing ever." And the permanent presence in this particular context is obviously woman, both in her way of experiencing life and in her character as an imprint—a message from the world—for the male to assimilate. The Neanderthal graves and bear sanctuaries, our earliest certain evidences of religious ritual, point to an attempt to cope with the imprint of death. But the mystery of the woman is no less a mystery than death. Childbirth is no less a mystery; nor the flow of the mother's milk; nor the menstrual cycle—in its accord with the moon. The creative magic of the female body is a thing of wonder in itself. And so it is that, whereas the men in their rites (as initiates, tribal dignitaries, shamans, or what not) are invariably invested with

* Supra, pp. 329–331.

magical costumes, the most potent magic of the womanly body inheres in itself. In all her primary epiphanies, therefore, whether in the paleolithic figurines or in the neolithic, she is typically the naked goddess, with an iconographic accent on the symbolism of her own magical form.

Woman, as the magical door from the other world, through which lives enter into this, stands naturally in counterpoise to the door of death, through which they leave. And no theology need be implied in this, but only mystery and the wonder of a stunned mind before an apprehended segment of the universe—together with a will to become linked to whatever power may inhabit such a wonder. Let us recall the charge of the Blackfoot conductor of the buffalo to his two wives, that they should remain in the lodge that day and pray. "Pray," is perhaps merely the word of the modern interpreter; better might have been the phrase, "perform their magic," for, as we have seen, the men's role in the hunt had to be supported by the magic of their women. However, in the regions of the Great Hunt, where an essentially unbroken masculine psychology prevailed, supported by tokens of prestige, skillful achievement, and the firm establishment of a courageous ego, the feminine principle could be only ancillary to the purposes conceived and executed by the males. The goddess and her living counterparts could give magical support to the men's difficult tasks but not touch their ruling concept of the nature of being. In the mythologies of that world, or conceived in the spirit of that world, therefore, the fundamental theme is always achievement: achievement of eternal life, magical power, the kingdom of God on earth, illumination, wealth, a good-natured woman, or something else of the kind. The dominant principle is *do ut des:* "I give so that thou mayest give"—"I give to Thee, O God, so that Thou, in turn, mayest give something nice to me—whether in this life or in the next."

In the milder regions of the plant-dominated tropics, on the other hand, the feminine side was not simply ancillary but could even establish—out of its own mode of experience—the dominant pattern of the culture and its myth. And this is the force that comes to view in the myth of the serpent and the maiden, where the basic elements are: (1) the young woman ready for marriage (the nymph), associated with the mysteries of birth and menstruation, these mysteries (and the womb itself, therefore) being identified with the lunar force; (2) the fructifying masculine semen, identified with the waters of the earth and sky and imaged in the phallic, waterlike, lightninglike serpent by which the maiden is to be transformed; and (3) an experience of life as change, transformation, death, and new birth.

The analogy of death and resurrection with the waning and waxing of the moon; the analogy of the water's disintegration and fructification of the seed with the shadow swallowing and releasing the moon, and therewith, as it were, the moon's sloughing of its skin of death; furthermore the resemblance of both of these cycles, plant and lunar, to the passing and rising of the generations, as well as to certain spiritual experiences of melancholy and rapture intrinsic to the psyche—these perceived analogies must have constituted then, as they do still, a source both of fascination and of inspiration to at least the more thoughtful members of the species, who at that time may well have constituted an even larger proportion of the population than today.

A diffusion of this mythology and its ritual enactment of the mystery of the monster serpent and the maiden from the mythogenetic zone of Province *a* must have carried it in due course to Province *b*, and then eastward into the circum-Pacific area, as well as northwestward from Province *a* to the Mediterranean. So that the curious myth at the opening of our chapter, of the young woman whose serpent husband gave fire to their children, is almost certainly a descendant of the same tradition that in the Mediterranean sphere produced the legends of Persephone and Eve.

The amazing fact, however, is that in the Admiralty Island version, which is a comparatively primitive variant remaining on a proto-neolithic level, the antithesis that gave Nietzsche so much to think about, between the myths of the feminine Fall and masculine fire-theft, is dissolved—in a single image, full of seeming import, which contains both themes.

It is through just such shifts of emphasis that primitive myths, and the myths of alien worlds, enable us to read anew the once pliant images in our own tradition, which the centuries have embalmed.

II. The Birth of Civilization in the Near East (c. 7500–2500 B.C.)

The concept of the "mythogenetic zone" applied to the stages of our subject already viewed will clarify the main outlines of this natural history of the gods.

Stage I we have termed the Stage of Plesianthropus. There can be no question as to where myths and rites arose during this period, if at all. Whatever part of the earth the students of paleontology may ultimately recognize as having been the "zone of hominization"—the part of the earth in which our species stepped away from its less playful, more grown-up, more serious-minded, economically oriented fellows, and began to play games of its own invention instead of only those of nature's—we shall recognize as our primary "mythogenetic zone."

The brain capacity of Plesianthropus does not promise much in the way of stimulating ideas; nor is the evidence rich enough to give us more than clues for romantic guesses. Yet both the pygmoid and the gigantic hominids of that time must have responded—as all animals do—to the sign stimuli not only of their environments but also of their own bodies and social situations. Also, no less than Köhler's chimpanzees, they must have enjoyed the playful invention of new situations, games, and organizations. Such games, it is true, are not yet rites. But if the brain of Plesianthropus was capable of playing with patterns of thought as well as with patterns of movement, the ground was present for a "seizure" on this level. An individual "seizure"—comparable, on the mental plane, to the chimpanzee's "seizure" by the round polished stone * —would have been a pointer, already, toward the mentality of shamanism, while a group "seizure"—again on the mental plane, but comparable to the fascination of the chimpanzees for their dervish dance or for their dance around the pole †—would have

* Supra, p. 358.
† Supra, pp. 358–359.

produced something like a popular cult. The game, if communicated, would then have established a tradition. And the endurance of the tradition would have depended upon the force of its appeal—that is to say, its power to evoke and organize life energy. In short, if, besides inventing patterns of movement, Plesianthropus was capable also of patterns of thought (mythological associations to go along with his ritual games), the first chapter of our science would have begun.

The only tangible evidence of anything of the kind, however, is that curious separation of heads and tails from animal skeletons observed and described by Professor Dart. Theorizing on the basis of this evidence, one might suggest, hypothetically, that the cult of the animal offering with its game of "life beyond death and a pleasant journey home" had already opened its prodigious career. The psychological force of such a play is epitomized in Róheim's formula: "Whatever is killed becomes father." The veneration of the food animal, according to this formula, is simply inevitable in a hunting community—provided the inhabitants are actually hominids, not beasts. And that Plesianthropus was a kind of man seems to be indicated by the fact that he brained his prey with a club—with a tool, that is to say—instead of his empty hands and naked teeth.

Stage II, that of Pithecanthropus (c. 400,000 B.C.), reveals a two-pronged diffusion from the "zone of hominization" (which was probably South and East Africa): (1) northward into Europe (Heidelberg Man), and (2) eastward through the tropical arc to Java (Pithecanthropus), and then northward up the Pacific coast to Peking (Sinanthropus). For the primitive mythology of the animal-head cult (if such existed), zones (1) and (2) would thus have been "zones of diffusion."

However, two new phenomena now appear, and these would seem to indicate the emergence of two new "mythogenetic zones." The first phenomenon is the elegant development of the hand ax in the western sector of the tropical arc (Africa to western India) and in Europe; the second, the appearance of fire in the gruesome den of Peking Man. Professor J. E. Weckler has observed that throughout much of the early glacial period the eastern end of the tropical arc was cut off from the west by desert and ice, and that, consequently, two separate provinces of human evolution were delineated.[6] In the west, as we have already noted,* stone tools developed into beautiful, symmetrically balanced forms, some of which are so large and elegant as to suggest implements for ritual use. In the east, on the other hand, stone tools remained in a relatively primitive state—but fire was discovered and put to use. The mythology and ritual lore of the hand ax, which in later myth and cult became linked to the idea of thunder (Thor's hammer, the bolt of Zeus, Indra, etc.), would have begun, then, in the west, while the mythologies and ritual practices associated with fire would have sprung—like the sun—from the east. We do not know what the early mythologies may have been; but I think it interesting that the bolt in later myth is generally associated with a god, whereas fire in the east is frequently the gift, or even the very body, of a goddess. We have already spoken of the Ainu goddess of the hearth, and have remarked also that the Ainu name of this goddess, Fuji, appears in the name of the sacred volcano Fujiyama. In Hawaii the goddess Pele is the goddess of the dangerous yet beloved volcano Kilauea, where the old chieftains dwell forever, playing their royal games in the flames. And in Malekula, in Melanesia, the journey of the dead leads to and through the goddess guardian of the path to a volcano. In Japan the sun is a goddess and the moon a god; so too in Germany, where the sun is female (*die Sonne*) and the moon a male (*der Mond*)—while in France, beyond the Rhine, the sun is *le soleil,* and the moon, *la lune.*

There is, in fact, a great mythological area east of the Rhine, where the myth of the moon brother and sun sister is told. Briefly, the tale is of a young woman who at night was visited by a lover whom she never saw. But one night, determining to learn his identity, she blackened her hands in the coals of the fire before he came and, embracing him, left the imprint on his back. In the morning she saw the marks of her own palms on her brother and, screaming with horror, ran away. She is the sun, he the moon.

* Supra, p. 386.

And he has been pursuing his sister ever since. One can see the hand marks on his back, and when he catches her there is an eclipse. This myth was known to the North American Indians, as well as to the northern Asian tribes, and may indeed be of immense age.

It would surely be ridiculous to press the contrast of the feminine fire and the masculine bolt on back to a couple of hypothetical mythogenetic zones of about 400,000 B.C.—but a polarity of some kind is surely indicated in the evidence, and who will say that in the deepest levels of our two culture worlds of East and West (which harbor even greater differences than anyone today cares to think) the dialogue could not still be in progress of the God of the Bolt and the Goddess Fire?

Stage III, that of Neanderthal Man (c. 200,000–75,000/25,000 B.C.), reveals in Central Europe the earliest dependable evidence found anywhere of an establishment of myth and rite: ceremonial burials with grave gear, and bear-skull sanctuaries in high mountain peaks. Professor Weckler has suggested that Homo neanderthalensis may have come from the Oriental zone, pressing west across the tundras into Europe, where he was the first to use fire.[7] Sinanthropus, it will be recalled, who had already captured fire as early as c. 400,000 B.C., was a cannibal; so also Neanderthal Man: we have mentioned the evidence of the opened skulls at Krapina and Ehringsdorf.* But in Java too a number of such opened skulls have been found among the remains of Solo (Ngandong) Man, Neanderthal's Oriental contemporary; and these were opened precisely in the way of the skulls of the present-day headhunters of Borneo.† Neanderthal and Solo Man, therefore, may have practiced some form of ritual cannibalism in connection with an early version of the headhunt; and if so, the formula should perhaps be carried back even to the period of Plesianthropus, who killed and beheaded men as well as beasts—in which case, this grim cult might reasonably be proposed as the earliest religious rite of the human species.

* Supra, p. 373.
† Supra, loc. cit.

But now, with respect to the earliest employment of fire, a curious problem arises when it is realized that although the heavy-browed family of Sinanthropus crouched around its hearth as early as c. 400,000 B.C. and that of Neanderthal Man c. 200,000, those lusty brutes gobbled their meals of fresh meat and brains—whether human or animal—absolutely raw. For it was not until the period of the far more highly developed races of the temple caves, c. 30,000–10,000 B.C., that the art of roasting was invented.

But then, why the hearths?

It has been suggested that they were used to heat the caves,[8] and this, indeed, would seem to have been the only practical end to which they were turned. However, even if this were the case, one would still have to ask by what accident Sinanthropus could have learned that the blast of a forest, prairie, or volcanic fire could have been turned to such congenial use.

A possible answer is provided by the Ainu ritual of the mountain bear ceremonially entertained during his night-long conversation with the goddess of the hearth; for the fire in that context was not a mere device for the provision of heat but the actual presence of a divinity. The earliest hearths, too, could have been shrines, where fire was cherished in and for itself in the way of a holy image or primitive fetish. The practical value of such a living presence, then, would have been discovered in due time.

The suggestion is rendered the more likely, furthermore, when it is considered that throughout the world the hearth fire remains to this day a sacred as well as secular institution. In many lands, at the time of a marriage, the kindling of the hearth in the new home is a crucial rite, and the domestic cult comes to focus in the preservation of its flame. Perpetual flames and votive lights are known practically everywhere in the developed religious cults. The vestal fire of Rome, with its attendant priestesses, was neither for cooking nor for the provision of heat. And we have already learned of the holy fire made and extinguished at the times of the installation and murder of the god-king.

The hearth, then; the mountain sanctuary of the bear; and the ceremonial burial with grave gear, animal sacrifice, and perhaps occasional ritual cannibalism—these, in the period of Neanderthal

Man, supply our chief clues to the religious life of a broad middle paleolithic province, documented from the Alps to the Arctic Ocean, eastward to Japan and south to Indonesia. But where the mythogenetic zone and where the diffusion zones within this vast area may have been we do not know—though, surely, the earliest points of reference thus far discovered are the bear-skull sanctuaries of the Central European peaks.

And finally, as to the question of other possible mythogenetic zones and ritual syndromes developed during the course of this long period, whether in Africa, western Europe, or Southwest Asia, nothing has yet been found that could be read as evidence. However, it is entirely possible that the cults of the female statuettes and temple caves, which appear abruptly in the following period, were in the process of formation during this earlier, darker day, but have left no evidence; for where wood is abundant as a material for sculpture, and leaves, bark, feathers, etc., for ritual masks, no remains survive. Some part of the great primary field of the tropics, therefore, may have been the mythogenetic zone for the earlier stages of the cults that abruptly appear, already fully formed, in the documented late paleolithic areas of the golden age of the Great Hunt.

Stage IV, then (c. 30,000–10,000 B.C.), reveals the mythology of the naked goddess and the mythology of the temple-caves.

The richest finds of the first of these two complexes have turned up in the Ukraine, though the range extends westward to the Pyrenees and eastward to Lake Baikal. Provisionally, therefore, the Ukraine may be designated as the mythogenetic zone; and this likelihood is rendered the more evident when it is considered that many of the basic elements of the complex were to reappear in the neolithic goddess-cults of the fifth millennium B.C., directly to the south, on the opposite flank of the Black Sea.

The relationship of these two goddess-cults to that of the Ainu fire-goddess is probably extremely remote: they appear to have stemmed from different mythogenetic zones. Nevertheless, in the areas of their diffusion they undoubtedly met and possibly were amalgamated. And finally, of course, both represent the imprint of the "permanent presence" previously discussed, namely, woman.

The second mythology of this important era, that of the great temple-caves, is definitely centered in northern Spain and southern France—the so-called Franco-Cantabrian zone—and though the cult may have commenced as a provincial form of some earlier masked ritual of the men's dancing grounds developed in areas to the south, it achieved here a character and ritual investment of such force that the area must be regarded as our first precisely pin-pointed mythogenetic zone; one, furthermore, from whose truly marvelous amplifications of the symbology of the labyrinthine chambers of the soul every one of the high religions and most of the primitive, also, have received instruction.

What a coincidence of nature and the mind these caves reveal! And what an evocation it must have been that drew forth these images! Apparently the cave, as literal fact, evoked, in the way of a sign stimulus, the latent energies of that other cave, the unfathomed human heart, and what poured forth was the first creation of a temple in the history of the world. A shrine is one thing, a temple another. A shrine is a little place for magic, or for converse with a divinity. A temple is the projection into earthly space of a house of myth; and as far as history and archaeology have yet shown, these paleolithic temple-caves were the first realizations of this kind, the first manifestations of the fact that there is a readiness in man's heart for the supernormal image, and in his mind and hand the capacity to create it. Here, therefore, nature supplied the catalyst, a literal, actual presentation of the void. And when the sense of time and space was gone, the visionary journey of the seer began.

The fashioning of an image is one thing, the fashioning of a mythological realm another. And the remarkable fact, it seems to me, is that, for all their complication, these caves—or at least a number of them—are conceived as units, with outer and inner chambers of increasing power. Consider, for example, the composition of the upper cave at Lascaux, with its scenes of the happy hunting ground and its curious wizard beast with the pointing-stick horns; and then below, in the crypt, the shaman and Master Bull, upon whose magical accord the whole happy hunt above depends. Or consider at Trois Frères the long flume of the difficult approach—the difficult journey—leading to the great chamber of the animals, where the only form with emphasizing paint upon it was the dancing shaman. In this latter case we are dramatically confronted by a new thing in the world: the use of a change of art technique to render a magnification of power. And then finally, at the cavern of Tuc d'Audoubert, the visitor passes, first, through beautifully painted chambers and then, clambering through a very small entrance—which the boys who discovered the cave called "the cat's hole," and going through which their father, the Count Bégouën, got stuck and had to forfeit both his shirt and his trousers—one arrives in the sanctuary of the connubium of the two divine bison, who are rendered not in paint but in bas relief, not in two dimensions but in three; so that here, once again, the possibilities of art were being exploited, in a way never known before, to communicate the sense of a heightening of the spiritual power sphere. The placement of the shaman in the crypt of Lascaux, the emphasized form of the dancing shaman of Trois Frères, and the plastic rendition of the bison pair of Tuc d'Audoubert speak volumes for the degree of esthetic sensibility of the artists of these caves, who were greater men by far than mere primitive magicians, conjuring animals. They were mystagogues, conjuring the minds of men.

And so it is, I believe, that we can say that in the mythogenetic zone of the Franco-Cantabrian caves the rendition in art of the mythological realm itself was achieved for the first time in the history of the world. All cathedrals, all temples since—which are not mere meeting houses but manifestations to the mind of the magical space of God—derive from these caves. And I would say, also, that we have here our first certain sign of the operation of the fertilized masculine spirit, the upbeat to *La Divina Commedia* and to all those magical temples of the Orient wherein the heart and mind are winged away from earth and reach first the heavens of the stars, but then beyond. Though within the earth in these caves, we have left it, on the wings of dream. And this, already, is the wondrous flight so beautifully rendered in Gregory of Nyssa's image of the "wings of the dove," as the primary symbol of the Holy Spirit, whereby our nature, "transforming itself from glory to glory," moves on without bound or ultimate term toward no limit. "For the soul turned toward God, fully committed to its desire for incorruptible beauty, is moved by a desire for the transcendent ever anew, and this desire is never filled to satiety. That is why the dove never ceases to move on toward what is before, going on from where it now is, to penetrate that further to which it has not yet come."[9] It flies into the shadows, and the shadows continually recede, yet are ever there; for the shadows through which the dove is flying—now and forever—are neither more nor less than "the incomprehensibility of the essence or being of the divine."

Stage V is represented by the Capsian. The vast diffusion of the microliths, from Morocco to Ceylon and from South Africa to northern Europe, charts the horizon of this new influence. But a much more limited center of creative force is indicated by the distribution of the art works of the period, the chief centers of which are in North Africa and eastern Spain—though with echoes of diffusion southward to the Cape and eastward into those regions that were soon to become the matrices of the next great mythopoetic transformation. The Capsian art, as we have said, is in clear contrast to the Magdalenian. In its passage from north to south, the paleolithic tradition renounced the task of projecting magical realms. Instead, it now is presenting the earthly scenes of a mythologically inspired community almost on the level, we might say, of women's gossip, or of ethnology. We see the exterior, not so much the interior, of that long-forgotten period of mankind's spiritual as well as physical development.

Can it be said, then, that we have the evidence here of an impact from the north upon the south? I believe it can. And I would say also that in Stage IV of our sketchy history we had the evidence of an impact from the south upon the north. For it is surely remarkable that in precisely those areas on either side of the Mediterranean where a possibility of cross-fertilization existed in that period of no sailing craft—that is to say, on either side of the comparatively narrow barrier of Gibraltar—the two most impressive heightenings of the paleolithic world of thought and performance come into view.

North Africa, in any case, can be provisionally regarded as the mythogenetic zone of the Capsian rites illustrated on its open-faced rock walls. And if we may judge from the evidence of a number of the scenes, the underlying mythology was almost exactly that which we have already seen represented also in the ritual of the Congo Pygmies.* Their picture of a gazelle struck by the rays of the sun and the magical cry of the woman with her lifted arms were vestiges in the twentieth century A.D. of the world's most advanced thinking of the tenth century B.C.

But in this art we are on the brink of a prodigious transformation, certainly the most important in the history of the world. For among the beasts represented we can identify precisely those types of cattle and sheep that are about to appear as the barnyard stock of the neolithic. Indeed, an only slightly later level of engravings on the same North African rock walls—in the same sites—shows the same animals domesticated. Furthermore, on several of the older engravings of the Capsian period appear superimposed engravings of planetary symbols; for example, on a rock wall in the Sahara-Atlas range, at Jebel Bes Seba, the disk of the sun superimposed upon the head of a ram [10]—reminding us that in Egypt the sun-god Ammun presently would be represented as a ram.

In the broadest terms, the apogee of the Capsian phase of the epipaleolithic, mesolithic, proto-neolithic stage of development (however one may like to name it) we can associate with a time, about 10,000 B.C., "when," as Dr. Henri Frankfort declares, "the Atlantic rain storms had not yet followed the retreating ice cap northward; when grasslands extended from the Atlantic coast of Africa up to the Persian mountains; and when, in this continuum, the ancestors of both the Hamitic- and the Semitic-speaking peoples roamed with their herds." [11]

The herds were followed by hunters first, we may imagine, precisely as were the bison of the North American plains, and the first step toward domestication can have been taken when—as sometimes

* Supra, pp. 296–298.

happened on the plains—a hunting band remained close to a single herd for some time, as if it were a kind of living larder, fighting off alien groups wishing to poach upon it, and killing only a few of its number from day to day. When the possibility of corralling such a herd then dawned on some bright mind—or number of minds—the idea would have spread like wildfire from one extreme of the herding continuum to another—just as, in the tropical arc, the idea of domesticating plants must have spread.

And now, it seems to me extremely significant that the neolithic came into being almost precisely at the point where the hunting continuum described by Dr. Frankfort ("from the Atlantic coast of Africa up to the Persian mountains") and the tropical arc of our primary diffusion (from South and East Africa, through Arabia, Palestine, Mesopotamia and Iran, to India and Southeast Asia) * intersect; namely, the area that old Professor James Henry Breasted used to call "the Fertile Crescent." It is entirely possible that the idea of domestication passed from one of these two spheres to the other—from the herders to the planters, or vice versa. But in any case, it is surely no accident that the neolithic dawned—and with it civilization—in the Near East, and precisely at the point where the semi-primitive, proto-neolithic arts of plant and cattle cultivation would have met.

Stage VI, the birth of civilization in the Near East, we have outlined in Part Two, Chapter 1. The mythogenetic zone is the Fertile Crescent and its flanking mountains, from the Nile up the coast to Syria, then down to the Persian Gulf. And the phases of the development, sketched in the broadest lines, are four:

1. The proto-neolithic (c. 7500–5500 B.C.), the phase of the Natufians, which can now be described as an advance from the Capsian, with the promising, highly significant addition of a grain or grass harvest to the provisions of the hunt. As I have observed, we do not know whether a planting had preceded the harvest or whether the animals killed were yet domesticated. But if the Natufians were not domesticating, they were nevertheless slaughtering the pig, goat, sheep, ox, and an equid of some sort, the same

* Cf. supra, pp. 362 and 385.

beasts that were later to constitute the basic barnyard stock of all the higher cultures. And if they were not planting, they were nevertheless harvesting some variety of wild or primitive grain. As we have said, the first discoveries of their remains were made in the Mount Carmel caves in Palestine. But similar finds have turned up since, from Helwan in Egypt to Beirut and Yabrud, and as far west as to the Kurdish hills of Iraq.

2. The basal neolithic (c. 5500–4500 B.C.), when the foundations of a well-established barnyard economy based on grain agriculture and stock-breeding were already a firmly established pattern and the new style of village living had already begun to spread from the primary zone. The chief crops were wheat and barley, and the animals domesticated were the pig, goat, sheep, and ox, the dog having already joined the human tribes by the time of the Capsian period, as a companion of the hunt. Pottery and weaving had been added to the sum of human skills; likewise the arts of carpentry and house-building. And then suddenly—very suddenly—the evidence of a new great leap ahead appears in the pottery, the finely fashioned, very beautiful painted pottery of the next phase:

3. The high neolithic (c. 4500–3500 B.C.), when the elegant geometrically organized designs of the pottery styles of Halaf, Samarra, and Obeid appear. As we observed in Part Two, Chapter 1, this sort of geometrical organization of a field was a new thing in the world at that time and its appearance poses a psychological problem. For why should it have been that just when a settled style of village life came into being, an art of abstract forms geometrically organized came into being too? The answer, I believe, is that in the period of the earlier hunting societies there was no differentiation of social functions except along sexual or age lines, every individual was technically a master of the whole cultural inheritance, and the communities were therefore constituted of practically equivalent individuals; whereas in the larger, more greatly differentiated communities of the high neolithic, there had already begun that tendency toward specialization which in the next period was to reach a climax. On the level of a primitive society adulthood consists in being a whole man.

In the later, differentiated type of society, on the other hand, adulthood consists in acquiring, first, a certain special art or skill, and then the ability to support or sustain the resultant tension—a psychological as well as sociological tension—between oneself (as merely a fraction of a larger whole) and others of totally different training, powers, and ideals, who constitute the other necessary organs of the body social. The sudden appearance in the high neolithic of a geometrically composed art form, wherein disparate elements were brought and held together as a balanced whole, seems to me to indicate that some such psychological problem must already have begun to emerge.

We have already noted, too, that in the pottery styles of this period various symbols appear: in the Halaf style of the northwestern area, just southward of the Taurus (Bull) Mountains of Anatolia (now Turkey), the form of a bull's head in association with figurines of the goddess, and with clay figures of the dove, cow, humped ox, sheep, goat, and pig. It was just to the north of this fruitful area, beyond the Black Sea, in the Ukraine, that a great number of paleolithic figurines of the goddess had appeared in the Aurignacian. That a connection must be supposed would seem to be clear.

Furthermore, we have noted that the symbols stressed in the Halaf ware are not quite the same as those of the Samarra style, which, with its chief area of distribution farther south and eastward, extended into Iran. The obvious conclusion to be drawn is that a number of mythological systems had been caught in the vortex of the new mythogenetic zone, and this conclusion is supported by the evidence of the later, literate period, when the earliest written documents appear, first in Sumer and then in neighboring Egypt. The impression one gets from these is of a considerable hodge-podge of differing mythologies being coordinated, synthesized, and syncretized by the new professional priesthoods. And how could the situation have been otherwise, when it was the serpent of the jungle and the bull of the steppes that were being brought together? They were soon to become melted and fused—recompounded—in such weird chimeric creatures as the bull-horned serpents, fish-tailed bulls, and lion-headed eagles that from now on would constitute the typical apparitions of an extremely sophisticated new world of myth.

4. In the epoch of the hieratic city state (3500–2500 B.C.), the basic cultural traits of all the high civilizations that have flourished since (writing, the wheel, the calendar, mathematics, royalty, priestcraft, a system of taxation, bookkeeping, etc.) suddenly appear, prehistory ends, and the literate era dawns. The whole city now, and not simply the temple compound, is conceived of as an imitation on earth of the cosmic order, while a highly differentiated, complexly organized society of specialists, comprising priestly, warrior, merchant, and peasant classes, is found governing all its secular as well as specifically religious affairs according to an astronomically inspired mathematical conception of a sort of magical consonance uniting in perfect harmony the universe (macrocosm), society (mesocosm), and the individual (microcosm).* A natural accord of earthly, heavenly, and individual affairs is imagined; and the game is no longer that of the buffalo dance or metamorphosed seed, but the pageant of the seven spheres —Mercury, Venus, Mars, Jupiter, Saturn, the moon, and the sun. These in their mathematics are the angelic messengers of the universal law. For there is one law, one king, one state, one universe. And beyond the walls of our little city state is darkness; but within is the order intended from all eternity for man, supported by the pivot of the king, who in his saintly imitation of the moon has purged from his heart all deviant impulse and been transubstantiated. He is the earthly moon, according to that magical law wherein A *is* B. His queen is the sun. The virgin priestess who will accompany him in death and be the bride of his resurrection is the planet Venus. And his four chief ministers of state—the lords of the treasury and of war, prime minister, and lord executioner—incarnate the powers, respectively, of the planets Mercury, Mars, Jupiter, and Saturn. Sitting about him in his throne room—when the moon is full and he therefore reveals himself, wearing, however, the veil that protects the world from his full radiance—the king and his court are the heavens themselves on earth.

* Cf. supra, pp. 146–150.

What a marvelous game!

In the neighboring pinpoint on the map, perhaps, the king would be the sun, his queen the moon, and the virgin priestess the planet Jupiter; the game would go by a different set of rules. But no matter what the local rules, wherever this mad dream was played to the limit, the mesocosm of the local state, conceived as a reflection of the universe, was actually a reflection of something from deep within man himself, pulled from his heart as the paintings were in the great caves, evoked now by the void of the universe itself—the labyrinth of the night and its threading adventurers on their mysterious journeys, the planets and the moon.

Moreover, in the symbolism of this new and larger play of destiny, the earlier themes were all subsumed—those of both the monster serpent and the animal master—to produce a far more sophisticated, multidimensional symbolic play, qualitatively different and far more potent, both to evoke and to order the multifarious energies of the psyche, than anything the primitive world had ever produced.

Perhaps the most amazing revelation that has ever come to us of what mythology meant in that remote, heaven-guided age, when the awesome mystery of the planets was enacted on earth by divine kings who at death took with them—back into the night sea—the whole cast of characters of their pageant, has been that of the "royal tombs" of Ur in the cemetery of the sacred Sumerian city of the moon-god Nanna. The excavated graves, as Sir Leonard Woolley, their discoverer, declares, included burials of two sorts: those of commoners and those of kings—or perhaps, as certain others now suggest, not of kings but of their substitutes, the priests who assumed their roles when their moment came to die. And it was noted that whereas the older of the private graves, though clustered around the royal tombs, were respectful of their sanctity, the newer graves invaded the royal burials, as though, their memory having faded, there had been left in later ages only a vague tradition that this was holy ground.[12]

The first of the royal tombs discovered had been plundered by grave robbers, so that little remained for the twentieth century

A.D.; however, something more than even the boldest imagination might have conceived soon came to light. Wrote Sir Leonard Woolley, describing the course of his dramatic discovery:

> We found five bodies lying side by side in a shallow sloping trench; except for the copper daggers at their waists and one or two small clay cups they had none of the normal furniture of a grave, and the mere fact of there being a number thus together was unusual. Then, below them, a layer of matting was found, and tracing this along we came to another group of bodies, those of ten women carefully arranged in two rows; they wore head-dresses of gold, lapis lazuli, and carnelian, and elaborate bead necklaces, but they too possessed no regular tomb furnishings. At the end of the row lay the remains of a wonderful harp, the wood of it decayed but its decoration intact, making its reconstruction only a matter of care; the upright wooden beam was capped with gold, and in it were fastened the gold-headed nails which secured the strings; the sounding-box was edged with a mosaic in red stone, lapis lazuli and white shell, and from the front of it projected a splendid head of a bull wrought in gold with eyes and beard of lapis lazuli; across the ruins of the harp lay the bones of the gold-crowned harpist.
>
> By this time we had found the earth sides of the pit in which the women's bodies lay and could see that the bodies of the five men were on the ramp which led down to it. Following the pit along, we came upon more bones which at first puzzled us by being other than human, but the meaning of them soon became clear. A little way inside the entrance to the pit stood a wooden sledge chariot. . . . In front of the chariot lay the crushed skeletons of two asses with the bodies of the grooms by their heads, and on the top of the bones was the double ring, once attached to the pole, through which the reins had passed; it was of silver, and standing on it was a gold "mascot" in the form of a donkey most beautifully and realistically modeled.
>
> Close to the chariot were an inlaid gaming-board and a collection of tools and weapons, . . . more human bodies, and then the wreckage of a large wooden chest adorned with a figured mosaic in lapis lazuli and shell which was found empty but had perhaps contained such perishable things as clothes. Behind this box were more offerings. . . . The objects were removed and we started to clear away the remains of the wooden box, a chest some 6 feet long and 3

feet across, when under it we found burnt bricks. They were fallen, but at one end some were still in place and formed the ring-vault of a stone chamber. The first and natural supposition was that here we had the tomb to which all the offerings belonged, but further search proved that the chamber was plundered, the roof had not fallen from decay but had been broken through, and the wooden box had been placed over the hole as if deliberately to hide it. Then, digging round the outside of the chamber, we found just such another pit as that 6 feet above. At the foot of the ramp lay six soldiers, orderly in two ranks, with copper spears by their sides and copper helmets crushed flat on the broken skulls; just inside, having evidently been backed down the slope, were two wooden four-wheeled wagons each drawn by three oxen—one of the latter so well preserved that we were able to lift the skeleton entire; the wagons were plain, but the reins were decorated with long beads of lapis and silver and passed through silver rings surmounted with mascots in the form of bulls; the grooms lay at the oxen's heads and the drivers in the bodies of the cars. . . .

Against the end wall of the stone chamber lay the bodies of nine women wearing the gala head-dress of lapis and carnelian beads from which hung golden pendants in the form of beech leaves, great lunate earrings of gold, silver "combs" like the palm of a hand with three fingers tipped with flowers whose petals are inlaid with lapis, gold, and shell, and necklaces of lapis and gold; their heads were leaned against the masonry, their bodies extended onto the floor of the pit, and the whole space between them and the wagons was crowded with other dead, women and men, while the passage which led along the side of the chamber to its arched door was lined with soldiers carrying daggers and with women. . . .

On the top of the bodies of the "court ladies" against the chamber wall had been placed a wooden harp, of which there survived only the copper head of a bull and the shell plaques which had adorned the sounding-box; by the side wall of the pit, also set on the top of the bodies, was a second harp with a wonderful bull's head in gold, its eyes, beard, and horn-tips of lapis, and a set of engraved shell plaques not less wonderful; there are four of these with grotesque scenes of animals playing the parts of men. . . .

Inside the tomb the robbers had left enough to show that it had contained bodies of several minor people as well as that of the chief person, whose name, if we can trust the inscription on a cylinder seal, was A-bar-gi; overlooked against the wall we found two model boats, one of copper now hopelessly decayed, the other of silver wonderfully well preserved; some 2 feet long, it has high stern and prow, five seats, and amidships an arched support for the awning which would protect the passenger, and the leaf-bladed oars are still set in the thwarts; it is a testimony to the conservatism of the East that a boat of identical type is in use today on the marshes of the Lower Euphrates, some 50 miles from Ur.

The king's tomb-chamber lay at the far end of this open pit; continuing our search behind it we found a second stone chamber built up against it either at the same time, or more probably, at a later period. This chamber, roofed like the king's with a vault of ring arches in burnt brick, was the tomb of the queen to whom belonged the upper pit with its ass-chariot and other offerings: her name, Shub-ad, was given us by a fine cylinder seal of lapis lazuli which was found in the filling of the shaft a little above the roof of the chamber and had probably been thrown into the pit at the moment when the earth was being put back into it. The vault of the chamber had fallen in, but luckily this was due to the weight of earth above, not to the violence of tomb-robbers; the tomb itself was intact.

At one end, on the remains of a wooden bier, lay the body of the queen, a gold cup near her hand, the upper part of the body was entirely hidden by a mass of beads of gold, silver, lapis lazuli, carnelian, agate, and chalcedony, long strings of which, hanging from a collar, had formed a cloak reaching to the waist and bordered below with a broad band of tubular beads of lapis, carnelian, and gold: against the right arm were three long gold pins with lapis beads and three amulets in the form of fish, two of gold and one of lapis, and a fourth in the form of two seated gazelles, also of gold.

The head-dress whose remains covered the crushed skull was a more elaborate edition of that worn by the court ladies: its basis was a broad gold ribbon festooned in loops round the hair—and the measurement of curves showed that this was not the natural hair but a wig padded out to an almost grotesque size. . . . By the side of the body lay a second head-dress of a novel sort. Onto a diadem made apparently of a strip of soft white leather had been sewn thousands of minute lapis lazuli beads, and against this background of solid blue were set a row of exquisitely fashioned gold animals, stags, gazelles, bulls, and goats, with between them clusters of

> pomegranates, three fruits hanging together shielded by their leaves, and branches of some other tree with golden stems and fruit or pods of gold and carnelian, while gold rosettes were sewn on at intervals, and from the lower border of the diadem hung palmettes of twisted gold wire.
>
> The bodies of two women attendants were crouched against the bier, one at its head and one at its foot, and all about the chamber lay strewn offerings of all sorts, another gold bowl, vessels of silver and copper, stone bowls, and clay jars for food, the head of a cow in silver, two silver tables for offerings, silver lamps, and a number of large cockle-shells containing green paint . . . , presumably used as a cosmetic.[13]

"Clearly," writes Sir Leonard at the conclusion of this vivid description of his truly astounding discovery, "when a royal person died, he or she was accompanied to the grave by all the members of the court: the king had at least three people with him in his chamber and sixty-two in the death-pit; the queen was content with some twenty-five in all." [14]

Several more such tombs were discovered, some even larger than the dual burial of King A-bar-gi and his queen Shub-ad—he and his court having been buried first and she and hers above, as when the moon sets and the planet Venus follows. In the largest tomb the bodies of sixty-eight women were found, "disposed in regular rows across the floor, every one lying on her side with legs slightly bent and hands brought up near her face, so close together that the heads of those in one row rested on the legs of those in the row above." [15] Twenty-eight of these women had worn hair-ribbons of gold, and all but one of the rest precisely the same type of ribbon of silver. All had been clothed in red cloaks, having beaded cuffs and shell-ring belts, and they had been adorned with great lunate earrings and multiple necklaces of blue and gold. Four were harpists, and these were grouped together with a copper caldron beside them, which Woolley associates with the manner of their death, suggesting that it contained the drink that bore this multitude through the winged gate to the other world.

"Clearly," he writes,

> these people were not wretched slaves killed as oxen might be killed, but persons held in honor, wearing their robes of

> office, and coming, one hopes, voluntarily to a rite which would in their belief be but a passing from one world to another, from the service of a god on earth to that of the same god in another sphere. . . . Human sacrifice was confined exclusively to the funerals of royal persons, and in the graves of commoners, however rich, there is no sign of anything of the sort, not even such substitutes, clay figurines, etc., as are so common in Egyptian tombs and appear there to be reminiscent of an ancient and more bloody rite. In much later times Sumerian kings were deified in their lifetime and honored as gods after their death: the pre-historic kings of Ur were in their obsequies so distinguished from their subjects because they too were looked upon as superhuman, earthly deities; and when the chroniclers wrote in the annals of Sumer that "after the Flood kingship again descended from the gods," they meant no less than this. If the king, then, was a god, he did not die as men die, but was translated; and it might therefore be not a hardship but a privilege for those of his court to accompany their master and continue in his service.[16]

"It is safe to assume," he says in conclusion, "that those who were to be sacrificed went down alive into the pit. That they were dead, or at least unconscious, when the earth was flung in and trampled down on the top of them is an equally safe assumption . . . , they are in such good order and alignment that we are driven to suppose that after they were lying unconscious someone entered the pit and gave the final touches to their arrangement. . . . It is most probable that the victims walked to their places, took some kind of drug—opium or hashish would serve—and lay down in order; after the drug had worked, whether it produced sleep or death, the last touches were given to their bodies and the pit was filled in." [17]

And what of the one young lady without a ribbon either of gold or of silver? Actually, she had had a ribbon of silver on her person. It was discovered among the bones of her skeleton at about the level of the waist: "carried apparently in the woman's pocket, it was just as she had taken it from her room, done up in a tight coil with the ends brought over to prevent its coming undone." [18] She had been late, apparently, for the ceremony and had not had time to put it on.

Here, then, is the prototype of the miserable little Shilluk affair of the king buried with a living virgin, whose bones then would be gathered with his into the hide of a bull. For it was the moon-bull, the symbol of the lunar destiny of all things and the mathematics of the universe, that sang to these people their song of dreams. A magical equation had been conceived: the bull and the cow (as in the cavern of Tuc d'Audoubert) : : the monster serpent and the maiden (as in the ritual of the Dema) : : the moon and the planet Venus (which as evening and as morning star is the herald both of night-sleep-death and of dawn-rebirth) : : the fertilizing waters of the abyss and the seed that is to bear much fruit : : the king and the queen.

Among the cylinder seals of Mesopotamia, where many of the basic motifs of the earliest mythology of this dawning age were aphoristically illustrated, there is an image, more than once encountered, in which, on a fleece-covered couch having legs shaped like those of a bull, a male and female lie extended with a priest officiating at their feet. "It seems certain," Dr. Henri Frankfort observes, "that we have here the ritual wedding of the god and goddess." [19] But in the period of the hieratic city state (though not in the later periods of Mesopotamia) the god and goddess were incarnate in the king and queen. In the queen's chamber of the royal tomb, as we have seen, there was "the head of a cow in silver." The king's chamber had been plundered, but there were harps fashioned in such a way that their bodies terminated in beautiful heads of gold—the heads of bulls with lapis lazuli beards: mythological bulls (supernormal images) from which the music of the myth and this ritual of destiny derived. It is not known by what means the kings were killed (or the priests who may have been serving by this time as their substitutes, about 2500 B.C.); but the manner of Shub-ad's death is perfectly clear. "On the remains of a wooden bier lay the body of the queen, a gold cup near her hand." [20] Her court was interred above his, but her own tomb had been sunk to the level of A-bar-gi's and placed beside it.

The myth being enacted in this mad rite was that of the ever-dying and resurrected god, "The Faithful Son of the Abyss," or

"The Son of the Abyss who Rises," Damuzi-absu, or Tammuz (Adonis). The queen of heaven, the daughter of God, goddess of the morning and evening star, the hierodule or slave-girl dancer of the gods—who, as the morning star, is ever-virgin, but, as evening star, is "the divine harlot," and whose names in a later age were to be Ishtar, Aphrodite, and Venus—"from the 'great above' set her mind toward the 'great below,' abandoned heaven, abandoned earth, and to the nether world descended," to release her brother and spouse from the land of no return.

By chance a fragment of her legend from the period of the tombs of Ur survives; and we have, also, just such a hymn as the tongues of the women of the gold and silver ribbons sang to the harps of the moon-bull that were found still in the grasp of the girl-harpists' skeleton arms:

Mayest thou go, thou shalt cause him to rejoice,
O valorous one, star of Heaven, go to greet him.
To cause Damu to repose, mayest thou go,
  Thou shalt cause him to rejoice.
To the shepherd Ur-Nammu mayest thou go,
  Thou shalt cause him to rejoice.

To the man Dungi mayest thou go,
  Thou shalt cause him to rejoice.
To the shepherd Bur-Sin mayest thou go,
  Thou shalt cause him to rejoice.

To the man Gimil-Sin mayest thou go,
  Thou shalt cause him to rejoice.
To the shepherd Ibi-Sin mayest thou go,
  Thou shalt cause him to rejoice.[21]

The five last titles are the names, in order, of the last kings of the Third Dynasty of Ur (about 2150–2050 B.C.)* and express well the fundamental concept of this whole archaic world, which was that the reality, the true being, of the king—as of any individual—is not in his character as individual but as archetype. He

* The dating of the dynasty varies according to the current authority. The dates above are from S. N. Kramer, *Sumerian Mythology* (*Memoirs of the American Philosophical Society*, Vol. XXI, 1944), p. 19. Henri Frankfort terminates the period 2025 B.C. (*The Birth of Civilization in the Near East* [London: Williams and Norgate, 1951], p. 77). Woolley's dates were 2278–2170 B.C. (*The Sumerians* [1928], p. 22).

is the good shepherd, the protector of cows; and the people are his flock, his herd. Or he is the one who walks in the garden, the gardener; the one who gives life to the fields, the farmer of the gods. Again, he is the builder of the city, the culture-bringer, the teacher of the arts. And he is the lord of the celestial pastures, the moon, the sun. The five kings—Ur-Nammu, Dungi, Bur-Sin, Gimil-Sin, and Ibi-Sin—are the same, namely, Damu, the ever-living, ever-dying god; just as the Queen is Inanna, the naked goddess, whom we have known since the beginning of time.

From the "great above" she set her mind toward the "great below,"
The goddess, from the "great above" she set her mind toward the "great below,"
Inanna, from the "great above" she set her mind toward the "great below."

My lady abandoned heaven, abandoned earth,
To the nether world she descended,
Inanna abandoned heaven, abandoned earth,
To the nether world she descended,
Abandoned lordship, abandoned ladyship,
To the nether world she descended.

The seven divine decrees she fastened at her side,
The shugurra, the crown of the plain, she put upon her head,
Radiance she placed upon her countenance,
The rod of lapis lazuli she gripped in her hand.

Small lapis lazuli stones she tied about her neck,
Sparkling stones she fastened to her breast,
A gold ring she gripped in her hand,
A breastplate she bound about her breast.

All the garments of ladyship she arranged about her body,
Ointment she put upon her face.
Inanna walked toward the nether world.[22]

Thus our precious fragment begins. The goddess is walking to the nether world, which is ruled by the dark side of her own self, her sister-goddess Ereshkigal. And she comes to the first gate.

When Inanna had arrived at the lapis lazuli palace of the nether world,
At the door of the nether world she acted evilly,

In the palace of the nether world she spoke evilly:
"Open the house, gatekeeper, open the house,
Open the house, Neti, open the house, all alone I would enter."

Neti, the chief gatekeeper of the nether world, answers the pure Inanna:
"Who, pray, art thou?"

"I am the queen of heaven, the place where the sun rises."

"If thou art the queen of heaven, the place where the sun rises,
Why, pray, hast thou come to the land of no return?
How has thy heart led thee to the road whose traveler does not return?"

The pure Inanna answers him:
"Ereshkigal, my elder sister,
The lord Gugalanna, her husband, has been killed:
I have come to attend the funeral."

The chief gatekeeper of the nether world, Neti, answers the pure Inanna:
"Stay, Inanna, let me speak to my queen."

He goes, and returns. Neti, the chief gatekeeper of the nether world, speaks to the pure Inanna:
"Come, Inanna, enter."

And the following dialogue then comes to pass.

Upon her entering the first gate,
The shugurra, the "crown of the plain" of her head, was removed.
"What, pray, is this?"
"Extraordinarily, O Inanna, have the decrees of the nether world been perfected,
O Inanna, do not question the rites of the nether world."

Upon her entering the second gate,
The rod of lapis lazuli was removed.
"What, pray, is this?"
"Extraordinarily, O Inanna, have the decrees of the nether world been perfected,
O Inanna, do not question the rites of the nether world."

Upon her entering the third gate,
The small lapis lazuli stones of her neck were removed.

"What, pray, is this?"
"Extraordinarily, O Inanna, have the decrees of the nether
world been perfected,
O Inanna, do not question the rites of the nether world."

Upon her entering the fourth gate,
The sparkling stones of her breast were removed.
"What, pray, is this?"
"Extraordinarily, O Inanna, have the decrees of the nether
world been perfected,
O Inanna, do not question the rites of the nether world."

Upon her entering the fifth gate,
The gold ring of her hand was removed.
"What, pray, is this?"
"Extraordinarily, O Inanna, have the decrees of the nether
world been perfected,
O Inanna, do not question the rites of the nether world."

Upon her entering the seventh gate,
All the garments of her body were removed.
"What, pray, is this?"
"Extraordinarily, O Inanna, have the decrees of the nether
world been perfected,
O Inanna, do not question the rites of the nether world."

Thus, naked, the goddess came before her sister and the seven judges of the nether world, Ereshkigal and the Anunnaki.

The pure Ereshkigal seated herself upon her throne,
The Anunnaki, the seven judges, pronounced judgement be-
fore her,
They fastened their eyes upon her, the eyes of death,
At their word, the word that tortures the spirit,
The sick woman was turned into a corpse,
And the corpse was hung from a stake.[23]

But death, as we are taught in all the mythological traditions of the world, is not the end. The lesson of the moon-god, three days dark, is still to be told. Inanna's corpse remained on the stake.

After three days and three nights had passed,
Her messenger Ninshubur,
Her messenger of favorable winds,
Her carrier of supporting words,
Filled the heaven with complaints for her,

Cried for her in the assembly shrine,
Rushed about for her in the house of the gods,
Like a pauper in a single garment he dressed for her,
To the Ekur, the house of Enlil, all alone he directed his step.

Ninshubur, known too as Papsukkal, "chief messenger of the gods," and Ilabrat, "the god of wings," was told by the goddess before her departure that if she did not return he should "Weep before Enlil (the air-god), weep before Nanna (the moon-god), and if these failed to respond, then weep before Enki, the lord of Wisdom (the serpent), who knows the food of life and the water of life. He," she said, "will surely bring me to life."

The clay figurines of Ninshubur, the messenger, found in foundation boxes beneath the doors of temples, show him without wings but bearing a staff or wand in his right hand.[24] He is the prototype of Hermes (Mercury), the Olympian messenger of the gods and the guide of souls to the underworld, who also brings souls to be born again and so is regarded as the generator both of new lives and of the New Life. Hermes' staff, it will be recalled, is the caduceus, with entwined serpents. But the meaning of these serpents is precisely the same as that of the ritual and myth we are now discussing: namely, it is a reference to the divine, world-renovating connubium of the monster serpent with the naked goddess in her serpent form.

Wishing to be certain of the reference of the sign of the caduceus, Dr. Henri Frankfort once sent an inquiry to the British Museum of Natural History. "The symbol in which you are interested may well represent two snakes pairing," Mr. H. W. Parker, Assistant Keeper of Zoology, replied. "As a general rule the male seizes the female by the back of the neck and the two bodies are more or less intertwined. . . . Vipers are said to have the bodies completely intertwined." "This, then," comments Dr. Frankfort, "explains most satisfactorily why the caduceus should have become the symbol of our god, who is thus characterized as the personification of the generative force of Nature." [25]

Hermes, the Greek carrier of the serpent staff—which is both beautiful and terrible and both bestows sleep and awakens—is the inventor of the lyre and of the art of making fire with the fire-sticks. He is, furthermore, the archetypal trickster god of the ancient world. We think of the bull-voiced lyres of the graves of Ur and of the Greek orgies where "bull-voices roared from somewhere out of the unseen" (Aeschylus, Fragment 57). We think of the young boy and girl of the fire-sticks in Africa, and their shocking rite.* And we think, too, of Coyote-trickster, who turned himself into a girl and became pregnant. Hermes, too, is androgyne, as one should know from the sign of his staff.

When the messenger, Ninshubur, then, Hermes' protoype, had wept to no effect first before Enlil and then before the moon-god, Nanna, of the city of Ur, he turned to Enki, "Lord of the Waters of the Abyss," who, when he had heard, cried out:

"What now has my daughter done! I am troubled,
What now has Inanna done! I am troubled,
What now has the queen of all the lands done! I am troubled,
What now has the hierodule of heaven done! I am troubled."

He brought forth dirt and fashioned two sexless creatures, two angels. To the one he gave the food of life; to the other he gave the water of life. And then he issued his commands.

"Upon the corpse hung from a stake direct the fear of the rays of fire,
Sixty times the food of life, sixty times the water of life, sprinkle upon it,
Verily Inanna will arise."

Upon the corpse hung from a stake they directed the fear of the rays of fire,
Sixty times the food of life, sixty times the water of life, they sprinkled upon it,
Inanna arose.

Inanna ascended from the nether world,
The Anunnaki fled,
And whoever of the nether world had descended peacefully to the nether world;
When Inanna ascended from the nether world,
Verily the dead hastened ahead of her.

* Supra, p. 169.

Inanna ascends from the nether world,
The small demons like reeds,
The large demons like tablet styluses,
Walk at her side. . . .[26]

The conclusion of the piece is missing. But the import of the image is clear enough. It is a theme that has been given many turns in the course of the centuries since. One thinks, for example, of Mary Magdalene at the tomb, weeping outside the tomb; and as she wept she stooped to look within. But she saw two angels sitting in white where the body of Jesus had been, one at the head and one at the feet, and they said to her, "Woman, why are you weeping?" She answered, "Because they have taken away my Lord, and I do not know where they have laid him." Saying which, she turned around and saw Jesus standing, but did not know that it was Jesus. He said to her: "Woman, why are you weeping? Whom do you seek?" And supposing him to be the gardener, she said, "Sir, if you have carried him away, tell me where you have laid him, and I will take him away." He said to her, "Mary!" She turned, and she said to him in Hebrew, "Teacher!" Jesus said to her, "Do not hold me; for I have not yet ascended to the Father; but go to my brethren and say to them, I am ascending to my Father and your Father, to my God and your God." Then Mary Magdalene went and said to the disciples, "I have seen the Lord." [27]

III. The Great Diffusion

Huizinga, in his highly suggestive study of the play element in culture, *Homo Ludens,* points out that the Dutch and German words for "duty," *Plicht* and *Pflicht,* are related etymologically to our English "play," the words being derived from a common root.[28] English "pledge," too, is of this context, as well as the verb "plight," meaning "to put under a pledge, to engage" (as in "to plight troth," "a plighted bride"). We may recall here Huizinga's reference to the Japanese "play language," or "polite language" (*asobase-kotoba*), where it is not said that "you arrive in Tokyo," but that "you play arrival"; not that "I hear your father is dead," but that "I hear your father has played dying." [29] "The play-concept as such is of a higher order than seriousness," Huizinga declares. "For seriousness seeks to exclude play, whereas play can very well include seriousness." [30]

The royal tombs of Ur illustrate the capacity and spirit of the world's first aristocracy for play: pledging in play and then playing out the pledge. And it was in their utterly wonderful nerve for this particular game that the world was lifted from savagery to civilization. In such a performance the question of belief is of secondary moment and effect. The principle is that of the masque, the dance, the pageant, the motion pattern through the form of which a new power for life is evoked. An image is conceived, a supernormal image, surpassing in scope the requirements of food, clothing, shelter, sex, and a pleasant hobby for one's leisure time. Nerve is required to move into such a game and to play out the fraction of one's part in the picture. But then, behold! a transformation of life, an increment such as before had not been even imagined, and therewith a new horizon, both for man and for his gods. It was in the marvelous talent of the Sumerians for their extremely demanding divine play that civilization was born as a function of an aristocracy of spirit. And it was continued as such in many parts of the world up to a very recent date.

Now, as Sir Leonard Woolley has already shown, the effigies of servants at their tasks in certain Egyptian tombs indicate that at one time the courts of the Nile too went with their kings into the underworld. Likewise, in the royal tombs of ancient China ceramic effigies have been found. In fact, in China the practice of human sacrifice at royal entombments persisted until well into the twelfth century A.D.; and in the neighboring island empire of Japan an impressive instance of the custom of voluntary "dead following" (*jinchu,* "loyalty") came to the notice of the world as late as 1912, when the general Count Nogi, the hero of Port Arthur, put himself to death at the precise hour of the burial of his Mikado, Meiji-tenno, and the Countess Nogi then killed herself to accompany her spouse.

It is clear from the evidence that the ritual of "dead following" was a generally honored social and religious practice, not only in the cities of the Near East, where the epochal transition was made from savagery to civilization, but also wherever the earliest carriers of the new game of destiny settled in their astonishingly broad and rapid conquest of new fields. The diffusion of their influence can be readily traced in the four directions—or rather, to the points between—somewhat as follows.

THE SOUTHWESTWARD DIFFUSION

Already we have heard something of the early diffusion of this high culture complex to the Sudan. Far to the south, in the area marked by the great stone temple ruins of Zimbabwe, in South Rhodesian Matabeleland, ritual regicide appears to have been practiced until as late as 1810. The stars and a sacred oracle were consulted by the priests every four years and, without fail, the verdict would be "death for the king." The custom there was that the king's first wife—who had assisted him with the making of the sacred first fire of his reign—should strangle him with a cord made of the foot-sinew of a bull. The night should be a night of the new moon. The corpse should be taken by the priests that night to a hut on the summit of a mountain and there placed on a platform beneath which a great leathern sack should be hung. The first day, the entrails of the king were removed and tossed into the sack; the second, the body was stuffed with herbs and leaves and sewn up again. On the third day, the skull was opened from behind and its contents were emptied into the sack. The fourth day, the corpse was lashed in a crouch position, swathed with cloth in such a way that the toe- and fingertips with their nails should protrude, and then wrapped in the fresh hide of a jet-black bull with a white mark on its forehead. Every night for a full year a priest would open the bull hide and massage the mummy in such a way that its liquid and maggots as well as toe and fingernails should drop into the sack. And when this year was accomplished—once again on a night of the new moon—the favorite wife of the king (not she who had strangled him, but another) was compelled to submit to the removal of her clothing, piece by piece, after which she was strangled, naked. The body was brought into a cave on the east slope of the mountain; the king's body into one on the west. And when the king had been immured, the dead queen was clothed and likewise immured. The most elaborate ceremonies, however, were reserved for the transportation of the sack from the charnel hut on top of the mountain to a holy cave in its side. Three people were slain as sacrifices and the sack was sealed within the cave—with a hollow reed leading from the chamber to the outer world. A priest watched this reed until, one day, the king's soul emerged from it in the form of a worm, beetle, lizard, snake, or some other small dragon; whereupon the reed was removed, the hole was sealed, and offerings were made that should be annually renewed.[31]

"In all of our mappings of historical culture movements in Africa," Frobenius writes, "no distribution is repeated more frequently than that of a broad plain down the east coast from the Nile to the Zambesi—that is to say, running in a north-to-south direction and lying close to the Eritrean shore—and then two tongues extending westward from this belt across the continent, the one in the north reaching as far as to Senegal. [See map, p. 167.] These two transverse areas reveal divergencies, which, however, are by far neither as numerous nor as important as the signs of inner accord and unity." [32]

And elsewhere he writes:

> The fragments of mythology and ritual that have come to light in southeast Africa, in the nuclear zone of the southern part of the Eritrean sphere, compel us to reconstruct an image that resembles that of the Sumerian and the Indian Dravidian lore of life and the gods as closely as one egg resembles another. The moon-god imaged as a great bull; his wife, the planet Venus; the goddess offers her life for her spouse; and everywhere, this goddess, as the Morning Star, is the goddess of war, as Evening Star a goddess of illicit love, and a universal mother besides; in all three zones (Africa, Dravidian India, and Sumer) the drama of the astral sky is the model and very destiny of all life, and when projected as such upon earth gave rise to what may have been the very earliest form and concept of the state—namely, that of a sacred, cosmic, priestly image. Is it too bold, given these circumstances, to speak of a Great Eritrean Culture Zone, which in ancient times comprised the shores of the Indian Ocean? [33]

We can regard this Great Eritrean area as the first zone of diffusion of the mythology of our mythogenetic Fertile Crescent; for a basal neolithic culture stratum has been identified as early as about 4500 B.C. in the Nile Valley; and a high neolithic about 4000. Furthermore, there is now dependable C-14 evidence that something of the neolithic had reached Northern Rhodesia as early as c. 4000 B.C.,[34] while the arts of the Bronze and Iron Ages surely were established in Sudanese Napata by, respectively, c. 750–744 and c. 397–362 B.C.[35]

The chief Egyptian sites of the basal stratum are on the left bank of the Nile, at Merimde, in the Delta region, and at Fayum, somewhat farther south, as well as on the right bank, about two hundred miles up the river, at Tasa. The assemblages differ slightly among themselves but in their culture level are about equivalent, the characteristic features being a rough black pottery; excellent basketry; spindle whorls for the fashioning of linen; palettes for cosmetics; burial in a contracted posture (at Tasa) or as in sleep, facing east (Merimde); bone, ivory, and (at Fayum) ostrich-shell beads; boar's-tusk and tiny stone-ax (celt) amulets (at Merimde); wheat stored in silos; and a barnyard stock of swine, cattle, sheep, and goats. C-14 dates for Fayum range c. 4440–c. 4100 B.C.

Merimde and Fayum, owing to an encroachment of the desert, were abandoned toward the close of this period, while at Tasa a new racial stock appeared with a high neolithic style of culture, the so-called Badarian. A beautiful red-to-brown pottery shaped and fired with a skill never excelled in the Nile Valley, clay and ivory female figurines (the first in Egypt), pottery models of boats, and the first signs of copper give the clue to the level of this culture. In the hunt the Badarians used the boomerang, and their racial traits suggest Frobenius' Great Eritrean zone. Cattle and sheep, as though deified, were sometimes given ceremonial burial, and human remains faced west, not east, toward the land of the setting, not the rising, sun. No bones of the pig have been discovered among their remains, and this may signal the commencement of a tradition of abstention from the flesh of swine. An association of the pig with some despised alien or socially inferior group, or with a mythology of the underworld, would suffice to account for such an avoidance—which, in any case, cannot possibly have been rationalized, in the usual modernist way, as a prophylaxis against a possible case of trichinosis. The boar's tooth, as we have just seen, was a fetish of the Merimde of the Delta, while, in contrast, the sacred beasts of the Badarians of the Upper Nile were the bull and ram.

A second high neolithic stratum overlies the Badarian—the Amratian, where five new types of pottery appear, decorated with figures and geometrical designs that do not have the elegance, formal beauty, or mathematical regularity of those of Mesopotamia, but on the other hand are extremely interesting for their obvious derivation from the Capsian art style of North Africa and Eastern Spain. The human forms, furthermore, show that the manner of dress had not changed. The men still wore decorated penis sheaths and were otherwise stark naked, with grass sandals and with feathers in their hair. The women wore linen aprons, and frequently shaved their heads to wear wigs. The physical type was about that of the Capsians: 5 feet 3 inches tall, slender, slightly built, with a long, small skull, small features, and straight hair. The bodies were tattooed. Figures of clay and ivory; copper, sometimes used now for small tools; papyrus-bundle boats; a number of types of arrowhead, and many elegant stone blades characterize the assemblage. Imports of malachite from Sinai, gold from Nubia, coniferous wood from Syria, and obsidian from Armenia and the Aegean speak for a development of trade—while in the graves we find that dogs were buried with their masters (perhaps as guides to the land of the dead), as well as statuettes of women and servants.[36]

But then, abruptly, something new in the Delta: hieroglyphic writing, the calendar, the mythology of the sun-god Horus and resurrected god Osiris, trading fleets sailing the seas to Crete, Syria, and Palestine, flying the signal flags of their nomes, the harpoon flag and the fish flag! There is an elegance in the arts and life style of pre-dynastic and dynastic Egypt completely different from those of the mythogenetic zone of Southwest Asia. Furthermore, in Egypt the new arts were applied to life in new ways. The mythology was adjusted to a geography in which the fertility of the earth sprang from the Nile, not from the clouds; and to a protected land—a grandiose oasis—unified and held in form with comparative ease, in contrast to the motherland of Southwest Asia, where city was to battle city and then empire empire for millenniums. But a complete contrast in style does not rule out in any way our recognition of the impact of a new idea, derived by diffusion from an alien land. Nor is the diffusion random; it is selective. The wheel appeared in Sumer about 3200 B.C., but not in Egypt until fourteen hundred years later. For the Nile supplied the best possible transportation; and it was not until the light war chariot, maneuverable in battle and drawn by steeds, had been invented that the wheel recommended itself as a valuable addition to the culture of the Pharaohs. The date of the introduction of writing, the calendar, and their associated arts to Egypt was c. 2800 B.C. that of the wheel, c. 1800 B.C.

The basic myth of dynastic Egypt was that of the death and resurrection of Osiris, the good king, "fair of face," who was born to the earth-god Geb and sky-goddess Nut. He was born together with his sister-wife, the goddess Isis, during the sacred interval of those five supplementary days that fell between one Egyptian calendric year of 360 days and the next.* He and his sister were the first to plant wheat and barley, to gather fruit from trees, and to cultivate the vine, and before their time the races of the world had been savage cannibals. But Osiris's evil brother, Set, whose sister-wife was the goddess Nephthys, was mortally jealous both of his virtue and of his fame, and so, stealthily taking the measure of his good brother's body, he caused a beautifully decorated sarcophagus to be fashioned and on a certain occasion in the palace, when all were drinking and making merry, had it brought into the room and jestingly promised to give it to the one whom it should fit exactly. All tried, but, like the glass slipper of Cinderella, it fitted but one; and when Osiris, the last, laid himself within it, immediately a company of seventy-two conspirators with whom Set had contrived his plot dashed forward, nailed the lid upon the sarcophagus, soldered it with molten lead, and flung it into the Nile, down which it floated to the sea.

* Cf. supra, p. 147.

Isis, overwhelmed with grief, sheared off her locks, donned mourning, and searched in vain, up and down the Nile; but the coffer had been carried by the tide to the coast of Phoenicia, where, at Byblos, it was cast ashore. A tamarisk immediately grew up around it, enclosing the precious object in its trunk, and the aroma of this tree then was so glorious that the local king and queen, Melqart and Astarte—who were, of course, a divine king and queen themselves, the local representatives, in fact, of the common mythology of Damuzi and Inanna, Tammuz and Ishtar, Adonis and Aphrodite, Osiris and Isis—discovering and admiring its beauty, had the tree felled and fashioned into a pillar of their palace.

The bereaved and sorrowing Isis, meanwhile, wandering over the world in her quest—like Demeter in search of the lost Persephone—came to Byblos, where she learned of the wonderful tree. And, placing herself by a well of the city, in mourning, veiled and in humble guise—again like Demeter *—she spoke to none until there approached the well the handmaidens of the queen, whom she greeted kindly. Braiding their hair, she breathed upon them such a wondrous perfume that when they returned and Astarte saw and smelt the braids she sent for the stranger, took her into the house, and made her the nurse of her child.

The great goddess gave the infant her finger instead of breast to suck and at night, having placed him in a fire to burn away all that was mortal, flew in the form of a swallow around the pillar, mournfully chirping. But the child's mother, Queen Astarte, happening in upon this scene, shrieked when she spied her little son resting in the flame and thereby deprived him of the priceless boon. Whereupon Isis, revealing her true nature, begged for the pillar and, removing the sarcophagus, fell upon it with a cry of grief so loud that the queen's child died on the spot. Sorrowing, then, the two women placed Osiris's coffer on a boat, and when the goddess Isis was alone with it at sea, she opened the chest and, laying her face on the face of her brother, kissed him and wept.

The myth goes on to tell of the blessed boat's arrival in the marshes of the Delta, and of how Set, one night hunting the boar

* Cf. supra, pp. 183–185.

by the light of the full moon, discovered the sarcophagus and tore the body into fourteen pieces, which he scattered abroad; so that, once again, the goddess had a difficult task before her. She was assisted, this time, however, by her little son Horus, who had the head of a hawk, by the son of her sister Nephthys, little Anubis, who had the head of a jackal, and by Nephthys herself, the sister-bride of their wicked brother Set.

Anubis, the elder of the two boys, had been conceived one very dark night, we are told, when Osiris mistook Nephthys for Isis; so that by some it is argued that the malice of Set must have been inspired not by the public virtue and good name of the noble culture hero, but by this domestic inadvertence. The younger, but true son, Horus, on the other hand, had been more fortunately conceived—according to some, when Isis lay upon her dead brother in the boat, or, according to others, as she fluttered about the palace pillar in the form of a bird.

The four bereaved and searching divinities, the two mothers and their two sons, were joined by a fifth, the moon-god Thoth (who appears sometimes in the form of an ibis-headed scribe, at other times in the form of a baboon), and together they found all of Osiris save his genital member, which had been swallowed by a fish. They tightly swathed the broken body in linen bandages, and when they performed over it the rites that thereafter were to be continued in Egypt in the ceremonial burial of kings, Isis fanned the corpse with her wings and Osiris revived, to become the ruler of the dead. He now sits majestically in the underworld, in the Hall of the Two Truths, assisted by forty-two assessors, one from each of the principal districts of Egypt; and there he judges the souls of the dead. These confess before him, and when their hearts have been weighed in a balance against a feather, receive, according to their lives, the reward of virtue and the punishment of sin.[37]

The myth is clearly of the family of Damuzi-absu and Inanna. However, the symbolic animal involved—at least in this version of the great adventure—was not the moon-bull, as in the Mesopotamian myths and rites of the royal tombs of Ur, but the pig, as in the Greek rituals of Persephone and Melanesian of Hainuwele. For Set, as we have just seen, was hunting the boar on the night of the full moon when he found and dismembered the body of Osiris. Comparably, according to Ovid, the young Adonis, beloved of Venus-Aphrodite (the classical counterpart of both Isis and Inanna), was killed by a wild boar when out hunting.[38] And the Phrygian ever-dying and resurrected divinity, Attis, following one version of his legend, was likewise gored by a boar—but, according to another, was himself a pig.[39] Apparently, therefore, we have here the evidence either of two periods or of two provinces of the same essential myth; one associating the bull, but the other a boar, with the force of the abyss.

THE NORTHWESTWARD DIFFUSION

"There is a land called Crete in the midst of the wine-dark sea," we read in the *Odyssey*, "a fair land and a rich, begirt with water, and therein are many men innumerable, and ninety cities. And all have not the same speech, but there is confusion of tongues; there dwell Achaeans and there too Cretans of Crete, high of heart, and Cydonians there and Dorians of waving plumes and goodly Pelasgians. And among these cities is the mighty city Cnossus, wherein Minos when he was nine years old began to rule, he who held converse with great Zeus. . . ."[40]

Professor Bedřich Hrozný has pointed out that in Cnossus, the capital of ancient Crete, the kings ruled "through periods of nine years" and that Homer's reference to the nine years of Minos must be a reflection of this circumstance.[41] Frazer, in *The Golden Bough,* in his chapters on "The Killing of the Divine King," states that the period of the rule of Minos was eight years and suggests that the Athenian legend of the tribute of seven youths and seven maidens sent to Cnossus periodically to be consumed by the Minotaur may have had some connection with Cretan ceremonials devoted to the renewal of the kingly power. "At the end of each period," says Frazer in his discussion of King Minos, "he retired for a season to the oracular cave on Mount Ida, and there communed with his divine father Zeus, giving him an account of his kingship in the years that were past, and receiving from him instructions for his guidance in those which were to come. The tradition plainly implies," he continues, "that at the end of every eight years the king's sacred powers needed to be renewed by intercourse with the godhead, and without such a renewal he would have forfeited his right to the throne." [42]

Nine years or eight; in either case, the Cretan tradition gives evidence of an actual or modified periodic regicide, and we may think, therefore, of the late Athenian legend of Theseus' victory over the Minotaur at the opening epoch of the Occidental, humanistic tradition, as a northern, European prototype of the Nubian victory of Far-li-mas and the princess Sali over the priests whose function it was to constrain man to heed the revelation of God's writing in the sky.

We have already mentioned both the diffusion of the Halaf ware motifs of the bull and the naked goddess, the maltese cross, double ax, and beehive tomb, from the Syrian area to Crete, and the further diffusion of the Cretan motifs of the labyrinth and megalithic mound burial westward, through Gibraltar to Ireland. A second way of diffusion was by land, largely up the valleys of the Danube and Dniester, the former leading to the heart of Central Europe—south Germany, Switzerland, and southern France—and the latter to the Vistula and the Baltic. For already, in the fourth millennium B.C., radiations from the Tigris-Euphrates were crossing the Caucasus to the northern shores of the Black Sea and radiations from the Aegean had begun to penetrate the Balkans.

Indeed, a secondary mythogenetic zone of prodigious import for the future is to be seen developing now, immediately northwest of the nuclear matrix of the Fertile Crescent. Here a vigorous population of mesolithic hunters were receiving ideas and new techniques from the great centers of the south much in the way of our Apache Indians of Part Three.* And retaining all their savagery while finding their powers of attack and plunder increased, they soon became a source of really terrible danger to the farming villages and merchant cities of the primary zone. Their style was pastoral, not sedentary, stressing stock-breeding, not agriculture; and even though they had not yet mastered the warrior's mount, the horse, they were adequately mobile with their

* Supra, pp. 238–239.

oxen carts and could readily surprise and overwhelm a sleeping town. They could also drive and scatter their less advanced paleolithic cousins to the wastelands of the arctic north. And they could move eastward as well, toward China. We may think of the arc above the Black Sea as their matrix—Bulgaria, Rumania, and the Ukraine—the lands of the lower Danube, Dniester, Dnieper, and Don. But the reach of their influence has been traced from the arctic to the tropics, and from Ireland to the South China Sea.

Richly furnished royal burial mounds (known variously as kurgans, barrows, or tumuli); smaller graves containing skeletons in the crouch position liberally sprinkled with red ocher; ceremonially buried bulls; a type of pottery bearing cord-marked and incised, zigzag, triangular, and stippled decorations; another type incised with loops and spirals; copper tools and beads, spiral earrings, and hammer-headed pins of bone and copper mark the passage of these folk as they pass from their homeland in the Caucasus area, westward along the northern shore of the Black Sea, and then, on the one hand, southward into Rumania, Bulgaria, and the Balkans, and, on the other, northward to the Baltic, southern Scandinavia, northern France, and the British Isles.[43] The dating of this diffusion, c. 2500–1500 B.C., is about the same as that of the seaways from Crete westward and the megalithic "giant graves" of France, Spain, Portugal, southern Scandinavia, Denmark, northern Germany, and the British Isles.

Up the Danube, meanwhile, a gradual advance of the peasants, slow wave upon wave, gradually conquered the greater part of Europe. Their various potteries again show incised, but also gracefully painted designs in meanders, spirals, and linked spirals. In the area of the Swiss lakes a folk who wore as amulets boars' tusks, as well as fragments of human skull, dwelt in pile dwellings over the water, while planting crops ashore of emmer and wheat, millet and flax.

In the Aegean itself, this was the great period of the flowering of the Bronze Age civilizations, with the powerful city of Troy (Hissarlik II) as one of the leading trading centers, and the fleets of the Cycladic Isles and Crete as the dominant conveyors oversea. Wherever tin was found, there was a mining outpost in continuous—even if remote—commercial contact with the major centers; and two important areas of such mining enterprise were Transylvania, in what is now Rumania, and Cornwall, in southwestern England. The gold of Ireland, furthermore, was abundant and greatly prized, and this too conduced to a maintenance of cultural bonds; while the precious amber of the Baltic flowed in a slow but steady trickle southward, through Central Europe, to the Adriatic.

We may take the Irish royal burial mound of New Grange as a typical monument of the period and a sign or marker, furthermore, of the reach of the northwestward diffusion. This tomb is the largest of a number in a broad area on the river Boyne, about five miles above Drogheda, known as *Brugh na Boinne* ("Palace of the Boyne") and traditionally associated with a mysterious personage called variously *Oengus an Brogha* ("Oengus of the Palace") or *Oengus mac in Dagda* ("Oengus, Son of the Good God"). The height of the burial mound of New Grange, which originally must have been greater, is now some forty-two feet, while the diameter is nearly three hundred. Originally the whole hemispherical surface was covered with a layer of quartz fragments, so that, sparkling in the sun, the monument would have been seen for many miles around. Moreover, a curb of slabs, about a hundred in number, some four feet in breadth and six to ten feet long, forms an unbroken ring around the structure and on certain of these formidable rocks engraved designs appear of zigzags, lozenges, circles and herring bones, spirals and linked spirals. A rough and narrow passage, roofed and walled by great slabs, some as long as fifteen feet, penetrates the southeast quarter of the mound, from behind an extremely handsome engraved curbing stone; and at the end of this tunnel is a cross-shaped burial chamber, where the remains of the kings were placed, probably in urns.

The relics, however, and everything else portable, were removed in the year 861 A.D., when the grave was plundered by Scandinavian pirates, so that today nothing remains but the eerie passage, 62 feet long, and the chamber, 21 feet from side to side and 18 feet in depth,[44] with its curious labyrinthine spirals on the walls and ceiling, an interesting floor stone with two worn sockets, where a man might have been made to kneel, and the still more interesting circumstance that precisely at sunrise, one day in eight years (or, at least, so the local story goes), the morning star may be seen to rise and cast its beam precisely to the place of the stone with the two worn sockets. The tale may be true or not, but the coincidence of eight years with the period assigned by Frazer to the reigning term of the kings of Crete gave me a shock when I heard it; and here it is, therefore, for the reader to take or to leave as he likes—or to go to Ireland, perhaps, to prove.

These grave tumuli in Ireland are associated with the fairy folk, who of old were the mighty Tuatha De Danann, "the tribes or folk of the goddess Danu."[45] Defeated in a great battle by the Milesians (the legendary ancestors of the Irish people, who are supposed to have arrived by sea from the Near East, via Spain, about a thousand years before the birth of Christ), the people of the goddess withdrew from the surface of the land to the *sid* (pronounced shee), the fairy hills, where they dwell to this day in Elysian bliss, and without touch of age, as the fairy folk. Deep under ground they have built themselves timeless abodes, glorious with gold and ablaze with the light of glittering gems.[46]

Danu, their mother, is again our goddess of many names. She is Anu, a goddess of plenty, after whom two hills in Kerry are called "the Paps of Anu," but who is said also to have been a savage woman devouring human beings.[47] Brigit, the goddess of knowledge, poetry, and the arts, was another aspect of this great "mother of gods," who had two sisters of the same name, connected with leechcraft and smithwork; and her worship is continued in the Irish devotion to Saint Brigit, at whose shrine in Kildare a sacred fire was maintained by nineteen nuns in turn, and on the twentieth day by the saint herself. "Similar sacred fires were kept in other monasteries," writes one of the chief authorities in this field, Dr. J. A. MacCulloch, "and they point to the old cult of the goddess of fire, the nuns being successors of a virgin priesthood like the vestals, priestesses of Vesta. Brigit . . . must have originated in a period when the Celts worshiped goddesses rather than gods, and when knowledge—leechcraft, agriculture, inspiration—were women's rather than men's. She had a female priesthood and men were perhaps excluded from her cult, as the tabued shrine at Kildare suggests." [48]

Other famous figures of the rich fairy lore of the *sid* are Aine, the fairy queen at whose seat, Knockainy in Limerick, some of the rites connected with her former cult are still performed, on Midsummer Eve, for a fruitful harvest, and who, at one time, according to local legend, was the captured fairy-bride of the Earl of Desmond; further, Morrigan, Neman, Macha, and Badb, the goddesses of battle; likewise, the hags, the fairy mistresses, and the washers at the ford, the banshee; and again, the White Women who assist in spinning. Among the Celts of ancient Gaul a feast and sacrifice were offered for every animal taken in the chase, to a goddess whom the Romans equated with Diana, who was thought of as rushing through the forest with an attendant train, the leader of the "furious host"; and when the great pagan days were ended she became the leader of the witches' revels. In a bronze statuette this same goddess of the Celts is shown riding a wild boar, "her symbol," as MacCulloch tells us, "and, like herself, a creature of the forest, but at an earlier time itself a divinity of whom the goddess became the anthropomorphic form." [49]

In fact, according to an Irish folktale told to this day in the peasant cottages of Connaught, the ancient hero Oisin—one of the sons of the fabulous giant Finn MacCool—was for many days annoyed in his fort and palace at Knock an Ar by a supernatural female with a pig's head, who was always making up to him and coming toward him, and this he did not particularly like. And it was usual in those days—as the tale goes on to tell—for the great warriors to go hunting on the hills and mountains; and whenever one of them did so he never neglected to take with him five or six strong men to bring home the game. And yet it so happened that on a day when Oisin had set out with his men and dogs to the woods in this way, he ranged so far and killed so much game that when it was brought together the men were so weak, tired, and hungry that they were unable to carry it, but went away home and left him, with his three dogs, to shift for himself. However, the female with the pig's head—who was the daughter of the king of the Land of Youth and herself, indeed, the queen of Youth—had been following closely in the hunt all day, and when the men departed she came up to Oisin.

"I am very sorry," Oisin said to her, "to leave behind anything that I've had the trouble of killing."

And she replied, "Tie up the bundle for me and I'll carry it to lighten your load."

So Oisin gave her a bundle of the game to carry and took the remainder himself; but the evening was warm and the game heavy, and when they had gone some distance, Oisin said, "Let us rest a while." Both threw down their burdens, and put their backs against a great stone that was by the roadside. The woman was heated and out of breath and opened her dress to cool herself. Then Oisin looked at her and saw her beautiful form and her white bosom.

"Oh then," said he, "it's a pity you have the pig's head on you; for I have never seen such an appearance on a woman in all my life before."

"Well," said she, "my father is the king of the Land of Youth, and I was the finest woman in his kingdom and the most beautiful of all, till he put me under a Druidic spell and gave me the pig's head that's on me now in place of my own. And the Druid of the Land of Youth came to me afterward and told me that if one of the sons of Finn MacCool would marry me, the pig's head would vanish and I should get back my face in the same form as it was before my father struck me with the Druid's wand. When I heard this I never stopped till I came to Erin, where I found your father and picked you out among the sons of Finn MacCool, and followed you to see would you marry me and set me free."

"If that is the state you are in, and if marriage with me will free you from the spell, I'll not leave the pig's head on you long."

So they got married without delay, not waiting to take home the game or to lift it from the ground. That moment the pig's head was gone and the king's daughter had the same face and beauty that she had before her father struck her with the Druidic wand.

"Now," said the queen of Youth to Oisin, "I cannot stay here long, and unless you come with me to the Land of Youth we must part."

"Oh," said Oisin, "wherever you go I'll go and wherever you turn I'll follow."

Then she turned and Oisin went with her, not going back to Knock an Ar to see his father or his son. That very day they set out for the Land of Youth and never stopped till they came to her father's castle; and when they arrived, there was a welcome before them, for the king had thought his daughter was lost. That same year there was to be a choice of a king, and when the appointed day came at the end of the seventh year all the great men and the champions and the king himself met together at the front of the castle to run and see who should be the first in the chair on the hill; but before a man of them was halfway to the hill, Oisin was sitting above in the chair before them. After that time no one stood up to run for the office against Oisin and he spent many a happy year as king in the Land of Youth.[50]

THE SOUTHEASTWARD DIFFUSION

The archaeology of India entered a new phase in the early twenties of the present century when a dramatic revelation of archaic cities antedating the arrival of the Vedic Aryans occurred at three widely separated sites in the Indus Valley: Mohenjo-daro, Chanhu-daro, and Harappa—the first two being in the lower quarter of the valley and the last in the Punjab, far to the north. The dating is c. 2500–1200/1000 B.C.; but earlier levels, since discovered in India, suggest a neolithic base going back perhaps to the fourth millennium. The beasts domesticated were the humped, long-horned Indian bull, a short-horned bull, the pig, buffalo, dog, horse, sheep, and elephant. Spinning and weaving were known, and the metals were gold, silver, copper, tin, and lead. Side by side with the metal tools, however, were knives made of flakes of chert, as well as stone axes and maces, revealing that even in the latest levels of this culture province the influence of the neolithic age had not completely passed.

Four stages can be readily distinguished in the Indian series.

1. The pre-Harappan simple village cultures of perhaps the late

fourth millennium B.C. Derivation, by way of Iran, from the Mesopotamian mythogenetic zone is indicated by the painted pottery styles, but the level of civilization was considerably below that of the contemporary high neolithic and hieratic city states of Mesopotamia.* The architecture is poorly developed; metal is either unknown or little used; and the industries are chiefly of pottery, chert, and shell. The familiar triangular, zigzag, meander, checker, lozenge, and double ax motifs appear, as well as—once again—a series of crude female statuettes, often associated with figures of the bull, and some even with evidences of human sacrifice.

2. The so-called Harappa stage of the great cities of Mohenjo-daro, Chanhu-daro, and Harappa (c. 2500–1200/1000 B.C.), which bursts abruptly into view, without preparation, already fully formed and showing many completely obvious signs of inspiration from the earlier high centers of the West, yet undeniable signs, also, of a native Indian tradition—this too already well developed. As Professor W. Norman Brown has suggested,[51] a native Indian center (i.e., a mythogenetic zone) somewhere either in the south or in the Ganges-Jumna area would seem to be indicated, where the characteristically Indian traits, unknown at this time farther west, must have come into form. For on two of the stamp-seals of the period we find figures seated on low thrones in the meditating yoga posture. One of these is flanked by two kneeling worshipers and rearing serpents, while the other, with two gazelles reposing beneath his seat, is surrounded by four wild beasts—a water buffalo, rhinoceros, elephant, and tiger. It is well known that precisely these compositions are associated in later Hindu and Buddhist art both with the god Shiva and with the Buddha. One can only suppose that the practice of yoga must already have been developed and associated with the concept of a heightened state of consciousness, not only worthy of worship but also capable of quelling and fascinating the animal world—like the music of Orpheus in the later tradition of the Greeks. The presence of serpents in the attitude of attendant worshipers or protectors, furthermore, indicates that the well-known serpent-

* Cf. supra, pp. 140–150.

daemon (*nāga*) motif that plays such a conspicuous role in later Indian religion had already been evolved—no doubt from the primitive theme of the monster-serpent of the abyss. We have referred to the imagery of the god Vishnu reclining on the Cosmic Serpent, which in turn is floating on the Cosmic Waters.* The supporting energy and substance of the universe, and consequently of the individual, is imaged in India in the figure of the serpent. And the yogi is the master of this power, both in himself (in his control of his own spiritual and physical states) and in the world (in his magical mastery of the phenomena of nature).

The seated yogi among the beasts wears on his head a curious headdress with a high crown and two immense horns, which, as Heinrich Zimmer has pointed out,[52] resembles to a striking degree one of the most prominent symbols of early Buddhist art, the sign of the so-called "Three Jewels" (symbolizing the Buddha, the doctrine, and the order of the Buddha's followers), which is in the form of a kind of trident. The Hindu god Shiva carries a trident also; and among the Greeks, as we know, this same sign was the attribute of Poseidon (Neptune), the god of the watery deep.

Another important art miniature of the period is a well-formed stone torso, 3¾ inches high, of a male dancer in a posture suggesting that of the later dancing Shiva of the South Indian bronzes. The figure, apparently, was ithyphallic, which would have accorded with Shiva's character as a phallic as well as meditative god. And yet another dancer—a beautifully cast copper female nude, 4¼ inches high—indicates, further, that already in the second millennium B.C. the temple dance had been developed, which in India, until most recent times, has been one of the principal liturgical arts.

But with this we are back on familiar ground. For have we not read that Inanna, the queen of heaven, who abandoned heaven, abandoned earth, and to the nether world descended, was the hierodule, the slave-girl dancer, of the gods? Among the stamp seals of the Harappa culture there is one showing the apparition of a goddess wearing a headdress of three horns, somewhat like that of the god whom we have just discussed; and there is a wor-

* Supra, p. 234.

shiper obeisant before her, accompanied by a strange sort of man-faced chimera, while a chorus of exactly seven pigtailed attendants stands in the foreground in a measured row. Ceramic female figurines discovered in dwellings likewise point to an extension of the cult of the goddess from the Near East. However, there have been found, in addition to these images, a number of simple sexual symbols: cone-shaped or phallic erect stones, denoting the male, and circular stones with a hollow center, representing the female. Such primitive forms (known as *liṅgam* and *yoni*) are still the most common objects of worship in India, whether in temples, in the open country, or in the household cult. Surviving from the tradition of the neolithic, they outnumber statistically all the other types of Indian sacred images, and occur most commonly in association, specifically, with Shiva and his goddess, Devi.

In brief, then, the evidence indicates that in the course of the third millennium B.C. a powerful influence from the Mesopotamian mythogenetic zone, on the levels of the high neolithic and of the hieratic city state, reached India by way of Iran. It touched here, however, another mythogenetic zone of considerable force—of which, up to this time, there had been left no indubitable archaeological evidence.

Among the leading elements of this suddenly revealed native Indian mythogenetic complex we may number: the serpent, as a development of the primitive proto-neolithic monster serpent of the tropical planters; the yogi, as a higher transformation of the shamanistic techniques and experiences of ecstasis; the goddess, though in what way or to what degree differently conceived and developed from the goddess of the Mediterranean sphere we cannot say; and the abstract symbol of sexual union (*liṅgam* and *yoni* in conjunction) as a primary symbol of the divine connubium through which the world is simultaneously generated and dissolved.

Among the elements and ideas imported, on the other hand, were certainly writing, the art of the stamp-seal, polychrome pottery, wheeled vehicles, metalcraft, grain agriculture, stock-breeding, the idea of the city, and—possibly—the hieratic city state.

Almost without question, also, the later Indian ideas of duty (*dharma*) and the round of rebirth (*saṁsāra*), the cosmic mountain crowned with the city of the gods, the underworlds of suffering and upper worlds of bliss, the kingly solar and lunar dynasties, and the sacral regicide were derived from Mesopotamia; likewise the sacred bull and cow as theriomorphic counterparts of the *liṅgam* and *yoni*. But a characteristic inflection was given to all these, in which it is difficult not to recognize a native Indian impulse, and which, even though not earlier represented in tangible evidence, may well derive at least from late Capsian (mesolithic) times. A number of the seals, it should furthermore be noted, show the forms of certain trees and plants that are regarded as sacred in India to this day. And, finally, some of the bulls look like unicorns—though perhaps only as a consequence of inept perspective.

3. Fom the middle of the second millennium onward, an epoch-making new development: the entry into India of the Vedic Aryans (remote cousins of the Homeric Greeks, who were penetrating the Balkans at the same time, both perhaps being direct descendants of the people of the kurgans and ocher graves discussed in the description of the northwestward diffusion). With the coming of these Aryans the higher civilization of the Indus cities was destroyed and a new age initiated, in which the male gods of a nomadic herding people for a time triumphed—and seemed to have triumphed forever—over the goddess of the soil-rooted city states. The Vedic heroic age is to be dated c. 1500–500 B.C. and the archaeology of this millennium is practically a total blank; for the early Indo-Aryans, like the early Greeks, neither built in stone nor committed their traditions to writing. Their sacred books (the Vedas, Brahmanas, and Upanishads), no less than their two great epics (the *Mahābhārata* and *Rāmāyaṇa*), were communicated only orally until some time following the third century B.C.; so that everything not regarded as worthy of a special school of rememberers was lost.

4. A period from c. 500 B.C. to c. 500 A.D., when the Aryan, Vedic tradition and the earlier so-called Dravidian, Harappa traditions gradually combined to form the great structures of modern

Hinduism and Indian medieval Buddhism. Whereupon India became the primary mythogenetic zone of the whole later Orient, sending its philosophically illuminated mythologies and mythologically illustrated philosophies northward and eastward into Tibet, Mongolia, China, Korea, and Japan; southward and eastward to Ceylon, Burma, Cambodia, Thailand, and Indonesia; and even westward, though with less force, into the Alexandrian sphere. The principal figures in this development were Gautama Buddha (563–483 B.C.); the Buddhist Emperor Ashoka (c. 274–237 B.C.), who sent, according to his own report, missions to Ceylon, Macedonia, and Alexandrian Egypt; the anonymous author of the Hindu *Bhagavad Gītā;* the Buddhist Emperor Kanishka (c. 78–123 A.D.), in whose time the Buddhist law was carried to China; the Buddhist philosopher Nagarjuna (c. 200 A.D.), whose paradoxical teachings of the "full void" represent perhaps the culmination of the history of metaphysical speculation; the myriads of anonymous craftsmen, to whom the world owes the glorious art of India's Maurya, Andhra, and Gupta periods; and again, those anonymous priests and poets through whom India's medieval Puranic and Tantric traditions were developed. Through all these the compound inheritance of the two great mythogenetic zones of the hieratic city state and the yogic awakening of the serpent power were wrought into mankind's most radiant vision of the harmony of being.

THE NORTHEASTWARD DIFFUSION

1. The Basal Neolithic. The Bronze Age was already in full flower in Crete, Egypt, and Mesopotamia when the elements of the basal neolithic reached the Far East. A coarse, unglazed pottery, shaped by hand by a coiling process and decorated with impressions or with lumps and strips of clay stuck on before firing, is the characteristic sign of this earliest northeastern stratum of diffusion. The dwellings were sometimes built on piles along the waterways (reminding us of the pile dwellings of the Swiss lakes) and a kind of millet was the basic crop (again reminding us of the Swiss lakes). But in the earliest stages no signs of cattle, sheep, or goats appear, the dog and pig being the only domesticated beasts; and even later, when cattle were introduced, pigs continued to preponderate. Oswald Menghin, therefore, has proposed that western China may have been the initial center of swineherding, which then would have been diffused in two directions: southeastward to Indo-China, Indonesia, Melanesia, and from Indo-China westward into India; and directly westward into Europe, the Near East, and Africa.[53]

However, the very early appearance of the pig in the Near East, in the earliest proto- and basal neolithic strata,* makes it difficult to imagine how the relationship of such a Chinese origin to the early Western data might be interpreted. Heine-Geldern links the herding of swine to the basal neolithic of the Near East, while Jensen, as we have already seen, associates the pig with the earliest planting cultures of the tropical zone. Apparently all that is certain is that the beast appears throughout the whole extent of the basal neolithic, whereas sheep, goats, and cattle enter into the northeastward province of this broad domain only centuries later; that in the rites of Persephone and Demeter, as well as in the myths of Attis, Adonis-Tammuz, and Osiris, the legends of Odysseus and Circe, and Irish fairy-lore, the pig and wild boar appear in roles that suggest a very early association with themes that were later adjusted to a cattle-herding complex; that in China and Southeast Asia the pig remained important even after cattle had been introduced; and that throughout Oceania the role of the pig in both ritual and myth is of supreme moment.

Professor Heine-Geldern has suggested—with a magnificently organized assemblage of evidence—that this basal neolithic complex of the Far East (the place of origin of which has not been definitely fixed, though it would seem sensible to place it, provisionally at least, in the Afro-Asiatic Near East, as suggested in Section I of this chapter) reached the Pacific by way of China and Japan, then spread southward across Formosa, the Philippines, Celebes, and the Moluccas to New Guinea and Melanesia, and even touched, finally, the primitive Australians and—as shown earlier † —the Andamanese. Its form of boat was the plank-boat with no out-

* Supra, pp. 136–139.
† Supra, pp. 368–369.

riggers, and its characteristic ground ax a roughly ovoid-cylindrical type.[54] Many signs exist throughout the area of an early matriarchal social organization, with female shamans and perhaps even female rulers, while among the mythological and ritual motifs that were almost certainly associated with this Far Eastern basal neolithic complex are the immolated maiden and the fire goddess. "Society in the Far East during the New Stone Age," as Professor Carl W. Bishop has observed, "seems indeed to have borne a decidedly feminine cast." [55]

However, all consideration of the proto- and basal neolithic of the Far East is rendered difficult, first by the paucity of archaeological material from the provinces in question, and second by the vivid character of the bit that we have recently learned concerning the period immediately subsequent to the basal, when a powerful high neolithic center suddenly burst into view in the western provinces of China, largely influenced by a cultural impact from the Southeast European, Danube-Dniester zone.

2. The High Neolithic. The most important archaeological site in the whole of the Far East is at Anyang, in the northeastern corner of Honan, where the Swedish geologist J. G. Andersson (the same to whom we owe the find of Choukoutien),* discovered three superimposed strata of pottery, representing the earliest levels of the Chinese high neolithic and hieratic city state, as follows: the painted pottery of the Yangshao culture level (c. 2200–1900 B.C.), the black pottery of the Lungshan culture level (c. 1900–1523 B.C.), and the white pottery and bronze sacrificial vessels of the Shang culture level (1523–1027 B.C.).[56]

Pigs, cattle, and dogs were the domestic beasts of the Yangshao complex, with a considerable emphasis on the pigs, and the chief crop was a millet or primitive wheat. Among the other elements carried from the Southeast European, Danube-Dniester zone were a number of distinctive painted pottery motifs (e.g., the double ax, spiral and swastika, meander and polygonal designs, concentric-circle and checker patterns, wavy-water lines, angular zigzags, and organizations of bands),[57] spear- and arrowheads of slate, a way of building pile dwellings along river and lake shores,

* Supra, pp. 360–361.

arrowheads and awls of bone, as well as a particular technique for cutting stone and a kind of square-cut ax made by this technique, which, in the further course of its migration, was to appear throughout the Malay Peninsula, Indonesia, and a good part of Melanesia, as well as in a modified form throughout Polynesia. The headhunt, too, was a component of this barbarous bronze-age culture of the steppes and followed the square-cut ax into Indo-China and Oceania—though apparently not to the northern sphere of Yangshao.[58] For a second, parallel phase of the same stream of life that brought the Yangshao complex to Kansu, Shensi, Shansi, and Honan (not reaching, however, as far as to Shantung) turned south into the Malay Peninsula. "This branch," writes Heine-Geldern, "before coming to Further India, must have passed through western China." [59] "It must have been a folk and culture wave of prodigious force," he then goes on to say, "which arrived in East Asia from the West in the late neolithic, transformed its entire ethnic and cultural structure, laid the foundations of Chinese culture and the Chinese empire as well as of the Further Indian and Indonesian cultures, and finally went on even to Madagascar, New Zealand, East Polynesia, and in all probability America as well. Relatively small groups are enough to give an impulse that will continue to work for millenniums and across continents and across seas." [60]

It is, in short, to the impact of this Yangshao-Austronesian culture wave that a great part of the broad diffusion to which I have devoted Part II of this study must now be attributed. The headhunt, the pig, pile dwellings, megaliths, and their associated rites of animal sacrifice came together on this wave from the West. In the Southeast Asian zone a secondary neolithic complex, involving rice-culture and the water buffalo, was encountered and absorbed, and on the great riverways of the Irrawaddy, Salween, Me-nam, Me-kong, etc., a characteristic boat, the outrigger canoe, was developed, which then bore the assemblage not only westward to Madagascar but also far eastward to Easter Island, and no doubt beyond. The basic rites of the cannibals of Ceram, and the Panpipes as well of Brazil as of the Solomon Islands, were almost certainly transported by this culture wave; for it achieved in Indonesia an impressive adaptation to the highways of the sea. The island of Java, in particular, abounds in examples of the characteristic square-cut ax of this brilliant day in many significant modulations, including a number of perfectly magnificent ceremonial forms which Heine-Geldern has described as marking the high point of the Indonesian neolithic stonecraft. A considerable cultural peak was achieved; the population of the area was relatively dense; trade was vigorously plied; and the impress of this specific center can be readily discerned from Madagascar to Easter Island and from New Zealand to Japan.

Furthermore, if we may judge of the date of this important prehistoric cultural movement from the carefully checked evidences of the Chinese Yangshao stratum (c. 2200–1900 B.C.), its period of florescence must have been early in the second millennium B.C. —in plenty of time for the delivery to the coast of Peru of those telling calabashes of Huaca Prieta.* And to mark a still further point of coincidence, we may recall that the formidable culture center in the Black Sea area from which this broadly influential Far Eastern complex came was sending its spreading rings westward into Europe as well as eastward to Honan. We have already noted that c. 2500–1500 B.C. its impulse reached both the Baltic and the Balkans. V. Gordon Childe has remarked that when pig bones are found among the remains of the ancient dwelling places of eastern Sweden, they belong to a cultural horizon contemporary with the middle (i.e., high) neolithic and illustrate the start of a secondary (or even tertiary) neolithic culture, "the first steps in swine-breeding by autochthonous hunter-fishers." [61]

May we, then, think of the Panpipe of Arcadian Greece as an inkling of the same great diffusion as that represented by the Panpipes of Melanesia and Brazil—on the opposite rim of the spreading ring of waves? It is not our only sign of such diffusion, by any means; for, indeed, have we not already had Persephone and Hainuwele to teach us? Or shall we say that all these correspondences of archaeology and mythology, now adequately identified in the farthest flung branches of our science, which so neatly gear even as to date and would readily clarify an other-

* Supra, pp. 205–206.

wise inscrutable enigma, must be overlooked as simply accidents of chance? The purely psychological reading of these parallels will not do at all, since a clearly, even though sparsely documented historical sequence has to be recognized, with its perfect coincidence of dates: the kurgan, barrow, or tumuli people entering Europe c. 2500–1500 B.C.; the Yangshao culture stratum of China, c. 2200–1900 B.C.; a parallel cultural development in Java, with a mastery of the seaways; and then at Huaca Prieta those grinning calabashes, c. 1016±300 B.C., to mark the smuggling of an alien agriculturalist across the Pacific into the New World.

But what, then, was the meaning of this ritual of the sacrificial pig, lamb, goat, or bull, which, having come into form as a basic feature of the high neolithic, was diffused, one way or another, throughout the world?

On the Melanesian island of Malekula, in the New Hebrides, halfway between Fiji and the Solomon Islands, an extremely complicated system of men's rites involving the sacrifice of many sacred pigs is celebrated among megalithic shrines that closely resemble those of prehistoric Ireland. John Layard in his richly illustrated *Stone Men of Malekula* [62] has given evidence enough to establish such an association, and, as Heine-Geldern has sufficiently shown, there was indeed a late diffusion in several waves of a megalithic culture complex into this part of the world, where the great stones are associated with the ceremonious pledging of a covenant, the offering of a sacrificial beast (originally a bull, states Heine-Geldern, but, in peripheral areas, the pig), memorials to the honored dead, and to capture of heads in the headhunt.[63]

According to Layard the Malekulans attribute their own megalithic tradition of the pig sacrifice to a mythical family of five culture-bringers, who were brothers and "white men" with aquiline noses. Their chief, the creator and giver of all good things, is represented constantly, Layard declares, "as sailing in a canoe, and in almost all, if not in all, areas where he is known, he is represented as having finally sailed away over the horizon to an unknown destination. In his heavenly aspect he is invariably associated with light and, in one way or another, with the sun and moon." [64] But he is also said to have been buried sitting on a stone seat within a stone chamber covered by a mound of earth and loose stones—"in other words," as Layard points out, "what we in Europe would call a chambered round-barrow"; and his body and that of his wife are said to be incorruptible. The alleged undecayed bodies of this culture-bringer and his wife are ritually washed at certain festival times for the purpose of ensuring the continuance of the human race.[65]

This highly interesting, theoretically challenging megalithic complex of Malekula is brought to focus in a context of ceremonials known as the Maki, which lasts from fifteen to thirty years and when finished is immediately recommenced. It serves on the one hand the aims of the community, inasmuch as it magically fosters the fertility of the race, but on the other hand the personal fame and ambition of the individual, since it is a rite of a strongly competitive kind, in which the men of the village, breeding up and sacrificing numberless boars, vie for status both in this world and in the next.

We have been introduced already to one of the chief elements of the mythology of the Maki.* When a Malekulan dies, we have noted, and commences his journey to the land of the dead, the female guardian of the cavernous entrance to the other world draws a labyrinth on the ground across his way and as he approaches erases half. To pass, he must know how to reconstruct the labyrinth. And he must also offer a pig for the guardian to eat in lieu of himself. But this can be no simple, ordinary pig. It is to be a boar bred up by his own hands and ritually consecrated, time and again, in the ceremonials of the Maki, at every stage of the development of its greatly cherished tusks. And hundreds of other boars must have been sacrificed in the course of these ceremonials, so that the beast offered represents the whole life-effort, as well as the ritual status, of the voyager.

At the beginning of its days the upper canine teeth of a male pig are removed ceremonially, so that the lower, meeting no resistance,

* Supra, pp. 68–70.

may continue to grow. These lower tusks then curve outward, down, and around, in such a way as to circle back, penetrate the lower jaw, and form a ring. Such growth requires at least seven years, and every stage represents an increment in spiritual and therefore economic worth. But one circle is not the highest stage of achievement. Two are not uncommon and with great good fortune even three can be attained. The pain to the animal is so great, meanwhile, that it puts on little flesh and from the standpoint of a gourmet would be a miserable morsel; but in the realm of the spirit we are not to think as gourmets. These radiant pigs are not physical food; they are spiritual food. They represent the moon, that glowing orb with which the sea-voyaging ancestral "white man," the founder of the cult, is himself identified. For, as Layard explains their power: "The really fundamental concept of the tusks is not that they should form a spiral but simply that they should be curved or crescent shaped, thus representing, on one symbolic level, the waxing and waning moon, both represented together on either side of the mouth of the same sacrificial animal. . . . The black body of the boar between them corresponds to the 'new' or 'black' invisible moon at the time of her apparent death." [66]

The boars, then, are the moon at the moment of its death, consumed by the goddess guardian of the underworld. Their tusks point to the continuance of life, however, waxing and waning over the ground of death. Thus, in their own way, they symbolize the mystery that we have already discussed in connection with the planting-world mythology of the serpent and the maiden. The boar sacrifice, symbolically, is equivalent to the sacrifice of the maiden. But the boar is a male; furthermore, it is a figure derived from the domain of masculine interest, the animal world, the world of the hunt, the world of domesticated flocks. Sows are neither sacrificed nor eaten. Their flesh is taboo, even despised. And the staple food of this society is the yam, cultivated by the women, to which breadfruit, shellfish and fish, turtle eggs, prawns, eels, flying fox, and other bits of wild game may be added. So that, from the physical point of view, all is well enough cared for by the women—the circumstance being precisely that described by

Father Schmidt in his characterization of the natural supremacy of the female among primitive planters. However, with the pig, the Maki, and the rites of the men's lodge, a masculine, mythological, "spiritual" counterforce is brought to bear against the feminine power. The chief divinity concerned is female, indeed—the guardian of the gate, who eats. But she is cheated, overcome, by the rites. She consumes the boar, but the man escapes. She consumes the black boar, but the radiant tusks survive and are hung as signs of man's immortality from the roof beams of the cult houses. Women, furthermore, being without souls, are not deeply concerned in this spiritual game. They acquire rank along with their husbands as the men, through sacrifice, proceed up the mystical ladder of their masonic lodges; but the cult itself is a man's affair, and through it the role and importance of woman have been systematically reduced, so that she cannot even figure now as the sacrifice. It is the boar, not the sow, that is killed; and when a human offering is to be made, it is no longer a maiden but a man or boy.

In the first phase of a Maki ceremony the focal center is a dolmen, a kind of table of stone, formed of a great slab supported by stone uprights, symbolizing three things: a stone grave, the cave through which the dead must pass on their journey to the other world, and the womb through which the living may achieve rebirth. A wooden figure is erected before this symbolic structure, to represent all the male ancestors who have gone through this rite in the past and to serve also as the gable post of a roof thatched over the dolmen. The main beam of this roof terminates in a carved image of the mythological hawk whose spirit hovers over the ceremonies. And since no portion of the cult structure is ever removed, the ground all about is strewn with the rotting remains of earlier times.

The crucial rite before the dolmen occurs when a man seeking to elevate himself in the power scale ceremonially approaches, in imitation of the soul approaching the cavern entrance to the other world. His mother's brothers block the way, just as the female guardian spirit will block his way at the time of death. And he then makes copious offerings to them of boars—and these go to his credit in the spiritual account that will be closed only when he dies and is buried together with his supreme pig.

The values of the offerings are reckoned by the tusks; and according to these values a man's rank is made. Without tuskers he can neither enter the land of the dead nor be reborn, cannot even marry. Moreover, since in the course of a ceremonial as many as five hundred pigs may be offered in a day, it is clear that any man who takes seriously the salvation of his eternal soul must be considerably occupied with the spiritual exercise of breeding, trading, and reckoning his pigs, which, indeed, serve as money in Malekula, so firmly fixed and well known are their relative values—just as, in the higher cultures, gold, which is of no more practical value than a Melanesian pig, supplies the basic standard of all monetary worth because of its mythological reference to the sun. Gold is of incorruptible character, untarnished by the touch of time. The kingly crown of gold, symbolizing the secular power as well as spiritual authority of the character on whom it sits, corresponds to the boar's-tusk decorations of a cloud-catching Melanesian. And just as a man with a golden crown—or even a golden cigarette case—may regard himself as having gained the fruit of his birth, so likewise the Melanesian Maki-man with a fine display of the skulls of one-, two-, and three-circle tuskers along the roof beam of his family home.

The natives declare that their boar offerings have taken the place of human sacrifices; yet to this day a personage of great purpose, seeking the paramount crown, may offer a young human being along with a fine three-circle tusker, and thus perform a feat of as great value as can be expected of an aspirant, either in heaven or on earth. The human victim of such an offering is generally a bastard, bred and reared solely for sacrifice, kept healthy and given the greatest affection, while being kept ignorant of the fate in store. The boy and the very precious three-circle tusker, painted exactly alike, are led together to the dolmen, when "suddenly, those dancing behind the boy seize him, and slipping over his blue-painted neck a rope dangling from the hawk image, jerk it so that he is left hanging, whereon the sacrificer, lifting his club, sacrifices him by striking him on the head. The victim is then lowered and the three-circle tusker he led in is clubbed also and left on the victim's body to die." The boy's body is given to the makers of the ancestral image to eat, and the man who has made the sacrifice assumes the title of *Mal-tanas,* "Lord of the Underworld. " "He communicates with the unearthly," we are told. "He may do as he wishes; he may even do what is not done. No man dare be hated by him." [67] And after the killing, the new Lord of the Underworld remains for thirty days on the stone platform, eating only yams. His limbs are covered with armlets of the most valuable shell beads, and he has pigs' tusks as bangles from elbow to wrist. He is a very picture of that immortal person for whom death has no sting.

And with this, I believe, we have our final clue to the ritual sacrifice of the royal tombs of Ur, as well as to the "fury for sacrifice" that beset, at one time or another, every part of the archaic world in the various high periods of its numerous cultures. A magical power is gained according to the measure of one's sacrifice. The ultimate sacrifice is, of course, one's self; yet the value even of this self is to be measured according to the orders of sacrifice accomplished during life and made by one's survivors at one's mortuary feast. The most potent supporting offering of this sort is another human being—one's son, one's slave, one's prisoner of war. But the next in order is some beast that one has raised oneself and cared for as one's own. Moreover, wherever such animal offerings are rendered, the beast is of a species mythologically associated with deity. We have mentioned the Capsian petroglyphs in North Africa, showing a ram with the sun between its horns and the figure of the moon-bull on the sacred harps of Ur, as well as the bulls' heads on the high neolithic pottery of the Halaf style. Let us add, now, the rites of the Minotaur in the bull rings of Crete, whence the imagery was carried with the megalithic culture complex to Spain, where, even today, we may see the brave moon-bull with its crescent horns slain by the solar blade of the sparkling matador, just as the paleolithic bulls in the deep temple caves of the neighboring Cantabrian hills and Pyrenees are slain by the solar power of the shamans. And in Malekula, at the other end of the line, the same symbolism is rendered in the megalithic rites of the sacrifice of the lunar boar.

The offered beast is a captured quantum of divine power, which, through its sacrifice, is integrated with the giver. The giver climbs, so to say, on the rungs of his sacrifice. And the Maki is a great ladder of such rungs.

When the aspirant has accomplished his ultimate sacrifice, he is identified with the hovering hawk, the mythological bird that is carved on the roof beam over the dolmen, and the old man presiding at the rite, who has invested him with the power-name of the boar that has just been killed, which now is the name of his own new life, "springs into the air, with extended arms and fluttering hands, in imitation of the hawk." At other times, "it is the sacrificer himself, who, mounted on his stone platform at the supreme moment of sacrifice, spreads out his own arms in imitation of a soaring hawk and sings a song about the stars." The word *Na-mbal,* "hawk," may be used as a personal name by the man who has achieved such rank. Other lofty names are "the face of the sun," "catches clouds," "at heaven's zenith," "holy ground on top," and "lord of the above." [68] Moreover, this yearning upward, which, as we have seen, was characteristic also of the shamanism of the north, is rendered here in the symbolism of the great dolmens and monoliths themselves—some of the platforms that play a part in the second phase of the Maki being of such a height that they overtop the trees.[69]

In this second phase, the structure on which the offering is made is a high platform of stone, raised behind the dolmen, on the summit of which the culminating boar offering takes place, the kindling of the new fire, and the assumption of the new name. The mythological reference of this tower and its sacrificial fire is to a large volcano on the neighboring island of Ambrim, which is supposed to be the happy land of the living dead. Abiding in that fire is bliss; there is no fear of being consumed.

A number of variant images are given of the voyage of the dead to their happy land. According to one, the soul entering the cave is immediately blocked by the guardian spirit, Le-hev-hev, to whom the boar-offering is presented to be consumed in lieu of the soul itself; and the voyager, then allowed to pass, goes through the cave and emerges on the coast, along which he walks to a certain rocky place, well known, where he lights a fire to summon the ferryman. The latter comes in a ghost canoe, which is called "banana peel" and might be any little bit of bark from the banana tree, floating on the water. The waiting soul, then, is ferried to the great volcano—which is called "The Source of Fire"—and there the ghosts dance every night and sleep all day. But according to a second version, the fire of the volcano is spread over the whole path and the boar is placed in the grave to appease this fire. "The guardian," they say, "stands upright in the midst of the path of fire, then rushes forward to consume us; but is content to eat the boar." [70]

We are far, indeed, in these myths and rites from that profound feminine experience of immolation and transformation which the noble Abyssinian woman, earlier quoted (from Frobenius), expressed when she remarked on the utter triviality of the male's mode of experience and understanding. "His life and body are always the same. . . . He knows nothing." They represent, in fact, a masculine transformation of the planters' myth of the immolated maiden, through a force derived from the northern, shamanistic sphere.

The mythogenetic zone of this high neolithic mythology of acquisitive sacrifice was the Black Sea area: first the southward shore of Anatolia and the Taurus mountains, where the figure of the bull in association with the naked goddess first appears about 4500 B.C., on the painted pottery of the Halaf style; and then, with an even stronger stress on the values and anxieties of the male ego, in the barbaric steppe lands of the lower Danube, Dnieper, Dniester, and Don valleys, from which, as we have just seen, the wielders of the square-cut ax broke away, in the third millennium B.C., to reshape the world.

3. The Hieratic City State. In the *Historical Records* of Ssu-ma Ch'ien (c. 145–86/74 B.C.) we are told of the concern of the legendary Chinese "Yellow Emperor," Huang Ti, for accurate astronomy. The supposed date of this fabulous ruler would place him half a millennium earlier than the period of the painted-pottery culture of Yangshao. He is, however, a sheer invention of the later Chinese scholars. And yet his supposititious interest in astronomy represents a basic inheritance of the Celestial Empire and, indeed, derives from a very early date. "Huang Ti," we are told, "commanded Hsi Ho to take charge of the observation of the sun, I Chang the observation of the moon, and Yu Chu the observation of the stars."[71]

The sun as the source of light, heat, and dryness represents in China the masculine, positive force of the universe, the *yang,* while the moon, governing moisture, shadow, and cold, stands for the negative, feminine, the *yin*. These, interacting, produce the order, sense, direction, or way, *tao,* of all things, which is represented geometrically as an ever-turning circle, mixed of black and white, of *yin* and *yang:*

Below the sun and moon are the five planets, each affiliated with an element. Mercury is the planet of the element water, the element of the north; Venus of metal, the element of the west; Mars of fire and the south; Jupiter of wood, which is east; and finally Saturn, the planet of the element earth, which is of the center. In India, too, there is a doctrine of five elements, old enough to have been studied by the Buddha (563–483 B.C.) and traditionally attributed to a still more ancient sage named Kapila, who may have lived as early as the eighth century B.C. The five elements in the Indian tradition are associated with the five senses: ether, the first, is the element of hearing; air, the second, the element of touch; fire, of sight; water, of taste; and earth, of smell. In the Occident, however, since the period of the Buddha's contemporary, Empedocles (c. 500–430 B.C.), we have heard only of four elements: fire (which is hot and dry), air (which is hot and moist), water (which is cold and moist), and earth (which is cold and dry). The systems differ, yet they are derived from the same root.

And how far back should this root be dated?

A clue is given by the harps in the royal tombs of Ur, to the sound of which the king and his celestial court died, and which were fashioned in such a way as to suggest that their harmony was that of the moon-bull, whose body was their sounding chamber and on whose golden head the lapis lazuli beard of the heavenly principle was displayed. The five notes of the Chinese pentatonic scale are associated with the harmony of the five elements and the five planets.

In a Chinese musical treatise of the second century B.C. we read:

> If the note, Kung [C = the tonic], is disturbed, then there is disorganization, the Prince is arrogant.
>
> If the second note, Shang [D], is disturbed, then there is deviation: the officials are corrupted.
>
> If the Chiao [E] is disturbed, then there is anxiety: the people are unhappy.
>
> If the Chi [G] is disturbed, then there is complaint: public services are too heavy.
>
> If the Yü [A] is disturbed, then there is danger: resources are lacking.
>
> If the five degrees are all disturbed, then there is danger: ranks encroach upon each other—this is what is called impudence—and, if such is the condition, the destruction of the Kingdom may come in less than a day. . . .
>
> In periods of disorder, rites are altered and music is licentious. Then sad sounds are lacking in dignity, joyful sounds lack calm. . . . When the spirit of opposition manifests itself, indecent music comes into being . . . when the spirit of conformity manifests itself, harmonious music appears. . . . So that, under the effect of music, the five social duties are without admixture, the eyes and the ears are clear, the blood and the vital spirits are balanced, habits are reformed, customs are improved, the Empire is in complete peace.[72]

The five social duties here associated with the pentatonic scale are the "five activities of high importance under heaven" announced in the Confucian Doctrine of the Mean. They are, namely, "the obligations between prince and minister; between father and son; between husband and wife; between elder and younger brothers; and between friends. Those," we read, "are the five obligations that have great effects under heaven."[73]

"Tuned to the tone of Heaven and Earth," we learn from another text of the second century B.C., "the vital spirits of men express all the tremors of Heaven and Earth, just as several cithars, all tuned on Kung, vibrate when the note Kung resounds. The fact of harmony between Heaven, Earth, and Man does not come from a physical union, from a direct action; it comes from a tuning on the same note producing vibrations in unison. . . . In the Universe there is no hazard, there is no spontaneity; all is influence and harmony, accord answering accord." [74]

But this, precisely, was the view of the Greek Pythagoras (582–c. 507 B.C.), an echo of whose lore we have already heard in Plato's words concerning the pristine accord of man's nature with "the harmonies and revolutions of the world." And the concept of musical accord in India is the same, where it is said that "all this universe is but the result of sound." [75]

The Chinese terms for heaven are *t'ien* and *shang ti*. The first is impersonal, denoting "what is above"; the second, personal, and translated "lord." "It is called Heaven (*t'ien*) when viewed from the point of its overshadowing the entire world," states a commentator to the *Wu Ching;* "it is called Lord (*ti*) when viewed from the point of its rulership." [76]

The lord and ruler of the earth, the emperor of China—which is regarded as the "middle kingdom" of the world—occupies his throne with the approval, or by the mandate, of heaven. He is the tonic note or pivot of the earthly harmony and, when attuned, his empire prospers. In the fabulous prehistoric period of Huang Ti the people were able to control their passions perfectly, and there was such an accord between Heaven and earth that the middle kingdom became an earthly paradise. Its inhabitants did not have to eat; merely to sip the dew was enough. The four benevolent animals, the unicorn, dragon, tortoise, and phoenix—the four lords, respectively, of the warm-blooded quadrupeds, scaly animals, mollusks, and birds—appeared and took up their abodes in the gardens of the palace. Boons, moreover, proceeded from the understanding of the emperor, who taught the arts of divination and mathematics, composed the calendar, invented musical instruments of bamboo, taught the use of money, boats, and carriages, and the arts of work in clay, metal, and wood. He established the rituals of address to *shang ti,* built the first temple and the first palace, studied and taught the properties of healing herbs. And when he died, at the age of one hundred and eleven, he left a nation established in a harmony that survived, in the main, for some four thousand years.

But on the other hand, when an emperor becomes unworthy of the mandate of heaven, inauspicious omens presently appear, and the Son of Heaven may be overthrown. We recognize, therefore, a deep and real anxiety in the words of the Emperor Ming (227–239 A.D.), following the solar eclipse of the year 233.

"We have heard," states Ming Ti,

> that if a sovereign is remiss in government, God terrifies him by calamities and portents. These are divine reprimands sent to recall him to a sense of duty. Thus, eclipses of the sun and moon are manifest warnings that the rod of empire is not wielded aright. Our inability to continue the glorious traditions of Our departed ancestors and carry on the great work of civilization ever since We ascended the throne has now culminated in a warning message from on high. It therefore behoves Us to issue commands for personal reformation, in order to avert impending calamity. The relationship, however, between God and man is that of father and son; and a father, about to chastise his son, would not be deterred were the latter to present him with a dish of meat. We do not therefore consider it a part of Our duty to act in accordance with certain memorials advising that the Grand Astrologer be instructed to offer up sacrifices on this occasion. Do ye governors of districts, and other high officers of State, seek rather to rectify your own hearts; and if anyone can devise means to make up for Our shortcomings, let him submit his proposals to the throne.[77]

The coming of this concept of the hieratic city state to China is to be dated from the period of the black ware of the Lungshan culture (c. 1900–1523 B.C.), which now appears to have stemmed from the same centers of northern Iran and southern Turkestan (Tepe Hissar, Turang Tepe, Shah Tepe, Namazgah Tepe, Anau, etc.) [78] that sent the concept into India for the formation of the Harappa style.* The characteristic fortress-city of this Chinese

* Supra, pp. 435–438.

stratum is perfectly quadrangular in form, bounded by a powerful wall of pounded earth, and of considerable size. Sheep and horses have been added to the earlier barnyard stock of cattle, pigs, and dogs, and two of the pottery shards discovered show that writing was now known—in two scripts that have not yet been deciphered.

The evidence of the next stratum, though, is much more abundant: the level, namely, of the white pottery of the Shang Dynasty (c. 1523–1027 B.C.). Here the basic socio-political structure of the later Chinese empire can be seen to have been already laid. Bronze-casting, tools and weapons of bronze, war chariots drawn by yoked steeds, a highly developed writing system, chamber burials and human sacrifices, an impressive architecture, gabled and colonnaded, advanced stone carvings, oracle bones, and a great passion for the hunt as a royal sport mark the flowering of an elegant, highly developed civilization, following essentially the lines laid down some fifteen hundred years earlier in Ur, Kish, Lagash, Erech, and Nippur in Mesopotamia.

An important feature of considerable interest, however, is the novel art style that appears at this time; for although many of its themes are derived directly from the West (entwining serpents, antithetical beasts with a human figure between, and the hero subduing beasts, for example), the style itself and the manner of composition through which its themes are rendered not only are distinctive but also represent the earliest appearance anywhere of certain basic traits characteristic of the circum-Pacific arts, whether in the Old World or in the New. The first of these is the principle of the totem pole, a piling up of similar forms in vertical series. A second device consists in splitting the body to be represented, either down the front or down the back, and opening it like a book. A third renders in a particular way decorative organizations of angular spirals and meanders. Furthermore, many of the Shang face-formations and body postures are unmistakable, in whatever cultural context they may appear.

Professor Heine-Geldern, tracing the trans-Pacific courses of the various Far Eastern cultural influences, has pointed out, among other significant signs of a long-continued impact on America:

art motifs of the Chinese eighth century B.C., from the coastal states of Wu and Yüeh, in the Chavín culture of the same period in the Central Andes (goldwork and fine weaving now appearing in America for the first time); art motifs of seventh- and sixth-century China in the Salinar culture of the North Central Andes, dating from the first centuries A.D.; art motifs of seventh- to fourth-century China in the Tajín culture of Middle America, dating from c. 200–1000 A.D.; the art of the late Chou Dynasty bronzes and jades (fifth to third centuries B.C.) reflected in the Ulúa style of Middle America (c. 200–1000 A.D.); a brief break in the contact of the Chinese with America after 333 B.C., when the seafaring state of Yüeh, in the southeast, lost its independence and the Dong-son folk of Vietnam, in northeastern Indo-China, took over the commerce with such effect that their influence can be recognized from Panama to Chile and the Argentine, particularly in techniques of metallurgy and ornamental metal designs; during the period of the Han Dynasty (202 B.C.–220 A.D.), a resumption of the Chinese voyages, and after c. 50 A.D., with the conquest of Tonkin and North Annam by China, a probable end of the Dong-son trans-Pacific sailings; and finally, with the fall of the Han Dynasty, a passing of the lead from China to the Hinduized peoples of Southeast Asia, where Cambodia was the chief power from the seventh to tenth centuries A.D.—the contacts of these voyagers with America perhaps then continuing until the death of Jayavarman VII of Angkor, about 1219 A.D.[79]

And so, we are not surprised to learn that the great high priest and monarch of the Golden Age in the Toltec city of Tula, the City of the Sun, in ancient Mexico, whose name, Quetzalcoatl, has been read to mean both "the Feathered Serpent" and "the Admirable Twin," [80] and who was fair of face and white of beard, was the teacher of the arts to the people of pre-Columbian America, originator of the calendar, and their giver of maize. His virgin mother, Chimalman—the legend tells—had been one of three sisters to whom God, the All-Father, had appeared one day under his form of Citlallatonac, "the morning." The other two had been struck by fright, but upon Chimalman God breathed and she conceived. She died, however, giving birth, and is now in heaven, where she is revered under the honorable name of "the Precious Stone of Sacrifice," Chalchihuitzli.

Quetzalcoatl, her child, who is known both as the Son of the Lord of the High Heavens and as the Son of the Lord of the Seven Caves, was endowed at birth with speech, all knowledge, and all wisdom, and in later life, as priest-king, was of such purity of character that his realm flourished gloriously throughout the period of his reign. His temple-palace was composed of four radiant apartments: one toward the east, yellow with gold; one toward the west, blue with turquoise and jade; one toward the south, white with pearls and shells; one toward the north, red with bloodstones—symbolizing the cardinal quarters of the world over which the light of the sun holds sway. And it was set wonderfully above a mighty river that passed through the midst of the city of Tula; so that every night, precisely at midnight, the king descended into the river to bathe; and the place of his bath was called "In the Painted Vase," or "In the Precious Waters." But the time of his predestined defeat by the dark brother, Tezcatlipoca, was ever approaching; and, knowing perfectly the rhythm of his own destiny, Quetzalcoatl would make no move to stay it.

Tezcatlipoca, therefore, said to his attendants, "We shall give him a drink to dull his reason and show him his own face in a mirror; then, surely, he will be lost." And he said to the servants of the good king, "Go tell your master that I have come to show him his own flesh!"

But when the message was brought to Quetzalcoatl, the aging monarch said, "What does he call my own flesh? Go and ask!" And when the other was admitted to his presence: "What is this, my flesh, that you would show me?"

Tezcatlipoca answered, "My Lord and Priest, look now at your flesh; know yourself; see yourself as you are seen by others!" And he presented the mirror.

Whereupon, seeing his own face in that mirror, Quetzalcoatl immediately cried out, "How is it possible that my subjects should look upon me without fright? Well might they flee from before me. For how can a man remain among them when he is filled as I am with foul sores, his old face wrinkled and of an aspect so loathsome? I shall be seen no more, I shall no longer terrify my people."

Presented the drink to quaff, he refused it, saying that he was ill; but urged to taste it from the tip of his finger, he did so and was immediately overpowered by its magic. He lifted the bowl and was drunk. He sent for Quetzalpetlatl, his sister, who dwelt on the Mountain Nonoalco. She came, and her brother gave her the bowl, so that she too was drunk. And with all reason forgotten, the two that night neither said prayers nor went to the bath, but sank asleep together on the floor. And in the morning Quetzalcoatl said, in shame, "I have sinned; the stain of my name cannot be erased. I am not fit to rule this people. Let them build a habitation for me deep under ground; let them bury my bright treasures in the earth; let them throw the glowing gold and shining stones into the Precious Waters where I take my nightly bath."

And all this was done. The king remained four days in his underground tomb, and when he came forth he wept and told his people that the time had come for his departure to the Red Land, the Dark Land, the Land of Fire.

Having burned his dwellings behind him, buried his treasures in the mountains, transformed his chocolate trees into mesquite, and commanded his multicolored birds to fly before him, Quetzalcoatl, in great sorrow, departed. Resting at a certain place along the way and looking back in the direction of Tula, his City of the Sun, he wept, and his tears went through a rock; he left in that place the mark of his sitting and the impress of his palms. Farther along, he was met and challenged by a company of necromancers, who prevented him from proceeding until he had left with them the arts of working silver, wood, and feathers, and the art of painting. As he crossed the mountains, many of his attendants, who were dwarfs and humpbacks, died of the cold. At another place he met his dark antagonist, Tezcatlipoca, who defeated him at a game of ball. At still another he aimed with an arrow at a large *pochotl* tree; and the arrow too was a *pochotl* tree, so that when he shot it through the first they formed a cross. And so he passed along, leaving many signs and place-names behind him, until, coming at last to where the sky, land, and water come together, he departed.

He sailed away on a raft of serpents, according to one version, but another has it that his remaining attendants built a funeral pyre, into which he threw himself, and while the body burned, his heart departed and after four days appeared as the rising planet Venus. All agree, however, that he will presently return. He will arrive with a fair-faced retinue from the east and resume sway over his people; for although Tezcatlipoca had conquered, those immutable laws that had determined the destruction of Tula assigned likewise its restoration.

Quetzalcoatl was not dead. In one of his statues he was shown reclining, covered with wrappings, signifying that he was absent or "as one who lays him down to sleep, and that when he should wake from that dream of absence, would rise to rule again the land." [81] He had built mansions underground to the Lord of Mictlan, the lord of the dead, but did not occupy these himself, dwelling, rather, in that land of gold where the sun abides at night. This too, however, is underground. Certain caverns lead to it, one of which, called Cincalco, "To the Abode of Abundance," is south of Chapultepec; and through its gloomy corridors men can reach that happy land, the habitation of the sun, which is still ruled by Quetzalcoatl. Moreover, that land is the land from which he came in the beginning. . . .

All this, which in so many ways parallels the normal imagery of the Old World culture-hero myths, telling of the one who is gone, dwells underground in a happy, timeless land, as lord of the realm of the happy dead, like Osiris, but will arise again, we can read without surprise. But what is surprising indeed was the manner of Quetzalcoatl's actual return. The priests and astrologers did not know in what cycle he was to appear; however, the name of the year within the cycle had been predicted, of old, by Quetzalcoatl himself. Its sign was "One Reed" (*Ce Acatl*), which, in the Mexican calendar, is a year that occurs only once in every cycle of fifty-two. But the year when Cortes arrived, with his company of fair-faced companions and his standard, the cross, was precisely the year "One Reed." [82] The myth of the dead and resurrected god had circumnavigated the globe.

Conclusion

THE FUNCTIONING OF MYTH

1. The Local Images and the Universal Way

"What is important," said a white-bearded Hindu pilgrim as the train pulled into Benares, "is not the object worshiped, but the depth and sincerity of the worship." And yet he was getting off at Benares, after a long and arduous trip, to worship Shiva in his spiritual capital.

Two aspects of every ritual tradition are recognized in Indian thought, and they correspond to Adolph Bastian's "elementary ideas" (*Elementargedanke*) and "ethnic ideas" (*Völkergedanke*), which we discussed in the opening pages of this book. It will be recalled that according to Bastian the elementary ideas are never experienced directly, in a pure state, abstracted from the locally conditioned ethnic ideas through which they are substantialized, but, like the image of man himself, are to be known only by way of the rich variety of their inflections in the panorama of human life. We may therefore think of any myth or rite either as a clue to what may be permanent or universal in human nature (in which case our emphasis will be psychological, or perhaps even metaphysical), or, on the other hand, as a function of the local scene, the landscape, the history, and the sociology of the folk concerned (in which case our approach will be ethnological or historical). The corresponding Indian terms designating these two aspects of mythology and rite are, respectively, *mārga*, meaning "path" or "way," the path or way to the discovery of the universal, and *deśī* (pronounced "day-shee"), "of the region, local, or ethnic," the peculiar, sectarian, or historical aspect of any cult, through which it constellates a folk, a nation, or a civilization.

I should like to join these two Indian terms to Bastian's; for they not only corroborate his insight but also suggest better than the Western terms the psychological force, or way of service, of the two aspects of a mythological image. Functioning as a "way," mythology and ritual conduce to a transformation of the individual, disengaging him from his local, historical conditions and leading him toward some kind of ineffable experience. Functioning as an "ethnic idea," on the other hand, the image binds the individual to his family's system of historically conditioned sentiments, activities, and beliefs, as a functioning member of a sociological organism. This antinomy is fundamental to our subject, and every failure to recognize it leads not only to unnecessary argument, but also to a misunderstanding—one way or the other—of the force of the mythological symbol itself, which is, precisely, to render an experience of the ineffable through the local and concrete, and thus, paradoxically, to amplify the force and appeal of the local forms even while carrying the mind beyond them. The distinctive challenge of mythology lies in its power to effect this dual end; and not to recognize this fact is to miss the whole point and mystery of our science.

We have to recognize, therefore, that even where a single deity is worshiped, the varieties of religious experience represented by the worshipers may differ to such an extent that it is only from the most superficial sociological point of view that they can be said to share the same religion. They are held together sociologically by their god, or gods, yet psychologically are on different planes.

"Among the Dakota Indians," we hear, for example, from Paul Radin, "what the ordinary man regards as eight distinct deities, the priest and thinker takes to be aspects of one and the same deity." [1]

Comparably, in the contemporary world of cross-cultural communication, where the minds of men, leaping the local fences, can recognize common fields of experience and realization under alien forms, what many priests and sociologists regard as eight distinct deities, the comparative mythologist and psychologist can take to be aspects of one and the same. The nineteenth-century saint and sage Ramakrishna stressed this psychological—as opposed to ethnological—orientation when he spoke of the ultimate unity of all religions.

"A mother prepares dishes to suit the stomachs of her children," he said. "Suppose she has five children and a fish is brought for the family. She doesn't cook pilau or kalia for all of them. All have not the same power of digestion. She prepares for some a simple stew; but she loves all of her children equally. . . . Do you know what the truth is?" he asked. And he answered his own question:

> God has made different religions to suit different aspirants, times and countries. All doctrines are only so many paths; but a path is by no means God himself. Indeed, one can reach God if one follows any of the paths with wholehearted devotion. You have no doubt heard the story of the chameleon. A man entered the wood and saw a chameleon on a tree. He reported to his friends. "I have seen a red lizard." He was firmly convinced that it was nothing but red. Another person, after visiting the tree said, "I have seen a green lizard." He was firmly convinced that it was nothing but green. But the man who lived under the tree said, "What both of you have said is true. But the fact is that the creature is sometimes red, sometimes green, sometimes yellow, and sometimes has no color at all." [2]

Every student of comparative mythology knows that when the orthodox mind talks and writes of God the nations go asunder; the *deśī,* the local, historical, ethical aspect of the cult symbol is taken with absolute seriousness and the chameleon is green, not red. Whereas, when the mystics talk, no matter what their *deśī,* their words in a profound sense meet—and the nations too. The names of Shiva, Allah, Buddha, and Christ lose their historical force and come together as adequate pointers of a way (*mārga*) that all must go who would transcend their time-bound, earth-bound faculties and limitations.

We have summarized in Parts Two to Four the history and

distribution of the mythological forms according to the plane of interest of history and ethnology. It remains now to indicate very briefly the psychological levels in terms of which symbols are experienced and utilized. And here it will be useful to turn to India for a system of classification. For in India, where an essentially psychological orientation to the forms of myth has prevailed for millenniums in the disciplines of yoga, and a vast number of native and alien cults have existed side by side, a cross-cultural, non-sectarian, syncretic analysis of myth and ritual in psychological terms has yielded a number of very clear, well-defined orders of comparative interpretation—of which we may choose the simplest for our present introductory sketch of a unitary mythological science.

II. The Bondages of Love, Power, and Virtue

In classical Indian philosophy a distinction is made between the ends for which men strive in the world and the aim of absolute release from these ends. The ends for which men strive in the world are three—no more, no less; namely: love and pleasure (*kāma*), power and success (*artha:* pronounced "art-ha"), and lawful order and moral virtue (*dharma*).

The first, *kāma,* corresponds to the aim or interest conceived by Freud to be fundamental to all life and thought, and—as a vast literature of psychoanalytic research now lets us know—anyone motivated by this urge, whether he be the patient or the doctor, sees sex in everything and everything in sex. The symbolism of mythology, like the world itself, means sex and nothing else to such a psyche: food, shelter, sex, and parenthood. And all mythology and cult then (including the cult of psychoanalysis itself) is simply a means to the harmonious realization of this vegetal system of interests.

The second category of worldly aims, *artha,* "power and success," corresponds to that conceived by the philosophy of Friedrich Nietzsche and the later psychology of Alfred Adler [3] to be the fundamental impulse and interest of all life and thought; and again, we have a considerable clinical literature to let us know that any psyche fully mastered by this drive, desiring to conquer, eat, consume, and turn all things into itself or into its own, discovers in the myths, gods, and rituals of religion, no more than supernatural means for self- and tribal aggrandizement.

These two systems of interest, then—the erotic and aggressive—may be taken to represent, together, the sum of man's primary biological urges. They do not have to be infused; they are implicit at birth and supply the animal foundations of all experience and reaction.

We have already observed that in many animal species the innate releasing mechanisms (IRMs) respond immediately and appropriately to specific stimuli of which the individual animal in question has had no previous experience, the reacting, "knowing" subject in such cases being not the individual but the species; whereas in others an individual experience (an "imprint") supplies the sign stimulus to which the affected IRM thereafter responds. And we have observed, further, that in the species man the majority of the responses are to sign stimuli established by imprint. But then we found that such imprints are in large measure constant to the species, so that a considerable series can be named of fundamental imprints or engrams to which the whole race responds. In other words, we found that there are certain fundamental biological urges ingrained from birth in the human central nervous system and that these are released by sign stimuli which, in the main, are also constant to the species, though not innate. And so we may say that a substantial trans-cultural system of constants has been found to exist, on the level of which no greatly significant historical or sociological differentiations can be discerned.

Furthermore, we now must note, in addition, that these two elementary systems of interest, *kāma* and *artha,* pleasure and power, do not necessarily support each other but often are in conflict. For example, even among the fish, the little fellow known as the stickleback has a highly effective concealing color pattern outside of the breeding season, but when he is ready for mating everything changes. As Professor Tinbergen describes the case: "The back is much darker than the ventral side, thus counterfeiting the effect of dorsal illumination ('counter-shading'), and the sides show a pattern of vertical bars, thus breaking up the visual outline of the body ('disruptive pattern')."[4] During the short courtship period, however, the coloration of the little fish changes, "leaving the back a radiant bluish-white, while the ventral side becomes deep red. The result is a total reversal of the countershading while the disruptive coloration disappears. The fish is now very conspicuous indeed, which is an adaptation to attract females. At the same time such a male is extremely mobile and practically loses its escape reactions. There are indications that these adaptations serving cooperation between the sexes render him very vulnerable to predators like cormorants and herons.

"Such a conflict between various 'interests,' of which this is only a random example, is in fact a basic phenomenon of adaptiveness," Tinbergen declares; and he concludes: "The conflict is resolved by all animals in such a way as to compromise between the different demands."[5]

And in man, too, there has to be a compromise. So that in the psyche itself, even before the factor of the social norms and *mores*—the aim of *dharma*—is introduced, an elementary problem of balance and harmonization exists, which has to be solved—and solved, and solved again, since man, unlike the stickleback, has no mating season, but is ever alert to the values and offerings of both worlds.

Dharma, the sense of duty, the knowledge of one's duty and the will to abide by it, is not innate, but the aim instilled in the young by education. Since the period of the Renaissance, we of the West have come to believe that the proper aim of education is the inculcation of information about the world in which we live. This, however, was not the aim in the past, nor is it the aim in the Orient (in which I include Russia) to this day. The aim of education in the primitive, archaic, and Oriental spheres has always been and will no doubt continue to be, for many centuries, not primarily to enlighten the mind concerning the nature of the universe, but to create communities of shared experience for the engagement of the sentiments of the growing individual in the matters of chief concern to the local group. The unsocialized thought and feeling of the very young child are egocentric but not socially dangerous.

When the primary urges of the adolescent remain unsocialized, however, they become inevitably a threat to the harmony of the group. The paramount function of all myth and ritual, therefore, has always been, and surely must continue to be, to engage the individual, both emotionally and intellectually, in the local organization. And this aim is best effected—as we have seen—through a solemn conjuring up of intensely shared experiences by virtue of which the whole system of childhood fantasy and spontaneous belief is engaged and fused with the functioning system of the community. The infantile ego—uncommitted, unaware of itself as distinct from the universe and ranging without bounds, without regard for the conventions of the local scene (like those Greenland Eskimo puppies who could not learn until adolescence the political geography of the packs) *—is dissolved for recombination in a ritual and actual experience of death and resurrection: death of the infantile ego and resurrection of the socially desirable adult. So that, thereafter, the man is neither physically nor spiritually a general model of the species Homo sapiens, but specifically an example of a certain local type, developed to function in a certain way in a certain field.

Kāma, artha, and *dharma,* then—pleasure, power, and the laws of virtue, the two primary systems of interest of the raw individual controlled by the *mores* of the local group—are the fields of force composed in every functioning system of mythology on its plane of address to the common man, the hard-headed, tough-minded, honest hunter, his wife, and his family. And so that the pedagogically furnished system of the law (*dharma*) should have the weight and authority to work upon the two others (*kāma* and *artha*), it is presented as the will and nature of some unimpeachable higher might—which, according to the level of development of the group in question, may be represented as the will and magic of the "ancestors," the will of an omnipotent all-father, the mathematics of the universe, the natural order of an ideal humanity, or an abstract, immutable imperative seated in the moral nature of every man who is properly a man. The main point throughout, however, is that this third, socially presented principle

* Supra, p. 36.

should have sovereignty over nature's two, and that the members of the group who represent it should have the whip hand. Attitudes of love, fear, servitude, pride in achievement, and identification with the law itself are variously fostered by the rites through which the local *dharma* is imprinted; and the individual, assaulted from every side—no less from inside than from out—is either beaten into form or rendered mad.

We should not judge the case of the past, however, by the present. Among the paleolithic nomads the groups were relatively small and the demands of *dharma* relatively simple. Furthermore, the roles to be played accorded with the natural capacities of the male and female organisms, which had evolved and been gradually shaped under conditions of the hunt during the course of a period of some six hundred thousand years. With the turn, however, to agriculture, c. 6000 B.C., and the rapid development then of sedentary, highly differentiated, and very much larger social units (up to, say, four or five hundred souls), the problem not only of enforcing but also of rationalizing a *dharma* in which inequality and yet coordination were of the essence became acute. It was then—by a stroke of intuitive genius—that the order of the universe, in which inequality and coordination are of the essence, was taken as a model, and mankind was put to school to the stars. In every one of the archaic systems the mythology of a natural harmony coordinating mankind and the universe poured its force into the various social orders, so that the sheer brutality of the interplay of the three mutually antagonistic interest systems of *kāma, artha,* and *dharma* was softened, beautified, and significantly enriched by the operation of a fourth principle, that of the mind's awe before the cognized mystery of the world.

And it is now to this fourth principle that we must turn our regard; for although it is true that the full extremes of dedication to this principle have been realized only in the Orient, it is also and equally true that its force, in what may be termed the minor, first stages of its mysteries, inhabits, and has always inhabited, mythology wherever it has lived, and will today, as its spirit is recaptured, make it evident that science itself is now the only field through which the dimension of mythology can be again revealed.

III. The Release from Bondage

In the period of the hieratic city states man's awe before the discovered order of the universe moved him to match that order in a mime, based on what he conceived to be celestial laws, which should bring into play in his own field of *kāma, artha,* and *dharma* the force of a superior principle. Comparably, in the earlier periods of the paleolithic and mesolithic gatherers, hunters, and primitive planters, a sense of awe before the closely watched wonders of the animal and plant domains had produced the mimes of the buffalo dance and the sacrificed seed. Through such half-mad games and plays ordered human societies were constellated in which the mutually contradictory interests of the elementary and social urges were resolved. And the higher principle according to which they were thus resolved was not in any sense a function or derivative either of any one of them or of their combination, but an actually superior, superordinated principle *sui generis,* which we have already seen illustrated in the round dance of Köhler's chimpanzees: that principle of disinterested delight and self-loss in a rhythm of beauty, which now is termed aesthetic and which used to be called, more loosely, spiritual, mystical, or religious. The biological urges to enjoy and to master (with their opposites, to loathe and to fear), as well as the social urge to evaluate (as good or evil, true or false), simply drop away, and a rapture in sheer experience supervenes, in which self-loss and elevation are the same. Such an impact is "beyond words"; for it is not such as can be explained by a reference to anything else. The mind is released—for a moment, for a day, or perhaps forever—from those anxieties to enjoy, to win, or to be correct, which spring from the net of nerves in which men are entangled. Ego dissolved, there is nothing in the net but life—which is everywhere, and forever. The Zen masters of China and Japan have called this state the state of "no-mind." The classical Indian terms are *mokṣa,* "release," *bodhi,* "enlightenment," and *nirvāṇa,* "transcendence of the winds of passion." Joyce speaks of "the luminous silent stasis of esthetic pleasure," when the clear radiance of the aesthetic image is apprehended by the mind, which has been arrested by its wholeness and fascinated by its harmony. "The mind," he says, "in that mysterious instant Shelley likened beautifully to a fading coal."

The impulse to art—the impulse to echo, through accord, an apprehended order of beauty—underlies the grandiose formation of the archaic orders of society; and, as we have seen, whole populations could be caught up in such a picture and given form, a new form, in which, paradoxically, all was surrendered and yet a heightened life was gained. We cannot suppose, however, that all who participated in the mime experienced its wonder in aesthetic terms. For the majority its value must have been only magical: a power to produce the fruits of their three elementary orders of desire. And yet, we cannot assume out of hand that there was none capable of disinterested wonder; for whence, then, would the rapture have sprung from which the social forms themselves derived? The words of our two Eskimo shamans, Igjugarjuk and Najagneq, have let us know that primitive man could bring his mind to rest in the mystery of the universe and therewith attain to a knowledge that can be justly called wisdom. His technical and scientific knowledge was limited to the horizon of his pitiful temporal community, but his wisdom, his enlightenment, his sense and experience of the mystery and power of the universe, was of eternal worth.

We have already pointed to the deep psychological cleavage separating the tough-minded "honest hunters" from their feared yet indispensable tender-minded shamans. We must now observe that for these two types, throughout the course of history, mythology and cult have had precisely opposite meanings, values, and effects. The benefits of religion for the majority have been primarily of the orders of *kāma, artha,* and *dharma.* The cult has served as a magical device to assure an abundance of food and youngsters, power over enemies, and the linkage of the individual to the order of his society. It has served, that is to say, as a means to engage him in the *deśī,* the local, ethnic context, and has supplied, in compensation, assurance of a continuance of the goods of *kāma, artha,* and *dharma* beyond the grave. One's little offerings of finger-joints, pigs, sons and daughters, or even of oneself, seem to have meaning in a sort of mystical barter system; and one's peccadillos, missed by the police, can be counted on to eat from within, like rats, doing the work of the law. But then, perhaps, on occasion, in the precincts of the temple, dancing ground, or some sacred site, the fleeting wisp of a sense of some mystery beyond, in the face of which all of this is trivial nonsense, may be experienced and therewith—even if only for a second—the interest of the fourth end for which men may live will have been attained.

The Way of Suffering of the shaman is the earliest example we know of a lifetime devoted to the fourth end: the serious use of myth hermetically, as *mārga,* as a way to psychological metamorphosis. And the remarkable fact is that the evidence points irrefutably to an achievement—at least in many cases—of a perceptible amplification of the individual's horizon of experience and depth of realization through his spiritual death and resurrection, even on the level of these first primitive explorations. The shaman is in a measure released from the local system of illusions and put in touch with mysteries of the psyche itself, which lead to wisdom concerning both the soul and its world; and he thereby performs the necessary function for society of moving it from stability and sterility in the old toward new reaches and new depths of realization.

The two types of mind, thus, are complementary: the tough-minded, representing the inert, reactionary; and the tender, the living progressive impulse—respectively, attachment to the local and timely and the impulse to the timeless universal. In human history the two have faced each other in dialogue since the beginning, and the effect has been that actual progress and process from lesser to greater horizons, simple to complex organizations, slight to rich patterns of the art-work which is civilization in its flowering in time.

Once this point is made, I think, it speaks for itself. The dual service of myth as contributory to the ends of *kāma, artha,* and *dharma,* and, on the other hand, as a means of release from these ego-linked obsessions, is now perfectly obvious. And that in the latter service it is functioning as art can hardly be denied. Can mythology have sprung from any minds but the minds of artists? The temple-caves of the paleolithic give us our answer.

Mythology—and therefore civilization—is a poetic, supernormal image, conceived, like all poetry, in depth, but susceptible of interpretation on various levels. The shallowest minds see in it the local scenery; the deepest, the foreground of the void; and between are all the stages of the Way from the ethnic to the elementary idea, the local to the universal being, which is Everyman, as he both knows and is afraid to know. For the human mind in its polarity of the male and female modes of experience, in its passages from infancy to adulthood and old age, in its toughness and tenderness, and in its continuing dialogue with the world, is the ultimate mythogenetic zone—the creator and destroyer, the slave and yet the master, of all the gods.

REFERENCE NOTES

PROLOGUE: TOWARD A NATURAL HISTORY OF THE GODS AND HEROES

1. Thomas Mann, *Joseph and His Brothers,* Vol. I, *The Tales of Jacob* (New York: Alfred A. Knopf, 1936), p. 3.
2. Thomas Mann, "Freud and the Future," *Life and Letters Today,* Vol. 15, No. 5 (Autumn 1936), p. 89.
3. *Udāna* 6.4.66–69; cf. Eugene Watson Burlingame, *Buddhist Parables* (New Haven: Yale University Press, 1922), pp. 75–76.
4. Cf. A. Meillet and Marcel Cohen, *Les Langues du monde* (Paris: H. Champion, 1952), p. xxiii.
5. Sir William Jones, "Third Anniversary Discourse" (February 2, 1786), *Works,* ed. Lord Teignmouth (London, 1807), Vol. III, p. 34.
6. Franz Bopp, *Über das Conjugationssystem der Sanskritsprache in Vergleichung mit jenem der griechischen, lateinischen, persischen und germanischen Sprache* (Frankfurt am Main, 1816).
7. Arthur Schopenhauer, Parerga II, par. 185, *Werke,* Vol. VI, p. 427.
8. Leo Frobenius, "Die Masken und Geheimbunde Afrikas," *Abhandlungen der Königlichen Leop.-Carol. Deutschen Akademie der Naturforscher,* Bd. LXXIV, Nr. 1 (Halle, 1898).
9. St. Thomas Aquinas, *Summa contra Gentiles,* Ch. v.
10. Wilhelm Wundt, *Völkerpsychologie* (Leipzig: W. Engelmann, 5 vols., 1900–1909; 10 vols., 1911–1920); *Probleme der Völkerpsychologie* (2nd ed.; Stuttgart: Alfred Kroner Verlag, 1921), pp. 1–37.
11. Jean Martin Charcot, *Nouvelle iconographie de la Salpêtrière* (1888–1895); *Leçons du mardi à la Salpêtrière* (1889–1890).
12. Carl G. Jung, *Wandlungen und Symbole der Libido,* first published in two parts in the *Jahrbuch für psychoanalytische und psychopathologische Forschungen* (Leipzig, III–IV, 1912), and republished the same year as a book by Deuticke Verlag, Leipzig and Vienna. English translations: *Psychology of the Unconscious,* translated by Dr. Beatrice M. Hinkle (New York: Moffatt Yard and Company, 1916), and *Symbols of Transformation,* translated by R. F. C. Hull, from the 4th edition, revised, 1952 (New York: Pantheon Books, The Bollingen Series XX, 1956).
13. Sigmund Freud, *Totem und Tabu,* first published in two parts in *Imago* (Bd. 1–2, 1912–1913); republished as a book by H. Heller und Compagnie, Leipzig, 1913; *Gesammelte Schriften,* Vol. X (Vienna, Psychoanalytischer Verlag); English translations by Dr. A. A. Brill, *Totem and Tabu* (New York: New Republic, 1931), by James Strachey (New York: W. W. Norton and Company, 1952).
14. Mann, "Freud and the Future," p. 87.
15. Ibid., p. 89.

PART ONE: THE PSYCHOLOGY OF MYTH

INTRODUCTION: THE LESSON OF THE MASK

1. Mann, "Freud and the Future."
2. Leo Frobenius, *Paideuma, Umrisse einer Kultur- und Seelenlehre,* 3 Aufl. (Frankfurt, 1928), pp. 143–45.
3. J. Huizinga, *Homo Ludens,* translated by R. F. C. Hull (London: Routledge and Kegan Paul, 1949), p. 5.
4. Ibid., p. 22.
5. Ibid., p. 23.
6. Ibid., p. 25.
7. Heinrich Zimmer, *Philosophies of India,* ed. Joseph Campbell (New York: Pantheon Books, The Bollingen Series XXVI, 1951).
8. Swami Nikhilananda, translator, *The Gospel of Sri Ramakrishna* (New York: Ramakrishna-Vivekananda Center, 1942), p. 396.
9. Ibid.
10. Ibid., pp. 778–79.
11. Huizinga, op. cit., pp. 34–35.
12. Cited by Clement of Alexandria, *Exhortation to the Greeks,* p. 61 P.
13. *Kena Upaniṣad* 1.3.
14. Immanuel Kant, *Prolegomena zu einer jeden künftigen Metaphysik, die als Wissenschaft wird auftreten können,* paragraph 58.

CHAPTER 1: THE ENIGMA OF THE INHERITED IMAGE

1. C. G. Jung, *Psychologische Typen* (Zurich: Rascher Verlag, 1921), p. 598.
2. Adolf Bastian, *Das Beständige in den Menschenrassen und die Spielweite ihrer Veränderlichkeit* (Berlin: Dietrich Reimer, 1868), p. 88.
3. A. R. Radcliffe-Brown, *The Andaman Islanders* (2nd printing; London: Cambridge University Press, 1933), pp. 233–34.
4. N. Tinbergen, *The Study of Instinct* (London: Oxford University Press, 1951), pp. 7–8.
5. Ibid., p. 150.
6. Ludwig Bolk, *Das Problem der Menschwerdung* (Jena: Gustav Fischer, 1926), pp. 32–33.
7. Konrad Lorenz, "Psychologie und Stammesgeschichte," in *Die Evolution der Organismen,* Gerhard Heberer, ed. (2d ed.; Stuttgart: Gustav Fischer Verlag, 1954), p. 161; as cited by Herbert Wendt, *In Search of Adam* (Boston: Houghton Mifflin Company, 1955), p. 144.
8. A. E. Housman, *The Name and Nature of Poetry* (London: Cambridge University Press; and New York: The Macmillan Company, 1933), pp. 45–46.
9. Ibid., p. 34.
10. Ibid., pp. 35 and 37.
11. Tinbergen, op. cit., p. 44.
12. Adolf Portmann, "Die Bedeutung der Bilder in der lebendigen Energiewandlung," *Eranos-Jahrbuch 1952* (Zurich: Rhein-Verlag, 1953), pp. 333–34.
13. Tinbergen, op. cit., p. 197.
14. Géza Róheim, *Psychoanalysis and Anthropology* (New York: International Universities Press, 1950), pp. 403–404.
15. E. Kaila, "Die Reaktionen des Säuglings auf das menschliche Gesicht," *Annales Universitatis Aboensis,* Turku, Vol. 17 (1932).
16. R. A. Spitz and K. M. Wolf, "The Smiling Response," *Genetic Psychology Monographs,* Vol. 34 (1946).
17. Adolf Portmann, "Das Problem der Urbilder in biologischer Sicht," *Eranos-Jahrbuch 1949* (Zurich: Rhein-Verlag, 1950), p. 426.
18. Konrad Lorenz, "Die angeborenen Formen möglicher Erfahrung," *Zeitschrift der Tierpsychologie,* Bd. 5 (1943), pp. 235–409.
19. Ralph Linton, *The Study of Man* (New York and London: D. Appleton-Century Company, 1936), p. 108.

CHAPTER 2: THE IMPRINTS OF EXPERIENCE

1. James Joyce, *A Portrait of the Artist as a Young Man* (London: Jonathan Cape, 1916), p. 252.
2. *Timaeus* 90D.
3. Nicholas of Cusa, *De Visione Dei,* translated by Emma Gurney Salter (London and Toronto: J. M. Dent and Sons; New York: E. P. Dutton and Company, 1928), pp. 25–27.
4. *Kena Upaniṣad* 1.3.
5. H. Ostermann, *The Alaskan Eskimos, as Described in the Posthumous Notes of Dr. Knud Rasmussen. Report of the Fifth Thule Expedition 1921–24,* Vol. X, No. 3 (Copenhagen: Nordisk Forlag, 1952), pp. 97–99.
6. Cited by C. G. Jung, *Seelenprobleme der Gegenwart* (Zurich: Rascher Verlag, 1931), p. 67.
7. Apuleius, *The Golden Ass,* translated by W. Adlington, Book XI.
8. Adolf Portmann, "Die Erde als Heimat des Lebens," *Eranos-Jahrbuch 1953* (Zurich: Rhein-Verlag, 1954), pp. 473–94.
9. Géza Róheim, "Dream Analysis and Field Work in Anthropology," *Psychoanalysis and the Social Sciences* (New York: International Universities Press, 1947), Vol. I, p. 90.
10. Ovid, *Metamorphoses* III, 173 ff.
11. Heinrich Zimmer, *The King and the Corpse,* ed. Joseph Campbell (New York: Pantheon Books, The Bollingen Series XI, 1948), pp. 311–12.
12. Ovid, *Metamorphoses* III, translated by Frank Justus Miller (Cambridge, Mass.: Harvard University Press, Loeb Classical Library), 188–93.
13. Hans Weinert, "Der fossile Mensch," *Anthropology Today* (Chicago: University of Chicago Press, 1953), p. 108.
14. Henry Fairfield Osborn, *Men of the Old Stone Age* (3d ed.; New York: Charles Scribner's Sons, 1918), pp. 214–22, 513–14; also Carleton S. Coon, *The Story of Man* (New York: Alfred A. Knopf, 1954), pp. 67–69.
15. Jean Piaget, *The Child's Conception of the World* (New York: Harcourt, Brace and Company, 1929), p. 231.
16. Ibid., pp. 245–46.
17. Ibid., p. 233.
18. Melanie Klein, "Early Stages of the Oedipus Complex," *International Journal of Psycho-analysis,* Vol. ix (1928); also *The Psychoanalysis of Children* (London: Hogarth Press, 1932), pp. 179–209.
19. W. F. Jackson Knight, "Maze Symbolism and the Trojan Game," *Antiquity* VI (December 1932), pp. 445–58; 450, note 3.
20. Ibid., p. 446.
21. Ibid., p. 450, note 3.
22. Virgil, *Aeneid* VI. 255–63.
23. John Layard, "Der Mythos der Totenfahrt auf Malekula," *Eranos-Jahrbuch 1937* (Zurich: Rhein-Verlag, 1938), pp. 274–75.
24. Morris Edward Opler, *Myths and Tales of the Jicarilla Apache Indians. Memoirs of the American Folklore Society,* Vol. XXXI (1938), p. 18.
25. Ibid., pp. 153, 184.
26. Sigmund Freud, *Neue Folge der Vorlesungen zur Einführung in die Psychoanalyse* (Vienna: Internationaler Psychoanalytischer Verlag, 1933), pp. 33 ff.
27. Radcliffe-Brown, op. cit., p. 194.
28. Opler, op. cit., p. 67.
29. Ibid., pp. 67–68.
30. Bronislaw Malinowski, *Sex and Repression in Savage Society* (London: Routledge and Kegan Paul, 1927), pp. 142–43.
31. Géza Róheim, "The Oedipus Complex, Magic and Culture," *Psychoanalysis and the Social Sciences* (New York: International Universities Press, 1950), Vol. II, pp. 173–228.
32. Ibid., *War, Crime, and the Covenant. Journal of Clinical Psychopathology,* Monograph Series No. 1 (Monticello, N.Y.: Medical Journal Press, 1945), p. 61.
33. Ibid., p. 57.
34. *Hamlet* I.v.96–106.
35. Piaget, op. cit., pp. 92–96.

36. Ibid., pp. 97–98.
37. *A Catechism of Christian Doctrine,* Prepared and Enjoined by Order of the Third Plenary Council of Baltimore. Kinkead's Baltimore Series of Catechisms, No. 3 (New York: Benziger Brothers, 1885), Question 888.
38. *The Gospel of Sri Ramakrishna,* p. 206.
39. Piaget, op. cit., p. 241.
40. *Der Hl. Gertrude der Grossen Gesandter der göttlichen Liebe, nach der Ausgabe der Benediktiner von Solesmes übersetzt von Johannes Weissbrodt* (12th ed.; Freiburg: Verlag Herder, 1954), Book I, Ch. 21, p. 116.
41. *Bṛhadāraṇyaka Upaniṣad* 4.3.21.
42. Quoted by D. T. Suzuki, *Mysticism: Christian and Buddhist* (New York: Harper and Brothers, 1957), p. 180.
43. E. H. Whinfield, translator, *The Rubáiyát of Omar Khayyám,* verse 400.
44. Piaget, op. cit., p. 256.
45. Ibid., pp. 366–67.
46. Ibid., pp. 361–62.
47. *Kiddushin* 71a.
48. *Soferim* iv.
49. John 1:1–4.
50. Genesis 1:3.
51. Piaget, op. cit., p. 72.
52. Ibid., p. 64.
53. Ibid., p. 72.
54. Ibid., p. 368.
55. Baldwin Spencer and F. J. Gillen, *The Native Tribes of Central Australia* (London: Macmillan and Company, 1899), pp. 215–216; also Géza Róheim, *Psychoanalysis and Anthropology,* p. 76.
56. Spencer and Gillen, op. cit., pp. 218–30.
57. Cf. E. F. Worms, "Northwest Australian Prehistoric Rock Carvings and Cave Paintings," *Vth Session of the International Congress of Anthropological Sciences* (Philadelphia, 1956); also *Anthropos,* Vol. L (1955), pp. 546–566.
58. Spencer and Gillen, op. cit., pp. 244–46.
59. Ibid., p. 246, note 1.
60. Ibid., pp. 246–49.
61. Géza Róheim, *The Eternal Ones of the Dream* (New York: International Universities Press, 1945), p. 74.
62. Ibid., p. 75.
63. Ibid., pp. 74–75.
64. Ibid., p. 73.
65. *Nonni Dionysiaca* 6.121; *Orphei Hymni* 39.7; 39.253; O. Kern, *Orphicorum fragmenta* 34, 35, 54; Clement of Alexandria, *Exhortation to the Greeks,* ii, p. 15 P.
66. E.g., Jane Ellen Harrison, *Themis: A Study of the Social Origins of Greek Religion* (London: Cambridge University Press, 1927).
67. Spencer and Gillen, op. cit., p. 257.
68. Róheim, *The Eternal Ones of the Dream,* p. 164.
69. Ibid., p. 165.
70. Cf. Robert H. Lowie, *Primitive Religion* (New York: Boni and Liveright, 1924), p. 211.
71. Róheim, *The Eternal Ones of the Dream,* p. 174.
72. Ibid., p. 177.
73. Genesis 2:21–24.
74. *Symposium* 189D ff. *The Dialogues of Plato,* translated by Benjamin Jowett (New York: Random House, 1937).
75. John C. Ferguson, *Chinese Mythology. The Mythology of All Races,* Vol. VIII (Boston: Marshall Jones Company, 1928), p. 111.
76. *Bṛhadāraṇyaka Upaniṣad* 1.4.1–5.
77. T. G. H. Strehlow, *Aranda Traditions* (Melbourne: Melbourne University Press, 1947), pp. 7–8, abridged.
78. Snorri Sturluson, *The Prose Edda,* "Gylfaginning," translated by Arthur Gilchrist Brodeur (New York: American-Scandinavian Foundation, 1929), pp. 17–18.
79. Ibid., VIII, p. 21.
80. *Ṛg Veda* X. 90.
81. Stephen Herbert Langdon, *Semitic Mythology. The Mythology of All Races,* Vol. V (Boston: Marshall Jones Company, 1931), pp. 277–325.
82. Cf. Ernst Benz, "Theogonie und Wandlung des Menschen bei Friedrich Wilhelm Joseph Schelling," *Eranos-Jahrbuch 1954* (Zurich: Rhein-Verlag, 1955), pp. 316, 338.

83. Spencer and Gillen, op. cit., pp. 360, 373.
84. Róheim, *Psychoanalysis and Anthropology,* pp. 77–78.
85. Spencer and Gillen, op. cit., p. 364.
86. Ibid., p. 365.
87. Ibid., pp. 363–67, slightly modified, with insert from p. 350.
88. Henrik Ibsen, *Peer Gynt,* last two verses, translated by William Archer.
89. A. Capus, "Contes, Chants et Proverbes des Basumbua dans l'Afrique Orientale," *Zeitschrift für afrikanische und oceanische Sprachen* (Berlin, 1897), Vol. III, pp. 363–64.
90. Abraham Fornander and Thomas G. Thrum, *Fornander Collection of Hawaiian Antiquities and Folk-lore. Memoirs of the Bernice Pauahi Bishop Museum,* Vol. V, Part III (Honolulu, 1919), p. 574.
91. Martha W. Beckwith, ed., *Kepelino's Traditions of Hawaii* (Honolulu: Bernice Pauahi Bishop Museum, Bulletin 95, 1932), p. 52.
92. Martha W. Beckwith, *Hawaiian Mythology* (New Haven: Yale University Press, 1940), p. 157.
93. Fornander and Thrum, op. cit., pp. 572–76.
94. Sturluson, op. cit., "Gylfaginning," XLI.
95. Ibid., "Gylfaginning," XXXVI.
96. Ibid., "Skaldskaparmal," XXXIII.
97. Ibid., "Gylfaginning," XVI.
98. *Poetic Edda,* "Hovamol" 139, translated by Henry Adams Bellows (New York: American-Scandinavian Foundation, 1923), p. 60.
99. C. G. Jung, *Modern Man in Search of a Soul* (New York: Harcourt, Brace and Company, 1936), pp. 125–26.
100. Ibid., p. 129.
101. Ibid., pp. 129–30.
102. Ibid., p. 123.
103. Leo Frobenius, *Monumenta Africana. Erlebte Erdteile,* Bd. VI (Frankfurt am Main: Frankfurter Sociatäts-Druckerei, 1929), pp. 435–66.
104. Ibid., p. 439.
105. Spencer and Gillen, op. cit., pp. 497–511.
106. Frobenius, *Monumenta Africana,* pp. 457–60.
107. John Layard, *Stone Men of Malekula* (London: Chatto and Windus, 1942), pp. 530–31.

PART TWO: THE MYTHOLOGY OF THE PRIMITIVE PLANTERS

CHAPTER 3: THE CULTURE PROVINCE OF THE HIGH CIVILIZATIONS

1. D. A. E. Garrod and D. M. A. Bate, *The Stone Age of Mount Carmel* (London: Oxford University Press, 1937).
2. Cf. Leo Frobenius, *Ausfahrt. Erlebte Erdteile,* Bd. I (Frankfurt am Main, 1925), pp. 155–428; and Adolf Jensen, *Das religiöse Weltbild einer frühen Kultur* (Stuttgart: August Schröder Verlag, 1949).
3. Meillet and Cohen, op. cit., pp. 649–73.
4. Cf. V. Gordon Childe, *New Light on the Most Ancient East* (New York: D. Appleton Century Company, 1934); Henri Frankfort, *The Birth of Civilization in the Near East* (London: Williams and Norgate, Ltd., 1951); Robert J. Braidwood, *The Near East and the Foundations of Civilization* (Eugene, Ore.: University of Oregon Press, 1952); Robert J. and Linda Braidwood, "The Earliest Village Communities of Southwestern Asia," *Cahiers d'histoire mondiale,* Vol. I, No. 2 (Paris, October 1953), pp. 278–310; E. A. Speiser, "The Beginnings of Civilization in Mesopotamia," *Journal of the American Oriental Society,* Supplement No. 4, 1939; Robert W. Ehrich, ed., *Relative Chronologies in Old World Archaeology* (Chicago: University of Chicago Press, 1954).

5. M. E. L. Mallowan and J. Cruickshank Rose, "Excavations at Tall Arpachiyah," *Iraq,* II.1, 1935.
6. Robert Heine-Geldern, "The Origin of Ancient Civilizations and Toynbee's Thesis," *Diogenes,* No. 13 (University of Chicago Press, Spring 1956), pp. 90–99.
7. Timaeus 90.C–D, translated by Francis Macdonald Cornford in *Plato's Cosmology* (New York and London: Humanities Press, 1952), p. 354.

Chapter 4: THE PROVINCE OF THE IMMOLATED KINGS

1. Leo Frobenius, *Märchen aus Kordofan. Atlantis,* Vol. IV (Jena: Eugen Diederichs, 1923), pp. 9–17.
2. Diodorus Şiculus, *Bibliotheca historica* III.5–6.
3. Frobenius, *Märchen aus Kordofan,* p. 19.
4. Cf. Joseph Campbell, "Editor's Introduction," *The Portable Arabian Nights* (New York: The Viking Press, 1952), p. 22, citing John Payne, *The Book of the Thousand Nights and One Night* (London, 1882–1884), Vol. IX, pp. 261–392.
5. Jeremiah Curtin, *Myths and Folklore of Ireland* (Boston: Little, Brown and Company, 1890).
6. Standish H. O'Grady, *Silva Gadelica* (London: Williams and Norgate, 1892).
7. Joseph Campbell, "Folkloristic Commentary," *Grimm's Fairy Tales* (New York: Pantheon Books, 1944), p. 833, citing Johannes Bolte and Georg Polivka, *Anmerkungen zu den Kinder- und Hausmärchen der Brüder Grimm* (Leipzig, 1912–1932), Vol. IV, pp. 443–44.
8. 'Ali Abū-l Hasan ul-Mas'ūdī, *Marūjudh-Dhahab* (*Les Prairies d'or*), C. Barbier de Maynard and Pavet de Courteille, eds., 9 vols. (Paris: Imprimerie Impériale, 1861–1877), Vol. 4, pp. 89–90.
9. Frobenius, *Märchen aus Kordofan,* p. 22.
10. Ibid., pp. 20–21.
11. Sir James George Frazer, *The Golden Bough* (one-volume edition; New York: The Macmillan Company, 1922), p. 267.
12. Frobenius, *Monumenta Africana,* pp. 318–22.
13. Duarte Barbosa, *Description of the Coasts of East Africa and Malabar in the Beginning of the Sixteenth Century* (London: The Hakluyt Society, 1866), p. 172; cited by Frazer, op. cit., pp. 274–75.
14. Leo Frobenius, *Schicksalskunde im Sinne des Kulturwerdens* (Leipzig: R. Voigtlanders Verlag, 1932), p. 127.
15. Leo Frobenius, *Monumenta Terrarum: Der Geist über den Erdteilen. Erlebte Erdteile,* Bd. VII (Frankfurt am Main: Forschungsinstitut für Kulturmorphologie, 1929), 392–94, citing, among others, E. Pechuël-Lösche, *Volkskunde von Loango* (Stuttgart: Strecker und Schröder, 1907), pp. 155–92, who, in turn, cites O. Dapper, *Beschreibung von Afrika* (1668) and the Abbot Proyart (1776).

Chapter 5: THE RITUAL LOVE-DEATH

1. Paul Wirz, *Die Marind-anim von Hollandisch Süd-Neu-Guinea* (Hamburg: L. Friedrichsen and Company, Vol. I, 1922, Vol. II, 1925).
2. Ibid., Vol. II, pp. 40–44.
3. Jensen, op. cit., pp. 34–38.
4. After ibid., p. 39.
5. Ibid., pp. 168–70.
6. Cf. Adolf E. Jensen, "Die mythische Weltbetrachtung der alten Pflanzer-Volker," *Eranos-Jahrbuch 1949* (Zurich: Rhein-Verlag, 1950), pp. 440–47.
7. Frazer, op. cit., p. 386.
8. *Homeri Hymnus in Cererem* 2; also Ovid, *Metamorphoses* V, 385 ff.

9. Frazer, op. cit., p. 470.
10. Jane Ellen Harrison, *Prolegomena to the Study of Greek Religion* (3d ed.; London: Cambridge University Press, 1922).
11. Scholiast to Lucian, *Dial. Meretr.* II.1, translated by Jane Ellen Harrison in ibid. (1st ed., 1903), p. 122.
12. Hippolytus, *Philosoph.* 5, 8.
13. Walter Otto, "Der Sinn der eleusinischen Mysterien," *Eranos-Jahrbuch 1939* (Zurich: Rhein-Verlag, 1940), pp. 99–106.
14. *Ephemeris archaiologikē, 1883, Archaiologikē hetaireis en Athēnais* (Athens: Carl Beck, 1884), p. 81.
15. Frazer, op. cit., pp. 479 ff.
16. Ovid, *Metamorphoses,* IV.665 ff.
17. Carl Kerényi, "Kore," in C. G. Jung and Carl Kerényi, *Essays on a Science of Mythology* (New York: Pantheon Books, The Bollingen Series XXII, 1949), pp. 179–87.
18. Jensen, *Das religiöse Weltbild einer frühen Kultur,* pp. 66–77.
19. Edward Winslow Gifford, *Tongan Myths and Tales* (Honolulu: Bernice Pauahi Bishop Museum Bulletin 8, 1924), p. 181.
20. J. F. Stimson, *The Legends of Maui and Tahaki* (Honolulu: Bernice Pauahi Bishop Museum Bulletin 127, 1934), pp. 28–35. The account is from a chant from the Tuamotus, here abridged from Stimson's text and rendered in narrative style.
21. Ibid., p. 3.
22. E.g., Captains James Cook and James King, *A Voyage to the Pacific Ocean* (London: G. Nicol and T. Cadell, 1784), Vol. II, Ch. X.
23. Gifford, op. cit., p. 183.
24. William Wyatt Gill, *Myths and Songs from the South Pacific* (London: Henry S. King and Company, 1876), pp. 77–79.
25. Ananda K. Coomaraswamy, *The Ṛg-Veda as Land-náma-bók* (London: Luzac and Company, 1935).
26. Thomas Thrum, *More Hawaiian Folk Tales* (Chicago: A. C. McClurg and Company, 1923), pp. 235–41.
27. W. J. Thomson, *Te pito te Henua, or Easter Island* (Washington, D.C.: Smithsonian Report, 1889), pp. 518–19, as cited by Werner Wolff, *Island of Death* (New York: J. J. Augustin, 1948), p. 179.
28. Meillet and Cohen, op. cit., p. 649.
29. Ibid., pp. 663–64, 671.
30. A. V. Kidder, "Looking Backward," *Proceedings of the American Philosophical Society,* LXXXIII, No. 4 (1940), pp. 527–37, cited by Clyde Kluckhohn in *Anthropology Today,* p. 512n.
31. Leo Frobenius, *Geographische Kulturkunde* (Leipzig: Friedrich Brandstetter, 1904), p. 450.
32. Cf. A. L. Kroeber, *Anthropology* (1st ed.; New York: Harcourt, Brace and Company, 1923), p. 491.
33. Cf. ibid., Fig. 36 (Spinden's diagrammatic representation of the development of native American culture) and p. 352 (Kroeber's own guess).
34. Frederick Johnson, "Radiocarbon Dating," *Memoirs of the Society for American Archaeology,* No. 8 (Salt Lake City, 1951), pp. 10–18.
35. Cf. Carleton S. Coon, op. cit., p. 149, and Harry L. Shapiro, "Les Iles Marquises: Prehistory of Polynesia," *Natural History,* May 1958, p. 265.
36. Gordon R. Willey, "Archaeological Theories and Interpretation: New World," *Anthropology Today,* p. 375.
37. Wendell C. Bennett, "New World Culture History: South America," *Anthropology Today,* pp. 220–21.
38. Julian H. Steward, "South American Cultures: An Interpretative Summary," *Handbook of South American Indians* (Washington, D.C.: Bureau of American Ethnology, Bulletin 143, Vol. V, 1949), p. 749.
39. Ibid., p. 769.
40. Carl O. Sauer, "Cultivated Plants in South and Central America," *Handbook of South American Indians,* Vol. VI (1950), p. 506.
41. Ibid., pp. 533–38.
42. Ibid., pp. 524–25.
43. Ibid., p. 497.
44. Ibid., p. 527.

45. Ibid., p. 494. See also, however, Paul C. Mangelsdorf, "New Evidence on the Origin and Ancestry of Maize," *American Antiquity,* XIX, No. 4 (1954).
46. Sauer, op. cit., pp. 499–500, 502–503, 510, 513.
47. Paul Rivet, "Early Contacts between Polynesia and America," *Diogenes,* No. 16 (Winter 1956), p. 82.
48. Ibid., pp. 78–87.
49. Kroeber, op. cit., pp. 226–27.
50. Robert Heine-Geldern and Gordon F. Eckholm, "Significant Parallels in the Symbolic Arts of Southern Asia and Middle America," *Selected Papers of the XXIXth International Congress of Americanists,* Vol. I, *The Civilization of Ancient America* (Chicago: University of Chicago Press, 1951); Robert Heine-Geldern, "The Origin of Ancient Civilizations and Toynbee's Thesis," loc. cit.; Charles Wolcott Brooks, "Reports of Japanese Vessels Wrecked in the North Pacific from the Earliest Records to the Present Time," *Proceedings of the California Academy of Sciences,* Vol. 6 (1875).
51. See Gordon F. Eckholm, "A Possible Focus of Asiatic Influence in the Late Classical Cultures of Mesoamerica," *Memoirs of the Society of American Archaeology,* Vol. XVIII, No. 3, Part 2 (January 1953), pp. 72–89.
52. Compare, for example, in *Anthropology Today,* the articles by Wendell C. Bennett ("New World Culture History: Middle America"), Alex D. Krieger ("New World Culture History: Anglo-America"), and Gordon R. Willey ("Archaeological Theories and Interpretation: New World"). A helpful chart and discussion will be found in Miguel Covarrubias, *The Eagle, the Jaguar, and the Serpent* (New York: Alfred A. Knopf, 1954), pp. 73–89. Further guidance will be found in Philip Ainsworth Means, *Ancient Civilizations of the Andes* (New York and London: Charles Scribner's Sons, 1931); P. Alden Mason, *The Ancient Civilizations of Peru* (London: Penguin Books, 1957); Sylvanus Griswold Morley, *The Ancient Maya* (Stanford: Stanford University Press, 1946); G. C. Vaillant, *The Aztecs of Mexico* (Penguin Books, 1950); Miguel Covarrubias, *Indian Art of Mexico and Central America* (New York: Alfred A. Knopf, 1957); and Gordon R. Willey and Philip Phillips, *Method and Theory in American Archaeology* (Chicago: University of Chicago Press, 1958). For the most recent study and C-14 datings of the Olmec complex, see Philip Drucker, Robert F. Heizer, and Robert J. Squier, *Excavations at La Venta Tabasco, 1955* (Washington: Bureau of American Ethnology, Bulletin 170, 1959).
53. Eckholm, loc. cit.
54. Willey, op. cit., p. 37.
55. Mentor L. Williams, ed., *Schoolcraft's Indian Legends* (East Lansing, Mich.: Michigan State University Press, 1956), pp. 58–60.
56. Theodor Koch-Grünberg, *Zwei Jahren unter den Indianern: Reisen in Nordwest-Brasilien 1903–1905* (Berlin: Ernst Wasmuch A. G., 1910), pp. 292–93.
57. Frazer, op. cit., pp. 589–91.
58. E. de Jonghe, "Histoyre du Méchique, Manuscrit français inédit du XVIe siècle," *Journal de la Société des Américanistes de Paris,* Nouvelle Série, Tome II, No. 1 (1905), pp. 28–29; cited by Jensen, *Das religiöse Weltbild einer frühen Kultur,* p. 119.

PART THREE: THE MYTHOLOGY OF THE PRIMITIVE HUNTERS

Chapter 6: SHAMANISM

1. From Robert H. Lowie, *Primitive Religion* (Black and Gold Library; New York: Boni and Liveright, 1924), p. 7. Copyright: (R) 1951 by Robert H. Lowie.
2. Ruth Benedict, *Patterns of Cul-*

ture (Boston: Houghton Mifflin Company, 1934), pp. 59–60.
3. Alex D. Krieger, op. cit., *Anthropology Today*, p. 251.
4. Opler, op. cit., p. 1.
5. *Vajracchedika* 32.
6. *The Tempest* IV.156–58.
7. Opler, op. cit., pp. 1–18, greatly condensed.
8. Ibid., p. 17.
9. *Rāmāyaṇa* 1.45, 7.1.
10. Opler, op. cit., p. 26.
11. John 12:24.
12. Natalie Curtis, *The Indians' Book* (New York: Harper and Brothers, 1907), pp. 38–39.
13. Knud Rasmussen, *Across Arctic America* (New York and London: G. P. Putnam's Sons, 1927), pp. 82–84. Copyright G. P. Putnam's Sons, Inc. Reprinted by permission of the publisher.
14. Ibid., pp. 84–85.
15. Ibid., pp. 85–86.
16. E. Lucas Bridges, *The Uttermost Part of the Earth* (New York: E. P. Dutton and Company; London: Hodder and Stoughton, 1948), p. 262.
17 Ibid., pp. 284–86.
18. Ibid., p. 264.
19. Ibid., pp. 232, 302–304.
20. Ibid., p. 290.
21. Ibid., p. 261.
22. G. V. Ksenofontov, *Legendy i rasskazy o shamanach u. yakutov, buryat i tungusov*. Izdanie vtoroe. S predisloviem S. A. Tokareva (Moscow: Izdatel'stvo Bezbozhnik, 1930); translated (into German) by Adolf Friedrich and Georg Buddruss, *Schamanengeschichten aus Siberien* (Munich: Otto Wilhelm Barth-Verlag, 1955), pp. 211–12.
23. Mircea Eliade, *Le Chamanisme et les techniques archaïques de l'extase* (Paris: Payot, 1951).
24. William James, *Pragmatism* (New York: Longmans, Green and Company, 1907), p. 12.
25. Paul Radin, *Primitive Man as Philosopher* (New York and London: D. Appleton and Company, 1927).
26. Eliade, op. cit., p. 40.
27. Spencer and Gillen, op. cit., pp. 523–25.
28. Géza Róheim, *Social Anthropology* (New York: Boni and Liveright, 1926), pp. 350–51.
29. Róheim, *The Eternal Ones of the Dream*, p. 191.
30. Ksenofontov, op. cit., pp. 213–14.
31. Uno Holmberg (Harva), *Finno-Ugric, Siberian Mythology. The Mythology of All Races*, Vol. IV (Boston: Marshall Jones Company, 1927), p. 499.
32. B. Munkácsi, *Vogul Népköltési Gyüjtemény*, Vol. III (Budapest, 1893), p. 7, cited by Géza Róheim, *Hungarian and Vogul Mythology* (Locust Valley, N.Y.: Monographs of the American Ethnological Society, J. J. Augustin, 1954), p. 22.
33. Munkácsi, op. cit., Vol. II, Part 1, 1910–1921, p. 066, cited by Róheim, op. cit., p. 30.
34. Ksenofontov, op. cit., pp. 179–181.
35. Ibid., pp. 181–83.
36. Jensen, *Das religiöse Weltbild einer frühen Kultur*, p. 131.
37. Ksenofontov, op. cit., pp. 160–161.
38. Ibid., p. 163.
39. Ibid., p. 163.
40. Ibid., p. 161.
41. Ibid., p. 133.
42. Ibid., pp. 146–47.
43. Adapted from George Bird Grinnell, *Blackfoot Lodge Tales* (New York: Charles Scribner's Sons, 1892), pp. 153–54.
44. Ibid., pp. 155–56.
45. After Paul Radin, *The Trickster* (New York: Philosophical Library, 1956), p. 8.
46. Ibid., pp. 22–23.
47. Ibid., pp. 25–27.
48. After Grinnell, op. cit., pp. 137–142.
49. After Radin, *The Trickster*, p. 53.
50. V. L. Serosevskii, *Yakuty* (Petrograd, 1896), p. 653.
51. Jung, "On the Psychology of the Trickster Figure," in Radin, *The Trickster*, pp. 197–99.
52. Charles Du Fresne Du Cange, *Glossarium Mediae et Infimae Latinitatis* (1733), s.v. *festum asinorum*.
53. Jung, op. cit., p. 209.
54. "Skazaniya buryat, zapisanniyia raznymi sobiratelyami," *Zapiški Vostocno-Sibirskago Otdela Russkago Geografičeskago Obsčestva*, I.2 (Irkutsk, 1890), pp. 65–66.
55. V. I Anucin, "Ocerk samanstva u yeniseyskich ostyakov," *Sbornik*

Muzeya po Antropologii i Ethnografi pri Akademii Nauk, II.2 (Petrograd, 1914), p. 14.

56. See, for example, George Bird Grinnell, *Blackfeet Indian Stories* (New York: Charles Scribner's Sons, 1917), pp. 145–46; and, for an extensive bibliography, Stith Thompson, *Tales of the North American Indians* (Cambridge, Mass.: Harvard University Press, 1929), p. 279, note 30, "Earth Diver."
57. After James A. Teit, "Thompson Tales," in *Folk-tales of Salishan and Sahaptin Tribes*, Franz Boas, ed., p. 2; *Memoirs of the American Folk-lore Society*, Vol. XI (1917); cited by James G. Frazer, *Myths of the Origin of Fire* (London: Macmillan and Company, 1930), pp. 173–74.
58. John R. Swanton, *Myths and Tales of the Southeastern Indians* (Washington, D.C.: Bureau of American Ethnology, Bulletin 88, 1929), p. 46; cited by Frazer, *Myths of the Origin of Fire*, p. 147.
59. Livingston Farrand, "Traditions of the Chilcotin Indians," *The Jessup North Pacific Expedition*, (New York: Memoir of the American Museum of Natural History, 1900), Vol. II, Part I, p. 3; cited by Frazer, *Myths of the Origin of Fire*, pp. 182–83.
60. Adapted from James A. Teit, "Kaska Tales," *Journal of American Folk-lore*, Vol. XXX (1917), p. 443.
61. Radcliffe-Brown, op. cit., pp. 202–203.
62. Aeschylus, *Prometheus Bound*, 937 ff., translated by John Stuart Blackie.
63. Job 42:5–6.
64. See Carl Kerényi, *The Gods of the Greeks* (London and New York: Thames and Hudson, 1951), pp. 215–16, citing *Hesiodi Opera et Dies* 50, *Hygini Astronomica* 2.15, and *Scholium Vergilius Eclogae* 6.42.
65. Sturluson, op. cit., "Gylfaginning," LI, pp. 78–79.
66. Nietzsche, *Thus Spake Zarathustra*, Prologue 2.

Chapter 7: THE ANIMAL MASTER

1. Grinnell, *Blackfoot Lodge Tales*, pp. 229–30.
2. After ibid., pp. 104–107, 220–24.
3. Dr. G. Lalanne, "Bas-reliefs à représentations humaines," *L'Anthropologie* (1911), pp. 257–60; "Bas-reliefs à figurations humaines de l'abri sous roche de Laussel (Dordogne)," ibid. (1912), pp. 129–48; Dr. G. Lalanne and chanoine J. Bouyssonie, "Le Gisement paléolithique de Laussel," ibid., Tome L (1950).
4. Lowie, op. cit., p. 6.
5. Ibid., p. 4.
6. Cf. Herbert J. Spinden, "First Peopling of America as a Chronological Problem," *Early Man*, George Grant MacCurdy, ed. (Philadelphia, New York, and London: F. B. Lippincott Company, 1937), pp. 105–14.
7. *Bhagavad Gītā* 2:17–18.
8. Ovid, *Metamorphoses*, XV, 165–168.
9. Rasmussen, op. cit., p. 80.
10. Grinnell, *Blackfoot Lodge Tales*, pp. 221–22.
11. Leo Frobenius, *Das unbekannte Afrika* (Munich: Oskar Beck, 1923), pp. 34–35.
12. Leo Frobenius, *Atlantis*, Vol. I, *Volksmärchen der Kabylen* (Jena: Eugen Diederich, 1921), pp. 14–15.

Chapter 8: THE PALEOLITHIC CAVES

1. Abbé H. Breuil, *Four Hundred Centuries of Cave Art* (Montignac, Dordogne: Centre d'études et de documentation préhistorique, no date), Figs. 86 and 89 and p. 118.

2. Ibid., Figs. 114 and 115, and pp. 134–37.
3. Ibid., pp. 135–37.
4. Géza Róheim, *Magic and Schizophrenia,* posthumously edited by Warner Muensterberger (New York: International Universities Press, 1955), pp. 36–37. For further examples and discussion, see Róheim, "The Pointing Bone," *Journal of the Royal Anthropological Institute,* Vol. LIV (1925), p. 90.
5. Róheim, *Psychoanalysis and Anthropology,* p. 131.
6. Spencer and Gillen, op. cit., p. 287, Fig. 47; p. 295, Fig. 52; pp. 332–33, Figs. 66 and 67; p. 518, Fig. 102.
7. Leo Frobenius, *Kulturgeschichte Afrikas* (Zurich: Phaidon-Verlag, 1933), pp. 131–32.
8. Breuil, op. cit., pp. 146–47.
9. Ibid., p. 236.
10. This account of the discovery is based on that given by Count Bégouën to Dr. Herbert Kühn at the time of the latter's visit to the cave in 1926. From Herbert Kühn, *Auf den Spuren des Eiszeitmenschen,* published by F. A. Brockhaus, Wiesbaden, Germany, 1953, pp. 88–90.
11. Ibid., pp. 91–94, abridged.
12. Breuil, op. cit., pp. 152–75.
13. Kühn, op. cit., p. 96.
14. Breuil, op. cit., p. 176.
15. Kühn, op. cit., pp. 94–95.
16. Coon, op. cit., p. 103.
17. Moritz Hoernes and Oswald Menghin, *Urgeschichte der bildenden Kunst in Europa* (Vienna: Anton Schroll and Company, 1925), pp. 116–17; Georges H. Luquet, *L'Art et la réligion des hommes fossiles* (Paris: Masson et Compagnie, 1926), p. 126.
18. Frobenius, *Das unbekannte Afrika,* pp. 27–28.
19. Oswald Menghin, *Weltgeschichte der Steinzeit* (Vienna: A. Schroll and Company, 1931), p. 148.
20. Franz Hančar, "Zum Problem der Venusstatuetten im eurasiatischen Jungpaläolithikum," *Praehistorische Zeitschrift,* XXX–XXXI Band (1939–40), 1/2 Heft, pp. 85–156.
21. Ibid., p. 151.
22. Ibid., p. 152.
23. Bridges, op. cit., pp. 412–14.
24. Ibid., p. 166.
25. Spencer and Gillen, op. cit., p. 426.
26. Ibid.
27. E. F. Worms, "Prehistoric Rock Carvings and Cave Paintings in Northwestern Australia," paper read at *Fifth International Congress of Anthropological and Ethnological Sciences,* Philadelphia, 1956.
28. W. Schmidt, *Der Ursprung der Gottesidee,* 12 vols. (Munster in Westfalia; Aschendorff, 1912–1955).
29. Ibid., "The Position of Women with Regard to Property in Primitive Society," *American Anthropologist,* Vol. 37 (1935), pp. 244–56.
30. E.g., Bronislaw Malinowski, *The Sexual Life of Savages* (one-volume edition; New York: Eugenics Publishing Company, 1929), pp. 179–86.
31. Schmidt, *Der Ursprung der Gottesidee,* Vol. II, "Die Religionen der Urvölker Amerikas," pp. 995–96.
32. Genesis 3:16.
33. Osborn, op. cit., pp. 284–87.
34. Ibid., pp. 364–70.
35. Cf. Coon, op. cit., pp. 34–35.
36. Hančar, op. cit., p. 106.
37. Ibid., pp. 135–37.
38. C. von den Steinen, "Prähistorische Zeichen und Ornamente," *Bastian-Festschrift* (Berlin, 1896), cited by Hančar, op. cit., p. 130.
39. V. A. Gorodcov, *Archeologija,* 1923, Kamennyie period, p. 281; cited by Hančar, op. cit., p. 130.
40. P. P. Jefimenko, *Soobščeniya Gosudarstvennoi Akademii Istorii Material'noi Kul'turi* (Leningrad-Moscow, 1931), 11–12, p. 60.
41. *Ipek* (*Jahrbuch für prähistorische und ethnographische Kunst*) (Leipzig, 1931), p. 65.
42. Hančar, op. cit., p. 94; also Herbert Kühn, "Das Problem der Urmonotheismus," *Akademie der Wissenschaften und der Literatur in Mainz, Abhandlungen der Geistes- und Sozialwissenschaftlichen Klasse,* 1950, Nr. 22, pp. 1665–66.
43. N. N. Cheboksarov and T. A. Trofimova, "Antropologicheskoe

inzushemie Mansi," *Kratie soobščenia* II, M.K. 9, as reported by F. Field and E. Prostov, "Results of Soviet Investigations in Siberia," *American Anthropologist,* Vol. 44 (1942), p. 403 n.
44. Spinden, op. cit., map, p. 108.
45. William S. Webb and Charles E. Snow, *The Adena People* (Lexington, Ky.: Department of Anthropology and Archaeology, University of Kentucky, Reports in Anthropology and Archaeology, Vol. VI, 1945); and William S. Webb and Raymond S. Baby, *The Adena People, No. 2* (Columbus, O.: Ohio State University Press, 1957).
46. W. A. Ritchie, *Recent Discoveries Suggesting an Early Woodland Burial Cult in the Northeast* (Albany, N.Y.: New York State Museum and Science Service, Circular 40, 1955).
47. Henry (Hinrich Johannes) Rink, *Tales and Traditions of the Eskimo* (Edinburgh and London: William Blackwood and Sons, 1875), pp. 39–40.
48. *Katha Upaniṣad* 3:14.
49. Chrêtien de Troyes, *Le Chevalier de la charrette* (Wendelin Foerster's ed.; Halle: Max Niemeyer, 1899), pp. 107 ff., ll. 302 ff.
50. Kroeber, op. cit., p. 41.
51. A. C. Haddon, *The Races of Man* (London: Cambridge University Press, 1924), p. 95.
52. Kyosuki Kindaiti, *Ainu Life and Legends* (Tokyo: Tourist Library 36, 1941), p. 50.
53. J. Bachelor, article "Ainus," *Encyclopaedia of Religion and Ethics,* ed. James Hastings (New York: Charles Scribner's Sons, 1928), Vol. I, pp. 249–50; and Kindaiti, op. cit., pp. 52–54.
54. Kindaiti, op. cit., pp. 51–52.
55. Bachelor, op. cit., p. 245.
56. Ibid., p. 239.
57. Frobenius, *Kulturgeschichte Afrikas,* map, p. 88.
58. Weinert, op. cit., p. 108.
59. Osborn, op. cit., pp. 257–58.
60. Emil Bächler, *Das alpine Paläolithikum der Schweiz* (Basel, 1940).
61. Konrad Hörmann, *Die Petershöhle bei Velden in Mittelfranken* (Abhandlungen der Naturhistorischen Gesellschaft zu Nürnberg, 1923).
62. Osborn, op. cit., pp. 221, 513–14.
63. Ibid., p. 222.
64. Ibid., p. 223.
65. Piaget, op. cit., p. 367.
66. Kindaiti, op. cit., pp. 41–47.
67. Oswald Menghin, "Der Nachweis des Opfers im Altpaläolithikum," *Wiener Prähistorischer Zeitschrift,* 1926, pp. 14 ff.
68. A. Gahs, "Kopf-, Schädel- und Langknochenopfer bei Rentiervölkern," *Festschrift: Publication d'hommage offerte au P. W. Schmidt* (Vienna: Mechitharisten-Congregations-Buchdruckerei, 1928), pp. 231 ff.
69. A. J. Hallowell, "Bear Ceremonialism in the Northern Hemisphere," *American Anthropologist,* 1926, pp. 87 ff.
70. Uno Holmberg, "Über die Jagdriten der nördlichen Völker Asiens und Europas," *Journal de la Société Finno-Ougrienne,* Vol. 41 (Helsinki, 1925–1926), pp. 1–53.
71. Lothar Friedrich Zotz, *Die schlesischen Höhlen und ihre eiszeitlichen Bewohner* (Breslau, 1937); *Die Altsteinzeit in Niederschlesien* (Leipzig, 1939). Also, Wilhelm Koppers, "Künstlicher Zahnschliff am Bären im Altpaläolithikum und bei den Ainu auf Sachalin," *Quartär,* 1938, pp. 97 ff.
72. Kühn, "Das Problem des Urmonotheismus," pp. 1646–47.
73. Comte Bégouën, "Les modelages d'argile de la caverne de Montespan," *Comptes rendus des séances de l'Académie des Inscriptions et Belles Lettres,* 31 août and 26 octobre, 1923, 14 p., pp. 349–50, 401. A photograph of the object will be found in Abbé Breuil, op. cit., p. 237.
74. Frobenius, *Kulturgeschichte Afrikas,* pp. 83–85.
75. Ibid., p. 83.
76. Ibid., p. 81.
77. Ibid., p. 81.
78. Piaget, op. cit., pp. 361–62.
79. Ostermann, op. cit., p. 128.
80. Leo Frobenius, *Der Kopf als Schicksal* (Munich, 1924), p. 88; as quoted by Carl Kerényi, "Kore," op. cit., pp. 141–42.
81. Cf. Lidio Cipriani, "Excavations in Andamanese Kitchen Mid-

dens," *Acts of IVth International Congress of Anthropological and Ethnological Sciences* (Vienna, 1952), Vol. II, pp. 250–53.

PART FOUR: THE ARCHAEOLOGY OF MYTH

CHAPTER 9: MYTHOLOGICAL THRESHOLDS OF THE PALEOLITHIC

1. Wendt, op. cit.
2. E. von Eickstedt, "Gedanken uber Entwicklung und Gliederung der Menschheit," *Mitteilungen der Anthropologischen Gesellschaft in Wien,* IV, pp. 231–54.
3. Pierre Teilhard de Chardin, "The Idea of Fossil Man," *Anthropology Today,* pp. 97–98.
4. Hans Weinert, "Der fossile Mensch," *Anthropology Today,* p. 102.
5. Wolfgang Köhler, *The Mentality of Apes* (2d ed.; New York: Humanities Press, 1927), p. 95.
6. Ibid., pp. 314–15.
7. W. Krickeberg, in *Buschan's Illustrierter Völkerkunde* (2d ed.; Stuttgart: Strecker und Schröder, 1922), p. 57; cited by Schmidt, op. cit., Vol. VI (1935), pp. 28–31.
8. Steward, *Handbook,* Vol. V, p. 748; also, W. F. Libby, *Radiocarbon Dating* (Chicago: University of Chicago Press, 1952), Sample No. C-485.
9. Krieger, *Anthropology Today,* p. 240.
10. José Imbelloni, "The Peopling of America," *Acta Americana,* I, 3 (1943), pp. 321–22.
11. Harold S. Gladwin, *Men out of Asia* (New York: McGraw-Hill Book Company, 1947), pp. 65–74.
12. Paul Rivet, *Les Origines de l'homme américain* (Montreal: Editions de l'Arbre, 1943), pp. 74–88.
13. L. S. B. Leakey, *Olduvai Gorge: A Report on the Evolution of the Hand-axe Culture in Beds I–IV* (London: Cambridge University Press, 1951).
14. Coon, op. cit., pp. 55–56.
15. Ibid., p. 57.
16. Radcliffe-Brown, op. cit., p. 129.
17. Ibid., p. 193.
18. Cipriani, op. cit., pp. 251–52.
19. Radcliffe-Brown, op. cit., p. 307.
20. Ibid., p. 405.
21. Ibid., p. 327.
22. Ruth Underhill, "Withdrawal as a Means of Dealing with the Supernatural," paper read at *Fifth International Congress of Anthropological and Ethnological Sciences,* Philadelphia, 1956.
23. Weinert, op. cit., p. 115.
24. Ibid., p. 117.
25. G. H. R. von Koenigswald, "A Review of the Stratigraphy of Java and Its Relations to Early Man," *Early Man,* p. 31.
26. Breuil, op. cit., pp. 32–33.
27. Herbert Kühn, *Die Felsbilder Europas* (Stuttgart, 1952), p. 12.
28. Carleton S. Coon, reviewing Glyn Daniel, *Lascaux and Carnac,* in *Natural History: The Magazine of the American Museum of Natural History,* Vol. LXVI, No. 7 (September 1957), p. 341.
29. Osborn, op. cit., p. 490.
30. Weinert, op. cit., pp. 117–19.
31. Hančar, op. cit., p. 132.
32. Osborn, op. cit., pp. 333–38.
33. Ibid., p. 382.
34. Frobenius, *Kulturgeschichte Afrikas,* pp. 66–70.
35. Ibid., Plates 1–26.

CHAPTER 10: MYTHOLOGICAL THRESHOLDS OF THE NEOLITHIC

1. J. Meier, "Mythen und Sagen der Admiralitäts-insulaner," *Anthropos,* Vol. II (1907), p. 654.
2. Robert Heine-Geldern, "Urheimat und früheste Wanderungen der Austronesier," *Anthropos,* Vol. XXVII (1932), p. 556.
3. Menghin, *Weltgeschichte der Steinzeit,* p. 604.
4. Heine-Geldern, "Urheimat und

früheste Wanderungen der Austronesier," p. 607.
5. P. Bley, "Sagen der Baininger auf Neupommern," *Anthropos,* Vol. IX (1914), p. 198.
6. J. E. Weckler, "The Relationships between Neanderthal Man and Homo Sapiens," *American Anthropologist,* Vol. 56, No. 6 (December 1954), pp. 1003–1025.
7. Ibid.
8. Coon, op. cit., pp. 60–63.
9. *Two Rediscovered Works of Ancient Christian Literature: Gregory of Nyssa and Macarius* (Leiden: Brill, 1954), XLIV, 1033 D-1036 A; cited by Jean Daniélou, "La Colombe et la ténèbre dans la mystique byzantine ancienne," *Eranos-Jahrbuch 1954,* p. 417.
10. Frobenius, *Kulturgeschichte Afrikas,* Plate 19.
11. Henri Frankfort, "A Note on the Lady of Birth," *Journal of Near Eastern Studies,* Vol. III, No. 3 (July 1944), p. 200.
12. Sir Charles Leonard Woolley, *Ur of the Chaldees* (London: Ernest Benn Ltd., 1929), pp. 33–34.
13. Ibid., pp. 46–56, with omissions.
14. Ibid., p. 57.
15. Ibid., p. 58.
16. Ibid., pp. 64–65.
17. Ibid., pp. 59–60.
18. Ibid., p. 63.
19. Henri Frankfort, "Gods and Myths on Sargonid Seals," *Iraq,* Vol. I, No. 1 (1934), p. 8.
20. Woolley, op. cit., p. 52.
21. H. de Genouillac, *Textes réligieux sumériens du Louvre* (Paris: Paul Geuther, 1930), text no. 5374, lines 191 ff., as cited and translated by Langdon, op. cit., p. 345, abridged.
22. Kramer, op. cit., pp. 88–89, abridged.
23. Ibid., pp. 91–93, abridged.
24. Langdon, op. cit., pp. 176–77.
25. Frankfort, *Iraq* I, 1, op. cit., p. 12.
26. Kramer, op. cit., pp. 90–95, abridged.
27. John 20:11–18.
28. Huizinga, op. cit., p. 39.
29. Ibid., pp. 34–35.
30. Ibid., p. 45.
31. Leo Frobenius, *Erythräa: Lande und Zeiten des heiligen Königsmordes* (Berlin-Zurich: Atlantis-Verlag, 1931), pp. 133–36.
32. Frobenius, *Das unbekannte Afrika,* p. 132.
33. Frobenius, *Erythräa,* pp. 329–30.
34. J. D. Clark, ed., *Proceedings of the Third Pan-African Congress on Prehistory* (1955) (London: Chatto and Windus, 1957), p. 428.
35. G. A. Wainwright, as cited by Basil Davidson, "Aspects of African Growth before A.D. 1500," *Diogenes 23* (Fall 1958), p. 88.
36. See Childe, op. cit., pp. 52–84.
37. A number of versions of the myth existed. I have followed, in the main, that of Plutarch, as summarized by Frazer, *The Golden Bough,* pp. 362–67.
38. Ovid, *Metamorphoses,* X, 708 ff.
39. Frazer, *The Golden Bough,* p. 471.
40. *Odyssey* XIX, 172–78, translated by S. H. Butcher and Andrew Lang (London: Macmillan and Company, 1879).
41. Bedřich Hrozný, *Ancient History of Western Asia, India, and Crete* (New York: Philosophical Library, 1953), p. 198, note 1.
42. Frazer, *The Golden Bough,* p. 280.
43. Marija Gimbutas, "Culture Change in Europe at the Start of the Second Millennium B.C." *Fifth International Congress of Anthropological and Ethnological Sciences,* Philadelphia, 1956.
44. R. A. S. Macalister, *Newgrange, County Meath* (Dublin: Government Publications, official handbook, no date).
45. J. A. MacCulloch, *The Religion of the Ancient Celts* (Edinburgh: T. and T. Clark, 1911), p. 63.
46. P. W. Joyce, *A Social History of Ireland* (London: Longmans, Green and Company; Dublin: M. H. Gill and Son, Ltd., 1913), Vol. I, pp. 251–52.
47. MacCulloch, op. cit., p. 67.
48. Ibid., p. 69.
49. Ibid., p. 42.
50. After Curtin, op. cit., pp. 327–32.
51. W. Norman Brown, "The Beginnings of Civilization in India," *Supplement to the Journal of the*

American Oriental Society, No. 4 (December 1939), p. 44.
52. Heinrich Zimmer, *The Art of Indian Asia*, edited and completed by Joseph Campbell (New York: Pantheon Books, The Bollingen Series XXXIX, 1955), Vol. I, p. 27.
53. Menghin, op. cit., pp. 319, 322–24.
54. Heine-Geldern, "Urheimat und früheste Wanderungen der Austronesier," loc. cit., p. 608.
55. Carl W. Bishop, "The Beginnings of Civilization in Eastern Asia," *Supplement to the Journal of the American Oriental Society*, No. 4 (December 1939), p. 49.
56. Li Chi, *The Beginnings of Chinese Civilization* (Seattle: University of Washington Press, 1957), p. 14; and Heine-Geldern, "The Origin of Ancient Civilizations," loc. cit., pp. 89–90. See also Walter A. Fairservis, Jr., *The Origins of Oriental Civilization* (New York: The New American Library, Mentor Books, 1959), pp. 82–141; especially p. 140, note, discussing the revised dating of the Chinese dynasties.
57. G. D. Wu, *Prehistoric Pottery in China* (London: Kegan Paul, Trench, Trubner and Company, 1938), Figs. V–LII; and compare Hrozný, op. cit., Figs. 5 and 8.
58. Heine-Geldern, "Urheimat und früheste Wanderungen der Austronesier," loc. cit., pp. 598–602.
59. Ibid., p. 598.
60. Ibid., p. 599.
61. Childe, in *Anthropology Today*, p. 209.
62. Layard, *Stone Men of Malekula*.
63. Robert Heine-Geldern, "Die Megalithen Südostasiens und ihre Bedeutung für die Klärung der Megalithenfrage in Europa und Polynesien," *Anthropos*, Vol. XXIII (1928), p. 303.
64. Layard, *Stone Men of Malekula*, pp. 209–10.
65. *Ibid.*, p. 210.
66. John Layard, "The Making of Man in Malekula," in *Eranos-Jahrbuch 1948* (Zurich: Rhein-Verlag, 1949), p. 235.
67. Layard, *Stone Men of Malekula*, pp. 620–21, note 6.
68. Ibid., pp. 733–34.
69. Ibid., p. 734.
70. Layard, "Der Mythos der Totenfahrt auf Malekula," loc. cit., pp. 253–61.
71. Ssu-ma Ch'ien, *Historical Records* (Shih Chi), ch. vii.
72. *Notes on Music* (Yo Chi)—a chapter interpolated in the *Record of Rites* (Li Chi), as cited by Maurice Courant, "Essai sur la musique classique des Chinois," *Encyclopédie de la musique et dictionnaire du Conservatoire* (Paris, 1924), Vol. I, p. 206, and by Alain Daniélou, *Introduction to the Musical Scales* (London: The India Society, 1943), pp. 16–17.
73. *Doctrine of the Mean* (Chung Yung), XX, 8, translated by Ezra Pound in Confucius, *The Unwobbling Pivot* (New York: New Directions, 1951).
74. *Record of Rites* (Li Chi), as cited by A. Préau, "Lie Tseu," *Le Voile d'Isis*, Nos. 152–53 (1932), pp. 554–55, and by Alain Daniélou, op. cit., pp. 6–7.
75. *Vākya Pādukā* 1.124.
76. Lü Shih, commentary to the *Wu Ching*, as cited by Daisetz Teitaro Suzuki, *A Brief History of Early Chinese Philosophy* (2nd ed.; London, Probsthain and Company, 1914), p. 175.
77. H. A. Giles, *Confucianism and Its Rivals* (London: Williams and Norgate, 1915), p. 180.
78. Heine-Geldern, "The Origin of Ancient Civilizations," loc. cit., pp. 82–83, 89.
79. Ibid., pp. 93–94.
80. Daniel G. Brinton, *American Hero-Myths* (Philadelphia: H. C. Watts and Company, 1882), pp. 65–67.
81. Torquemada, *Monarquia Indiana*, Lib. VI, Cap. XXIV, cited by ibid., p. 134.
82. After Brinton, op. cit., pp. 9–136, condensed, and Bernardino de Sahagun, *Historia General de las Cosas de Nueva España* (Mexico, 1829), Lib. III, Cap. xii–xiv, condensed.

CONCLUSION: THE FUNCTIONING OF MYTH

1. Paul Radin, *Primitive Man as Philosopher*, p. 241.
2. *The Gospel of Sri Ramakrishna*, p. 559.
3. Alfred Adler, *Understanding Human Nature* (Garden City, N.Y.: Garden City Publishing Company, 1932); *Menschenkenntnis* (Leipzig: S. Hirzel, 1927).
4. Tinbergen, op. cit., pp. 153–54.
5. Ibid., p. 154.

REFERENCE NOTES TO THE FOREWORD OF THE 1969 EDITION

1. G. H. Curtis, "Clock for the Ages: Potassium Argon," *National Geographic Magazine*, Vol. 120, No. 4 (1961), pp. 590–592.
2. L. S. B. Leakey, "The Astonishing Discovery of 'Nutcracker Man,'" *Illustrated London News*, Vol. 235, No. 6267 (1959), pp. 217–19; "The Newly Discovered Skull from Olduvai: First Photographs of the Skull," *ibid.*, Vol. 235, No. 6268 (1959), pp. 288–289; "Recent Discoveries at Olduvai Gorge," *Nature*, Vol. 188, No. 4755 (1960), pp. 1050–52; "Finding the World's Earliest Men," *National Geographic Magazine*, Vol. 118, No. 3 (1960), pp. 420–35; "New Links in the Chain of Human Evolution: Three Major New Discoveries from the Olduvai Gorge, Tanganyika," *Illustrated London News*, Vol. 238, No. 6344 (1961), pp. 346–48; L. S. B. Leakey, P. V. Tobias, and J. R. Napier, "A New Species of the Genus *Homo* from Olduvai Gorge," *Nature*, Vol. 202, No. 4927 (1964), pp. 7–9.
3. Carleton S. Coon, *The Origin of Races* (New York: Alfred A. Knopf, 4th printing, 1966), pp. 302–304.
4. James Mellaart, "Hacilar: A Neolithic Village Site," *The Scientific American*, Vol. 205, No. 2 (August 1961); and by the same author, *Çatal Hüyük: A Neolithic Town in Anatolia* (New York: McGraw-Hill Book Company, 1967); *see also* Kathleen M. Kenyon, *Archaeology in the Holy Land* (New York: Frederick A. Praeger, 1960).
5. Mellaart, *Çatal Hüyük*, p. 22.
6. Betty J. Meggers, Clifford Evans, and Emilio Estrada, *Early Formative Period of Coastal Ecuador: The Valdivia and Machalilla Phases* (Washington, D.C.: Smithsonian Institution, 1965).
7. *See* Richard S. MacNeish, "The Food-gathering and Incipient Agriculture Stage of Prehistoric Middle America," in Richard Wauchope (ed.), *Handbook of Middle American Indians* (Austin: University of Texas Press, 1964–1967), Vol. I, pp. 413–26; Paul C. Mangelsdorf, Richard S. MacNeish, and Gordon R. Willey, "Origins of Agriculture in Middle America," *ibid.*, Vol. I, pp. 427–45; Philip Phillips, "The Role of Transpacific Contacts in the Development of New World Pre-Columbian Civilizations," *ibid.*, Vol. IV, pp. 296–315; and Daniel Del Solar, "Interrelations of Mesoamerica and the Peru-Ecuador Area," in *Kroeber Anthropological Society Papers*, No. 34, Spring 1966.

INDEX

Some other books published by Penguin
are described on the following pages.

Carl Gustav Jung

THE PORTABLE JUNG

Edited by Joseph Campbell

Joseph Campbell has assembled a comprehensive selection of the famous psychologist's writings. This volume aims to acquaint the reader with the elementary terms and themes of analytical psychology, trace the development of Jung's thought, and provide an introduction to his *Collected Works*. It goes a long way toward explaining Jung's over-all psychology.

Contents: The Stages of Life. The Structure of the Psyche. Instinct and the Unconscious. The Concept of the Collective Unconscious. The Relations between the Ego and the Unconscious. Aion: Phenomenology of the Self. Marriage as a Psychological Relationship. Psychological Types. The Transcendent Function. On the Relationship of Analytical Psychology to Poetry. Individual Dream Symbolism in Relation to Alchemy. The Spiritual Problem of Modern Man. The Differences Between Eastern and Western Thinking. On Synchronicity. Answer to Job. A chronology of Jung's life.

I. M. Lewis

ECSTATIC RELIGION

An anthropologist looks at states of spiritual exaltation and religious trance. Professor Lewis makes an important distinction between ecstatic experiences that reinforce official morality and established power and those that are a form of indirect protest on the part of the downtrodden–particularly women. This volume's wide-ranging subject matter includes reference to African shamanism; the classical shamanistic religions of Asia, the Arctic, and South America; Haitian voodoo; the cult of Dionysus; Christian mysticism; the contemporary counterculture; and the strange European phenomenon known as Tarantism. With twelve plates. I. M. Lewis is Professor of Anthropology at the London School of Economics.

J. M. Coles and E. S. Higgs

THE ARCHAEOLOGY OF EARLY MAN

A worldwide review of human development up to the introduction of agriculture. "The writers present, by continents and by countries, the basic evidence for the actitivies of the first men in their relation to the natural environment and to their natural competitors, the large mammals. . . . Stone, bone and other artefacts and the plans of houses and tent-sites are illustrated concisely and conveniently. . . . The economic aspects of these early hunting groups, from their beginnings to the end of the glacial conditions in temperate Europe about 10,000 years ago, are discussed at length and with illuminating insight."–Stuart Piggott

Kenneth Maddock

THE AUSTRALIAN ABORIGINES

A survey of Aboriginal society. The Aborigines are the only major hunting-and-gathering people to have survived into modern times. Although their civilization has been ravaged by the European settlement of Australia, it is beginning to assume a new importance because of recent worldwide trends in favor of cultural autonomy and decentralization for dispossessed peoples. In this very objective book, Kenneth Maddock examines all known aspects of the life of the Aborigines, including religion, social stratification, and attitudes toward land, sexuality, and death.

Edited by Teodor Shanin

PEASANTS AND PEASANT SOCIETIES

A collection of essays on the generic characteristics of peasant societies seen as distinct types of social organization. The twenty-eight writings are grouped by topic, and the editor's choices have been made to draw the reader's attention to the classical roots of the relevant sociological tradition and to break through linguistic frontiers that have hitherto prevented widespread appreciation of many European studies of peasantry. Part One considers peasant social structure. Part Two focuses on forms of production and exchange typical of peasant society. Part Three brings together contributions on the political sociology of peasantry approached as a class. Part Four discusses peasant cultural patterns. The fifth and last part looks at the peasantry as an object of policies in the modern state.

Georges Roux

ANCIENT IRAQ

This is the first complete political, cultural, and economic history of ancient Mesopotamia. Covering a period that ranges from prehistoric times to the Christian era, Dr. Roux describes the empires, dynasties, and religions of each millennium. Among the topics he discusses are the gods of Sumer, the Sumerian renaissance, the time of Hammurabi, the rise of Assyria, the house of Sargon, the Chaldaean kings, and the splendor of Babylon. That so vast a subject should make such fascinating reading is due not only to its intrinsic interest but also to the talent and discernment of a brilliant historian.

Edited by Max Marwick

WITCHCRAFT AND SORCERY

This collection of readings surveys the current status of worldwide witchcraft and sorcery. Part One reviews different approaches to the topic. Part Two samples the rich ethnography of witchcraft from magic in the ancient world to the Salem witch hunts. Theories of witchcraft are examined in Part Three, with emphasis on the relationships among cultist movements, persecution, and social stress. Part Four shows the contribution that the study of witchcraft can make to the understanding of various sociological problems.